THE SEPARATION OF THE PARTY AND THE STATE

To my family, especially my Parents and Vandita

The Separation of the Party and the State

Political Leadership in Soviet and Post-Soviet Phases

VINAYAK N. SRIVASTAVA
Institute for Social Sciences
New Delhi, India

Ashgate

Aldershot • Brookfield USA • Singapore • Sydney

Published by
Ashgate Publishing Ltd
Gower House
Croft Road
Aldershot
Hants GU11 3HR
England

Ashgate Publishing Company
Old Post Road
Brookfield
Vermont 05036
USA

British Library Cataloguing in Publication Data
Srivastava, Vinayak N.
The separation of the party and the state : political leadership in Soviet and post-Soviet phases
1.Kommunisticheskaia partiia Sovetskogo Soiuza 2.Soviet Union - Politics and government 3.Russia (Federation) - Politics and government
I.Title
324.2'1'75'0947

Library of Congress Cataloging-in-Publication Data
Srivastava, Vinayak N. (Vinayak Narain)
The separation of the party and the state : political leadership in Soviet and post-Soviet phases / Vinayak N. Srivastava.
p. cm.
Includes bibliographical references (p) and index.
ISBN 1-84014-709-1 (hard)
1. TSK KPSS--History. 2. Elite (Social science)--Soviet Union--Political activity. 3. Soviet Union--Politics and government--1985-1991. 4. Perestroika. 5. Elite (Social science)--Former Soviet republics--Political activity. 6. Post-communism--Former Soviet republics. 7. Post-communism--Asia, Central 8. Russia (Federation)--Politics and government--1991- 9. Asia. Central--Politics and government--1991- I. Title.
JN6598.K7S687 1998
324.247'075'09049--dc21 98-30878
CIP

ISBN 1 84014 709 1

Printed in Great Britain

Contents

Contents

List of Tables

Preface

This book is the first full length study of one of the most important political institution of the erstwhile Soviet political system - the Central Committee of the Communist Party of the Soviet Union (CPSU). It discusses the reforms which the institution and the political leadership comprising it underwent during Perestroika. Tracing the historical background of the evolution of the Central Committee since its early days up to the begining of Perestroika, the book undertakes a comparitive analysis of the Central Committee at the threshold of Perestroika and the principles governing its constitution - composition, organisation and working, its transformations until the time it ceases to exist, the issues involved in the reforms and their bearing on this metamorphosis.

The originality of this work lies in its main argument that the central reform during Perestroika was that of the Party and the State - a reform which ultimately resulted in the CPSU and its institutions, the Central Committee being one of the most vital among them, firstly, surrendering the monopoly over political power and control over the instrumentalities of the State and secondly, systematically deinstitutionalising and dismantling the formidable Soviet political system. These eventually succumbed to the subalteran and subterranean forces hitherto lying dormant and their political manifestations such as the resurgent nationalisms and sub-nationalisms and a disintegrating economy coupled with a state of socio-cultural entropy. The political demise of the Soviet Union and birth of fifteen nation-states with distinctive political identities from the debris of the former is perhaps one of the greatest political transformations of the latter half of the twentieth century.

The seeds of transformation and the shape of politico-economic and socio-cultural systems that emerged in successor States were laid down during the Soviet era - in particular during Perestroika itself. The carrier of these transformations have been, in several cases, Soviet era political leadership which has continued to determine the destiny of these nascent nation-states. Many of them have been key members of the Central Committee itself, thus underlining the continuity with the Soviet past. Changes, however, too had been crystallising during the Soviet era, more distinctly during Perestroika under the impact of the competing forces of conservatism and reformism. Thus, although it was the separation of the Party and the State during Perestroika that culminated in the disintegration of the Soviet political system, the successor States and their politico-economic and socio-cultural systems are evolving within the paradigm laid during Perestroika with erstwhile political leadership playing the crucial role. The continuity, therefore, is as striking, if not more, as the change is.

The book is based on a wide range of Russian and translated primary and secondary sources, biographical directories and databases, memoirs of leading political actors, published documents and interviews held in Moscow with the members of the highest CPSU leadership organs, academicians and journalists.

I would like to acknowledge my appreciation to a number of institutions which assisted me during the course of my research. My gratitude goes to the Kings College and to the Faculty of Social and Political Sciences, University of Cambridge; to the Ministry of Human Resource Development, Government of India; and to the staff of the Cambridge University Library and Lenin Library, Moscow.

My gratitude goes to Professor John Barber and Professor David Lane. I owe special thanks to Professor Vera Pavlovna and Irena Bausova.

1 Introduction: the Perspective

Institutions conduct the praxis of politics, state and governance. Individuals may be prominently situated in or above these institutions, they may sometimes seem to be the symbolic centre of power, yet, be they Kings or Prime Ministers, Presidents or General Secretaries, the institutions of the state and government are the real executor of the power and the governance. The institutionalised system with an institution or set of institutions evolve over a period of time to operationalise the dominant political ideology of a time and regime. This dominant political ideology, through a conscious or enlightened intervention or as an accepted value system which may be deemed to have existed since times immemorial and perceived as eternal, lays down the parameter, norms or paradigm governing a particular society in a specific time period. The institutions give a tangible shape and implement the perspective articulated by the dominant philosophy, generally imperfectly since the ideology defines the ideal type.

Social institutions influence the society, the economy, cultural and religious institutions, the spiritual aspect of the human life, as do the political institutions effect the political life of a country or a society. This is true for all kinds of political systems that have existed since human race learnt to govern itself and social and political organisations evolved into complex systems. Institutions, a network of these, have sustained all hitherto known types of political systems-tribal, monarchical, authoritarian, autocratic, militaristic, liberal-democratic types, parliamentary or presidential, nationalistic, socialistic or communist. These could be simple or complex in terms of their forms and composition. Tribal institutions were obviously simpler in nature as were those of monarchical, authoritarian, autocratic and militaristic political systems. Thus the Soviet political system too was based on a set of institutions - some more important than others, and perhaps had the distinction of having been the most extensively studied one, with a very large number of scholarly characterisations defining its nature.

The political system was unique, as was the political philosophy on which it was founded and was an uniquely Twentieth century phenomenon based on an alternative and more egalitarian theory of modernisation in its ideal form, the other mainstream one being that of liberal-democracy.

Marxism-Leninism provided the philosophical base to the institutions of the Soviet political system as John Locke and Hegel did for modern liberal-democratic institutions. The institutions were thus shaped by the conscious or enlightened motive force of the segments or social forces of these societies which acquired dominant political status, power and authority within their respective societies through conquest - with or without coercion. Institutions not amenable to their sectional interests were dismantled, retaining those which did and new ones were created. Institutions have never emerged spontaneously and have always throughout the history been crafted through the conscious political intervention. This was amply evident when the institutions of the Soviet political system emerged and evolved as indeed when they were sought to be changed in both forms and content and new ones established.

With the evolution of a society its institutions too either evolve to reflect emergent realities or perish. Sometimes their evolution may itself carry seeds of destruction and they may re-emerge in entirely new forms with different content. If an institution resist change for long it may ossify and simply become redundant at some point of time because political processes mutate in accordance to the growing maturity of a society, both social and political. Evolution can be deferred but can not be arrested. Revolutions may hasten the transformation spurring it to a rapid pace, whereas reforms result in phased or incremental changes. Both effect the institutions and are affected by them. Institutions may initiate either processes, modify as a consequence and are primarily effected by the changes unleashed. Supra-institutional changes originating outside and irrespective of them too influence the institutions.

Among the array of what can be called primary institutions of the Soviet political system, the Central Committee was a key one. Primary institutions would refer to those institutions which conducted the affairs of politics, State and governance in the Soviet political system. These included the Communist Party of the Soviet Union and its leadership organs like the Politburo, the Central Secretariat and the Central Committee, and State institutions like the Supreme Soviet, the Council of Ministers and the Presidency. The Central Committee, amongst all of these, was more important of these primary political institutions. The Central Committee, as an institution, and individually its membership, constituted the central component of power in the Soviet political system. Even when the Central Committee, as an institution, was less important having effectively been surpassed by other institutions or few individuals at the helm of affairs, yet it remained sufficiently important firstly, simply because it was the august assembly of most powerful individuals and secondly, as a consequence of the fact that its apparatus was the body which prepared, implemented and exercised supervision over all major decisions of state and governance. Even the decisions of State institutions like the Council of Ministers and the Supreme Soviet were prepared in the Central Committee departments, with or without their collaboration, not to mention those of the Politburo, the Central Committee and its Central Secretariat.

Without the active involvement of an institution like the Central Committee, no political reform programme could either be conceived or put into practice. Indeed the Central Committee as an institution initiated the reforms. It was the Central Committee plenum of March 1985 which declared its intentions to reform the Soviet political system and all its institutions, including the Party and its Central Committee. All the primary institutions were to be involved in one of the most important conscious attempts at political engineering ever undertaken. The Central Committee was to lead the changes. Obviously the institutional integrity of the Central Committee could hardly have remained unaffected. In fact, not only the Central Committee underwent dramatic transformation during six years of Perestroika, it lost its position as the primary institution of the Soviet political system and eventually disintegrated as the USSR crumbled.

One of the oft-debated issue about the Soviet political system was as to which of the two institutions - the Party or the state were more important. Whether the political system was a Party-led or a state-led system? Extensive scholarly debates were conducted on this issue. Some contended that the state has in practice replaced the Party as the most primary political institution, whereas the other's held that the state institutions were subservient to the Party and real power and authority lay with the Party institutions. The Party, in the latter's view, had supplanted the state organs, which merely rubber-stamped the decisions of the Party. These arguments were countered by the plea that actually the Party had lost its political role and character and the priorities of the state institutions had become its own. The Party worked towards implementing the decisions necessitated by the requirements of the Soviet state. The Party had been reduced to responding to the task of governing a complex and advanced industrial society with a multi-ethnic character perpetually in economic and military competition with economically advanced societies of the West. The Party therefore needed to be purged of its 'non-political' role of being executor of activities of the state institutions. In certain sense this role was also a consequence of the existing single-Party system and the status of the Communist Party of the Soviet Union (CPSU) as the only political Party.

The Party's political role, defined by its political ideology, therefore, degenerated into merely governing the Soviet society. Absence of a competitive political system left the only party with unchallenged political supremacy. The Party did not need to compete with other political forces to win the leadership of the Soviet society. In the long run such a monopoly of political power reduced the Party to a mere instrument of governance, alienated it from the Soviet people and prevented its periodic reforms or modernisation in accordance to the contemporary requirements keeping its basic political ideology unchanged. A competitive and pluralistic political system would have ensured such a modernisation, making the Party more competitive, less bloated and more effective. The Soviet political system was pluralistic. Pluralism, however, referred to the pluralism of numerous sectional interests that competed within the political system for optimal allocation of available resources, rather than pluralism of political ideologies, policies and political organisation. A communist political system denied the possibility of the pluralism of the latter variety since the triumph of the working class ideology and politics, was deemed to have superseded all ideologies and politics of antagonistic classes, be they bourgeoise, feudalism, monarchy etc.

Reforms under Perestroika were about the modernisation of the Party and its withdrawal from excessive involvement in the affairs of the state as also about putting in place new institutions of state which may depend increasingly less on the Party for the governance. In reality the institutions of the state acquired autonomy to the extent of depriving the Party any leverage over the former and weakening it greatly. The Party could not even direct the state institutions from a distance or influence their policies and activities to any significant extent. Institutions of the state came to be by and large under the influence of rival political ideologies and forces. Even those which were dominated by the Party were deeply divided since the Party itself was split - vertically and horizontally, into numerous ideologies and sub-ideologies exerting pulls and pressures in different directions. Thus in practice the institutions under the influence of the Party were either paralysed or ineffectual. Those under the influence of the political rivals of the Party, however, could pursue their political agenda much more vigorously utilising the more tolerant political dispensation under Gorbachev. The decline of primary Party institutions like the Central Committee was directly proportional to the ascendancy of other political forces, increasing separation of the Party and the state and the growing influence of the rival political ideologies over these state institutions.

Central Committee gave political legitimacy to the acts of the Party, State and government institutions. Its name added to the numerous decrees lent to them the weight of political authority and signalled authenticity of its contents. All important decisions were ratified by this body and thus became legal enactment which the Party and the State officials were obliged to act upon. Many activities of the state and Government institutions became more significant when the name of the Central Committee prefixed their decisions as in case of joint decrees of the Central Committee and the Union Council of Ministers or even those issued by other primary institutions like the central trade union or Komsomol even though it may not deliberate or discuss a specific decision, which would invariably be in line with its strategic decisions taken at its most important plenums. Its name added the requisite political authority to the decision.

These may, in all probability, have been prepared by the departments of the Central Committee itself. It has been argued that these departments were very powerful in the decision-making and the decision-implementing processes and they, not the members of the Central Committee played the key role in conducting the affairs of the Party, the State and the government. Other primary institutions like the Politbureau and the Central Secretariat could function with the help of these departments, circumventing the Central Committee many times. Yet even then these institutions, for most part of the Soviet history, could not avoid referring the most important issues and the basic perspective that governed the decision of the Party, the State and the Government to the Central Committee. The central apparatus or departments contained appointed career officials who would usually possess expertise in different areas dealt with by the Politbureau, the Central Secretariat and the Central Committee. Some of these officials had spend a very long time in their respective areas of work and provided indispensable service to the Party and its leadership institutions. They virtually worked as supra-institutions overseeing the working of various State and Government institutions on behalf of the Party leadership and in practice dealt with the nitty-gritty of day to day governance.

The Central Committee had representation of various Party, State and the government bodies, whose leaders would find a berth in this august body. Thus, most important Party officials, State officials, Ministers, Military officials, mass organisation officials, republican and regional leaders etc. would be represented in this primary institution. Whatever one may argue about the democratic or undemocratic nature of the body, it was a rational form of organisation in a single-Party political system, providing a common platform to the leaders of most important Party, State and Government primary and secondary institutions to deliberate upon the matters of policy and other vital issues. On important issues, however inadequately, this body did discuss them and sometimes did take far-reaching decisions, like for example that of launching the Perestroika. The Central Committee had undergone a whole process of evolution since its inception several decades ago. It had traversed a long path, defining its characteristics, from its emergence as the collective leadership of a small, and at that juncture, politically insignificant political formation to that of a very powerful single party led political system which became a key player in the international arena. This evolution was a chequered one. It changed from being the most significant primary institution within the Party to relatively less important and then again witnessing the revival of its political fortunes. Nevertheless it continued to play a role and never faced a threat to its existence until 1991.

Since the Congress consisted of delegates elected at lower levels of the Party and mass organisations, the Central Committee was thus indirectly elected and reflected the choice of the Party or at least its important section. Such forms of indirect elections have been employed by various political parties and its variants are practised even now. Such elections make the contest for leadership competitive and gives a chance to Party delegates to choose from different alternatives. Such a principal of electivity is the next best option to direct elections which may not be possible because of the size of the membership and provide a filter for the leadership contest. However, crucial to the democratic content of such indirect elections is that the delegates are elected in a direct election. After the 10th Party Congress, when the outgoing leadership initiated the system of presenting a slate of candidates, it took away or curtailed the right of the Congress to voluntarily choose from among the candidates. The list presented to be voted upon may have excluded some of those whom the delegates may have wished to be considered. Although the circumstances created by a Civil War aided by external powers in which the new regime found itself embroiled and factionalism within its ranks compelled the Party leadership to introduce such a measure, yet in the final analysis, a more democratic process of electing a leadership was the casualty. The earlier system was not restored even when a semblance of normalcy returned since Party leadership found in it a convenient way of perpetuating its dominance. Thus gradually the process of election was replaced by a process of selection irreparably damaging the inner party democracy.

Political pluralism as is well known, existed both within and outside the Party in the early days of the Soviet regime. There were numerous political parties active in the society and many ill-defined political formations within the Party itself encompassing a very wide range of socialist and non-socialist ideologies. However the Civil War created conditions in which the political rights were severely curtailed and activities of different political forces curbed, not to be revived again until the very last phase of Soviet rule. Nevertheless these existed at the subterranean level asserting themselves as dissidence in different forms and broadly as conservatism and subtle reformism within the Party. Multi-pluralism of early years was reduced to bi-pluralism of two broad tendencies termed popularly as 'conservatism' and 'reformism', particularly within the Party. Dissident movements adhering to different ideologies within the society were largely very low key and remained an underground phenomenon. Conservatism and reformism however could contest within the broad parameters of Soviet socialism. Both these tendencies were however restricted by the political conventions laid down over the years of existence of the Soviet political system. Nonetheless they competed for political control over the primary and secondary institutions of the society and an undeclared see-saw battle continued unabated between the two. Thus apart from the plurality of institutions, plurality of opinions, social, ethnic and cultural pluralisms, there existed clearcut political and ideological pluralism both within and outside the Party as an integral part of the Soviet political culture. These myriad ideologies and their political manifestations impinged upon the Soviet political system through formal and informal channels and influenced the decision-making process. Thus the political system was not a monolithic one as it appeared to be prima facie. It was a closed pluralistic system if not an open one. History is yet to record an absolutely monolithic system despite the dominance of a particular ideology and politics. However it was not a multi-party system as in open pluralistic political systems.

Political coalitions presuppose plurality. The plurality could be within the broad framework of an ideology or of varying ideologies. Within the Party, plurality was within the confines of the parameters laid down by Soviet socialism. Thus liberal-democracy, monarchism, nationalism, religion-based ideologies could not be allowed to compete openly within or outside the Party. However dissident movement outside the fold of the Party and other informal associations within the society could hardly be controlled from being practiced and even influenced the policies of the Party. Political coalitions within the Party could be worked out on the basis of common understanding on issues of mutual interest. In the absence of the formal channels like various political parties, these alliances were informal in nature and within the same political formation, the CPSU. Such coalition or coalitions could attempt to steer the Party and the society on a course defined by them. All political tendencies have social basis. For example, the conservatism was more evident within the Party and the state officials whereas reformism was amongst members of intelligentsia. Thus in ultimate analysis, broad social coalitions constituted the basis of these informal political coalitions. These were in reality quasi-coalitions since the partners neither had any legitimate shape as political formations in a single-party system nor were well-defined. These coalitions extended to various echelons of the Party including its leadership and in the society. Thus an informal political pluralism existed within the political system, which even though devoid of recognisable forms contested within the framework of a single-party system influencing effectively the policies and the decision-making. Hence the Soviet political system was pluralistic, and not monolithic, with differing political tendencies playing an important role in defining the system at a particular point of time.

Glasnost and Perestroika facilitated in activating the civil society. Innumerable dissident groups emerged in legimitate shape as informal organisations and associations which could now function openly. Several of these seem to have been sponsored by the reformist and non-reformist sections of the Party and its leadership supporting or opposing the policies being pursued by the latter. During Perestroika, the civil society was highly politicised and became important channel rallying anti-communist and anti-socialist political forces against the political society represented by the Party and the state leadership. Civil society however was characterised only by articulate segments of the society, particularly sections of intelligentsia. During Perestroika these sections came to be identified with the civil society. These included those sections which played the pivotal role in mobilising support for anti-CPSU political forces. Civil society thus came to be identified with anti-establishment social and political forces during Perestroika unlike the one in 1960s. The political movement of the civil society was initially led by the social and political forces wanting to reform the political system within the existing paradigm of socialism and under the leadership of the CPSU and Gorbachev. In latter stages these social and political forces were taken over by those with avowed anti-communist and anti-socialist ideologies that agitated for a systemic change and eventually succeeded. Thus the civil society played a crucial role in not only harbouring anti-CPSU political and social forces but in essentially wrecking the political society and the political system as a whole. Initially it provided legitimacy to Gorbachevian reforms and regime in the form of an informal social and political contract but ultimately abandoned both Gorbachev and his reforms opting for the dissolution of the political society led by him, the newly emerging framework of political institutions and that of the Soviet Union itself as a political entity.

Civil society has been projected as a non-class alternative to a class-based analysis of a political reality and processes. The contemporary concept of civil society seems to derive its meaning and definition from the emergence of a middle class, which although not owning any means of production or capital, constitutes that vital professional segment of the society engaged in industry, service sectors and even in agriculture, which possesses the knowledge and training so indispensable to run the economy and the society. With ongoing technological revolution these segments occupy a crucial position in any society and is burgeoning by the day. Although it may not be capital-owning or means of production-owning segments, it certainly aspires to that end. It is ambitious enough to be wanting to convert its skills into capital asset. It is these segments of the society who constitute the articulate and the vocal sections of the civil society. It was the professional, skill-owning middle-classes in the former Soviet Union which became the basis of an actively anti-establishment and anti-Party civil society. It was, of course, supported by a section of the working classes which engaged in major industrial actions against the political leadership, nonetheless intellectual, moral and political leadership was provided by the professional middle classes with intelligentsia as its key component. Intelligentsia could include academicians, journalists, technocrats, management personnel, writers, other literary figures, artists, agriculturists, administrators (the officialdom), scientists, students etc. Thus the civil society does not incorporate all sections and all the classes of a society as it appears to represent. The latter is virtual reality, whereas the reality is that it only includes a much smaller, nonetheless vital and a very articulate section of the society or in effect its social vanguard. Civil society institutions and its component segments represent very definitive class and sectional interests and politics which is coterminus with these. Therefore civil society and its institutions do not represent some universal values applicable to all or are value-neutral as they tend to present themselves. That is why the civil society in the former Soviet Union turned against its political society constituting the CPSU leadership when it felt that the promised reforms will not deliver its goals and objectives. The civil society went alongwith Gorbachev and his reforms to the extent they paved way for the restoration of the domination of its ideological values over those hitherto propagated by the existing political society. Once that objective had been achieved and the reforms did not proceed in the desired direction, the same civil society, that had hailed Gorbachev and his reforms as a harbinger of a new era in the former Soviet Union, turned against them mobilising popular opinion against Gorbachev, his vacillations and the inadequacy of the reforms taking advantage of the economic hardships which common people faced during economic transition. Hence the civil society played a politically partisan role during Perestroika. Civil society institutions included innumerable informal organisations, political, quasi-political, social and cultural clubs, discussion societies, educational and semi-educational institutions, religious organisations, ethnic, regional and sub-regional groupings, manifestly political and those professing social and cultural objectives, professional organisations or associations at work places, residents associations based in residential areas, minority groups - whether religious or social-cultural, economic activity based associations, for example those of cooperators and enterpreneurs, associations like students unions, those formed around a specific issue like the Memorial or around a set of issues and agenda whether political, social, cultural or scientific associations, those formed by writers, artists, literary figures and other sections of the cultural intelligentsia etc.

The Central Committee's transformation from a political body primarily to that administering a complex society is significant. Political and revolutionary notables who initially constituted this body, ensured that the Party effectively discharged its political role in the society. This role abated over a period of time as the Central Committee changed into chiefly an organ of governance. Its role was reduced to periodically issuing resolutions, whereas its membership, primarily from the most important Party and state officials, was preoccupied with running the behemoth, the Soviet political system. Single Party system had a dual impact on the course of Soviet history, as indeed on the Party and its leadership. One, most significantly, the Party was enjoined with the task of providing administrative infrastructure for governing the society, which it did from within its ranks thus enmeshing the Party and the state into each other. In contrast was the multi-party system in which the bureaucracy would not usually belong to a political party with a bureaucrat as an activist member, although the former may not be necessarily neutral. Secondly, its primarily political task of competing for popular support by campaigning for its policies and programmes was undermined by its role to permanently govern the Soviet society. It was reduced to an agency of governance rather than that of political leader of the society. Diminution of its political role alienated the Party, particularly its leadership, from the people. Political society was thus far removed from the civil society. No wonder political opinion turned against the Party and its leadership, particularly when Perestroika designed to revive the political role of the Party failed, resulting in socio-economic disruption and political chaos.

One of the key political issues was that of political federalism given the ethnic diversity within the political boundaries of the former Soviet Union. However a significant issue was that of federalisation within the Party and its leadership. Membership of the leadership was rarely determined by considerations of nationalities representation. As modernising ideologies, Communism and Socialism did not provide for the representation of political identities based on ethnicity or nationalism. Adherance to the ideology and proleterian internationalism was the criterion for the selection of the leadership. Since the leadership was selected from the top and not elected from within the rank and file, the latter being more susceptible to nationalist and other ethnicity-based ideologies and identities, such a factor played no role in choosing the leadership of the Party. However this could positively discriminate in favour of certain nationalities and ethnicities, wittingly or unwittingly, and against certain others particularly the smaller ones, thus leaving a lingering sense of injustice to a people or region. Thus Russian nationality was thought to be a disproportionately dominant one whereas smaller ones like those from the Baltics or Central Asian republics or Caucasus to be those not adequately represented. Such a situation also had to do with the ideology governing Soviet socialism which merely dismissed nationalism as a bourgeoise ideology and ethnicity as at best an expression of primordial identities thus preventing an adequate theoretical and political treatment of these vital and sensitive issues so close to popular political sensibilities. Federalisation of the Party could have allowed adequate representation of various peoples and regions constituting the former Soviet Union, in the Central Committee. This was particularly more important since the state institutions, which were more representative, wielded much less power and authority than the Party bodies like the Central Committee.

Federalisation however was antithetical to the unitary constitution of the Party, since the Party as a vanguard internationalist political force had superseded localised nationalisms and sub-nationalisms and provided a future model of the Soviet society composed merely of the Soviet citizen - the mythical Soviet man, who dissappeared under the relentless onslaught of the nationalist ideology, and not of Russians, Kazakhs, Georgians,

Latvians, Chechens, Tatars, Volga-Germans, Azeris etc. during Perestroika. Yet nationalities and sub-nationalities, regional and sub-regional identities were socio-geographical facts with political manifestations even within the Party, leaving aside the larger society. The party could not purge its own ranks of these phenomenon, neither could it contest them ideologically nor even understand the intricacies of the phenomenon and its long term political implications. Thus upsurge of national and sub-national ideologies during Perestroika, which eventually demolished the Soviet Union as a political entity, caught the Party leadership off-guard, completely unprepared to respond adequately. The evolution of the pattern of the constitution of the Party bodies, particularly the primary institutions such as the Central Committee, undermined not only its political character but also its representative one. The emergence of an ideal type Soviet citizen, 'the Soviet man' was part of a political-ideological discourse in the former Soviet Union. He was to be a believer in proletarian internationalism, in values of communism and socialism, in a vanguard role of the party, a selfless dedicated worker of these causes who placed the interests of the society and the collective before his individual one. The values of communitarianism were dearer to him over those of individualism. Soviet media did assiduously propagate the idea of such a 'Soviet man' constituting the Soviet society. 'Soviet man' was increasingly coming to compose the former Soviet Union if the Soviet media was to be believed. Alas, when the nationalist upsurge took place on the ruins of a disintegrated Soviet economy, the mythical 'Soviet man' was nowhere to be seen and instead the Soviet citizen was replaced by a Russian, Kazakh, Latvian, Georgian, Chechen, Tatar or some other nationalist or sub-nationalist. Subterranean ideologies of nationalism and subnationalism undermined the Party ideology of creating a 'Soviet man' based on the transnational proletarianism which derecognised the former.

Soviet republics were constitutionally recognised as separate nation-states with their own constitutions, flags, emblems, state and governmental structures etc. Formal political federalism was granted by law. They were given the right for self-determination- a radical legal instrument. The republics could secede and become independent nation-states. However, although in letter the nation-states existed or were permitted to be in making, in spirit compulsions of a unitary modernising ideology contradicted it. Both had their own rationale and both co-existed with the latter determining the dominant paradigm of the political constitution of the Soviet state. One feature, despite the latter's dominance and because of the explicit legal acceptance of desirability of independent nation-states or republics within the framework of a federal Soviet Union, praxis notwithstanding, was that a tradition of accepting the separate identities of these republics, culturally, socially and to some extent politically and historically did continue to exist. Or in other words, nationalisms and national-identities or perhaps more appropriately sub-nationalisms and sub-national identities in a federated Soviet Union, continued to exist, were accepted at a theoretical level and when the time came, during Perestroika, provided sufficient basis for national-assertions, sometimes as genuine responses to real or perceived injustices meted out to these nationalities in the past, and sometimes simply as a political instrument exploited by anti-communist or anti-socialist political forces that burgeoned as a multitude of national and/or democratic fronts in various union-republics. The successive Soviet regimes were wary of national assertions which they considered to be expression of bourgeoise-democratic ideology and thus inimical to socialist construction therefore giving less leeway to national aspirations. They, however, had utilised national sentiments and employed national symbols from time to time, as and when required, for example, during the Second World War. Nationalism thus was a potent mobilising political force and as such could not be ignored by the Soviet regimes. Thus nationalist undercurrents continued in a often symbiotic relationship with the Soviet socialism, internationalism and Soviet identity. The former was a political reality throughout the Soviet era and an uneasy relationship existed between the incipient nationalisms and the modernising and standardising ideology of Soviet internationalism.

The duality was characterised by the acceptance of federalism and federal structures in the Soviet state with the existence of Union-republics, a recognition of distinct national identities along with a vehement denial of federalism within the political force which governed the society, the Communist Party of Soviet Union, since the latter represented the goal of the non-national, internationalist, modernising ideology, that is of transcending nationalisms and creating a Soviet identity with the ideal Soviet man and woman. The party obviously was in the vanguard and bourgeoise phenomenon like nationalism and national identities had no room in its scheme of things. The party was understood to lead the way and its membership was meant to have purged itself of nationalist ideology, and the rest of the society was expected to follow suit. Thus a dichotomy between the leading political force and the society and organisation of the state resulted in a continual tension between the two. As long as the Party and its ethos dominated, nationalist streams were pushed underground.

During Perestroika, political pluralism challenged the Party and its ethos and subterranean nationalisms resurrected to the extent that not only the Party virtually split on nationalist lines in many Union-republics, the Party leadership was compelled to reorganise itself on national lines in complete travesty of its principled adherance to an unitary structure with so called national contingents of the Party. The Communist Party of Russia (RCP), for example, had to be established to fend-off challenge from Russian nationalist forces. Nationalism was thus legitimised under Perestroika as an acceptable political doctrine. Fault lines appeared in the Party along national lines and the Party split and disintegrated along these as did the Soviet society and the Soviet state. Federalism within the Party organisations only hastened the dissolution of Soviet Union since it was an overt acknowledgement of victory of nationalism over internationalism.

Nowhere was the unitarianism of the Party reflected in a more crystal clear manner as in the Central Committee. Several Union-republics and nationalities were over-represented, whereas some were under-represented or sometimes had no representation at all. This may not have appeared very significant prima facie since institutions and not the nationalities were the basis of representation. Yet it did contribute to the sense of discrimination of those union-republics and nationalities, particularly the smaller ones, which were under-represented or not represented at all. Plenum speeches did reflect republican or national interests and some could thus be denied the opportunity to express them at this vital forum. The Central Committee plenums were the nearest approximation of a forum at which interest articulation took place. However tacit or direct, the Central Committee members spoke about the interests of the constituencies they represented. In early days the plenums reflected political pluralism. Latter day plenum primarily discussed programmes, policies and their implementation or simply the diverse social interests. Political differences were discussed in nuances or couched expressions of different tendencies. Plenums endorsed important policy-decisions or any other issue of significance. Plenum resolutions gave a decision its seal of legitimacy. The decisions then became binding on the Party and the state and government institutions and their personnel. Since the distinction between the Party and the state and the government institutions was blurred to say the least, joint declarations and joint resolutions were a common phenomenon. The Central Committee thus lent its authority and legitimacy to important decisions of the state and government institutions. However this was also the clearest indicator of the integration of the Party and the state. Membership of various state and government institutions in the Central Committee could be explained as a necessary feature in a single-Party or a multi-Party system in which these leaders are generally a part of the leadership body of the governing party merely by virtue of the fact that the latter implements its policies through the former and need to get the feedback and policy and other inputs into decision-making process continually.

In the initial decade or so of its existence, the Central Committee was a pluralist institution in the sense that divergent political-ideological and diverse interests were present. These openly competed for their sectarian politics and sectional interests. It is in this sense that it was emerging as a 'parliament' of the Party, a uniquely 'Soviet parliament' different from what it is understood to be in the liberal-democratic systems - a body elected on the basis of adult franchise, having majority and minority representations signified by the political parties and their members elected to this institution on the basis of their ideologies, programmes and policies or personalities. Although in its early years the Central Committee was elected, albeit by the Congress delegates, it did represent different political-ideological tendencies, although broadly from within the social-democratic and left movement in Russia and Europe at that time. These tendencies lacked any definitive and independent organisational form and discipline of a political party, they did have differing perspectives, programmes and policies. Thus 'Soviet parliament' was a quasi-parliament working within a single political party system. It was better characterised as a 'supreme Party conference' in between Congresses. It did provide the best available democratic practice to intra-party functioning, particularly at the highest levels of leadership. An organisational mechanism of this kind could contain the diverse tendencies within the singular framework allowing them to compete for the political leadership of the Party and the society. However it may not have been consistent with the avowed and conscious decision to build a society and polity based on Bolshevik values - political, economic, social and cultural, as embodied in Marxism-Leninism and had come to define the programme and perspective of RSDLP (Bolshevik) during the course of its underground struggle, the revolution and subsequent bid to retain political power during the Civil War, a conflict which undermined the very existence of Bolsheviks and Bolshevism. These divergent tendencies were very much evident within the Politburo. Lenin with his political stature could arbitrate and steer the Party and the government during the critical years. With the untimely demise of Lenin, no single leader could acquire a similar status and the differences amongst divergent tendencies sharpened threatening a debilitating internal conflict within the leadership. In such a situation the role of arbitration fell upon the Central Committee as the 'Soviet parliament' to resolve the dispute amongst its highest standing committee, the Politburo. This perhaps again reflected working inner-Party democracy albeit partial.

The question of the legitimacy of a political system or a regime and its leadership is extremely crucial. Legitimacy amounts to the acceptance of a political system and its personnel by those over whom the institutions and their human components rule. It may be a democratic legitimacy or a non-democratic one. A democratic legitimacy in the modern sense in a liberal-democratic society is vested into periodic election of the leadership of the state and the government through universal adult franchise and the evolution of its institutions. However this is also a class-based legitimacy in which certain significant sections of the society are disenfranchised effectively in practice whereas in theory universal franchise is guaranteed. A government may derive legitimacy to rule even if it gets minority popular votes in a real sense although these may be the majority of the votes cast. Certain-types of politics and ideologies may not be allowed level playing fields thus making them conditional democracies since the broad socio-political consensus militates against them for right or wong reasons. The participants may have to abide by this broad consensus and conform to the ground rules laid down by the dominant politico-ideological framework governing a particular society. Political pluralism within a defined framework is the hallmark of this democratic legitimacy in a liberal-democratic society. This is then an incomplete and conditional democracy. Coercion and coercive apparatuses exist to regulate such a legitimacy. Coercion may or may not be exercised to varying degrees, but the threat of use of coercion complements other institutionalised means to ensure that the socio-political and economic norms and values do not deviate from those which the society either voluntarily believes or had been conditioned to believe in their correctness, universality and perpetuity. This has been true for all societies in history including the Soviet type of societies. Thus a sort of false-consciousness pervades each society and its members and is demystyfied periodically only to be replaced by another false-consciousness legitimating another variant of political system, personnel may or may not be the same, and dominant politico-ideological confluence. Personnel may be the same, although metamorphosed politically and ideologically. Thus one false or partial consciousness replaces the other. This however happens when a configuration of dominant social forces - their politics, economics and ideology, are replaced by another one. They may be those with recent origin, may be old but subordinated ones or may be a combination of old and new. Nonetheless, it is they who determine which the dominant set of norms and values governing the institutions of the society and the political system are going to be. These may be a radical departure from those that existed or a synthesis of past and present. 'Old' and 'new' are misnomers, since most of them may have co-existed in dominant or subordinate forms for long historical periods. These terms can only be used with precise demarcations over prolonged historical periods. For instance, there would be very little in common in 12th Century Russia and present day Russian terms of social, political, economic and even cultural (culture takes longest to change) values, norms and institutions of the society and the political system. Some clear continuity however may be traced between the late Tsarist period, particularly the 19th Century, and Soviet and post-Soviet periods.

Many sets of values and norms, Tsarist, communist, liberal-democratic co-existed and even institutions were sought to be replicated. They contested with the support of different social forces, old and new, religion being one of the major old social and ideological force, to establish their dominance over the society and pursue their class-oriented sectional agenda without any resistance. However each of them could rule as long as they were legitimate in the eyes of those over whom they ruled. This legitimacy could be derived from an ideology as in case of Marxism-Leninism or the goals the society (read dominant social forces) set for themselves as in the case of revolutionary ideals of Bolshevism, or a negative legitimacy of anti-communism and for restoration of a capitalistic social order as in post-Soviet Russia. Non-democratic legitimacy in a modern sense may be those of monarchy or other authoritarian or dictatorial regimes which may not undergo any process of consultation like for example periodic elections or referenda, yet the political system and its leaders are accepted as legitimate rulers by the society. Such a legitimacy may be based on ostensibly non-political factors like tribal-affinity, caste, community or religion. However, such non-democratic legitimacy was replaced by democratic ones even though the method of establishing such legitimacy differed from one place to another. Single-party political systems too conducted elections which were however not based on principle of pluralism as in liberal-democratic societies represented by different political parties contesting them. Yet as discussed elsewhere, pluralism and pluralistic tendencies were evident and in full play in these systems as well as contesting to win the leadership and set the political agenda, even if such a contest was not open and between political tendencies having distinct organisational forms, as for example in contemporary China or the former Soviet Union. An institution like the Central Committee had acquired its legitimacy because of its position as the leadership organ of the ruling Party in a single-Party political system, its history as an assembly of revolutionary notables that led the revolution and established the Soviet regime, because of its composition which included all the important political and administrative leaders of the Soviet Union and finally because all major policy decisions emanated from this institution.

The General Secretary of the Party primarily exercised the power and authority vested in the Central Committee. He was the sole arbiter between numerous institutions vying for resources within this institution. As a 'parliament' of numerous primary and secondary institutions the Central Committee was involved in coping with day to day inputs and demands at a very functional level, despite a functioning government and other state institutions. Its Apparatus replicated other primary and secondary institutions and not only laid down the guidelines but played a role in the actual process of policy-decisions and policy-implementation. It has however been a matter of debate amongst Soviet scholars as to whether the Central Committee and its departments were as powerful as they were made out to be or the state institutions, like the ministries and state bodies, had an autonomy of their own and functioned almost independent of and inspite of the Central Committee and were dictated by their own sectoral interests. The bodies like the Politburo and the Central Committee were said to be merely responding to their demands and were led instead of leading. The General Secretary, as a team leader, played the most significant role in the selection process. He derived his power and authority from his appointees, who in turn acquired theirs from him. That is why each transition witnessed a massive overhaul of this body by the incumbent leader. However this process was not as simple as the appointment of a new cabinet by the Prime Minister or President -elect as in Western democracies. Several times it entailed a long drawn out struggle for power to rid the body of inherited personnel testifying to the position of considerable power enjoyed by these members. In many cases they were backed by the institutions they represented and definitive policy-orientations signified by the previous regimes. Sometimes they could survive the purges and continued in some uneasy or latent compromises brought about within the body for long periods. Even removal of the appointed leaders of the central apparatus was a tedious process. The new General Secretary may usher in policy and programme changes, even those with ideological-political tenor, he had to contend with entrenched interests backed by definite social forces within the Party and the society.

Making of a single institution or a set of institutions takes a long period of time and conscious intervention. This process imparts integrity and coherence. Institution based governance is more democratic and participatory as against a personalised one. The former is a more modern system, is more rational and impersonal. One of the key problems with institution based governance is that they are relatively lethargic and may lack the activism of a personalised system of governance. However, the former, albeit slow in their responses, have greater inbuilt system of checks and balances and inflexibility than the latter thereby providing greater stability and predictability to the system of governance. Although a personalised system of governance, like in monarchies, dictatorships etc., too had some institutional framework sustaining them, these were more elementary in nature. Such institutions were tied to the individuals and personalities and would often disappear with them. Institutional system of governance however outlived individuals and personalities. The former emerged when both society and the required governance were much simpler. Institutional governance came with complex societies, a complex mode of governance and maturing of a political system. More and more political institutions emerged, be they political parties, parliaments, executive Presidencies, cabinets etc. They integrated and interacted churning out norms and principles needed to govern a political system. Some were flexible, addressed themselves to the changing requirements of the society and modified their forms and content, whereas others lapsed into institutional inertia, apathy and stagnation. In the long run institutions matured and mutated or perished. These changes however take place over a very long span of time and only when the institution or institutions become completely outdated, isolated and incapable of evolution. Sometimes the very characteristic and positive feature of institutional integrity and coherence become fetters. Tampering with these may result in breakdown of an institution or set of institutions. If they endeavour to change they may lose their institutional integrity and coherence and collapse. These may suitably evolve and retain their institutional integrity and coherence during the transitional phase and thus continue to be relevant. Former circumstances were responsible for the breakdown of Soviet political institutions including the Central Committee. It is a moot question as to whether these institutions may have continued to be relevant and survive and for how long if they had not embarked upon a path of reforms encountering a slippery phase of transition. One can attempt to draw certain conclusions with the benefit of the hindsight, however these would merely be conjectures based on analysis devoid of any factual sequence of events. Institutions, particularly political ones, acquire integrity and coherence when they articulate a certain set of coherent social interests. Soviet political institutions, including the Central Committee of the CPSU, acquired these two features on the basis of representing sectional class interests derived by virtue of the Soviet state being a proleterian and semi-proleterian state deriving ideological legitimacy from Marxism-Leninism. When it allowed the emergence of counter-sectional class interests represented by the bourgeoise and semi-bourgeoise and attempted to incorporate them within the existing framework, these political institutions, the Party and the Central Committee included, not only lost their integrity and coherence but became a battleground for conflicting political positions and diametrically opposite ideological, policy and programme orientation. They created conditions for the emergence of a counter ideological legitimacy and set of political institutions. They lost the battle to the latter partly because of the foregoing reasons of loss of institutional integrity and coherence and partly because these political institutions had not undertaken periodic reforms within their own paradigmatic framework defined by the ideology of Marxism and Leninism. They lost legitimacy within their own social and political constituencies which switched its political support to the counter ideology and institutions believing in the promises of a better life by the proponents of the latter. Later they used this newly acquired political legitimacy to destroy the existing political institutions.

Political structures refer internally to institutional organisation and a set of structures externally to institutional assemblage or matrix. A political system invariably is composed of a formation of institutions, each with its individual organisation and discipline, distinct from the other yet interlinked, interdependent and interacting. These provide the form to a political system and conduct the function of politics defining their contours over time. An institution itself may have component sub-structures as in the case of the Central Committee. These may undergo changes, reform, lose their political relevance and may be replaced by new ones. These are very much like the building blocks which makes a system more tangible and real. They may need to be repaired from time to time, may be overhauled or modified or demolished altogether. This comparison and the use of term 'structure' may be objected to and perhaps sought to be replaced by 'organisation' or 'assemblage' or 'matrix' or 'formation' or 'constitution' or 'configuration' since the former conveys an idea of greater rigidity than perhaps social or political institution display. However, such a term more clearly conveys an imagery of a more well defined configuration that has emerged over a sufficiently long historical span. This was the case with the Soviet political system and its institutions like the Central Committee. The Politburo and the Central Committee were primarily political institutions essentially taking fundamental political and policy decisions based on the political directives of the Party Congress. The Central Secretariat and the apparatus of the Central Committee were the primary administrative institutions. These institutions implemented the decisions of the Politburo and the Central Committee. They worked out the details adding content to the broadbased decisions, supervised their implementation and reviewed their success and failure. Thus the effective exercise of power was vested in the Central Secretariat and the apparatus of the Central Committee, whereas the Politburo and the Central Committee lend political authority to these bodies and the decisions. There was an overlap of membership between these bodies. They were helped by the Commissions in formulating decisions although the latter did not have any permanence. Thus the primary Party institutions were deeply involved in the activities of the state and governance as a result of the single-Party political system. These Party structures including that of the Central Committee evolved out of compulsions of governing a single-Party led political system. This unique characterstic further resulted in unwarranted centralisation of power and authority in those structures. They grew in complexity and scope with the Soviet society. However structural constraints coupled with centralisation restricted their capacity to provide adequate and good governance. In one sense, the crisis of Soviet political system was also the crisis of these institutions and that of good and adequate governance. Decentralised governance is a precondition for good governance. This was not the case with the Soviet Union despite a plethora of secondary and subordinate institutions right up to the villages and the settlements. Integration of the Party, and state and a single-Party political system effectively resulted in the centralisation of decision-making and hierarchy of process of implementation whereby the decision-making was primarily vested in primary institutions and implementation was the responsibility vested upto the lowest Party and state institutions. Thus the upper echelons had power without responsibility whereas the lower ones, in practice, responsibility without power. Amongst the primary institutions, those who exercised power like the Central Secretariat and the Central apparatus enjoyed greater power than the primary political institutions like the Politburo and the Central Committee which lend political authority to the exercise of power. Bureaucracies, in all political systems, since they are the implementing arm of any system of governance, enjoy more power than their political masters. In the case of the Soviet political system the political and the administrative arms of the Party were integrated at one level with the overlapping of the memberships. Those who were part of both enjoyed greater powers than ones who did not. Thus the primary structures overlapped at one level and functioned as the nerve centre of the Soviet political system.

As a primary political institution which ruled and not merely reigned, the Central Committee governed and administered. In a planned economy, which avowedly shunned market-orientation for ideological reason, economic life was an important area of preoccupation. Policy decisions on economy, fixing broad targets and overseeing the implementation were some of these. Given the magnitude of the decisions regarding economic priorities of a vast country like the Soviet Union, it constituted one of the most important tasks for the Party leadership. The entire economy was managed by the Party organisations on the helm of which stood the Central Committee because of hierarchical Party structure. Such a system of economic administration took its roots in the 1930s, did play a significant role in developing and industrialising a backward economy, and continued as an accepted practice throughout the existence of the Soviet Union. Although in latter decades, economic organisations, it is argued, acquired greater autonomy, competed for resources and imposed their priorities on the Party leadership, or in other words as the economy grew ever more complex, it became increasingly difficult for the Party and its leadership to exercise control over the burgeoning economy. However by this time the distinction between the Party, the state and the economy had all but completely eroded as a result of overlapping that it was very difficult to distinguish between the Party, the state and the economic leadership. Most economic interests were represented in the Party leadership and contested for the resources. At a very functional level the Party leadership was engaged in resource allocation and less in political activities except for issuing periodic political resolutions. Political activities of any political party ought to be involved actively engaging with political, social, economic and cultural needs of the society which in turn get reflected in the policy-decisions and undertaking mobilisational activities to enlist support for the Party's programme and policies. However, with political power ensured in a single Party system, this particular function of the Party had been reduced to formalistic pronouncements.

Hierarchical system of organisation and functioning allows for an activist functioning but chokes the upward transmission of popular aspirations and responses. This precludes a vital element of organisational functioning, particularly of those involved in public affairs, that of not only assessing the impact of a policy-decision, but also of vital input in policy-formulation. Modernising ideologies tend to have hierarchical structures in the political organisations espousing them because of the innate belief in the rationality of these ideologies. Since the practice of these ideologies is against the irrationality of some other forms and ideologies, they may be less sensitive towards them. The political leaderships are meant to be the ideal carriers of these modernising ideologies and therefore tend to set up practical goals to be implemented by other echelons. This may not be a good practice since it may end up antagonising those very people whom it seeks to convert, for in real sense the dominant ideologies may be those against whose irrationality the politically dominant modernising ideology may be working. In the absence of a proper feedback mechanism the political leadership may be practicing wrong political strategy and may not be properly aware of socio-economic-cultural aspirations of those ruled. Sometimes ideology precludes a sound practice of *real politik* and sets up goals which may either be too advanced or backward in relation to the stage of development a society is in. Such a development, a contentious term, may be in terms of levels of social, political, economic and cultural attributes of a society. Development in this context clearly relates to those attributes which have become and proven to have become obsolete in a given society. The index of development is dependent on the extent to which these variables constitute the dominant features of the society in question. For instance, a society which accepts monarchy as a political form of government or inhuman penal forms for crimes committed or violence as a normal social behaviour etc. would be low on the index of development.

In a liberal-democratic political system the dominant political parties were those owing allegiance to either aristocracy or nobility or to the newly emergent bourgeoise since emergence of political parties is a post-industrial revolution phenomenon. The parties essentially defended the interests of the erstwhile feudal classes which were gradually losing their political power and dominance to the emergent noveau-bourgeoise, historically an ascendant class, when the parties emerged, controlling the modern technology and means of production. These two socio-economic and political forces competed with each other, one to retain power and other to acquire the same. Their respective ideologies, the feudalism of aristocracy and nobility and liberalism of ascendant bourgeoise were locked in a political struggle for power and authority and political parties represented their sectional interests. The bourgeoise initially clamoured for greater political freedom and democracy against the autocracy of monarchies and feudal dominance. However these political freedoms were partial and did not include economic freedom. Hence on the one hand, political freedom and rights were considered legitimate by ideology of liberalism, on the other hand, exploitation of another class, which emerged as a result of industrial revolution and that era of capitalism, that of the working class was rampant. Lack of economic freedom and its economic dependence on the bourgeoise as a result of absence of any direct or indirect control over means of production rendered it vulnerable to universal exploitation. Although it did gain partial political freedom and rights, these were severely curtailed by its complete economic dependence on the bourgeoise. This, more numerous section of the society was disorganised and unable to represent its sectional interests and fight for its legitimate place in the society as the primarily productive class. There were no mainstream political parties in the modern sense representing them and their interests. It was only during the second half of the 19th Century that organisations and working class parties in the modern sense emerged and the works of Marx and Engels provided an ideological basis to many of them. These political parties based themselves on the exclusive ideology of proletarianism or working class interests and the world view and were avowedly against that of liberal-democratic ideology. The two were seen to be in perpetual conflict and political contest. Thus these constituted the third category of parties apart from those defending feudalism or advocating liberal-democratic values.

The working class party, for Lenin, was to be a revolutionary party unlike the reformist bourgeoise political parties. A revolutionary party endeavoured to replace a feudal or liberal-democratic regime with a working class rule. Thus it was to be an unconventional party, unlike the prevailing concept of a political party seeking evolutionary changes. The Party was not only a vehicle of revolutionary transformation externally, but an instrument to inculcate working class ideology and politics in its component class - the working class and its allies in peasantry and the middle classes. Thus the element of a conscious or enlightened mobilisation of class-based support was a distinct feature of such a party. It, although had a potential mass base, did not have an active mass support unlike bourgeoise or feudal-oriented political parties since these were dominant social, cultural and political ideologies exercising economic control as well. These were meant to provide a natural, normal and legitimate social system and society and since working class ideology militated against them, they obviously challenged the long existing values and thus destabilised the social order led by the former. Thus the task of a working class party was immensely harder. It had to organise the proletariat and semi-proletariat and inculcate working-class political consciousness based on the sectarian economic interests which came more easily to them. Only then the working class became class-for-itself from class-in-itself. It recognised its potential as a class and contested not merely for economic concessions but for winning over political power and running a working class state based on its ideology. Such a state was deemed to be more democratic since it was a rule by the majority for the majority. It was socialist because it imparted economic freedom alongwith the political freedom which had been won by the bourgeoise and further extended by the working class. However it was debatable if dominance of the ideology and politics of a single class - the working class and its allies automatically led to the emergence of a single-Party state and political system? It was also not clear if such a domination precluded the right of non-working class parties from existing and competing to acquire political power? Would such parties be dealt with by political coercion or through political competition? These questions had largely remained unresolved in the Marxist theory of those times and day.

The role of the state was crucial in a working class political system. Since it was a working class state it had the dual role of subordinating the antagonistic classes and functioning as a state engaged in production, distribution and welfare measures. Its former task included coercion, controlling the real and perceived enemies of the working class state, whereas the latter was a comprehensive act of mobilisation for production, equitable distribution through a state controlled distributive mechanism and discharging social welfare functions in the sphere of education, health, social justice and other indices of general well being. These were, apart from the usual functions of state common to most societies like maintaining law and order, general administration, running a legal justice system and internal and external security. However the role of the state was much more extensive and varied in a working class state since it is also involved in running and managing the economy in the absence of a private economic domain, particularly in macro sphere or the so-called commanding heights of the economy alongwith the responsibility of constituting and running a distributive mechanism catering to a complex society. Thus the state had to be perpetually extended to increase its areas of influence and activities to keep pace with a society that grew more and more complex and varied by the day, thereby stretching it to unviable lengths and becoming a source of constant tension between the ruler and the ruled. A simple society emerging from the shadows of feudalism as in the early periods of the Soviet regime up to the last phase of of Stalin's rule were easily manageable by the Soviet state using both coercion and consent. However relentless industrialisation and modernisation had given birth to an immensely complicated society with complex norms and values. It was much more demanding on its state, the only agency (apart from the Party, which in any case was not so distinct from the Soviet state) which had taken upon itself the role of sole provider. The resources obviously are more limited than the demands of a society at any point in time. In this case the Soviet state was the direct provider (unlike in other societies in which state does not directly perform this role) and thus the constant tension between the state and the society.

This continuous tension between the state and the society was the basis of a central question - Should the state gradually withdraw from its extensive commitments and remodel? If the state retreated then the Party too would, which had been integrated with the state historically? On the one hand this would most certainly diminish the power and authority of both the Party and the state, as it eventually did, whereas on the other hand, it afforded both the Party and the state a chance for renewal if they survived the transition, which neither ultimately did and perished. Simultaneous and integral to this process was the separation of the Party and the state. The Party was supposed to become a political force working out the policies but not executing them. The state was to decentralise and become more representative. Perestroika, in political terms was the separation of the Party and the state, withdrawal of the state from its multi-farious involvements, leaving the political field open to a plethora of political and ideological forces, plurality in the economy with a burgeoning private sector was to relieve the state from providing economic sustenance to society, and the Party was to give policy directions assuming that it continued to be the ruling force in face of massive and unmitigated erosion of its political primacy in the Soviet political system. The state was then not building socialism but modifying itself on the lines of a liberal-democratic state abandoning its uniqueness based on the concepts of a proletarian state and dictatorship of the proletariat. Quite obviously the economic changes during Perestroika were giving rise to new social classes and and political forces influencing the state and its policies. These included the nascent bourgeoise and professional middle-classes aspiring to be one. The modified state had to accomodate and respond to their aspirations. The state as it existed was indeed 'withering away' but not quite in the sense Marx would have wanted it to - by replacing it with a self-governing society. The Soviet state that 'withered away' was ultimately replaced by an authoritarian and narrow state with limited social support and therefore a more primitive and elementary form of state despite the trappings of liberal-democratic practices like elections and assemblies etc. Autarchy of the new state thus substituted quasi-authoritarianism of the old one. The new state continues to be a superimposed one, lacking significant social support and is precariously perched.

When the primary institutions undergo transformation, they threaten the survival of the very system they are designed to run. However the dilemma of whether to renew and improve the efficacy of institutions or to retain them and risk stagnation has always faced those who run the institutions. Institutions and the system they sustain evolve and come to acquire their form, content and function over a long historical period as in the case of institutions like the Central Committee and the Soviet political system. The Central Committee as it existed on the eve of Perestroika was a product of earlier decades of its existence and and an integral part of a single-Party political system. Reforms in the political system warranted institutional reforms of all its component institutions. The Central Committee was no exception. However attempting to reform this body meant disturbing the existing configuration discharging the political power and authority in the Soviet political system. This institution was at the centre of the institutional framework/arrangement engaged in the task of the state-craft. Thus institutional reforms could not have remained confined to a single institution and had to be extended to the whole gamut of primary institutions. Therefore the institutions were to metamorphose their organisation, their ethos, working, composition, in short, in all its ramifications. The two vital issues here were: in what direction and will they survive the transition? The initial direction of course was a reformed socialism allowing pluralism of ideas within the framework of political and ideological parameters of socialism and communism; a more open, democratic, representative, responsive political system and multiple economic forms - state, cooperative, private at a very elementary level, leaseholding etc.; a more federal political system based on a new union-treaty making republics more autonomous.

Although the transitional phase was deemed to be difficult, the reformist leadership did not envisage a total breakdown of the system. Conservatives, however, foresaw and foretold the possibility of a systemic disintegration. Institutions and institutional practices provide the glue that binds a system. Any radical tampering with them are bound to result in weakening the binding links. Any evolutionary transformation extending to a sufficiently prolonged historical period can prevent the erosion of binding linkages. Old linkages can be replaced by new ones and be consolidated further. New institutional arrangements and practices require prolonged periods to mature and institutionalise. Until then both are vulnerable and hold the possibility of disintegration bringing about systemic collapse. Systemic change as opposed to systemic collapse can prevent unintended and unforeseen consequences which may not be of a positive nature. Systemic changes however have to be evolutionary and incremental. Under Perestroika, an earlier phase of institutional reforms, particularly in primary institutions was evolutionary rather than revolutionary. Controlled systemic transformation rather than a radical one was the credo. However towards the final phase, pace of institutional reforms accelerated under both internally generated momentum and because of the impact of a radicalised external political environment. Political and ideological pluralism generated by Perestroika and glasnost destroyed thc carlier conception of one-Party democratisation within a socialist framework and these institutions were compelled to change willy-nilly in the direction dictated by an emerging multi-party, liberal-democratic political system along with resurgent nationalism and separatism.

2 Historical Background

Introduction

The Central Committee of the CPSU was dramatically transformed during Perestroika. From being a ruling institution it no longer remained the centre of power and authority towards the terminal years of the Soviet political system. The reforms which were designed to strengthen its position in a renewed power configuration within a reformed political system failed and reduced a once powerful political institution into a minor player in Soviet politics. How and why did this happen despite the radical changes this body underwent? Why did a political institution which was at the core of a supposedly monolithic political system come to abdicate power? Was it that the historically acquired characteristics it exhibited at the outset of Perestroika provided it with an inbuilt inflexibility preventing it from adjusting to change? Or was it the unintended consequences of the reforms which carried the seeds of its destruction? Could such a collapse have been prevented or did this institution, as a component part of a political system which had run its course, had to disintegrate? Did the reasons for its demise lay in the institutionalised political-administrative nature of the Central Committee? Did it exist only to discharge certain functions in Soviet society, which once removed from it deprived it of its raison d'être? Was it that having been denied its customary role and function in the political system, its collapse was inevitable? Or did the gradual dissolution of regulatory devices like the ban on factions and Democratic Centralism result in the interplay of conflicts between incipient political tendencies, bringing to the surface deep fissures, thus destroying its earlier coherence and integrity? Did personnel change, instead of contributing towards reforming this institution, in effect accelerate its disintegration? Was it that the reforms in the operational structures of the Central Committee, i.e. the Central Secretariat and the Central apparatus, instead of curing the malaise resulting from the command-administrative system, undermine them? Did the attempts to change its functioning result in making it effectively dysfunctional? Finally, to what extent did the central reform of the separation of the Party and the State, within the context of which the reforms were taking place, initially a one-Party democratisation and subsequently in an emerging multi-party system, contribute to the collapse of the Central Committee? Several vital questions underscored the importance of an institution which was an assembly of political and administrative leadership of the former Soviet Union.

The Central Committee of the CPSU was the designated supreme authority between congresses. It was the 'parliament' of leading institutions in the Soviet Union. These institutions represented the key functional elements of the political system, the demands of which were collated by this body. Its power and authority underwent fluctuations during the existence of the USSR. But it remained throughout a centre for political legitimation and thus of political authority, even in decline. It was also important because it incorporated an array of "expertise and experience", which could be used by the Politburo and the Central Secretariat in formulating policy.[1] Each "functional hierarchy" and each union republic was represented in the Central Committee. This membership corresponded to "the imputed status and importance" of a specific institution or region. Thus leading members of the Party, State institutions and mass organisations were represented in the Central Committee.[2] It was seen as "a composite" of the plenipotentiaries of major functional groups and "the principal medium" of the Politburo for a regular exchange of information with representatives of key interest groups. Thus its function represented "an institutionalisation of a high level of the communications network".[3] It was the recruiting ground for the Central Party leadership from which the Politburo and the Central Secretariat were elected. (It could not, however, elect new members, which was the prerogative of the Party Congress; members could only be promoted from among candidate members.) Meetings of the Central Committee had become ceremonial occasions,[4] where varied but not conflicting opinions would be expressed. The Central Committee served as a platform to announce policies and to ratify changes in the Politburo and Central Secretariat. The principle of Democratic Centralism welded together the structure of the Party and the Central Committee, though in practice the centralist element predominated over the democratic one. It forged the monolithic unity of the Party, and of the Central Committee, and ensured that channels of communications were vertical rather than horizontal.[5] All this however dramatically changed under the impact of the radical transformations unleashed during Perestroika.

Prior to the revolution, the Central Committee had been the decision-making body of the Russian Social Democratic Workers' Party. It was empowered to formulate policies between Congresses. In accordance with the principle of Democratic Centralism its decisions were binding.

Until the Tenth Congress, the election of the members of the Central Committee was not predetermined by the leadership. The Congress in practice had the final say in the composition. At the Tenth Party Congress in 1921, however, for the first time a slate of candidates was presented "to be voted on as a group by the Congress, a practice subsequently institutionalised."[6] Elections at Congresses allowed scope for the representation of different political tendencies in the Central Committee. These existed and manifested themselves from the early years of the revolution. By 1920, two significant opposition groups in the Party, the 'Democratic Centralists' and 'Workers' Opposition', had emerged. Different platforms were allowed to discuss the question of the role of trade unions and to mobilise support in local Party organisations for the election of delegates at the Tenth Party Congress. However the Kronstadt rebellion which occurred during this Congress sharply focused the question of inner-Party divisions, and the Congress resolved to ban factions in the Party.[7] The Fifteenth Congress in 1927 would be the last at which significant policy differences emerged; it marked the end of open opposition in the Party.[8] This did not however mean total consensus in the political leadership. Both reformism and conservatism, it has been argued, continued in a "latent conflict", representing a duality in Soviet political culture.

After 1953, these two tendencies emerged clearly in the Soviet politics, as forces of "innovation and tradition" in Soviet literature. The post-Stalin period up to the early 1960s has been seen as a period of triumph for reformism, with the rehabilitation of the Party as the ruling institution. Terror and political reprisals ended, and the participation of society in political and intellectual life increased. Khrushchev's reforms succeeded while they did not challenge the integrity and position of the central Party and State apparatuses; when they did he was deposed. Although with his fall, the reform movement suffered a political defeat, it had come to stay.

Conservatism and reformism as two distinct trends consolidated themselves within the Central Committee and the Party in the post-Stalin period. Conservatism had a strong political and social constituency from top to bottom of Soviet society, making the task of reform harder. But reformism continued to be tolerated by the Soviet leadership. Despite the dominance of conservatives after Khrushchev, they suffered from serious handicaps, the burden of the legacy of the past, of both the Stalin and Tsarist periods. Their programme could not resolve the problems of the economy and society. The Brezhnev period thus prepared the ground for a reformist upsurge of a qualitatively higher and deeper nature.

Political coalition was a pre-condition for the success of reforms. With the reformers in a minority, a coalition with moderate conservatives was important. In the 1960s, some evidence existed of an emerging consensus between moderate reformers and moderate conservatives, particularly among the intelligentsia, on certain issues of common interest. A basis was emerging for another phase of reform in Soviet society,[9] which culminated with the beginning of Perestroika. Another development was that "the glimmerings of a civil society were visible between 1962 and 1964," albeit one within the defined parameters of constructing communism.[10] Non-state, independent groups provided a basis in society towards which reformists could look for political support in meeting the challenge from the conservatives in the leadership. Thus reformists looked to civil society for "consent" in a Gramscian sense, and blurred the lines dividing political society (in this case the Soviet leadership) and civil society.[11] Under Gorbachev, political society came to be heavily dependent on civil society for sustenance and legitimacy, in sharp contrast to earlier Soviet history. Such consent was important in re-inforcing the legitimacy of the political order. It could come through reviving participatory politics, thus creating a new basis of legitimacy. New contradictions had arisen in the highly complex industrial society the Soviet Union had become. Existing institutions were proving inadequate to deal with the complexity of the tasks required. An extensive set of democratic, decentralised and responsive political institutions was needed. The demands and aspirations of Soviet citizens had to be articulated and fed into the system through them. Only then could the moribund political system revive and discharge its function of matching up to the complexities of Soviet society and acquire new legitimacy. This was where, for the Soviet leadership, the structures of the Party and its Central Committee were to play an important role. However, the question of political tendencies was linked, first and foremost, to the composition of the Central Committee, since this reflected the correlation of forces between them. The composition of the Central Committee constituted the political and administrative leadership. Already by the early 1920s the process of election of members of the Central Committee had given way to co-option or selection from above, and the post rather than their revolutionary or political record had become the chief criterion. This was an important factor in its conversion from an organ of political leadership to that of a collective of institutions. Monopoly control over power and the task of governance in extremely adverse circumstances were other factors contributing to this transformation. With its increasing size several posts which had not previously been represented in it came within its ambit.[12] No single institution or set of institutions could completely dominate this body for most of its existence

The Central Committee functioned as an alternative forum to the Politburo, Orgburo and Central Secretariat to deliberate and decide upon current matters. But it gradually lost its role to other bodies and met less and less frequently. From an average of meeting once a week in the six months prior to the Tenth Party Congress, the frequency soon fell to an average of little more than once a month. By the late 1920s it might not meet for several months. One reason may have been its size, which had increased substantially by 1927, making it impossible for it to monitor the day to day execution of its policies. However, its authority as the supreme body was accepted throughout the 1920s, and it acted as an arbiter of differences within the Politburo and continued to serve as a launching pad for major policy changes. Before Lenin's death it was emerging as a 'Soviet parliament'. On the eve of the Twelfth Party Congress, Lenin considered the Central Committee to be developing into "a kind of supreme Party conference". He recommended to the Congress that its plenums should be transformed into supreme Party conferences convened at bi-monthly intervals.[13] After his death, rivalries within the Politburo resulted in its role as "the supreme court of appeal"[14] becoming more prominent.

By the end of 1929, under Stalin, the role of the Central Committee as a 'Soviet parliament' had become redundant. Later it would be convened every few months to formally approve key decisions. Yet the role of the Central Committee in legitimating Soviet rule continued to be crucial.[15] The Central Committee was never subsequently allowed to resume its position as the supreme authority. The practice of the General Secretary ensuring that his supporters got elected to this body, resulting in the "circular flow of power"[16] also began.

By the Eighteenth Party Congress the Central Committee had become a collective of leaders of the "political-administrative structure".[17] After Stalin's death, Khrushchev attempted to strengthen the position of the Party. This, he believed, would strengthen his position, hence his insistence that the major decisions of the Party and the State be confirmed by Central Committee plenums. He used these to propagate his policies. In a major initiative the meetings and proceedings of the plenums received wide publicity and were published. Under Khrushchev the Party Apparatus started superseding the State Apparatus.[18] Attempts were made to revitalise the Central Committee by making the Presidium answerable to it on issues related to the composition of inner Party bodies. Khrushchev used Central Committee plenums to launch a series of reforms in agriculture, an area under his direct supervision.

The role of the Central Committee as 'Soviet Parliament' arbitrating in disputes in the Presidium was revived to some extent during the Khrushchev period. Moreover he built up a formidable support base within the Central Committee. Despite this the Presidium retained its role as the key policy-making body. Hence the importance of the Central Committee. In early 1957 Khrushchev reorganised industrial management and devolved the functions of the central government apparatus to local 'economic councils', subordinated to the Republican governments. These were supervised by provincial Party officials, winning him their support. He was now ensured of a majority within the Central Committee which he used to defeat opposition in the Presidium in June 1957. Thereafter, with the 'secured' dominance of Khrushchev in the Presidium, the Central Committee's 'parliamentary' role again abated. It would, however, meet periodically to function as a sounding chamber.[19] From 1958, Khrushchev, taking the support of the Central Committee for granted, initiated a high turn-over of the political elite.[20] From the 1960s he began inviting to the plenums non-Central Committee members, who were 'technical experts', sometimes not even Party members.[21] This was seen as undermining the integrity and the position of the Central Committee, which he had himself assiduously nurtured previously.

Article 25 of the new Party Statutes adopted at the 22nd Party Congress in 1961 proposed that one-quarter of the Central Committee and the Party Presidium was to be renewed at each regular election. Presidium members, except for "outstanding" politicians, were not to be elected for more than three terms. Similar and more drastic rules of turnover were introduced for lower levels. All this stemmed from Khrushchev's conviction that the fault lay with the individuals, not with the system. This was not to the liking of Party officials, including his own appointees in the Central Committee. They wanted settled, predictable careers and were unenthusiastic about his radical measures to implement his vision for the USSR. "He had power but he neglected authority",[22] and paid the price when he was easily removed from the office in October 1964 by the Central Committee he himself had strengthened.

Existing pressures for institutionalisation within the Soviet system, and the emergence of institutional integrity and coherence in which the Central Committee was of crucial importance, resulted in the end of Khrushchevism. In the post-Stalin era, of the two alternatives which presented themselves, one was the continuation of a personalised system of rule with a single directing centre. The other was institutionalising a system of relatively independent, individual structures with well defined areas of competence. These were to be governed by formal norms and informal conventions, co-ordinating among themselves. The interaction of institutions resulted in the generation and implementation of policies. In the latter system of rule, favoured overwhelmingly after Stalin, the emphasis was to be on collective leadership. The absence of a dominant leader removed the external source of intervention and allowed the consolidation and expansion of existing rules and conventions. Various bodies, including the Central Committee, became more coherent and integrated.

The members of these institutions on the one hand attempted to strengthen their respective institutions and on the other indirectly, contributed to the institutionalisation of the entire system, particularly at the higher levels. Khrushchev in several ways facilitated this process by attempting to restore the Party's importance as an institution. But many of his actions had the opposite effect, particularly that of increased mass participation in political life, attempting to expand the boundaries of decision-making, opening up the decision-making process to popular scrutiny and participation, and devolving many State functions to public or voluntary bodies. All this exposed officials at all levels to uncomfortable scrutiny and public accountability, and also questioned their rights and privileges. The institutional integrity of the Central Committee was eroded as a result of the frequent turnover of members. The downfall of Khrushchev was thus the combined consequence of questioning the personal security of the officeholders, and more importantly the result of the demands of the structures for greater institutionalisation.

Under Brezhnev's leadership, Khrushchev's measures which had undermined the institutionalisation process were revoked. The amendment to the Party Rules in 1966, for example, abolished the provision for compulsory turn-over in Party bodies and the provision that the General Secretary be elected by the Central Committee. Formal rules and informal conventions were introduced to strengthen and institutionalise the collective leadership. A policy of 'stability of cadres' ensured security of job tenure. This gave greater coherence to individual institutions. Positions which fell vacant were filled from within the organisation rather than by bringing in individuals from outside, resulting in a greater sense of institutional identification and loyalty. A decision-making style with emphasis on consensus and "a lowest common denominator approach" appeared at higher levels. A more regularised, albeit slow process of decision-making became institutionalised, involving consultation with all concerned organisations and institutions regarding policy matters.[23] This was evident in the Central Committee as well.

The process of institutionalisation brings us to the question of structures of the Party, particularly the Central Committee. The structures of any institution are significant because they play a regulatory role, determine the parameters of processes in accordance with the perceived or actual interests, and tend to get 'routinised'. They also tend to outlive their usefulness in their existing forms, thus necessitating periodic reforms to adjust them to new realities. However, the yearning of the political system for institutionalisation after Stalin had resulted in the absence of an inbuilt mechanism of institutional flexibility, producing institutional 'stagnation'. The structures of the Central Committee were part of this phenomenon. Hence the necessity for reforming them.

The organisational solidarity and discipline of the pre-revolutionary Bolsheviks was the forerunner of the apparatus which evolved after the revolution. No Party apparatus of full-time paid officials technically existed up to 1919. The Secretariat was set up at the Eighth Congress in March 1919 and was to establish and operate through a number of departments. By 1921 a Party apparatus led by the Secretariat had added administrative authority to the political authority of the Party leadership. By November 1923, the central apparatus had succeeded to a large extent in controlling the allocation of Party cadres within the State apparatus,[24] undertaken through the *nomenklatura* of the Central Committee.

The Eighth Party Congress did not demarcate the authority and powers of the Secretariat which developed in the course of practice. The Ninth Party Congress empowered it to deal with current administrative and executive questions. By 1922, the functions of the Secretariat included the mobilisation and allocation of Party personnel, the supervision of regional and local Party organisations via a corps of instructors, and propaganda and agitation activities. Party work in rural areas, and with women and national minorities, were monitored by special sections in the Secretariat. The apparatus gradually came to initiate, direct, and control most activities. Local secretaries came under the command of the central apparatus. The key function of the Central Secretariat was allotment of personnel and supervision of local Party organisations. After the Civil War, the Secretariat had the authority to make recommendations for appointments to the highest Party positions. However, in lower level appointments, where its recommendations were mandatory, the Secretariat had greater authority. The range of appointments by the Central Secretariat extended to the state apparatus as well by April 1923, controlling appointments to vital administrative and economic positions. Central representatives could veto the decisions of recalcitrant Party organisations. Local Party functionaries would report to the centre about work at conferences of Party secretaries, in written and oral reports. Through the departments, the central apparatus could control lower Party organisations, commissariats, trade unions, industry, co-operatives and leading Party workers. Thus emerged the hierarchical system of functioning.

The reorganisation of the Secretariat in 1930 divided the Organisation-Assignment section into two: the Organisation-Instruction section and the Assignment section. The former was concerned with the party apparatus and party organisation, and the latter with the administrative and economic apparatus. The assignment section was further subdivided into a number of subsections concerning various aspects of industry, transport, agriculture etc. These subsections appear to have been the forerunners of subsequent Central Committee departments. In 1934 another reorganisation of the Secretariat took place to ensure Party control over different branches of the economy and government. It was aimed at coping with a fast expanding economy which was rapidly developing and diversifying. Now all the activities concerning a particular sector of industry or administration, like personnel assignments or verification of fulfilment of decrees, were to be concentrated. Each branch of industry was to have a parallel branch in the apparatus. A return to the pre-1934 functional scheme took place in 1939. This again resulted in the diffusion of responsibilities for industrial performance throughout the Party apparatus, making it difficult to judge the overall performance of an industry, thereby creating its own problems.

The final reorganisation of the apparatus, before the basic structure stabilised, took place in 1948. It reverted almost completely to the principles of the 1934 reorganisation with the apparatus organised parallel to government and economic organisations. Industrial branch departments were recreated.[25] This again highlighted the ever present problem of effective Party control over the economy. The frequent reorganisations of the apparatus seemed indicative of the Party's attempt to control both industry and the rapidly expanding State administration.[26] The functional principle of organisation which existed from 1930 to 1934 and 1939 to 1948 turned out to be inadequate for control of the economy since the "advantages of specialisation in the choice of cadres and the enforcement of

Party decrees were lost".[27] The prestige and power of the Secretariat increased to an all-time high under Khrushchev, although some of its monitoring role was devolved to lower levels. However, continuity was also maintained. It was responsible for supervising lower Party organisations, checking the fulfilment of decrees by the Party and governmental organs, and acted as a channel of information for the Party leadership, raising issues to be discussed, preparing material for discussions and issuing resolutions and decrees.[28] Khrushchev's reforms in the central apparatus were overturned by Brezhnev, and the central apparatus reverted to its 1948 structure.[29] The Central Committee functioned through these structures.

Commissions of the Central Committee enjoyed a brief history under Khrushchev. The first, called the Commission on Questions of Ideology, Culture, and International Ties, was formed in January 1958. In this way three significant areas were taken outside the purview of the central apparatus. The Commission functioned for eight years and was abolished by a decree of the Politburo on the grounds of increasing the role and responsibility of the Central Committee departments.[30] The supremacy of the central apparatus was thus restored. A system of temporary commissions, particularly in the area of legislation and decision drafting, also existed. Institutions concerned with the issue under consideration were represented in these commissions. Experts participated as consultants or as members of the commissions, and were involved in drafting Central Committee decisions. Such temporary commissions were created in the central Party organs to conduct investigations and prepare proposals. These commissions, involved, apart from officials of the central apparatus, scholars, ministers and members of the central secretariat. Their reports would normally form the basis of discussions.[31] The experiences of these commissions seem to have been the forerunner of the idea of permanent commissions which came into existence under Perestroika.

One of the key functions of the Central Committee was its guidance of the economy. The Central Committee would lay down the instructions under which Gosplan would issue the guidelines regulating the plan and economic life. Regional Party organisations bore responsibility for general supervision of the economy in their respective areas at least from the early 1930s and could be reprimanded by the Central Committee for failures. In 1930, a special division of the Central Committee called the Assignment Department was responsible for selecting the entire administrative economic leadership, including factory directors. Such an arrangement more or less continued until 1939 when a Cadres Department of the Central

Committee came into existence. It was responsible for exercising general supervision over lower Party committees. The Central Committee could also rebuke a regional Party committee "publicly and sharply". The latter in turn could do the same to lower committees if they failed to adhere to the general line, made an inadequate decision or neglected economic affairs.[32] Thus a hierarchical system existed, governed by the principle of democratic centralism.

Although the existence of separate Soviet republics was recognised officially, the Eighth Party Congress, held in 1919, did not recognise federal rights for republican Party organisations which constituted part of a unitary structure.[33] However, it does not seem possible that lower Party organisations could have been controlled down to the smallest detail, which in practice left them a fairly large area of autonomy. Plenums were another important method of working for the Central Committee, although not only their frequency and nature, but also their significance, varied dramatically over different periods of history. In the last fifteen years of Stalin's rule only five plenary sessions were recorded. Under Khrushchev plenums were mainly used to "publicise declarations of policy, and to hear progress reports". Key Party decisions were issued in the name of the Central Committee, sometimes in conjunction with state institutions,[34] suggesting a close relationship between the two and posing one of the most important political problems for the Soviet leadership.

Marx and Engels did not develop a complete theory of political parties since modern ones only started taking shape towards the end of their lives. They were meant to be an expression of "classes and fractions of classes". However they advocated an independent proletarian Party, which was necessary for the working class to be able to act as a class against the parties of the propertied classes. For Lenin, the Party had a "major theoretical and practical importance". Although there were several models of the Party in Lenin's writings, the common element was "a centralised vanguard" which would attempt to "fuse" socialist theory and consciousness with the spontaneous working class movement. Given the Tsarist autocracy and difficulties for a working class Party to operate, he favoured "a narrow, hierarchically organised cadre Party". However, subsequently he favoured a mass Party based on the principle of democratic centralism in which the democratic element was dominant and the leadership was electable, accountable and removable. The Party was needed to bring class consciousness to the working class as distinct from trade union consciousness. A one-party system emerged in Soviet Russia in 1921, due to contingent historical circumstances, and was subsequently converted into a necessary feature of socialism.[35] The one-party system created the necessary conditions for the integration of the Party and the state over subsequent years.

The state for Marx was an institution defending not the general interests of society but the interests of property. It was an instrument of the ruling class which controlled the means of production. This formulation is called into question by the experience of contemporary political systems in which there exists a distance between the state and the economic classes. However, both Marx and Engels imputed to the state a considerable degree of 'relative autonomy' in certain circumstances. In a departure from, though not in contradiction to their basic conception of the state as a class state, Marx and Engels saw it as "an institution in its own right, with its own interests and purposes". There was no contradiction, since there existed a partnership between those who controlled the state and the means of production. The state was not a subordinate institution and one of its key tasks was to regulate class conflict and maintain social order.[36] Under Stalin the Soviet State came to wield immense powers and instead of 'withering away' was reinforced as the "'prime motor' for building socialism". It became a superimposed state and the question remained as to how the state in a Soviet type of society could be transformed "from an organ superimposed upon society into one completely subordinated to it".[37] This question in conjunction with that of the relationship between the Party and the State was of crucial importance to the reformist section of the Soviet leadership.

The relationship between the Party and State came into focus in the early years after the revolution. The Party now had to adapt itself from being an organisation of professional revolutionaries acting as the 'general staff' of the revolution to being a ruling party. The leading Party cadres became leaders of the executive committees of the Soviets. Party organisations were relegated to the background, and it was through the Soviets that the leadership controlled the provinces. It was at the Seventh Party Congress in March 1918 that Sverdlov, the key Party organiser, proposed that more attention should be given to the Party organisation and that the Party should undertake an important part of the work hitherto performed by the Soviets. Until 1919, local Party committees had no full-time staff and their work was mainly confined to propaganda. Sverdlov died in March 1919, bringing to the fore the question of Party and State relations.

The Eighth Party Congress held in the same month passed a "Resolution on Organisational Questions" addressing the question. This called for an end to the integration of the Party and the Soviets. Party committees were now to 'guide' and 'control' government institutions through directives given to the Party fractions working in them. At the same time they were to refrain from taking upon themselves detailed administrative work. In practice this was to be done by equipping the Party with a large and well organised apparatus and investing it with sufficient powers to be able to discharge its function of control through monitoring distribution of personnel. The Central Committee was to be authorised to assign personnel, its decisions being binding upon all. It was charged with "carrying on a decisive struggle against local separatism in these questions". Party bodies had been dependent on the Soviets for finances, something which hindered their revival. This practice was to stop. The process of revival was quite fast, and by 1921 Party officials were prominently placed in the executive committees and the secretaries of Party committees had replaced the chairmen of Soviets at local levels.

By March 1922, the process had gone far enough for the Eleventh Party Congress to resolve that it was necessary "to relieve the Party of a number of questions of a purely Soviet character which it has come to take upon itself..."[38], a problem which was to continue throughout the Soviet period. However, towards the end of his life, Lenin did argue for a "flexible amalgamation" of a Soviet institution with a Party institution in the case of Central Control Commission and Workers and Peasants Inspection, "if this (was) in the interests of our work".[39] At this early stage in a backward, peasant-dominated country, this was seen by him as a way of carrying forward the process of building socialism.

A duality of systems thus existed in the Soviet Union - that of the State and a parallel Party structure. The two bore complete responsibility for the implementation of important decisions of the leadership. If "one of the systems (got) out of line, the other rapidly (conformed)".[40] This relationship constituted the central problem of the Soviet political system. It essentially meant the relationship of the executive section of the Party, that is the party apparatus, with the State. Because of the absence of a properly functioning mechanism of inner-Party democracy, the Party as a whole could not be said to have been participating. The complexity of this question was compounded by the fact that this relationship varied from time to time and at different levels of administration. Khrushchev attempted to restrict the State by passing its several functions to trade unions and non-State bodies. However, this process was curtailed after him.

Under Brezhnev the position of State institutions was revitalised and revived. The Party through its guardianship of ideology was to lead "the institutions through which they (took) authoritative decisions", i.e. the State bodies. The Party was to formulate policy which the State organs were to implement. Soviet scholars insisted that Party resolutions only had the status of 'authoritative recommendations'. Only State institutions, particularly the Soviets, had the legal authority to take decisions. However, in practice the Party could ensure the compliance of its policies. Soviet scholars attempted to show that the CPSU was "a Party that rules but does not govern". The Party was not to be involved in details of administration, indulge in *podmena* or supplant the State. The Party was to formulate broad policies which should be implemented by State organs "formulating and applying specific decisions". In practice, however, these distinctions were blurred to say the least.

At central as well as local levels, executive institutions by virtue of being repositories of expertise and 'centres of specialised interests', were key actors in the process of policy formulation. An individual might be involved in all the processes in different capacities. Assuming that a State body rejected a Party policy, its members who were Party members were bound by the Party decision and thus obliged to implement it. Certain policy areas like foreign policy were exclusively in the domain of the Party. From the mid-1950s and 1960s, it sponsored efforts to develop State institutions. Yet the development of these institutions was controlled by the Party and limits were set to it. The policy of the Party towards the State was not uniform. Under Stalin, the representative side of the State was controlled while the administrative side, the ministries, grew to the extent of "virtually eclipsing the Party". The Party was generally more successful in exercising its influence over the representative wing of the State rather than the executive one. In the mid-1950s the attempt was made to revitalise the Party, while in the early 1960s the State was being weakened. Under Brezhnev, "competent management" was seen as an important characteristic of the State under developed socialism, or in other words, efforts were made to strengthen the State.

The key leaders of both representative and administrative institutions of the State at various levels were elected under the authority of the Party. They might simultaneously hold leading Party positions. Thus there was a large degree of overlapping or 'interlocking' between the personnel on Party committees and State institutions. In 1976, 79.3 per cent of the Central Committee members, and 63.9 per cent of candidate members and the entire Central Secretariat, were deputies of the USSR Supreme Soviet. Such an interlocking of membership strengthened the role of the Party in the State organs. The latter's experience could be incorporated into the Party's policy-making. This afforded State institutions the chance to influence Party policies. In the process of law-making, the issuance of broad guidelines by the Party, leaving subsequent drafting and adoption of legal measures to the State under the leadership of Party members would have given the State a degree of freedom. Although the Party authorities seemed to approve of it, this did not happen in practice. The apparatus of the Party, particularly the central apparatus, had its own staff. However, they relied on the state apparatus to obtain factual information and professional advice. It was at this stage that the latter could affect policy making, although the final word still lay with the Party. Legislation might be drafted by the Party organs and introduced in the Soviets for ratification, or the Party might at least examine legislation prepared in the state apparatus. Control over the Soviets was maintained through the Organisational department of the Party, which was responsible for maintaining 'everyday Party influence' in them, particularly at the central and republican levels.

The role of the Party to 'lead and guide' could often in practice become that of interference or *podmena*.[41] Several reasons were given for this. According to Fainsod such a system was deliberately designed to provide for "overlapping, duplication and parallel functions". For some Soviet scholars, it was due to either Party and State officials failing to appreciate the appropriate demarcation of functions or "structural imperfections" in the State and the economy, resulting in the Party taking over their functions. Lack of sufficient managerial skills had led to greater involvement of the Party in the affairs of the State in the past. Many Party officials were themselves technically qualified and had direct experience of such work. Coupled with the Party authority they had, this resulted in the Party organs' participation in the affairs of state and economy. The state and economic organs came to depend on them, with negative consequences. Thus the Party's vanguard role in practice led to *podmena*.[42]

Article 6 of the 1977 Constitution accorded to the Party the juridical sanction to control the State institutions. However the relationship was both "fused and confused" owing to the absence of separation of powers and precisely defined functions. The Party was accountable for the implementation of its policies. With its parallel structures of committees it was the most important source of authority. Despite the interference of Party officials the relationship between the two may not have been "unduly adversarial". In 1971, Party organisations in the ministries and departments were ordered to implement policy in accordance with Party directives. With the increasing role of experts, the "theoretical demarcation of the Party and

State spheres of competence" became blurred. The Party was supposed to act as "the supreme rational co-ordinator". However, under Brezhnev it "did not always generate a sufficient 'quantity of rational decisions'".[43] This system of Party control had played an important role in industrialisation and maintenance of social stability. However, its suitability in the contemporary Soviet Union with a highly developed and complex society and economy had become suspect.

With the strengthening of the role of the State under Brezhnev, the political and social role of the Party in society declined. The Party came to be preoccupied predominantly with its role as manager of the economy. Such a situation was the inevitable outcome of long years of the subordination of the social-political role of the Party to its economic one. The decline in the influence of the Party took place particularly rapidly in the 1970s and 1980s, being undermined by that of the ministries and local interests. In other words, the executive wing of the State was getting stronger. In the 1960s and 1970s, the *raikoms* of industrial *raions* and *obkoms* of regions with many union-level enterprises, especially in the defence industry, faced this situation. These Party committees were increasingly dependent on the directors of the enterprises and military commanders, and their influence over personnel nominations decreased. From the beginning of the 1970s, even the Central Committee was "reigning but not ruling". It was overshadowed by ministerial interests, a logical outcome of the primarily economic role played by the Party, since it was dependent on them for information and unable to implement its own resolutions. All decisions in the regions were in practice taken in the ministries, which were so powerful that, even during Perestroika, they could conceal information detrimental to them from the Politburo and the President.[44] Thus the question of revival of the role of the Party and separating it from the State could not wait any longer.

Conclusion

The Gorbachev reforms were therefore an attempt to reassert the position of the Party and rein in the State, particularly its executive wing. As such they were a continuation of the Khrushchev reforms. Only the reversal of the Party's integration with the State could rescue it as a political organism. How could this be done? For the reformists, by attempting to improve the economy, first and foremost, through economic reforms; revitalising the representative wing of the State, that is the Soviets; democratising the

Party; demarcating the functions of the Party and the State; subordinating the executive wing of the State to its representative one, and exercising overall supervision of the Party. This involved a process of virtually dismantling the system as it existed, and building new institutions and re-forging new relationships between them.

But opinions on reforms were far from unanimous, at least at the highest levels of the Party leadership, which reflected the diversity of positions within the party apparatus. Not all were happy at the prospect of the reforms, indeed a sizeable section was definitely not enamoured of them. A large section of the party apparatus was content with its role as a partner of economic and other state apparatuses. It represented a definite constituency in the Party and society whose interests were well served in the existing political system. On the other hand, a section of the leadership of the party and state apparatuses appreciated the necessity of reform if the political system, the economy and the influence of the Party were to survive and be revived. There thus existed a subtle plurality of opinions which was expressed in nuances and was broadly reformist and conservative.

Conservatives represented the entrenched interests of Party and economic apparatuses, which saw that reforms were an uncharted course and could seriously jeopardise the Soviet system, endangering their power and privileges. For the reformers political reforms were necessary to overcome the tenacity of methods of the command-administrative system of managing the economy and opposition to new methods by administrative personnel. The role of the executive apparatus had hypertrophied and despite the increasing numbers of individuals in different State and public agencies, which was as high as one-third of the adult population according to Gorbachev, the overwhelming majority had no real role to play in political life. According to him, under Brezhnev, the managerial apparatus consisting of 100 union and 800 republic ministries and departments for "all intent and purposes" began to dictate its will in the economy and political life. Since they were responsible for executing the decisions they could subvert them or determine, "what would be and what would not be".[45]

The Soviets and the Party could not be prevented from succumbing to the pressures of departmental interests. Public life was excessively statified. Power had veered to the executive side of the State. Thus the question of reorganising power and authority arose. Here again the question of power and authority between the Party and State, particularly the elective arm of the State, the Soviets, was of fundamental importance. The government, the Politburo, the Central Committee and Central Secretariat had been resolving numerous questions which should have been solved by lower Soviet, economic and other agencies. The Party bore responsibility for resolving every specific problem. The abnormality of the prevailing situation and the necessity of changing it, was acknowledged. However nothing had been done. In fact, the situation had become critical over the years with the Party becoming more and more involved in managing the economy. Demarcation of the functions of the Party and the State was vital to remedy such a situation. But this would be meaningless unless it reached the highest echelons of the existing power structure. Thus the Central Committee had to undergo a major transformation.

Notes

[1] R.J. Hill, *Soviet Union,-Politics, Economics and Society-From Lenin to Gorbachev*, Frances Pinter, (London, 1985), p. 85.

[2] R. V. Daniels cited in J.F. Hough and M. Fainsod, *How the Soviet Union is Governed*, Harvard University Press, (London, 1979), (hereafter J.F. Hough and M. Fainsod, 1979), pp. 452-453.

[3] M.P. Gehlen and M. McBride, "The Soviet Central Committee: an Elite Analysis", *American Political Science Review*, LXII 4, December 1968, p.1232.

[4] D.P. Hammer, *The USSR, The Politics of Oligarchy*, Westview Press, (London, 1986), pp. 86-87.

[5] R. Sakwa, *Soviet Politics, an Introduction*, (hereafter R. Sakwa, 1989) Routledge, (London, 1989), pp. 133-136.

[6] K. C. Farmer, *The Soviet Administrative Elite*, Praeger, (London, 1992), p. 109.

[7] T.H. Rigby, *Political Elites in the USSR*, Edward Elgar, (Hants, 1990), (hereafter T. H. Rigby, 1990) p. 52 and 56.

[8] B. Moore, Jr., "Development and Functioning of the Party"(1944), in A. Inkeles and K. Geiger, ed. *Soviet Society, A Book of Readings*, (hereafter Barrington Moore Jr. 1944), Constable and Company Ltd., (London, 1961), p.135.

[9] S. F. Cohen, "The Friends and Foes of Change: Reformism and Conservatism in the Soviet Union" in S. F. Cohen, A. Rabinowitch and R. Sharlet ed. *The Soviet Union Since Stalin*, Macmillan, (London, 1980), pp. 11-31.

[10] M. McCauley, "Khrushchev as Leader", in M. McCauley, ed. *Khrushchev and Khrushchevism*, Macmillan Press in association with the School of Slavonic and East European Studies, University of London, (London, 1987), (hereafter M. McCauley 1987), p. 27.

[11] T. Bottomore et al, ed. *A Dictionary of Marxist Thought,* (hereafter T. Bottomore, 1987) Oxford University Press, (Delhi,1987), pp. 194-195.

[12] E. Mawdsley, "Portrait of a Changing Elite: CPSU Central Committee Full Members, 1939-1990", in Stephen White, ed. *New Directions in Soviet History*, Cambridge University Press, (Cambridge, 1992), p.193-196.

[13] V.I. Lenin, "How We Should Reorganise the Worker's and Peasants Inspection", *Selected Works-III*, (hereafter, Lenin Selected Works-III), Foreign Languages Publishing House, (Moscow), pp. 824-25.
[14] The Twelfth Party Congress castigated the Politburo for not consulting the Central Committee and mandated that all the questions of fundamental importance be referred to the Central Committee plenum for discussions. M. Fainsod, *How Russia is ruled*, Harvard University Press (Cambridge, Massachusets, 1963), p. 185, hereafter, M. Fainsod, 1963).
[15] T.H. Rigby, 1990, pp. 148-151.
[16] R. V. Daniels, "Political Processes and Generational Change" in A.Brown ed., *Political Leadership in the Soviet Union*, Macmillan, (1989),(hereafter R.V. Daniels, 1989) pp. 109-121. The "circular flow of power" has been defined as follows:
" ... power in the Soviet system follows what may be imagined as a circular path, particularly evident at moments of the transfer of power, that runs down from the nominal leader by way of his power of bureaucratic appointment, over to the nominally representative structure of the party organisation, with its committees, and up to the Party Congress and the Central Committee that confirm the authority of the man in charge ..."
[17] *ibid.*, pp. 151-162.
[18] M.McCauley, 1987, pp. 18-19.
[19] T.H. Rigby, 1990, pp. 151-162.
[20] M. McCauley, 1987, pp. 21-24.
[21] G. Gill, "Khrushchev and Systemic Development", in Martin McCauley, ed. *Khrushchev and Khrushchevism*, Macmillan Press in association with the School of Slavonic and East European Studies, University of London, (London, 1987), (hereafter G. Gill, 1987), pp. 39-40.
[22] M. McCauley, 1987, pp. 21-24.
[23] G. Gill, 1987, pp. 30-45.
[24] M. McCauley, 1987, pp. 74-85.
[25] M. Fainsod, *How Russia is Ruled*, Harvard University Press, (Cambridge, Massachusets, 1963), pp. 179- 99.
[26] D. Lane and C. Ross, "The Composition of the Politburo of the CPSU: 1966 to 1991", p. 3. [Unpublished Paper].
[27] M. Fainsod, 1963, p. 204.
[28] *ibid.*, pp. 201-204.
[29] D.P. Hammer, *The USSR, The Politics of Oligarchy*, Westview Press Inc., Boulder, (Colorado, 1986), pp. 92-93.
[30]*Rabochaia tribuna*, 30 October 1990, p. 2 in *Foreign Broadcast Information Service, Soviet Union*, (hereafter *FBIS*), 7 November 1990, p. 47.
[31] J. F. Hough and M. Fainsod, 1979, pp. 435-437.
[32] B. Moore Jr., 1944, pp. 130-131 and p.136.
[33] D.J.R. Scott, 1965, p. 138.
[34] *ibid.*, pp. 145-146.
[35] T. Bottomore, 1987, pp. 360-361.
[36] *ibid.*, pp. 464-466.
[37] T. Bottomore, 1987, pp. 467-468.

[38] L. Schapiro, *The Communist Party of the Soviet Union*, Eyre & Spotiswoode, (London, 1960), pp. 241-245.

[39] "Better Fewer, But Better", *Lenin Selected Works-III*, pp. 836-37.

[40] D.J.R. Scott, 1965, pp. 138-140.

[41] R.J. Hill and P. Frank, *The Soviet Communist Party*, George Allen and Unwin, (London, 1981), pp.118-9. It referred "to a tendency on the part of the CPSU organs and officials to usurp the functions and authority of the State, to interfere in the work of professional administrators, or otherwise deal with matters that are properly the province of the State or economic management".

[42] *ibid.*, Chapter 5.

[43] R. Sakwa, 1989, pp. 139-43.

[44] A. Yakovlev, *Predislovie-Obval-Posleslovie*, Novosti, (Moscow, 1992), pp. 135-140.

[45] Gorbachev's Report Sizes Up Restructuring, *Current Digest of Soviet Press,* (hereafter *CDSP*) vol. XL, no. 26, 1988, pp. 7-25.

3 The Rise of Reformism

Introduction

The principal tendencies at the highest level of the leadership had started showing signs of conflict and this reflected in the changes the Central Committee underwent immediately prior to and at the 27th Party Congress in February 1986. Although conservatives and reformists were almost evenly balanced at the highest level, the election of Gorbachev as General Secretary in March 1985 tilted the balance in favour of the reformists. Major changes in the composition of the Central Committee took place at the Congress. Limited though they were, they propelled the process of reforms, bringing in a generation more favourable to reformism. No changes took place in the institutional organisation of the Central Committee. The reformist section of the leadership seemed to believe that changes in personnel would bring about the desired change. In any case, at this stage it was difficult for them to reorganise the institutionss of the Central Committee. In addition the agenda of reforms was limited, and the stress was on traditional means and themes. The economic had precedence over the political at this time.

Ascendancy of the Reformists

Problems in the economy brought into focus the question of what was to be done to improve it. The Soviet Union was seen as at the threshold of a crisis situation. Under Andropov "a coalition of reform-minded technocrats" had been put in place.[1] Andropov and subsequently Gorbachev talked of the possibility of "deep transformations" in the economy and "the need to make socialism credible in terms of its social and material achievements".[2] The key issue on the agenda for the reformists at this point was thus the economy. This also showed a concern that socialism could be justified only on the basis of an improved quality of life. The raison d'être for the Party was that it was building socialism that provided not only a socio-economically just society but also one with a qualitatively better life. The legitimacy of the Party was derived from this. The promises of 'developed socialism' had to be delivered. Moderate conservative and moderate reformist elements in the Party took this view. However, reformists did not envisage a systemic or a radical break from traditional norms and practices, hence the possibility of a coalition between moderate reformists and moderate conservatives existed. The shifts in policy framework and orientation were to be incremental. Gorbachev was elected as the leader of the Party supported by a coalition of moderate reformists and moderate conservatives at the March 1985 Central Committee plenum. That the election was a keenly contested one was indicated by Ligachev's remark later that "the decision could have been absolutely different".[3] Thus the alliance between moderate reformers and moderate conservatives which had been in the making under Brezhnev succeeded in defeating the more conservative section of the Party leadership. Gorbachev then set about consolidating the coalition. The coalition, however, was an inherently unstable one, as would be seen later as Perestroika developed. Anticipating the subsequent events one could contend that with the contours of a new system emerging, moderate reformists and moderate conservatives would enter a collision course resulting in dissolution of the alliance. In 1985, however, the contest was settled in favour of the reformists; it was decided within a small section of the Party leadership, which made the position of the new leader and his supporters rather precarious. The consensus was on intra-systemic economic reforms.

The Soviet economy had been in decline since the 1950s, hitting a new low in the 1970s with real economic growth stagnating. Some of Gorbachev's advisers suggested that the overall growth rate was zero in the period 1980-85.[4] The economy was oriented on extensive lines using up precious resources and labour, and there was an urgent need to switch to intensive methods of development. Labour productivity had fallen, along with the growth rate of other indices of efficiency. A resource surplus economy had become a resource shortage economy as a consequence. There was a disjunction between demand and supply with its inevitable social consequences. Gorbachev's solution at this stage was "the strategy of accelerating the country's social and economic development" which meant increased rates of economic growth. The economic reforms were to be coupled with an active social policy and socialist justice, which would involve updating the forms and methods of work of political and ideological institutions, the deepening of socialist democracy and overcoming inertia, stagnation and conservatism with a greater involvement of people.[5] This was to unfold a project of reforms, controlled and uncontrolled, having a dramatic impact on the Soviet political system, the Party and its Central Committee and indeed the entire Soviet Union.

At the 27th Party Congress, Gorbachev called upon the Party at all levels to work for the implementation of the Party's new line by democratising it, observing collective leadership, developing criticism and self-criticism, supervision and a responsible attitude to work. He exhorted the Congress to enhance the role of the Party and its organisations in every way. This was how the vanguard role of the Party was to be realised. The emphasis was on reactivating the Party. No organisation was to be outside supervision and criticism, nor was any Party official to be protected from responsibility. This was to apply to all ministries, departments, institutions and organisations. The role of the Party committees of ministries and departments was to be enhanced since an examination by the Central Committee of the reports sent by Party committees had shown that they were continuing to exercise their supervision rights very "timidly and cautiously".

Discussing the Party and the State relationship, Gorbachev said that the Party was to exercise political leadership, outline "the general prospects for development", undertake the selection and placement of cadres, and carry out general supervision. To resolve specific economic, social and cultural problems, extensive freedom was to be granted to state agencies and their personnel. Confusion between the functions of the Party committees, State and public agencies was to be eliminated. This would be a difficult task since it was hard "to detect the line at which Party supervision and the organisation of the fulfilment of practical tasks becomes petty tutelage, or even the supplanting of state and economic agencies".[6] It seemed the problem lay with State institutions, and the solution was seen as strengthening the role of the Party and its political leadership and supervision over them. This therefore also entailed the task of the demarcation of the Party and State. One of the consequences of the Party's involvement with economic and other state issues was that it shared the blame for the failures more directly, worked on issues more appropriately within the competence of state bodies and therefore in the process ignored its political and social role. The extent of the involvement of the Central Committee and the local Party bodies can be gauged from the following table listing the number of written and oral appeals received by them between 1980 and 1987:[7]

The 27th Party Congress resolved to stop the practice of day to day interference of the centre in the functioning of lower level units. Economic accountability and self-financing were to be introduced. Economic methods of management were to be introduced at all levels. Management was to be democratised and the role of labour collectives increased. Gosplan was to abandon current economic issues and concentrate on macro questions of planning and economy. The 'petty tutelage' of enterprises by ministries and departments was to be curtailed. The prevailing prejudice towards commodity-money relations and their role in planned economic management was to be overcome. National exclusiveness and parochialism were to be combated. Socialist democracy and the "socialist self-government of the people" were to be developed. The independence and activeness of local bodies of power, i.e. the Soviets, was to be increased.

Table 3.1 Number of Letters, and Oral Appeals to the Central Committee of the CPSU and Local Bodies

Year	Number of Letters	Number of Oral Appeals	Total
Number of appeals to the Central Committee in 1980	671,500	18,200	689,700
1985	767,300	27,600	794,900
1986	1,128,800	35,800	1,164,600
1987	966,900	32,100	999,000
Number of appeals to local Party bodies in 1980	1,864,200	1,349,000	3,213,200
1985	2,145,300	1,376,000	3,521,300
1986	2,283,500	1,367,800	3,651,300
1987	2,211,400	1,391,100	3,602,500

Source: Materiali Delegatu XIX Vsesoiuznoi Konferentsii KPSS, (Moskva, 1988), p. 245.

Democratic principles in management, the role of public organisations in administering the country, the role of labour collectives in public life and the economy were to be increased.[8] However opposition to the policy of reform was already evident in 1986. In his speech to the 27th Party Congress, Gorbachev talked of opposition to change. He complained that "there is a widely held tendency to view any change in the economic mechanism as if it were a deviation from socialist principles".[9] In short, conventional means were to be adopted with intra-systemic reforms. These were the key issues around which opinions polarised as the reforms progressed. They met with predictable resistance from the conservatives. Since the Central Committee was the battleground for the pro and anti-reform forces within the Party and the state institutions, therefore the reformist leadership embarked upon a predictable course of changes in its personnel composition. Such reforms were also based on the notion that changing the individuals would change the institutions. This notion was erroneous to the extent that the individuals formed and articulated their political positions on the basis of concrete socio-economic and political situations and the aspirations of old and new social forces prevailing in a particular historical epoch and social context. Therefore such changes may modify an institution only upto an extent. The new incumbents, whatever their persuasion, would have to ultimately respond to the circumstances prevailing, as did eventually happen. The Central Committee continued to be as divided on the political-ideological lines as it was at the outset of Perestroika and these divisions crystallised more sharply in its latter phases.

The Changing Composition of the Central Committee

Given the nature of the Soviet political system and the importance of the Central Committee in it, its composition was an obvious choice as a key area for reform.[10] This had been the traditional practice followed by successive General Secretaries. Hence, the 27th Party Congress introduced changes in the composition of the Central Committee. Although not dramatic, these could be characterised as a 'preparatory stage' of reform. A process of turnover, particularly at the lower levels, had preceded the 27th Party Congress. Already by the middle of 1985, 33 out of the 80 regional leaders elected to full membership of the Central Committee in 1981 had been replaced.[11] 31 or about 10 per cent of the Central Committee members had died and 54 or 17 per cent had retired by October 1985.[12] By February 1986, about one-third of the holders of the 300 or so posts that carried full membership of the Central Committee had been changed. Four republican Party leaders - from Georgia, Kirgizia, Tajikistan and Turkmenia - had been replaced.[13] Thus out of a total of 319 elected in 1981, only 234 or 73 per cent remained.[14] Such a large number of vacancies provided a major opportunity for Gorbachev to renew the Central Committee's composition.

The most marked feature of this Congress was the turnover in the Central Committee when compared with the 'stability of cadres' under Brezhnev. 44 per cent of the full and candidate members of the Central Committee elected in 1966 were still in it 15 years later.[15] At the 25th Party Congress in 1976, 89 per cent of the members were re-elected, with a similar number at the 26th Party Congress, if worker and peasant members are excluded from the count.[16] 80 per cent of all the members of the previous Central Committee were re-elected in 1981.[17] By 1982, an average full member of the Central Committee had been a member for almost 13 years.[18] In the four years preceding October 1985 only eleven candidate members had been promoted to full membership of the Central Committee, despite the provision in the Party statutes that vacancies in the Central Committee be filled from its candidate members.[19] At the 27th Party Congress itself, significantly, 30.6 per cent[20] or 97 out of 307 of the full members were new appointees, having never been members of the Party's leading bodies like the Central Committee or the Central Auditing Commission (CAC) in the past. These new appointments were significant because this was a completely new bloc of members which had no experience in the leading Party bodies. 104 or 40 per cent of the full members were new as compared to 17 per cent at the 26th Party Congress.[21] This Central Committee had 125 new full and candidate members, as compared to 82 elected at the 26th Party Congress.[22] Election of a large number of new Central Committee members committed to Gorbachev indicated the operation of the "circular flow of power"[23], something which would no longer exist by the 28th Party Congress.

Table 3.2 Composition of the Central Committee at the 26th and 27th Party Congresses

	26th Party Congress	27th Party Congress
Number of full Central Committee members	319	307
Newly elected members	82	125
Length of Service:		
Occupied the same position:5 years ago	231	172
10 years ago	153	109
15 years ago	86	61
20 years ago	54	29
25 years ago	15	19
30 years ago	10	5
Age		
Over 70	44	32

60 to 70	126	91
50 to 60	108	117

Source: M. Tatu, "The Central Committee Elected at the Twenty-Seventh Party Congress: Halfway Towards Rejuvenation", RL106/86, 10 March 1986.

Table 3.3 Representation of the most important non-Party institutions and their leaders in the Central Committee at primary (as full members) and secondary (as candidate members) levels

A- At the primary level

The Council of Ministers.
Chairman, Union of Journalists.
Chief of the General Staff of the Army.
Chairman, USSR State Committee for Television and Radio Broadcasting.
President USSR Academy of Sciences.
Commander-in-Chief, USSR Air Force.
Secretary, Union of Writers.
Chairman, USSR Committee for State Security.
Commander-in-Chief, USSR Naval Forces.
USSR Council of Defence.
Chairman, Presidium, USSR Supreme Soviet.
Commander-in-Chief, USSR Ground Forces.
Chairman, USSR State Committee for Foreign Economic Relations.
Chief of the Main Administration of the KGB.
Commander in Chief, Warsaw Pact Forces.
Chief, Rear Services, USSR Armed Forces.
Chief, Main Political Directorate of Soviet Army and Navy.
Chief Inspector, USSR Ministry of Defence.
Commander-in-Chief, USSR Strategic Rocket Forces.
Chairman USSR State Committee for Science and Technology.
Chairman, Military-Industrial Commission.
Chairman, USSR State Agro-Industrial Committee.
Chairman, USSR State Committee for Foreign Tourism.
USSR Procurator General.
Chairman, USSR Committee for People's Control.
Chairman, USSR State Planning Committee.

Chairman, USSR Supreme Court.
Chairman, Soviet Women's Committee.
Chairman, Council of Union, USSR Supreme Soviet.
Chairman, USSR Parliamentary Group.
Chairman, Soviet Committee for European Security and Cooperation.
Chairman, USSR State Committee for Material and Technical Supplies.
Chairman Council of Nationalities, USSR Supreme Soviet.
Commander-in-Chiefs of all important Regional Commands.

B- At the secondary level

Chief, Secretariat of the Chairman of the USSR Council of Ministers.
Board Chairman, USSR State Bank.
Chairman, USSR State Committee for Cinematography.
Board Chairman, 'Novosti' Press Agency (APN).
Chairman, USSR State Committee for Labour and Social Questions.
Chairman, State Committee for Prices.
Chairman, USSR Committee for Physical Culture and Sports.s
Chairman, USSR Olympic Committee.
Chairman, USSR State Committee for Standards.
Chief, USSR Central Statistical Administration.
Deputy Chairman, USSR State Committee for Utilisation of Atomic Energy.
Chairman, USSR State Committee for Publishing Houses, Printing Plants and the Book Trade.
Chairman, USSR State Committee for Supervision of Safe Working Practices in Industry and for Mine Supervision.

Source: Compiled from the list of full and candidate Central Committee members elected by the 27th Party Congress in S. Belitsky, V. Konavalev and H. Kraus, RL 145/86, 1April 1986 and RL151/86, 9April 1986.

The Central Committee elected at the 27th Party Congress included 220 new full and candidate members out of a total of 477 who had not been elected at the 26th Congress.[24] Thus the rate of renewal was 46.1 per cent from the 26th to the 27th Party Congress, as tables 3.4, 3.8 and 3.14 reveal. As table 3.8 shows, 230 or 72.1 percent in 1981 and 172 or 56.0 per cent in 1986 of the previous Central Committee members remained. 278 or 87.1 per cent in 1981 and 215 or 70.0 per cent in the 1986 Central Committee members were promoted from the candidate category or the CAC. A

Table 3.4 Occupational breakdown of the Central Committee elected at the 26th and 27th Party Congresses and after the 25 April 1989 Plenum

	1981	1986	1989
Total number of full members	319	307	251
Occupational Categories		Percentages	
Party Apparatus	43.6	44.5	33.9
State and Govt. Apparatus	31.0	28.9	27.5
Military	6.9	7.5	4.4
Diplomatic Services	4.1	3.5	7.2
KGB	1.6	1.3	1.2
Scientific and Cultural elite	3.4	3.5	5.2
Mass organisation	1.6	2.2	3.6
Workers and Peasants	6.0	8.5	14.3
Other	1.9	-	-
'Dead Souls'	-	-	2.8

Source: E. Teague, "Fall in Representation of Party Apparatus in CPSU Central Committee", Report on the USSR, 12 May 1989, p.4.

Table 3.5 Breakdown of professional representation of the full members of the Central Committee elected in 1976

Total Number of Full Members	287
Occupational Category	Percentage
Party Apparatus	41.81
Government	32.75
Military	6.96
Lower Foreign Affairs Official	5.92
Police	0.69
Media or cultural figures	1.74
Scientists or designers	3.13
Trade Unions	1.04
Workers	2.78
Peasant /Farm Management	0.69
Miscellaneous	2.44

Source: Compiled from J.F.Hough, 1982, Table 2.2, p. 46.

striking feature of the figures in table 3.8 is that the numbers promoted from previous Central Committees is much lower in 1956 and 1961 (the Khrushchev era) than between 1966 and 1981 (the Brezhnev era). The case is similar with those promoted from candidate membership or CAC. In both cases the figures are very low in 1961, much lower even compared to 1956,

Table 3.6 Party and State/Government representation in the Central Committee by geographical area

	Party			State/Government[25]		
	1981	1986	1990	1981	1986	1990
Central	63	49	25	123	124	36
RSFSR	80	87	48	21	18	15
Union Reps	68	77	64	35	35	23
Ukraine	24	25	14	6	7	4
Kazakhstan	14	16	12	3	3	4
Belorussia	5	7	6	3	4	2
Georgia	2	2	3	2	1	1
Azerbaijan	2	2	3	2	2	3
Latvia	2	2	4	2	2	1
Kirgizia	2	2	2	2	1	2
Moldavia	2	2	2	2	2	1
Lithuania	2	2	5	2	2	NIL
Tajikistan	2	2	NIL	2	2	2
Armenia	2	2	1	2	2	NIL
Turkmenia	2	2	1	2	2	1
Estonia	2	2	4	2	2	NIL

Source: Prepared from R V. Daniels, 1989, Table 4. 3, p. 103 and K.G. Saur, pp. 61-69.

indicating the high period of the Khrushchevian reforms, before rising phenomenally in 1966, when the Brezhnev era begins.[26] This reveals a similarity of approach under Gorbachev to the question of promotion of members from the candidate and CAC categories. Both Khrushchev and Gorbachev attached great significance to the renewal of the Central Committee as an important vehicle of reform.

Forty-nine per cent of candidate members of the previous Central

Table 3.7 Breakdown of the 24 full members of the Central Committee promoted at the 25 April 1989 Plenum

Occupational category	Number of new members elected	Percentage of the total number of replacements
Party Officials	6	25.00
State officials[27]	3	12.50
Govt. officials	2	8.33
Workers and peasants	7	29.16
Academicians	4	16.66
Diplomats	1	4.16
Military	1	4.16

Source: On the basis of the information available in Moscow Domestic Service, 1700 GMT, 25 April 1989, in FBIS, 26 April 1989, p. 44.

Table 3.8 Turnover in the Central Committee for the period 1956-90

Year	1956	1961	1966	1971	1976	1981	1986	1990
Central Commt members	133	175	195	241	287	319	307	412
No. held over from previous Central Commt.	79	66	139	149	201	230	172	38
Percent	59.4	37.7	71.3	61.8	70.0	72.1	56.0	9.2
Cand. Members	155	165	155	139	151	170	122	-
Number held over from cand. or CAC	94	97	170	195	251	278	215	20[28] *
Percent	70.7	55.4	87.2	80.9	87.5	87.1	70.0	11.4

Source: Taken from R.V.Daniels, 1989, p. 10 and updated.

Table 3.9 Carryovers from previous Central Committees to the Central Committee elected at the 28th Party Congress

Elected For The First Time In Year	Numbers	Percentage of Total Number Elected At The 28th Party Congress
1966	1	0.24
1971	1	0.24
1976	3	0.72
1981	3	0.72
1986	26	6.32
1987	1	0.24
1988	2	0.48
1989	9	2.18
1990	366	88.85

Source: Compiled from K.G. Saur, 1992, pp. 61-69.

Table 3.10 Representation of Republican-Communist Parties and their percentage of the total membership of the Central Committee

Number of the Central Comt. Members	Numbers	Percentage[29]			
	1990	1990	1971	1976	1981
Ukraine	40	9.70	15.6	15.1	15.1
Belorussia	12	2.91	5.2	4.0	4.0
Uzbekistan	18	4.36	4.1	4.0	4.0
Kazakhstan	22	5.34	8.3	7.9	8.7
Georgia	11	2.66	2.1	0.8	1.6
Azerbaijan	10	2.45	1.0	0.8	0.8
Lithuania	6	1.45	1.0	0.8	0.8
Moldava	7	1.69	1.0	0.8	0.8
Latvia	7	1.69	1.0	0.8	0.8
Kirgizia	8	1.94	1.0	0.8	0.8
Tazikistan	10	2.42	1.0	0.8	0.8
Armenia	7	1.69	1.0	0.8	0.8

Turkmenia	9	2.18	2.1	0.8	0.8
Estonia	6	1.45	2.1	1.6	1.6
Russia	124	30.09	53.1	60.3	58.7
Total	297	72.08			

Source: Prepared from the information in Moscow Television Service, 1722 GMT, 13 July 1990 in FBIS, 16 July 1990, pp. 7-9 and J. F. Hough, 1982, Table 2. 4, p. 49.

Table 3.11 Representation of other Party organisations in the Central Committee

Party Organisations	Number of Central Committee Members
Soviet Army and Navy	11
Frontier troops of the USSR KGB	1
Internal troops of the USSR MVD	1
Soviet Institution Abroad	1
Total	14

Source: Moscow Television Service, 1722 GMT, 13 July 1990 in_FBIS, 16 July 1990, pp. 7-9.

Committee were elected as full members in 1971 at the 24th Party Congress, 48 per cent in 1976 at the 25th Party Congress and 45 per cent in 1981 at the 26th Party Congress.[30] Compared to this only 10.75 per cent of the full members elected at the 27th Party Congress were candidate members of the previous Central Committee.[31] Table 3.2, comparing the change in the composition between the 26th and the 27th Party Congresses on the basis of length of service and age, gives a good idea of the increased rate of turnover at the 27th Party Congress.[32] Thus the normal reserve pool, namely the candidate members of the Central Committee and those who had worked in the highest echelons of the Party, was bypassed, in favour of personnel from lower levels. This 'new bloc' was thought of as more amenable to reform.. How reformist was this 'new bloc' ? A considerably higher turnover rate could also be interpreted as attempts to remove the conservative sections of the Party and make the Central Committee more reformist. Did conservatives continue to hold sway ? Did altering the composition at the 27th Party Congress set a far-reaching process of change in motion?

Table 3.12 Breakdown of the representation of Party officials in the 1990 Central Committee

Category	Percentage of the Total Number of Members from Party Category	Number of Central Committee Members
Central Party	16.78	23
Republican Party	18.24	25
Obkom	39.41	54
Gorkom	4.37	6
Primary Party org.	16.78	23
Kraikom	1.45	2
Raikom	2.91	4
Total		137 out of 412
Percentage of the total number of Central Committee Members		33.25

Source: K.G.Saur, 1992, pp. 61-69.

Table 3.13 Breakdown of State and Government officials in the 1990 Central Committee

State/Govt. Officials	Percentage of the Total Number of Central Committee Members	Number of Central Committee Members
Union Ministers	3.15	13
Heads and Deputy Heads of Union-republics	0.97	4
Republican Soviets	2.42	10
USSR Security Council	1.21	5
USSR Defence Council	0.24	1
Administrator of affairs for the USSR President	0.24	1
Rural Soviets	0.48	2
USSR Supreme Soviet	1.21	5
USSR State Organisations and Committees	1.94	8

Oblast Soviet	1.45	6
Republican Council of Ministers	1.69	7
KGB	0.48	2
USSR Congress of People's Deputies	1.21	5
Military	3.15	13[33]*
Krai Soviet	0.24	1
Presidential Adviser	0.48	2
President	0.24	1
Vice-President	0.24	1

Source: Compiled from the information given in K.G. Saur, pp. 61-69.

Table 3.14 Survival in the Central Committee by entry cohort 1952-90

Cent.Com. Entry Year	1952	1956	1961	1966	1971	1976	1981	1986	1990*
1952	125	79	40	36	23	15	12	3	-
1956	54	27	23	18	13	7	4	-	
1961	108	85	69	57	38	13	-		
1966	51	40	35	29	10	1			
1971	91	81	67	32	1				
1976	86	77	50	3					
1981	89	60	3						
1986	135	26							
1990[34]*	378								
Total:	125	133	175	195	241	287	319	307	412

Source: Prepared by updating the table 4. 7 in R.V. Daniels, 1989, p. 116, with data from K. G. Saur,1992, pp.61-69.

No major change took place in the norms of professional representation within the Central Committee from the 26th to the 27th Party Congresses. The proportion of the Party and State officials, military, diplomats, representatives of mass organisations and other categories did not change significantly.[35] The only changes which might have been of some importance were the addition of three members from agricultural management in 1986 as against none in 1981,[36] and an increase from six in 1981 to nine in 1986 in the number of members from the Academy of Sciences.[37] These may indicate greater stress on the affairs of agriculture and recognition of the increasingly important role the intelligentsia was expected to play in the course of the reforms. Apart from these, the overall pattern of representation followed the established norms of constituting the Central Committee.

The largest bloc was that of Party officials, which included Party leaders from the central, regional and local levels, officials of the Central Committee departments and the staff of the General Secretary. The second most important constituency was the central and regional State official category. It comprised Chairmen and deputy-Chairmen of the Council of Ministers, ministers, deputy-ministers, chairmen and deputy-chairmen of various State committees, members of the Supreme Soviet and so on. Military, diplomats and the intelligentsia (including those concerned with education, the media, the academy of Sciences and cultural life) were other influential categories.[38] Workers and peasants constituted another substantial group, although a quarter of them came from the management cadre of the industrial and agricultural sectors.[39] (For comparison, the percentage breakdown of the professional representation of the full members of the Central Committee elected in 1976 is shown in table 3.5.[40]) The most important institutions and their leaders apart from the Party, represented at two levels (the primary level or as full members and the secondary level or as candidate members), were as given in table 3.3.[41] During the election of the new Central Committee at the 27th Party Congress, this arrangement was virtually left untouched.

As noted earlier, no significant change took place in the norms of professional representation. The proportion of the 'central Party' category fell from 9.4 per cent to 9.0 per cent in 1981 and 1986 respectively. The representation of the 'regional Party' category reduced as well. The case was similar with the 'local Party' category which decreased from 1.7 per cent to 1.5 per cent in 1981 and 1986 respectively. The share of the 'mass representative' category increased from 8.1 per cent to 9.2 per cent respectively in 1981 and 1986. Representation of the 'central State' category went down from 25.1 per cent to 24.7 per cent in 1981 and 1986 respectively. Similarly the representation of the 'regional State' category registered a less dramatic decrease from 8.5 per cent to 7.8 per cent in the Central Committees elected at the 26th and the 27th Party Congresses. The military category was almost stationary with 7.7 per cent in 1981 and 7.6

per cent in 1986; similarly the diplomatic corps category, which increased from 4.7 per cent in 1981 and 4.8 per cent in 1986.[42] The representation of the working class and peasantry rose marginally from 30 in 1981 and 33 in 1986.[43] They continued to have a token representation in the Central Committee. There was no increase in the representation of the intelligentsia; its number remained constant at 27.[44] Only marginal changes took place in the gender composition of the Central Committee from the 26th to the 27th Party Congresses. The male component fell by 0.4 per cent.[45] Despite the claim of the equality of women in Soviet society, their representation was much less. This reflected the lack of a policy of promoting women to the highest echelons of the leadership. Significant changes did take place in the age structure. Although the increase in the number and percentage of members between the ages of 30-39 and 40-49 years was marginal, (2 or 0.4 per cent, and 5 or 0.9 per cent respectively), the increase in the age group of 50-59 years was more dramatic (51 corresponding to a 10.1 per cent increase). The number and percentage of individuals from the 60-69 age-group dropped by 15 or 3.6 per cent, however the reduction in the numbers belonging to the over 70 age group was more significant, falling by 36 or 7.8 per cent.[46] In the age structure, there was an almost four-fold increase in the number of members below 50 years and a sharp drop in the number above 60 years of age. The percentage of members above 60 years dropped from 50 per cent in 1981 to 38.6 per cent in 1986. That in the age-group 50-59 changed from 40 per cent in 1981 to 50.1 per cent in 1986.[47] This was Gorbachev's age-group and constituted the single largest bloc. Members in the 40 to 50 age group had been entering the Central Committee for some time. 80 per cent of the Central Committee elected for the first time at the 26th Party Congress was 55 years or younger when the year began, if new members from the military were excluded. More than 20 per cent of them were less than 50 years of age.[48] A younger Central Committee whose members' political outlook had been moulded under the influence of the Khrushchev reforms formed a significant part of this body. The generation of Gorbachev and those younger than him had their formative years, both politically and in general terms, during the Khrushchevian era. A whole new generation was coming to the leadership bringing with it a reformist outlook. The generational change here refers to the influx of a larger number of members who seemed to hold a reformist view at this point of time, although multiple generations were present at least in the period 1952 to 1986, and it may be misleading to talk of one dominant generation.[49] Representation of nationalities underwent only a minor change,[50] signifying the preservation of the Party's unitary character. Party organisations did not give any weightage to the national or sub-national make-up of the Soviet society while deciding the formation of the Party committees. The Central Committee members came from different backgrounds and institutions.

Members of the Central Committee Elected at 27th Party Congress - A Biographical Study

A sample of biographical information of 102 full Central Committee members elected at the 27th Party Congress was analysed to study the characteristics and the career trajectories of the members elected at this Congress. This provided a profile of the Central Committee. It included eight Central Party Officials belonging to the Central Secretariat and the apparatus, 13 Republican Party Officials including the first and the second secretaries, 35 Regional Party Officials, 16 Central Ministers, three Republican Ministers, three representing Central State Committees and the State apparatus, one Republican State institutions, one Lower Party Officials, two Diplomats, two from mass organisations, three Kolkhoz workers, five workers, four members of the Armed Forces, three representatives of academic institutions, two representatives of Higher Industrial Management, two from Regional Soviets, one each from the Party media and KGB.[51] These categories represented the posts held by them when they were elected full Central Committee members for the first time.

Five belonged to generation A (born between 1905-14), 28 to generation B (1915-24), 46 to generation C (1925-34), 21 to generation D (1935-44) and one to generation E (1945-54). The largest number were the so-called children of the Twentieth Party Congress. However a sizeable number still remained from the Stalin era.

With regard to the Party generation computed on the basis of the year an individual member entered the Party, none belonged to generation A, one and two to B and C respectively, 19 to D, 33 to E, 38 belonged to F(1955-64), eight to G(1965-74) and one to H (1975-84). Thus the highest number (71) had joined Party in the twenty years following the Second World War up to the Khrushchev era.

Only one was in his late thirties (37) at the time of becoming a full member of the Central Committee. 30 members were in their forties, 58 in their fifties, twelve in their sixties and one unknown. The overwhelming majority had thus become full members when in their forties or fifties. Again the majority belonged to Gorbachev's generation.

The Central Committee members were divided into three cohorts on the basis of the year they became full members. Those elected before 1966 belonged to the primary cohort (X), those between 1966 and 1982 were in the secondary cohort (Y) and those after 1982 belonged to the tertiary cohort (Z). Seven members were from cohort X, 44 from Y, 49 from Z category and one was unknown. The largest cohort thus belonged to the post-Brezhnev era although a sizeable number had also been members during his tenure. In that sense it was a partially renewed Central Committee.

The majority (80) had higher specialised education. 43 had a higher scientific and technical education, including engineering and sciences, metallurgy, aviation, military technology, geology, medicine; 15 had a higher agricultural education; 5 had a higher pedagogical education; six had a higher degree in economics; seven had degrees in other areas of social sciences and humanities such as history and philosophy, and four had a higher military education. Ten members had secondary, -mainly technical-education. Eleven had lower, again primarily technical, education. Thus the majority had a higher and chiefly scientific and technical education. Several had become members as a result of their careers in a specialised sector which led them to a post qualifying them for membership, e.g. ministers, Army, KGB, State Committees etc.

Seventy-six Central Committee members were Russians, eight were Ukrainians, four were Kazakhs, three were Azerbaijanis and the rest were from other nationalities. Hence, Russians were the dominant nationality. 49 Central Committee members were elected for the first time at the 27th Party Congress. Sixteen had been members for up to five years, 20 (up to ten years), seven (up to 15 years), five (up to 20 years), two (up to 25 years), one, N.K. Baibakov (up to 35 years) and one unrecorded. Thus the majority had little or no experience of being on the Central Committee.

Most of the Central Committee members had occupied the same post for some time before they became full members. Thus the position occupied as full members would be the same as the one held immediately prior to it, confirming that they became members by virtue of the posts they held. Occupancy of certain posts seems to have ensured greater likelihood of full membership of the Central Committee.

Some of the Republican Party Officials like A.M. Masaliev had virtually a complete Party career leading to the highest republican position. Others, like K.M. Makhkamov, had spent their entire career in State posts before becoming a republican Party official, in this case, first secretary of Tajik CP CC. Others like I.A. Mozgovoi had a mixed Komsomol, Party and State career. Some, like V.I. Brovikov, had also had a stint in the central apparatus. K.M. Bagirov, first secretary of the Azerbaijan CP CC, had started his career as a worker in an undertaking in Baku. Then he taught in a polytechnic institute followed by 14 years in a ministry and the Party. He then became the Sumgait obkom first secretary, then secretary and finally first secretary of the Azerbaijan CP CC. G.A. Aliev had a long career as the republican minister for internal affairs and head of the republican KGB before becoming first secretary of the Azerbaijan CP CC. He subsequently became First Deputy Chairman of the USSR Council of Ministers. Thus there were multiple career paths leading to the republican first secretaryship.

Regional Party Officials like N.I. Maslennikov had a predominantly Party career followed by a post in a republican State institution. In cases like those of M.S. Mendibaev and Ye.F. Muraev, it was preceded by a managerial career. In some cases they had a stint in ministerial positions as in the case of V.K. Mesiats. F.T. Morgun spent the first decade of his career in the agricultural sector. Another example of an official with a background in agricultural sector was V.P. Nikonov. After a long Party career, towards the latter stages of which he became a Central Committee member, he moved into higher agricultural management and ministerial positions before becoming a secretary of the Central Committee. This was followed by a decade in simultaneous Party and Soviet posts leading to a republican ministry before becoming regional first secretary. Similarly Ye.N. Auelbekov had started his career as higher agricultural management cadre. V.S. Murakhovski spent 11 years in Komsomol and State posts followed by a Party career of two decades, entering the Central Committee in the last years. Some like Yu.V. Petrov started their career as a worker, and spent about a decade in a lower managerial position before embarking upon a Party career including work in the central apparatus. A.N. Plekhanov moved from higher agricultural management, that is, director of a sovkhoz to a full-time Party career which started as the secretary of a kolkhoz-sovkhoz enterprise culminating in the first secretaryship of the Kurgan obkom just prior to becoming a Central Committee member. A.F. Ponamarev spent 5 years as chairman of a regional Soviet before becoming first secretary of the Belgorod obkom in 1983. He had a mixed earlier career in agricultural management, Soviets and the Party. F.V. Popov had a long career as a Party official followed by the chairmanship of a regional Soviet committee, then the post of RSFSR minister for Housing and Communal Services, before becoming first secretary of the Altai Territory executive committee. Thus again there were multiple entry points to the regional party first secretaryship. However most usually had long service in Party, Komsomol and State posts, while several entered via industrial and agricultural management.

Working class Central Committee members, like A.P. Miasnikov, spent most of their careers as workers. Kolkhoz representatives in the Central Committee would also have careers predominantly in agriculture as, for example, a collective farmer and combine operator, followed by lower level agricultural positions like team leader as in the case of Ye.N. Parubok. Another example was N.V. Perverzeva. After having spent 21 years as a collective farmer and eight years as a combine operator, she became field team leader of the harvesting transport group of a kolkhoz in 1974 before becoming a Central Committee member in 1982. These members, however, were not amongst the prominent members of this body.

Representatives from Academic institutions were generally senior academics, some of whom might hold academic-administrative positions such as directors of prestigious institutions. One example was B.Ye. Paton. An example of a member from the Party Media was V.G. Afanasiev, Chief Editor of *Kommunist*. He had started with an academic career and later embarked upon a journalistic career in the Party media.

Some Union Ministers had a long technical and technical-management career leading to a top management position such as general-director of an all-union enterprise before becoming a deputy minister. One example was Ye.K. Pervishin. Union-Minister for the Radio Industry, P.S. Pleshakov, spent a long time in various positions in an institute ending as its director before becoming deputy chairman of the State Committee of the USSR Council of Ministers on Radio Electronics. He subsequently became Deputy Minister in 1965, First Deputy Minister and then USSR Minister for the Radio Industry between 1974-87, becoming a Central Committee member in 1977. V.N. Poliakov started his career as a foreman, graduated from lower industrial management to higher management as general director of an amalgamated light vehicles manufacturing organisation before becoming Union Automobile Industry Minister in 1975 and a full Central Committee member in 1981. Another such example was N.A. Pugin. Most other ministers also came from higher industrial management such as B.V. Bakin, Yu.P. Batalin and O.D. Baklanov. Generally the ministry they headed would be directly related to their career experience. For example, B.P. Bugaev spend 24 years in the aviation career before becoming Union Minister for Civil Aviation. B.V. Balmont served eight years in the ministerial apparatus as head of the main administration of the Ministry of General Machine-Building, before becoming Union Minister. An example of the leaders of State committees was S.V. Bashilov. After serving for 26 years in higher industrial management, he joined the government apparatus as head of the department of government planning. He subsequently became a minister and Chairman of the USSR State Committee on Construction Work. Thus most ministers and State committee leaders were primarily technocrats or from management cadres. They were professionals in their specialised areas. These leaders represented the interests of the most important ministries and State committees.

An example of a central apparatus official was Ye.Z. Razumov, who after a long career in the Komsomol and as a Party official remained in the central apparatus for 22 years. O.B. Rakhmanin had a very long career in the central apparatus. He was first deputy head of a Central Committee department, but had worked in the central apparatus since 1963. The central apparatus would include mainly individuals with long Komsomol, Party or Party apparatus experience. A diplomat have had a long Party and Soviet career including a stint in the central apparatus, as in case of V.N. Bazovskii. Members from the Military and K.G.B had professional careers in these sectors, as in the cases of S.F. Akhromeev and F.D. Bobkov.

Some Central Committee members, such as N.S. Popov, were taken directly as representatives of Higher Industrial Management, having spent an entire career span in one factory (the Kirov Factory, Leningrad). He started as an engineer, rising to the highest management position.[52] Thus, although the composition of the Central Committee elected at the 27th Party Congress did not undergo any dramatic change, the first steps in the direction of reforming it were discernible. The changes, although small, carried in them the seeds of subsequent transformations.

The process of selection of the Central Committee did not alter. The delegates to the Congress were presented with an official slate of the names proposed. This slate, which would probably be prepared prior to a Party Congress, would be examined during the Congress by a meeting of the representatives from each of the oblast, territorial, and republican delegations. Robert Daniels' hypothesis of "job slot representation" as the basis of the selection of the Central Committee held good, by and large, despite a reduction in the number of representatives from the government and an increase in the mass representative category.[53] Such a criterion had continued since the late 1920s and had become a time honoured convention. The "job slot" system of status and representation was also observed in the case of various union-republics. This system had been deemed to be a "conservative and stabilising element in Soviet politics".[54] The Central Committee thus continued to be a collective of most important institutions and positions in the Soviet society. These institutions articulated and fed their demands into this institution and competed for the available resources both informally and formally. In that sense it was like an extended Cabinet, with its specialised bureaucracy, in which the process of policy-making and resource allocation was undertaken. This therefore emphasised its nature as an administrative and managerial institution in contrast to its political role which was secondary. Although a sizeable number of Party leaders were members of this body, they too did not have any significant political role to play because of the coalescence of the institutions of the Party and the state in a single Party political system. The Party leaders were the administrators and the economic managers in the first place. The Central Committee, however, did not undergo any major organisational changes and as an institution remained the same as that inherited from Brezhnev era.

Organisation of the Central Committee

Members of the Central Secretariat and the central apparatus were "described as executive agents of the collective Party committees". The former were elected whereas the latter appointed members. Most supervised a group of ministries or other institutions. The day to day conduct of the work of the central leadership organs automatically imparted significant influence to these bodies. Most Central Committee decrees were prepared by the Secretariat (with the help of the departments concerned) and approved by the Politburo. They were not usually discussed by Central Committee members in the plenums, which were normally held twice a year. Most activities in the name of the Central Committee were conducted by the Politburo or the Secretariat.[55] The Central Secretariat was supposed to be responsible particularly for "personnel assignment", "verification of decisions" and "current work within the Central Committee". According to Article 38 of the Party statutes in operation before Perestroika, the Secretariat did not formulate policy, which was the function of the Politburo.[56] Its role at the input level of policy-making was crucial since the Politburo relied on it in the process of policy formulation. Its key importance lay in its supervision of the nomenclature of both the Party and the State.[57] The Central Secretariat was assisted by the central apparatus which incorporated the relevant expertise for fulfilling the functions of the Secretariat.[58] The central apparatus could order the removal of a lower level official. It participated in decisions regarding the membership of the commissions responsible for drafting legislation. Although the two may not have been the "centre of policy initiation", their work was "connected specifically with the decision-making process within the Secretariat, the Politburo, and the Central Committee".[59] The dependency of the Central Secretariat on its apparatus gave the latter a significantly powerful position. The Secretariat had varying interests "often paralleling the government structure and acting in concert with it".[60] The Central Committee departments and the ministries acted "as the combined representative of the branch in the appropriation process".[61] A close relationship existed between the two, hence the vital place of the central apparatus in the Soviet political system. It was this joint responsibility that led to the deep involvement of the Central Secretariat and the apparatus in day to day governance, economic matters, agriculture and so on.

One of the primary functions of the apparatus was to process information from the hundreds of reports that were received from the entire country. Its task was to study the information received and brief the decision makers. Another important role was to disseminate information to lower levels, so that Party members were aware of the prevailing policies.[62] The Central Committee departments acted as "filters" which sifted the information coming from the ministries and lower Party organisations to the Politburo. Thus in both cases the central apparatus could be selective about what information reached the leadership, making the latter heavily dependent on the former. Indeed, there were complaints against the central apparatus for not providing full and objective information to the leadership regarding important matters. Change in the personnel of the Party apparatus was a priority at the outset of Perestroika and was seen as one of the basic means for the resolution of vital problems. Gorbachev, in a note written on 26 November 1985, blamed the departments of the Central Committee for not only believing the lies and half truths that emanated from some leaders of the central ministries and organisations, local Party committees and members of the Party apparatus, but also defending them.[63] The Politburo subsequently issued a decree on 29 November 1985 based on Gorbachev's note.[64]

As regards the relationship between the central apparatus and the ministries, the latter would send proposals to the departments where they would be examined. The department would then send a concrete proposal to the Central Committee signed by the head of the department and possibly the minister concerned. The final decision would be taken by the Politburo or the Central Secretariat depending on the importance of the issue. In the Politburo or the Central Secretariat a consensus decision would emerge, being signed by a few Politburo or Central Secretariat members. This would then go down as the decision of the Central Committee to institutions concerned such as ministries, Party organs and so on. The most important link in the process of implementation were regional Party committees.[65] The Central Secretariat and its departments were an integrated unit. The regional Party committees, with whatever autonomy they had in reinterpreting the central directives to the local interests, were under the command structure and control of the Central Secretariat. This provided an important power base which could in practice subvert and challenge the authority of the Politburo and the Central Committee. Gorbachev's April 1985 speech talked of a radical restructuring of the Party apparatus. An extensive campaign was conducted in the media against the Party apparatus. This provoked a major discussion at the Party Congress itself.[66] Criticism of the apparatus was to continue throughout Perestroika. However, no organisational changes were made at this juncture.

Important changes in the composition had been underway in the central apparatus well before Perestroika. The inspectorate of the central apparatus was revamped with members from Gorbachev's generation. Several of these, such as Ye. Stroev, V. Kuptsov, V. Bakatin, G. Revenko, K. Salikov, Yu. Litvintsev and V. Grigoriev, became prominent members of the Central Committee.[67] By the middle of 1985, Gorbachev had changed three heads of departments.[68] The status of the central apparatus was reduced by curtailing its representation in the Central Committee. At the 25th Party Congress in 1976, 17 members of the central apparatus were elected as full members of the Central Committee and 13 as candidate members, while at the 26th Party Congress 29 members of the central apparatus were elected as full members and 14 as candidate members, indicating its enhanced position.[69] This representation dropped at the 27th Party Congress. At the 27th Party Congress 15 leaders of the apparatus were elected as full members and eight as candidate members of the Central Committee.[70] Although a campaign of criticism was launched, and its composition and status changed, the central apparatus was preserved more or less in its inherited form.

The practice of working through resolutions, conferences and plenums[71] continued as in the past. However, resistance to the implementation of the resolutions and decisions was felt particularly strongly by the Party leadership and the Central Committee. The resolutions of the April 1985 Central Committee plenum and the 27th Party Congress, it was claimed, laid down the approach to bureaucracy on manifestations such as diktats, administrative arbitrariness in economic, social and moral spheres, and indifference to the rights and needs of the people. Bureaucracy was seen as having grown to dangerous proportions and as acting as a break on social progress.[72] The relationship between the Central Committee and lower Party organs also remained the same. Similarly the relationship between the Party and the State continued as before, except for a renewed call by Gorbachev at the 27th Party Congress for an increased political role for the Party, a demarcation of functions between the two, and an increased role for State institutions. Thus the reforms were still intra-systemic and very much within the defined paradigm. Economic reforms dominated the agenda of the Party during this period and no political reforms of any fundamental nature, except an increased emphasis on the separation of the Party and the state, were undertaken.

Conclusion

The reformist leadership recognised the importance of the central question of the separation of the Party and the State, and initiated reforms in the Central Committee which stemmed from this fundamental reform. The period from the 27th Party Congress to the 19th Party Conference prepared the ground for them. The deepening of the political reforms at this Conference started a new phase of Perestroika. However the period before the 27th Party Congress did not signify any dramatic reforms, but what it did show was the beginning of a more comprehensive reform process in the Soviet Union than had ever been undertaken or envisaged in the preceding two decades.

The first steps in the direction of reform began with the ascendancy of the reformist section of the leadership in a keenly contested leadership struggle. This struggle highlighted the problems of succession in state-socialist societies in which the two contending trends of conservatism and reformism were in conflict within the same institutional framework, and the norms of succession were not well defined. This was a consequence of the lack of a democratic mechanism within the single political party, and the prevailing dominance of the Party and the State apparatuses, which mediated the process of interest articulation, interest aggregation, decision-making and decision-implementation. Thus they played a key role in the selection process.

The first political steps of the alliance of moderate conservatives and moderate reformists was to consolidate its position within the leadership and undermine the legacy of 'Brezhnevism'. The latter constituted the political-ideological basis of the most conservative sections of the Party and the State apparatuses. Although limited in scope, the reform programme met with opposition both politically and economically, from even the highest levels. A solution was sought in changing the composition of the Central Committee. The significant features of these changes were that, apart from the rate of turnover, about one-third of the new members had never been members of leadership organs and very few were promoted from candidate membership. Despite its limitations, this was a major step in strengthening the position of the alliance within the Central Committee and in bringing in a large number of members whose political education had taken place under Khrushchev.

However, the constituent institutions of the Central Committee, like the central apparatus, despite a campaign against them and minor personnel changes, remained untouched. Nor did the working of the Central Committee and its relationship with State alter to any significant extent. The explanation for the piece-meal reforms lies in opposition from within the Party organisation. However, the significance of the central question of redefining the relationship of the Party and the State was recognised by the leadership. If the institutionalised power of those opposed to the reforms within the Party and the state organisations had to be undermined and reforms were to succeed, then the existing relationship between Party and State had to be fundamentally altered. The seriousness of the reformists' intentions, and the fact that they were not merely a slogan, were verified by subsequent developments.

Notes

[1] S. White, A. *Pravda*, Z. Gitelman eds., *Developments in Soviet Politics*, (hereafter S. White et al, 1990), Macmillan, (London, 1990), p. 15.

[2] T. McNeill, "Nikolai Ryzhkov: Gorbachev's New Economic Overlord", *Radio Liberty (hereafter RL) 146/85,* 8 May 1985, p. 1.

[3] E. K. Ligachev, *Zagadka Gorbacheva,* (hereafter E. K. Ligachev, 1992), Sibirski Centre, "Inter Book", (Novosibirsk, 1992), p. 62. Among the active supporters were S. Maniakin, F. Morgun and A. Filatov. He noted in his memoirs how the first secretaries of obkoms met him prior to the plenum and discussed the issue of leadership election. Gorbachev was the obvious choice. A group of them were prepared to speak out in favour of Gorbachev in case of opposition.

Moscow Domestic Service, 1400 GMT, 1 July 1988, in *FBIS,* 5 July 1988, pp. 102-103.

[4] P. Rutland, "Economic Management and Reform" in S. White et al, 1990, pp. 161-162.

[5] Gorbachev's Political Report, CDSP, Vol. XXXVIII, No. 8, 1986, p. 11-14.

[6] *ibid.*, 1986, pp. 32-34.

[7] *Materiali Delegatu XIX Vsesoiuznoi Konferentsii KPSS,* (Moskva, 1988), p. 245.

[8] Gorbachev Report, 1986, pp. 11-26.

[9] E. Teague, "Gorbachev's Speech to the Twenty-Seventh Party Congress: More Carrot and More Stick", *RL 96/86*, 25 February 1986, p. 3.

[10] For a comprehensive study of the membership of the Central Committee, see E. Mawdsley, "Portrait of a changing elite: CPSU Central Committee full members, 1939-1990", in S. White, ed. *New Directions in Soviet History*, Cambridge University Press, (Cambridge, 1992), pp. 191-206.

[11] E. Teague, "Gorbachev Consolidating His Position", *RL 201/85,* 20 June 1985, p. 4.

[12] A. Rahr, "More Personnel Changes in the Offing", *RL341/85*, 10 October 1985, p. 2.

[13] E. Teague, "Gorbachev's First Year: Domestic Policy", *RL82/86*, 19 February 1986, p. 1-2.

[14] A. Rahr, "More Personnel Changes in the Offing", *RL341/85,* 10 October 1985, p. 2.

[15] M. R. Beissinger, "The Leadership and the Political Elite", in J. Cracraft ed., *The Soviet Union Today-An Interpretative Guide*, (Chicago, 1988),(hereafter M.R. Beissinger, 1988) p. 38.

[16] J. F. Hough, "Changes in Soviet Elite Composition", in S. Bialer and T. Gustafson ed. *Russia at the Cross-roads: The 26th Congress of the CPSU,* George Allen and Unwin, (1982) (hereafter J. F. Hough, 1982), pp. 46-47.

[17] M. Tatu, "The Central Committee Elected at the Twenty-Seventh Party Congress: Halfway Towards Rejuvenation", *RL 106/86,* 10 March 1986, p. 2.

[18] M. R. Beissinger, 1988, p. 38.

[19] A. Rahr, "More Personnel Changes in the Offing", *RL 341/85,* 10 October 1985, p. 2.

[20] E. Teague, "Turnover in the Soviet Elite Under Gorbachev: Implications for Soviet Politics", *RL Supplement 1/86,* 8 July 1986, p. 17.

[21] *AFP*, 1918 GMT, 6 March 1986 in *FBIS*, 7 March 1986, p. O-2.

[22] M. Tatu, "The Central Committee Elected at the Twenty-Seventh Party Congress: Halfway Towards Rejuvenation", *RL 106/86,* 10 March 1986, p. 2.

[23] R.V. Daniels, pp. 109-121.

[24] E. Mawdsley, "The 1990 Central Committee of the CPSU in Perspective", Soviet Studies, vol. 43, no. 5, 1991, Table 2.

[25] Directors of large state farm and enterprises are included in this category.

[26] J. F. Hough,1982, p. 47.

[27] Directors of large state farm and enterprises are included in this category.

[28] * in this case the data is only of the candidate members promoted and not of Central Auditing Commission members.
[29] *These percentages do not include Central Committee members of different nationalities who were elected either in the Central list or from the list of representation of 'other party organisations' as given below. The list basically gives a break down of the percentage of 'provincial officials.'
[30] *ibid.*
[31] *ibid.*, p. 17.
[32] M. Tatu, "The Central Committee Elected at the Twenty-Seventh Party Congress: Halfway Towards Rejuvenation", *RL 106/86,* 10 March 1986.
[33] * 6 of the military members were associated with either the political wing of the military or the Party committees in it.
[34] *The figure for 1990 of 378 also includes those who first entered the Central Committee in 1987(1), 1988(2) and 1989(9) between the 27th and 28th Party Congress.
[R.V. Daniels has treated 125 members of 1952 as a single entry cohort, although 34 of them entered the Central Committee in 1939 or earlier.]
[35] E. Mawdsley, Table 4.
[36] *ibid.*, Table 6.
[37] *ibid.*, Table 7.
[38] *ibid.*, Tables 4,7,8 and 9.
[39] *ibid.*, Table 6.
[40] Calculated from J. F. Hough, 1982, Table 2. 2, p. 46.
[41] Taken from the list of members and candidate members of the Central Committee elected by the 27th Party Congress compiled by Sergei Belitsky, Valerii Konovalov and Herwig Kraus, *RL 145/86*,1 April 1986 and *RL 151/86*, 9 April 1986.
[42] E. Mawdsley, Table 4.
[43] *ibid.*, Table 6.
[44] *ibid.*, Table 7.
[45] E. Mawdsley, Table 11. For a detailed study on representation of women in the Central Committee elected in 1990, see P. Lentini, "A Note on Women in the CPSU Central Committee, 1990", *Europe - Asia Studies* (formerly *Soviet Studies*), vol. 45, no. 4, 1993, pp. 729-36.
[46] E. Mawdsley, Table 12.
[47] *ibid.*, Table 12.
[48] J. F. Hough, 1982, p. 39.
[49] E. Mawdsley, "Portrait of a changing elite: CPSU Central Committee full members, 1939-1990", in Stephen White, ed. *New Directions in Soviet History*, Cambridge University Press, (Cambridge, 1992), p. 204.
[50] E. Mawdsley, Table 13.
[51] In some cases they held more than one post.
[52] From information collected from V.G. Panov ed., *Ezhegodnik Bolshoi Sovetskoi Entsiklopedii,* 1987, Sovetskaia Entsiklopaedia, Moscow, 1987; *XXVI Syezd Kommunisticheskoi Partii Sovetskova Souiza otchet,* no. 2 and *A Biographical Directory of 100 Leading Soviet Officials,* compiled by Alexander Rahr, Westview Press, RFE/RL, 1990.

[53] R. V. Daniels, 1989, p. 105. "The unwritten code allocated to each functional hierarchy and to each union republic (and often province) a proportion of seats in the Central Committee corresponding to the imputed status and importance of the particular institution and region ... There is in practice an organic and automatic connection between this specific set of offices and the Central Committee as a well defined and quite stable set of leading job slots whose occupants enjoy the elite status conferred by Central Committee membership as long as and only as long as they occupy their respective offices". A similar observation was made by J. F. Hough and M. Fainsod, 1979, pp. 452-453, p.458.
[54] *ibid.*, p. 102-108.
[55] D. P. Hammer, *The USSR: The Politics of Oligarchy,* Westview Press, (1986), (hereafter D. P. Hammer, 1986)
p. 87.
[56] *ibid.*, pp. 89-90.
[57] R. J. Hill and A. Rahr, "The General Secretary, the Central Party Secretariat and the Apparat", in D. Lane, ed., *Elites and Political Power in the USSR*, Edward Elgar, (Hants, 1988), pp. 50-52.
See Also L. Shapiro, *The Government and Politics of the Soviet Union,* Hutchinson, (London, 1973); and W. Hahn, *Post-war Soviet Politics,* Cornell University Press, (London, 1982).
[58] J. F. Hough and M. Fainsod, 1979, pp. 410-420.
[59] *ibid.*, pp. 432-35.
[60] Lane D. and Ross C., The Composition of the Politburo of the CPSU: 1966-1991.
[61] *ibid.*, p. 444.
[62] D. P. Hammer, 1986, p. 89.
[63] *Izvestiia_Tsk KPSS*, no. 2, February 1989, pp. 39-41.
[64] *ibid.*, p. 39.
[65] Interview with Boris Kluev, former Instructor in the International department of the Central Committee, Moscow, August 1992.
[66] V. Shlapentokh, "The XXVII Congress - A Case Study Of the Shaping of a New Party Ideology", *Soviet Studies*, vol. XI, no. 1, January 1988, pp. 7-11.
[67] E. K. Ligachev, 1992, pp. 44-45.
[68] E. Teague, "Gorbachev Consolidating His Position", *RL 201/85,* 20 June 1985, pp. 4-5.
[69] J. F. Hough, *Changes in the Soviet Elite Composition*, in S. Bialer and T. Gustafson eds., *Russia at the Cross-roads: The 26th Congress of the CPSU,* George Allen and Unwin, (1982), Table 2. 2, p. 46.
[70] Calculated from *RL 145/86*, 1 April 1986, pp. 1-23 and *RL 151/86*, 9 April 1986, pp. 1-14. Compiled by S. Belitsky, V. Konalev and H. Kraus, Radio Liberty Bulletins.
[71] Four plenums were held in 1985, three in 1986, three in 1987 and five in 1988. G. Gill, *The Collapse of a Single-Party system, The Disintegration of the CPSU,* Cambridge University Press, (Cambridge 1994) (hereafter G. Gill, 1994), p. 89.
[72] "Materials of the 19th All-Union Conference of the CPSU", *Kommunist*, no. 10, 1988, p. 74.

4 Preparing for Systemic Political Reforms: between the 27th Party Congress and the 19th Party Conference

Introduction

Reforms introduced at the 27th Party Congress resulted in emerging differences in the coalition at the highest level. On the whole the reforms only had limited success as demonstrated by the working of the Central Committee and the nature of the relationship between the Party and the State. The period between the 27th Party Congress and the 19th Party Conference could at best be characterised as the preparatory stage for meaningful political reforms. The reforms were implemented through existing channels and traditional methods and therefore the systemic intrangisence effectively thwarted them. Nevertheless reformist measures generated a debate in society, the Party and the Central Committee, and created an opinion for effective political reforms. "Socialist pluralism" and glasnost were accepted as the vital kernel of these reforms accelerated further at the 19th Party Conference. The key political reform, one of far-reaching consequence, introduced at this Conference was that of the separation of the Party and the State at the highest level, that is the Central Committee itself.

According to Gorbachev, restructuring was said to be losing momentum. The centre for resistance, he declared, was in the Party and State apparatuses, in ministries and departments which tended to preserve their powers. They refused to devolve them to lower levels and either did not change their practice or had a conventional approach or positively resisted the reforms. The tendency was to strengthen the apparatuses further. The emphasis of reforms was on restructuring the style and methods of all the elements of the Party work with Party officials playing the key role. However, it was acknowledged by Gorbachev at the June

1986 Plenum that Party organisations had a tendency to simply ignore the decisions of a Congress. An authoritarian style of work, a negative attitude towards criticism, protecting wrongdoers and hiding failures, inducing economic managers to do report-padding and neglecting the development of initiative of Party organisations and people, in short, an administrative style of functioning, were not uncommon phenomena. Despite the Congress, the supreme decision-making body, enjoining the Party committees to undertake political methods of work, the latter continued to assume managerial functions. Party leaders would authoritatively speak on "the current economic campaign, of milk yields and weight gains, tons, and so on" yet were often at a loss while analysing the political and socio-economic phenomenon. entire Party functioned by a system of administrative fiat.[1] The integration of the Party and the Statc, both a cause and effect of the problem of governing a single-Party dominated political system, was in an advanced stage and therefore, the Gorbachevian leadership argued, necessitated political reforms. The existing practise of governance and the longstanding force of habit created a real bottleneck in implementing this central political reform, straining the coalition of moderate reformers and moderate conservatives and preparing the ground for the multiplicity of political tendencies which may compete for political dominance in the future. Customary methods of reforms were being counteracted and were ineffective, particularly at lower levels, both in the Party and the Soviets.

The economic reforms were opposed and the political reforms remained ineffective. The issue was whether to continue with the reforms or let them peter out. Reforms in personnel policy were thought to rescue the reforms package. The resolution of the January 1987 Central Committee plenum acknowledged that the acceleration of socio-economic development and the qualitative transformation of social life had encountered a braking mechanism. Conservatism, inertia and archaic modes of thinking continued. Change in personnel policy was seen as "a decisive means" of implementing the programme goals of the CPSU.[2] This was no panacea given that politics relied more on an arbitrary mechanism than institutional norms. Yet it marked a significant step in the direction of reform, particularly for the Central Committee.

Gorbachev's proposals included multiple candidacies in both the Party and local government. More non-Party members were to be elected to leading positions in the government and economy. Workers' participation was to increase in the election of enterprise directors. Co-operative forms of ownership were to be expanded with greater reliance on the market mechanism in the economy. Any number of candidates could be put forward by Party committee members, and the election was to be conducted by a secret ballot from raion to republic level. Gorbachev argued for the continuous renewal of higher Party organs, including the Central Committee, the Central Secretariat and the Politburo.[3] The controversial nature of this plenum was demonstrated by the high participation rate in its discussions. 34 members out of a total of 77 prospective speakers spoke,[4] compared to 13 at the 23 April 1985 plenum.[5] Gorbachev's proposals for a change in the process of electing Party officials were rejected.[6] The plenum decided to democratise the sphere of production and gradually introduce self-rule in workers' collectives and deepen inner-Party democracy. Control over the work of cadres was to be strengthened and glasnost promoted in the work of leading organs. The supremacy of the law was to be established and the legal system strengthened. Greater mass participation was to broaden the social base of Soviet democracy and ensure a constant influx of fresh forces at all levels of the Party, including its Central Committee.[7] These were recipes for dissension within the Central Committee. Ivan Polozkov warned against multi-candidate elections, expressing the resistance of Party officials, and several Central Committee members agreed with him.[8] Single Party democratisation and introduction of market economy was not acceptable to an influential section of the Central Committee. The conservative sections of the Party sensed that in the long run this could destabilise the very basis of the Soviet political and economic system jeopardising its long term viability. One could say with the benefit of the hindsight that they were not very far removed from an accurate judgement of the consequences of reforms. Whether the reforms were necessary for the survival and revival of the Soviet system or the nature of reforms and the methodology of their conduct was appropriate or not or the ethical and value-based dimension of politics (that the communist system was evil and less democratic as compared to Western liberal-democracies) warranted the reforms, constitute a different set of questions. The fact remains that the reforms culminated in destroying the integrity of the Soviet political system and restoration of a primitive form of market economy along with authoritarian and often radically nationalistic political regimes functioning in the name of liberal-democratic ideology and within liberal-democratic institutional forms. The worst nightmares of the conservative sections expressed during the course of the entire political-ideological conflicts throughout Perestroika proved to be true.

Another important political reform, though implemented unofficially, was the acknowledgement of pluralism, albeit a "socialist" one.

The impact of the acceptance of this concept had perhaps as deep ramifications as that of the introduction of glasnost. It signalled that the traditional repository of wisdom on political, economic and other aspects of Soviet life, the Party and the State apparatuses, could no longer exercise a monopoly over information. There could be any number of opinions on any issue and they need not essentially be "socialist" in reality. In any case the term "socialist" now had myriad meanings and even the Party leadership was not sure of how to define it. Depending on which political tendencies within the Party leadership was dominant at a particular point of time, the definition would be appropriately modified. However the pluralism coupled with glasnost undermined the monopoly of the apparatus over information and official ideology.

Pluralism had been a taboo until then in Soviet political discourse. At the plenum of February 1988 Gorbachev spoke positively about "socialist pluralism" and argued that "a socialist pluralism of opinion" already existed.[9] This stood in sharp contrast with the traditional theory of the "monolithic unity" of the Party and people. On the one hand, pluralism and glasnost would undermine the executive wing of the Party and the State which were resisting the reforms, on the other the Party could not possibly have played a political role without this. One-party democratisation as envisaged by the leadership would have had no meaning in the absence of these twin pillars. However there was no guarantee that the plurality of opinions would remain socialist, as indeed happened. The Theses of the Central Committee of the Party at the 23 May 1988 plenum gave official approval to "socialist pluralism".[10] The 19th Party Conference, recognising "socialist plurality", established its link with glasnost "as a means of collating and accumulating the entire diversity of interests and the socialist plurality of opinions that exist in Soviet society".[11] These were twin instruments to enable a democratised Party to play a more effective guiding role over the State by opening up channels other than the Party and the State apparatuses in a single-Party democracy assuming that ideologies and political and social forces antagonistic to the Party which had either emerged as a result of the ongoing economic reforms or had a subterranean existence as long as the Soviet Union had existed remained passive politically. These were thus important elements of the process of the separation of the Party and the State entailing the subordination of the executive wing of the two to their elective wings. They could, however, also destabilise the Soviet political system as it eventually did by opening the political space for alien ideologies.

Political pluralism was closely linked to the economic pluralism. Economic pluralism meant the emergence of new interests in society, and political pluralism would give them expression. Restructuring of the economy involved decentralisation of economic power, pluralism of all economic forms including property and the setting up of horizontal economic links. Political pluralism was not seen as necessarily leading to a multi-party system. The reformist leadership hoped that the expression of varied interests would be through the Party.[12] It was understood as pluralism of opinions[13] and as a means of democratisation within the one-party system.[14] Reformists argued that if monopolism could bring about decay in the sphere of economy, science and politics, the same would be true of a political party adhering to a single point of view. Consolidation was to include coexistence of different opinions.[15] Economic reforms had begun to give rise to new social forces like incipient bourgeoise in the cooperators, enterpreneurs and leaseholders etc. Regional and sub-regional interests were being asserted more forcefully and cohesively than ever before and provided a basis for ethnically oriented social forces. Those involved in parallel underground economy were tolerated more and more by the regime finding new acceptance and identification. A section of the Party, state apparatus, the mass organisation and the professional segments like the managers, engineers, technicians, doctors etc. were involved in commercial and service ventures and as beneficiaries of the economic reforms argued for expanding the reforms. At this stage most of these newly emerging social forces supported Gorbachevian reforms and the section of the political leadership aligned with him hoping to ensure increasing marketisation of the economy. Insignificant political and intellectual opinion at this stage was articulated in favour of a multi-party system. However glasnost was not yet in vogue and pluralism as a political concept was seldom articulated.

Thus at this stage of the reforms, the Party leadership envisaged one-party democratisation based on a democratic consensus. It meant the articulation of a multitude of political aspirations, even if they were contradictory, within a one-party system. Cognisance of social and political forces outside existing channels, those which had emerged as society grew more advanced and complex, could thus be facilitated, and could contribute to effective policy-making. Economic pluralism was to give rise to social class differentiation and therefore prepare the ground for the eventual emergence of a multi-party system. The CPSU could retain its character of a working-class led mass party functioning in a multi-party system, but could not contain within it the newly emerging political forces representing national-territorial aspirations and those of a nascent bourgeoisie. It could evolve into a mass political party of the working class, the peasantry and sections of the middle classes, functioning in a parliamentary political system with the Central Committee as its leadership organ. The emergence of socio-economic differentiation was still a long way off. In this period of transition the attempt of the reformist section of the leadership seemed to be to incorporate both socio-economic differentiation and national-territorial aspirations within it, as was made evident later by the changes in the Central Committee at the 28th Party Congress.

Although political conflict had taken place in the upper echelons of the Soviet leadership in the past, it had never been openly expressed. The leadership instead presented a public appearance of monolithic unity.[16] Different political opinions had existed in the Central Committee before Perestroika, but not in an organised form. The Party was primarily a coalition of different sections of society which were said to be non-antagonistic with a common strategic goal. The open formation of political and socio-economic based groups was thus forbidden, although many of these tendencies did express themselves informally. The absence of an institutionalised mechanism of intra-party democracy in a one-party system prevented the open articulation of varied political, social and economic tendencies. Although informal channels of articulation existed at input level they appeared to be limited in their scope. Because of the absence of open expression these tendencies seem to have led to a disbalance in society. In a competitive political system, competing forces result in the forging of a consensus and a compromise, thus maintaining the equilibrium of a social and political order.

During Perestroika the efforts of the Party in taking various social forces into account was admitted openly. This was an affirmation that new autonomous social forces had emerged outside the influence of the Party. An editorial in *Kommunist* in 1988 claimed that in order to build a higher form of society and direct the processes of democratisation, the Party tried to take into account different forces operating in society.[17] The new ideology of Perestroika was to acknowledge their coexistence and interaction in society. This could provide a deeper understanding of the contradictions in social development present at the start of Perestroika. Awareness of the contradictions was meant to facilitate effective policy making.[18] The existing political and State organisations were inadequate to cope with the demands of society, particularly in the absence of optimally representative democratic institutions. The existing ones were to be renovated rather than replaced during the reforms. All political institutions, whether liberal democratic or any other undergo periodic reorganisation to respond to new complexities of society if they want to continue their existence and the Soviet political institutions were no exceptions. Thus one-party democratisation could be seen as effort in that direction. However a political consensus within the Party, particularly its political leadership was an essential precondition for such a reform. Immediately after the January plenum, the coalition of moderate reformists and moderate conservatives at the highest levels of the leadership started showing signs of strain, as shown by the differences that emerged between Gorbachev, Yakovlev, Yeltsin and Ligachev.[19] However, not many differences were evident at the 19th Party Conference debates and were still subterranean.

The 19th Party Conference

The 19th Party Conference unveiled a comprehensive programme of political reforms with far-reaching effects, and at the same time intensified resistance to the reforms. The differences would subsequently become more open and manifest. Criticising the inherited political system, Gorbachev contended that it had not been able to prevent stagnation in the economic and social life of previous decades, and had led to the failure of earlier reforms. The Party, mainly the Party apparatus, had become economic managers and the role of the executive apparatus was hypertrophied. Public life was excessively dominated by the State. The political system itself therefore needed to be reformed.[20] Speeches by Central Committee members however did not indicate any sharp divergence of opinions, with some exceptions, because until now whatever reforms had been introduced were yet to become effective. The Party and the State apparatuses maintained their dominant position in the Soviet political system.

Gorbachev's report to the 19th Party Conference envisaged the development of "socialist democracy" which essentially meant one-party democratisation.[21] It did not, however, consider the possibility of a multi-party system as its basis, rather it attempted to develop an updated concept of socialist democracy. With the exception of L.I. Abalkin, director of the USSR Academy of Sciences Institute of Economics, there was a general consensus on this question. He implied that a multi-party system was a pre-condition for democracy, and questioned the possibility of democratisation in a single party system. Thus he argued for a Western-style multi-party system.

Abalkin's speech brought a rejoinder from A.M. Masaliev, first secretary of the Kirgiz Communist Party, who supported Gorbachev's position. V.I. Kalashnikov, first secretary of the Volgograd obkom, concurred.[22] I.K. Polozkov, first secretary of the Krasnodar kraikom, argued for the complete restoration of power to the soviets, as did D.K. Patiashvili. V.I. Mironenko, first secretary of the Komsomol, rejected the view that the multi-party system was "an indispensable condition of socialist pluralism".[23] Yakovlev did not foresee the possibility of a multi-party system "under conditions where socialist ownership predominates".[24] (Subsequently in his memoirs, Yakovlev claimed that at the end of 1985 he had written a note to Gorbachev arguing for "the necessity and urgency of dividing CPSU into two parties" which would occupy the "democratic space of rivalry". The two parties could have contested in elections and vied for power. This, in his retrospective view, could have democratised socialism.[25]) B. N. Yeltsin, now first deputy chairman of the USSR Gostroi, also did not favour a multi-party system. For V.G. Afanasiev, chief editor of *Pravda*, the emergence of political opposition was unlikely since there was "no social or class basis for it". In his opinion the press could play the role of a "socialist opposition".[26] Ye.M. Primakov, director of the USSR Academy of Sciences Institute of World Economics and International Relations, believed that "nationalistic and dogmatic elements of all hues could be the first to take advantages of the idea of a multi-party system" and give a "terrible blow" to Perestroika.[27] His words were indeed prophetic. It were "nationalistic and dogmatic elements of hues" that ultimately destroyed the Soviet political system.

One of the important corner-stones of reform was the economy. Its key elements were the transfer of enterprises to financial autonomy, self-financing and self-management. Enterprises which switched to these methods were given a positive appraisal by Gorbachev in his report to the Conference.[28] The control of numerous ministries and the central state agencies over the enterprises was to be reduced but no private ownership in any form was envisaged. Again a consensus existed among Central Committee members, with the exception of Arbatov, director of the Institute of the USA and Canada and the USSR Academy of Sciences. From the middle of 1987 when Yakovlev argued for deideologising the economy, the reform process at a political level had moved considerably for Arbatov to now contend that the success of Perestroika hitherto was "a recognition of the role of the commodity and money relationships of the market" in public consciousness and in political conceptions.[29] Deideologising essentially meant privatising the state-owned enterprises and contradicted the very basic tenet of socialism, that is social-ownership of the means of production. Market relations, a taboo for a long time, were to govern the economy. Thus although the official position maintained by Gorbachev and fellow reformists was that of undertaking economic reforms within the paradigm of socialism by granting them greater autonomy, the hidden unfinished agenda in the long-term was that of introducing full-fledged market economy and privatisation.

Other participants in the debate accepting the framework of the reforms proposed by Gorbachev included V.V. Bakatin, first secretary of the Kemerovo obkom.[30] D.K. Motornii, chairman of the Kirov kolkhoz, Kherson oblast, believed that the reforms had led to the "dynamic development" of the overall economy.[31] F.V. Popov, first secretary of the Altai kraikom, wanted to preserve the "leading role" of the centre but believed that the reforms were working.[32] A. A. Logunov, Rector of Moscow State University, argued for greater control and direction of the economic reforms. V.I. Melnikov, first secretary of Komi obkom, argued for a "fundamentally new economic management" with the republics too opting for self-financing and cost recovery.[33] K.M. Makhkamov, first secretary of the Communist Party of Tajikistan, opined the reforms so far had succeeded in arresting the economic and socio-political crisis.[34] Gumer Usmanov, first secretary of the Tatarstan obkom, too seemed to favour the proposed economic reforms.[35] Yu.A. Kvitinskii, Ambassador to the FRG, linked the economic reforms to political reforms which in this case meant the separation of Party and State and the reorganisation of the latter and not the introduction of a multi-party system as a section of the reformists would have liked.[36] V.K. Mesiats, first secretary of the Moscow gorkom, stated the basic accepted limit of the economic reforms, which was to develop the co-operative sector, collective and lease contract, transfer all sectors of the economy to economic accountability, self-financing and cost recovery.[37] Thus a broad consensus on economic reforms existed in the Central Committee of the CPSU.

The third issue was the nationality question. Gorbachev's report talked of reinterpreting the rights of the union-republics in the light of the economic reforms. Apart from fulfilling all-union obligations, the report argued for giving them the opportunity to increase production for their own requirements. The development of the multi-national state was envisaged, with a growth in national self-awareness seen as a positive phenomenon. The nationality problem was to be resolved within the framework of the union, taking into account the interest of all nations and ethnic groups and all the Soviet people. The internationalisation of the economy and social life was seen to preclude any form of national exclusivity.[38] Party officials from the republics favoured greater devolution of power to lower levels within the union framework. This was the reflection of the increasing national assertion within the Party leadership from the republics, which in turn underlined the growing nationalistic feelings and resurfacing of ethnic identities. The speeches of A.Kh. Vezirov, first secretary of the Azerbaijan Communist Party,[39] B.V. Kachura, secretary of the Ukrainian Communist Party,[40] Patiashvili[41] and S.K. Grossu reflected this view. G.A. Yagodin, chairman of the USSR State Committee for Public Education, believed that socialist internationalism was not "non-national" and was based "on national pride, progressive historical traditions, and respect for one's native language".[42] Ye.M. Primakov favoured the creation of "a single international alloy in the Soviet Union ... which will be much more monolithic than the sum of national formations leaning towards exclusiveness".[43] Thus nationalism and other political manifestations of ethnic identities were being accepted in the Soviet political discourse and in the understanding of the highest Soviet leadership and in the intellectual life. In the case of inter-ethnic relations, members of the Central Committee had a broad consensus on the renewal of the federation, which envisaged greater autonomy for the republics and the regions, and yet an important role for the union. These however were reluctant steps of a leadership departing from time honoured theory and practise as far as nationalism was concerned and proved woefully inadequate when the nationalist upsurge throughout the political boundaries of the former Soviet Union led by the political forces opposed to the party and the Soviet political system resulted in the latter's unceremonious disintegration. The party fractured along the national lines and so did the Soviet Union. A major section of each of these republican party organisations succumbed to the nationalist pressures, they either deserted the party or accepted their specific nationalisms as the dominant ideologies before finally abandoning any pretence of socialism or communism.

Hence, during the debate on key issues at the 19th Party Conference, there was no fundamental divergence of opinions between the Central Committee members, with a few exceptions. These exceptions however, did show that political-ideological concepts hitherto taboo were accepted in the Soviet intellectual discourse. The only clear political conflict that emerged during the Conference was between Ligachev and Yeltsin, who were to represent two very diverse and conflicting tendencies in the future. Yeltsin considered the existing policy of Perestroika to be declarative in nature, and said that it had been rushed through without proper analysis of the causes of stagnation, the existing situation in the society, and the errors of the Party. Hence, neither had the "tangible problems of the people" been solved, nor had any "revolutionary transformations" been achieved.[44] Ligachev objected to Yeltsin's assertion that Perestroika had been initiated without "a profound analysis", which was "sowing doubt about the correctness of the execution of the Party's political course".[45] Thus on the one hand ground was being prepared for a systemic change of far-reaching consequences although a majority of the Central Committee members argued for controlled reforms, on the other hand the coalition within the party, which introduced and led the reforms, was disintegrating. This would, in the post-19th Party Conference period, result in an increasing clash of political tendencies within the Party leadership and the rank and file.

The Working of the Central Committee

The Central Committee worked mainly through the resolutions issued in its authority within the policy framework laid down by the Party Congress or a plenum. These were prepared by the Central apparatus alongwith the Party and the state apparatuses. Only the most important ones were approved by a plenum. These resolutions could be issued jointly with other state institutions like the Council of Ministers or the mass organisations.[46] They contained detailed analysis of the area concerned, outlining the measures to be adopted by the Party and/or the State bodies. They were essentially directive despite the initiation of political methods of leadership.[47] The Central Committee was directly involved in a very wide range of issues under the purview of the State and government bodies.[48] The resolutions criticised the activities of ministers as well as the ministries.[49] Technical aspects of the economy and industry were discussed extensively in these resolutions. These also reviewed the implementation of past decisions and were circumvented by State agencies and lower Party organs when they failed to discharge essential functions.[50] The integration of the Party and the state was very sharply evident in the nature, content, mode of preparation and the role these resolutions performed in running the Soviet system including its day to day governance.

The practise of working through resolutions percolated down to the lowest Party and state organs. They too functioned by issuing edicts even though these did not work. Such a system continued well into the first phase of Perestroika upto the 19th Party Conference. Regional organs, whether Party or State, did not learn from the earlier experiences. These bodies therefore would not directly participate in solving the problems entrusted to them and their accountability remained upto the passing of the relevant resolution.[51] Local ispolkoms were particularly entrusted with the task of monitoring and certifying the readiness of the enterprises as a part of the transfer of power to the Soviets. The Central Committee would then issue a general joint resolution in the light of experiences in one oblast.[52] Lower Party and Soviet committees, however, would neglect their responsibilities, calling for the intervention of the Central Committee. The nominal transfer of power to the Soviets was in essence a transfer of power to its committees, which themselves had become inert organisations.

A wide range of issues was covered by these resolutions.[53] These could include issues which ought have been resolved by government agencies.[54] Between 1985 and 1988 there were at least fourteen more major resolutions or decisions of the Central Committee on the economy.[55] Resolutions were predominantly on the economy and agriculture, with very few on social and political issues or those concerning the Party; the Central Committee was involved in running the economy and the agricultural sector.[56] An analysis of these resolutions clearly highlighted the virtual absence of the social and political role which a political party in a single-party political system was required to play. Very few addressed these vital issues.

There were resolutions on inner-Party affairs, like that on the question of Party membership in the Tashkent oblast. Although addressed to a specific party organisation they were meant for wider application. This resolution said that not only the obkom but the republic as a whole had been following a policy of "artificially boosting" Party membership. Party organisations had given up monitoring the management and the apparatus. The tendency to have Party members even in minor posts had led to careerism. Admission to the Party was often linked to the appointment of an individual to a leading post. Despite the multi-ethnic composition of the oblast, ethnic minorities were not adequately represented. Several first secretaries of Party committees had not studied the question of Party membership themselves and therefore and did not know how to organise this work.[57] These problems were universal in nature and afflicted most Party organisations. A mechanical approach over regulating the selection and setting up of "control targets" for lower committees had resulted in an artificial increase in Party membership. This resolution exposed the problem of Party membership. Under conditions in which the Party and its leadership was preoccupied with economic issues, the mechanical supervision of the Party and the loss of its political role meant that Party membership had become an arbitrary affair in the hands of local leaderships.

On important social issues like housing allocation, a resolution of the Central Committee noted serious violations of the principle of social justice and housing legislation. Certain Party and Soviet committees were found to be violating the procedure for allocation of housing. Frunze gorispolkom, disregarding memoranda from the Kirgiz Communist Party and Council of Ministers, had allotted 78 apartments to those who already had good housing. In certain cases some economic functionaries, with the blatant support of local Soviet ispolkoms, allocated housing to organisations which were not entitled to it in exchange for services. It kept a large amount of housing in reserve, giving it to individuals who already had housing, or left housing unoccupied for long periods. The housing problem of war veterans and families of deceased soldiers and officers remained unresolved, and in several cases war invalids were given houses in suburbs or in "uninhabitable regions".[58]

Resistance to the implementation of the resolutions and decisions was felt particularly strongly by a section of the Party leadership and the Central Committee. The resolutions of the April 1985 Central Committee plenum and the 27th Party Congress, it was claimed, laid down the approach to bureaucracy on manifestations such as diktats, administrative arbitrariness in economic, social and moral spheres, and indifference to the rights and needs of the people. Bureaucracy was seen as having grown to dangerous proportions and as acting as a break on social progress.[59] The Central Committee plenum of June 1986 initiated the process of reform in the way the Party functioned. The plenum analysed the practical implementation of the reform process initiated by the 27th Party Congress and attacked the Party's administrative methods of working. It criticised certain lower Party committees and individual first secretaries, such as the Kursk obkom and its first secretary, A. Gudkov, and the Cherkassi obkom, for "unsuitable, unacceptable methods of working with cadres". *Pravda* in an editorial on the plenum on 25th June 1986 pointed out the clash between old and new ideas which had emerged in the Party.[60] The above instance also showed the practice of the Central Committee in taking a decision regarding the development of a region.

L.A. Onikov, an inspector at the Central Committee Propaganda department, in an interview in *Pravda*, talked about the failure of a resolution adopted in 1987 in the Vladimir oblast on glasnost. According to him it "essentially failed to provide the necessary guarantees of glasnost". The same question had to be addressed again in a resolution of the 19th

Party Conference.[61] Resolutions such as those on the Perm oblast, on admission to the Party in the Tashkent oblast, on Leningrad's Petrogradskii raikom, on glasnost in the Vladimir oblast, passed by the Central Committee after the 25th April 1985 plenum and the 27th Party Congress, and prior to the 19th Party Conference, were applicable throughout the Party but were virtually ineffective. According to an analysis of the stenographic records of the oblast and krai Party organisation plenums, held prior to the 19th Party Conference, the functioning of these Party organisations was practically unaffected by these resolutions.[62] The reforms and the expectation of Party leaders that it was possible to enhance the role of Party organisations and activate the Soviets through resolutions and exhortations proved not to be working at the lower levels. The reason lay in the Party and the Soviet committees and their structural and functional constraints. In the case of the Perm obkom, a resolution noted that it had been unable "to create a united front of all sectors in the struggle for acceleration". The situation had not changed in many enterprises. In the first ten months of the first year of the 12th Five Year Plan, an okrug and 11 cities and raions failed to fulfil the plan for industrial output sales. More than forty per cent of the enterprises working under new management conditions could not meet their delivery targets, and one in five could not meet the target for labour productivity growth. In the agro-industrial sector, work remained of a low standard and one third of farms were operating at a loss. Neither did state subsidies for meat and milk reduce, nor food supplies improve despite the existing potential. The situation was similar in the social sphere where targets of housing, schools, and hospitals were not fulfilled. Funds allocated for these purposes were not even utilised. The conclusion of the Central Committee was that this resulted from "the absence of any substantial change" in the method of working the obkom and its bureau which were marked by obsolete methods and approaches. However, the solution proposed by the resolution again consisted of traditional method of exhortations, that Party discipline and intra-Party democracy be strengthened and developed, the implementation of Party decisions and internal resolutions be effectively monitored, the role of Party committee plenums and Party conferences be increased, and the views of rank-and-file communists, workers, and specialists be sufficiently taken into account.[63] The problem with such an approach was that the institutionalised structures and practices and the persisting political culture of the Party and the State apparatuses constituted the nucleus of such arrangements. Apart from inertia, resistance ensued because any reform entailed deregulating their control and entrenched positions.

An example of the type of problem with the economic reforms was manifested at the Irbit Chemical-Pharmaceutical Plant in Sverdlovsk oblast. The Party bureau and the director kept away from, and even impeded, the introduction of composite teams formed in one of the shops according to the technological principle of the reforms which resulted in the abolition of the teams. Party member V.P. Bakharev, who initiated and actively worked to organise this, was charged with "disregard for the opinion of the labour collective", and was expelled from the Party and relieved of his position. The plant Party meeting, while not supporting his expulsion, recommended strict punishment. Irbitskii gorkom did nothing about it. Bakharev's petition to the Sverdlovsk obkom for a review of the decision resulted in the obkom officers forwarding his complaint to Irbitskii gorkom, from which they received a formal reply. This was filed without even being examined. Such actions of the Party bureau created "an unhealthy atmosphere" in the collective and the Party organisation. The Central Committee intervened and the Party bureau of the plant was held responsible. The secretary of the plant PPO, Dergachev, was removed and reprimanded, Poliakov, the director of the plant, was dismissed and reprimanded. The secretary of Irbitskii gorkom Volozhanin, received a strict reprimand, Sverdlovsk obkom was to decide if he could continue in his post, and Bakharev was reinstated.[64] This example showed how the Party and State apparatuses, particularly at the lower levels, could frustrate reforms which required the intervention of the Central Committee. There were many such examples. They raised the question of whether the existing structures and methods of working would be able to deliver the reforms. The only way the reforms could have been implemented would have been if the Central Committee had the omnipresent machinery to monitor and prevent such things. This meant strengthening the two apparatuses and further perfecting the administrative method.

The problem with the implementation of decrees of the Politburo, Central Secretariat and Central Committee was not a new one. These decrees were interpreted, distorted and diluted as they flowed down for implementation.[65] In the opinion of a former apparatus official, A. Fillipov, it was probably because of the difficulty the rank and file faced in fully understanding these resolutions. As these resolutions moved down the ladder of various Party committees, their essence was lost and their nature distorted.[66] Apart from administrative problems, the tendency was "to submerge the heart of the problem in general discussions and appeals not backed up by constructive decisions", as in the case of improving public health care.[67] A solution was seen in political methods of working combined with popular involvement.[68] The "political method" of working meant that sole reliance on the Party and state apparatuses for the implementation of the decrees was to be substituted by attempts to involve the population. In Soviet parlance, "administrative methods" referred to the role of the apparatuses in preparing and implementing the resolutions pertaining to almost all spheres of the Soviet life be it economy, general administration or social welfare functions. One of the pleas given by the reformists, within the Party, for launching major economic and political reforms was that the system of working through the apparatuses whose extensive network formed the building blocks of the Soviet political and economic system was unable to prevent the slide of the economy and society in general. Therefore other sections of the Soviet society had to be involved. At this stage of reforms neither a systemic change had been envisaged nor the groundwork for that undertaken by the reformists. This was a proposal of intra-systemic reform and hoped that economic and social problems would be resolved with least political changes like efforts to involve the Soviet society. However the institutional mechanisms for such an involvement were inadequate. Despite the extensive network of Soviets, the representative institutions were stymied by their subservience to the executive and absence of the principle of electivity. Hence the popular involvement in governing society was not forthcoming in any meaningful way.

The Central Committee and its Relationship with Lower Party Organisations and State and Government Agencies

The Central Committee "guided" lower Party committees and their leaders. This task stemmed partly from the non-fulfilment of resolutions and ensuing problems in the economy and agriculture, and partly from the inheritance of the past. It adopted resolutions critically, analysing their work chiefly in the economic sphere in accordance with the decisions of the 27th Party Congress and plenums. These resolutions gave detailed directives and guidelines to lower Party organs, including republican Party committees.[69] There were similar decrees for obkoms and kraikoms.[70] The organisational functioning of the Party organisations would be scrutinised.[71] Such resolutions were meant to serve as general resolutions applicable to other Party organisations.[72] The Party, government, the State agencies and their leaders could be "instructed" to rectify their shortcomings.[73] Thus one of the major tasks of the Central Committee was to take decisions for a republican or regional Party committee on various issues. A resolution on the activity of the Voronezh obkom listed its shortcomings in fulfilling the targets of two five-year plans to increase the production and procurement of animal husbandry products. The organisational and political work of the obkom, several gorkoms, raikoms and primary Party organisations in the labour collectives were also criticised.[74] This resolution was subsequently discussed at a Voronezh obkom plenum. In a classic example of reliance on the Central Committee to discover their own shortcomings, V. Ignatov, obkom first secretary, said:

> We have been given a graphic lesson ... in the results of tardiness in-restructuring and sluggishness in thinking, in the effects of general appeals and purely rhetorical goals, indifference, and complacency, and in the negative consequences with which miscalculations in cadre work are fraught.

Ignatov's statement reflected firstly the deep-seated problem pervading almost all the lower Party organisations, and secondly the belief that the problem lay with the personnel and the solution in "correctly calculating cadre work". The plenum criticised raikom secretaries for a technocratic approach to economic management and for assuming the role of economic managers.[75] The problem of reform of the lower Party organisations was further exemplified by the Kursk regional Party organisation. An administrative style of work was continuing and leaders of some Party organisations like the Oktiabrskii district committee discouraged criticism, tried to shelter "convenient" people, and hid failures. Economic managers were encouraged to do report-padding and did not stimulate the initiative of Party organisations.[76] In short, functioning at the lower levels did not seem to change much.

The large numbers of resolutions passed by the Central Committee indicated its excessive 'guidance' of lower Party organisations. It exhibited the latter's reliance on Central Committee directives further highlighting the problems of the lower Party committees in implementing decisions which were meant to accelerate reforms. It also revealed the problems of reforms within the existing organisational mechanism. Lower Party organisations in connivance with State institutions could either modify the content of resolutions in accordance with their local interests or simply soft-pedal their implementation. The Central Committee, however, seemed to continue attempting to ensure efficient socio-economic development by improving the organisational functioning of the Party. The Party's organisational mechanism was intended to play a more dominant role in the implementation of the reforms than the State and the government mechanism at this stage. The nature of resolutions suggests that in these initial years of Perestroika, the basic thrust of the Central Committee was to rely on and revitalise existing structures, particularly those of the Party, to ensure dynamism in the economy and the society.

It seems that after these methods of working, despite marginal initial successes, had failed to create a sustainable economic mechanism, the process of extending political reforms began. There were initial successes in the economic field. The growth of industrial output in 1986 was 4.9 per cent as against 3 per cent in the early eighties. Grain output increased by 30 million tonnes over the average annual harvest for the previous five years, and the real income of the population rose by 2.3 per cent.[77] By January 1988 industrial production registered an increase of 8.8 per cent, production of grain increased from 180.3 million to 210 million tonnes, and labour productivity in agriculture increased by 6.5 per cent. Machine production increased from 23 per cent to 47 per cent between 1985 and 1987.[78] In 1986 and 1987 steel production increased to 393 square metres and ready-made items to 58 million pieces.[79] Such developments do not seem to have satisfied the reform-minded leaders of the Party, who desired to put in place a sustainable economic mechanism which could be translated to a gradual transition to a market economy in place of social ownership of means of production - the fundamental cornerstone of a socialist economy. This led to an intensification of the political reforms, as pointed out by Oleg Bogomolov in *Kommunist*. According to him, one of the important features of the economic reforms was the attempt to create a system which was capable of self-regulation, permanent self-renewal, and adaptation to new situations. The new economic model meant a planned and regulated social market. These changes required corresponding changes in the superstructure. The political life of the society, it was argued, should open the way for the mechanism of self-regulation and self-evaluation of the economy.[80] It is oft-discussed that the Soviet Union under Gorbachev could have followed the Chinese model of reforms which ushered in economic reforms but kept the political reforms on a tight leash arguing that the latter could lead to political instability and thwart economic reforms. It seems that Gorbachev and his reformist colleagues had a Western social-democratic model in mind to replace the Soviet model of a single-Party political system and a socially-owned economy from the early days of Perestroika and by the 19th Party Conference some of his reformist colleagues could openly campaign for its introduction. Gorbachev however walked a tight rope and gave more concessions to the section of the Soviet leadership reticent about the reforms so that they did not rock the reformist boat as long as the CPSU was a viable political force. The reformists believed that the market reforms - controlled or otherwise, would not work and a sustainable economy could not be put in place as long as a multi-Party system was not ushered in and a Western style liberal-democracy replaced the existing Soviet political system. A multi-party system would introduce an element of competetiveness and remove the monopoly of the CPSU over the political life and the economy. The CPSU was still dominated by those sections of the Party which were sceptical of the economic and more so of political reforms which they thought would subvert the Soviet system itself in the long run.

Conferences

The practice of holding conferences at the Central Committee which monitored the implementation of resolutions was undertaken because of the existing administrative system of working.[81] This reflected the inherent problems of conducting reforms by administrative fiat since they could only be sustained beyond a certain point by perfecting administrative methods. The conferences on the economy included the leaders of Party committees of various levels such as Union-Republics, kraikoms and obkoms together with the participation of the ministries, departments, enterprises and so on.[82] The case was similar with conferences on agriculture.[83] Conferences were also used to work out the implementation of the decisions with broader participation. Leaders of the Party, government, State, mass organisations and experts were involved in them discussing important socio-economic issues.[84] The participation of Politburo and Central Secretariat members in these conferences indicated their importance. Furthermore, they would prepare for the forthcoming Central Committee plenums. Experts on a particular issue participated in the conferences. They were used both for preparing the materials for discussions and decisions, and for subsequently working out practical measures for their implementation.[85] Most of these conferences pertained to the economy and agriculture.[86]

Thus in the initial years of Perestroika the Central Committee attempted to implement reforms in an administrative way. A certain degree of efficiency and increased activity in terms of taking up issues and issuing directives on them could be seen. This yielded marginal success, particularly in the field of the economy. Yet a whole range of decisions met with resistance and were not implemented as desired. Although the Central

Committee appeared more efficient in its functioning, its decisions were lost in the quagmire of Party and State apparatuses, particularly at the lower levels. The reformist section of the Party leadership opted for greater political reforms, and a change in the methods of working was an integral part of it. It had concluded that earlier methods would not work.[87] There would therefore be an increased momentum towards reforms in the Central Committee's functioning in the post-19th Conference period.

Joint Resolutions

The practice of joint resolutions of the Central Committee and the USSR Council of Ministers on almost all important issues continued at the highest levels. These joint resolutions lent the authority of the Central Committee to the decisions. The system of joint resolutions was in keeping with the duality of the Party and the State institutions existing in the Soviet Union. These resolutions, apart from indicating the "supervisory" role of the Central Committee and its deep involvement in economic affairs, chiefly reflected systemic problems with them. Such a role resulted from the failure of the State and the government bodies at various levels, particularly ministries, departments, State committees and Soviet organs in fulfilling their responsibilities. Yet in the existing system the only way to improve its working was, ironically, by increasing the involvement of the Central Committee and the Party and perfecting the supervisory role. This, however, could not be the lasting solution and reinforced *podmena* (substitution).

There were numerous examples of such resolutions on the "integral programme of developing consumer goods production and the service sphere"; "on the development of the Omsk economy" and "on Further Improving the Economic Management Mechanism in the Country's Agro-Industrial Complex".[88] These resolutions laid down extensive guidelines and directives for State and government bodies.[89] The Central Committee instructed ministries to undertake measures on a particular issue.[90] It could thus take punitive action against individual leaders if it was deemed necessary. However, examples like these further underlined the problem with ministries and enterprises at various levels. The Central Committee "guided" the functioning not only of the central State and the government agencies, but also of union-republic ministries.[91] The five-year plans to be implemented by government and State agencies were worked out by the Central Committee. The ultimate authority to approve or disapprove a plan was vested in it.[92] Apart from the extensive involvement of the Central Committee, it showed that the regions were also within the ambit of direct supervision by the Central Committee.[93] While discussing the national economic plan for social and cultural construction in 1986, the Central Committee criticised several ministries, departments and Soviets for not restructuring their activity, asking the organisations concerned to undertake necessary measures to fulfil the plan.[94] Similarly the Councils of Ministers of several union and autonomous republics, krai ispolkoms and oblispolkoms were blamed for their failures.[95] However the pervasive problems of the State and the government institutions at various levels in not fulfilling decisions persisted. At one level it reflected the source of resistance to reforms, and at another the inherent shortcoming of this particular method of reform and system of governance. Although individual responsibility was important, the existing institutions and practices were proving inadequate. The stunted growth of the institutions of governance and their integration with the Party was reflected in the system of joint resolutions. The name of the Central Committee lent these institutions[96] political authority which they lacked in any significant measure. These institutions had been until now only meant to administer and implement and not to rule which only the Party bodies, particularly the highest ones did. It is infinitely simpler to administer and implement than to rule and the organisation of these institutions was accordingly simpler. The political authority did not vest with them but with the Party institutions in the Soviet political system. This however does not mean that the state institutions did not influence the Party decisions. Iindeed they did, particularly because of the integration of the Party and the State institutions, absence of any plurality - political or otherwise, the expertise they contained and there was as much involvement in the affairs of the society as that of the Party. However, the political authority and power rested only, and only, with the Party and the Party bodies. The institutions of the state acted in subordination to them.

Party and State

The process of separation of the Party and the State was initiated at lower levels by a resolution of the Central Committee in July 1986. It expressly forbade the Party from taking over the functions of the local Soviets and allowed the latter independence in their areas of competence. The practice of joint resolutions by the local Party and Soviet bodies was to be halted.

Closer collaboration between the Soviets, mass organisations and economic organs was to be ensured. An experimental process of the demarcation of the functions of the Party and the State bodies was initiated. However this demarcation was not yet to extend to the highest levels. The approach seemed to be to make the separation work at the lower levels where the greatest resistance to the reforms existed. The Party committees were obliged to increase the role of the sessions instead of orchestrating them. They were to allow much greater flexibility as to when and how long these were to be held. The responsibility of the Soviets to the electorate was to be increased in a decisive change from the practice of primary responsibility of the Soviets to the Party. The task of increasing the activity of the deputies was treated with some urgency.[97] However, the Party committees were to function with State bodies to implement reforms. For instance, a Central Committee resolution on law enforcement made the Party committees, along with the local Soviets, responsible for legality and law and order in their territories. They were to direct and co-ordinate the work of Party organisations, State institutions, and law enforcement organs in this work. Increased emphasis was put on the responsibility of local Soviets and their executive and administrative organs at all levels to ensure strict observance of the law by State institutions, economic organisations and their leaders. Local soviets were to influence the activity of internal affairs administrations and organs of justice. They were to monitor systematically reports by their leaders in the meetings of standing commissions, ispolkoms, labour collectives and places of residence. Party committees and Party bureaus were asked to increase the role of the Party members in the executive section of the State as exemplified by the case of law enforcement ministries and departments. The primary Party organisations were to influence actively "improvements in the work of the apparatus concerning the observance of Soviet law and the fulfilment of the Party and government directives, devoting particular attention to reinforcing official discipline among personnel".[98]

The question of the separation of the Party and State gained momentum from the 19th Party Conference. The Theses of the Central Committee for the 19th Party Conference, approved by the plenum on 23rd May 1988, outlined the process of the separation of Party and State. The Party was to refrain from passing resolutions "addressing direct instructions to state and economic bodies as well as to public organisations".[99] The reason for continuing substitution lay in the organisation of the Party committees, which needed to be changed. Until then, despite the creation of plenipotentiary State institutions, the Central Committee was holding conferences on subjects within the competence of the government and taking decisions on economic issues.[100] The reason given for the Central Committee attending day to day economic questions was that the "economic levers meant to stimulate the development of (the) economy and make it self-developing (were) not fully operational".[101] Many economic questions needed the involvement of the Central Committee in practice. The result was that the Party and its Central Committee were held responsible by the population for the failures of the State organs, which were not accountable. The latter did not show initiative and would rely not only on the instructions from the Party "but also wait for a Party worker or Party organ to come along, take them by the hand, and lead them through the fulfilment of those instructions".[102] Gorbachev in his report to the 19th Party Conference told how the Central Committee, apart from the Politburo and the Central Secretariat, had to deal with questions which could be resolved by local Soviets, and management or other bodies. He pointed out how the Central Committee received unnecessary telegrams from leading cadres and applications from citizens on issues "which should, in essence, be resolved on the spot, namely, in the town or the raion and even in the village".[103] A major problem with such Party involvement was that it reinforced rather than weakened the integration of the Party. Although the Party was asked to separate itself from the activities of the Soviets it was simultaneously made responsible for the proper conduct of the concerned activities. The Party was asked to act through the primary Party organisations and its members in various state institutions instead of substituting these bodies. How could the Party keep away from the responsibility of the discharge of various functions it had been used to undertaking for decades and could do so only at the peril of malfunctioning of the system? In that case who held the responsibility, the Party who had the organisational capability and the expertise to undertake such activities or the newly elected Soviet memberships with lot of enthusiasm for democracy but much less capabilities? How could the Party function only through its members or the primary organisations without the danger of substituting the Soviets? Therefore either the Party kept totally away or involved itself completely in the activities of the Soviets if it was to avoid the blame for failures which were not of its own making? Finally would not the sudden withdrawal of the Party result in disintegration of the existing organisation channels and modes of functioning creating a vacuum until the Soviets could function on their own? These were the dilemma's confronting the Party. No wonder the existing institutions and their organisation dissolved resulting in administrative anarchy for which eventually the Party was blamed by the people.

State institutions had ossified at all levels, particularly lower ones, in the absence of truly representative institutions and a workable mechanism to resolve the problems of the people. The problems of the rigid hierarchically structured system of the Party and the State, which prevented the development of initiative even of the leading cadres, became apparent. Institutional organisations were all too obviously inadequate. A centralised system had resulted in an inertia which could be overcome by devolution of power and responsibility. This could only be done by separating the Party and the State institutions, democratising the Party so that it could play an effective political role in feeding the political system with demands along with representative Soviets. An accountable executive wing of the State would then prioritise choices, and endeavour to fulfil them at all levels. However, the question remained whether this could be done in an evolutionary and orderly manner. Would not this de-institutionalisation result in a vacuum of power and authority? To whom would power and authority be devolved? The new institutions and institutional practices would obviously take time to evolve and consolidate. Would the transfer of power and authority go as intended or would there be unintended consequences? Would not the resistance to change from within the Party and the State structures and the emergence of competing values in a transitory system result in cleavages undermining the reforms? These questions persisted, yet the system needed to be reformed. The reformist section of the leadership considered that an orderly transition was possible.

The resolution "On the Progress of the Implementation of the 27th Party Congress Decisions and Tasks in Deepening Restructuring", passed at the 19th Party Conference, spelt out the intention of separating the Party and the State, and of making the Soviets sovereign at all levels. The main aim was to create a socialist law-based state. The Congress of People's Deputies, the new Supreme Soviet, the institution of the post of chairman of the Supreme Soviet, and the relationship among the top echelons of power, including the USSR Council of Ministers, were to be constitutionally regulated. The Party was to implement its policies through Communists working in State and economic organs and other organisations. It was to operate within the framework of the Constitution and the Soviet laws.[104] In his report Gorbachev underlined the question of the delimitation of the functions of the Party and State organs. He pointed out that this issue had been raised at different stages in Soviet history and every time this system had been acknowledged as "abnormal". He strongly argued for demarcation at the highest levels, with the Central Committee providing the political leadership.[105] It was this demarcation that indeed took place as never before, and the Central Committee was transformed.

Conclusion

The reforms introduced at the 27th Party Congress did not succeed as intended because of the method of their implementation and opposition from within the Party and State apparatuses. However, they did create an environment for further reform and an awareness of the problems and prospects of reform in the Party and in society. The channels of implementation were again through hierarchically organised apparatuses which stood to lose their economic and political power if the reforms succeeded. Greater autonomy to lower levels of economic units, an increased role for labour collectives and the loss of subsidies reduced the influence of central agencies like Gosplan, ministries and departments, depriving these apparatuses of economic and executive power. The development of socialist democracy which entailed increasing the role of Soviets as against executive committees, that of public organisations and labour collectives, would have resulted in a loss of political power. Hence the resistance and the failure of the reforms. More importantly, it meant the failure of the central reform of separating the Party and the State as envisaged by the 27th Party Congress. It became clear that institutions and institutionalised practices could not be changed through the resolutions. Until now, this primarily meant a separation and increased supervision of the Party committees vis a vis the State organs. However, the Party committees themselves along with their apparatuses were partners with State institutions in the process of appropriating the resources. Thus such a separation was meaningless and would not change anything in practice. The existing conception of the separation of Party and State had to change. Hence the necessity to change the system of election of Party committees and the Soviets. The process of elections within the Party committees and the Soviets would, it was hoped, result in qualitatively changing the nature of the two organs and subordinate their executive wings. The separation now would be between the Party as a political organism, as against the Party committees and its apparatus, and elected Soviets as against Soviet committees and other executive institutions of the State. This would result in a shift away from the command chain of administrative centralisation to independence and devolution of power and authority at all levels of Party and State institutions, particularly representative ones. Thus each level in the Party and the State would act in its defined area of competence, with the Party giving overall political leadership and framing appropriate policies. A democratised Party would now function through its members in the State institutions. However, the basic assumption of such a separation was that the Party would be the only political force and democratisation would take place within the single party. But such a reform necessarily required pluralism and glasnost. The contest in an elective system is not merely between individuals, but between policies and opinions on the issues of the day. And these could not be sustained without glasnost. The emergence of new socio-economic forces as a result of the economic reforms and as well as those hitherto unrepresented would thus find expression. They might be contradictory, yet it was hoped that they could be contained within a one-party system. Although in practice this did not remain the case, the reformist leadership pressed on with such a conception of separation, since it was deemed a transitional period. This, however, strained the alliance between moderate reformists and moderate conservatives at the highest level. Such a conception of separation of Party and the State was likely to undermine the system itself - its institutional organisation and the way they acted - as indeed it did.

Notes

[1] Gorbachev Speaks at the Central Committee Meeting, *Pravda*, 17 June 1986, pp. 1-4 in *FBIS*, 18 June 1986, pp. R4-R26. Gorbachev's Central Committee Speech, 1986.
[2] *Pravda*, 29 January 1987, pp. 1-2 in *FBIS*, 30 January 1987, pp. R1-R3.
[3] E. Teague, "Gorbachev Discusses Personnel Policy", *RL 38/87,* 28 January 1987, pp.1-4.
[4] *Pravda*, 30 January 1987, p. 1 in *FBIS*, 30 January 1987, p. R14.
[5] *Pravda*, 29 January 1985, p. 1 in *FBIS*, 24 April 1985, p. R1.
[6] E. Teague, "Signs of a Conservative Backlash", *RL 474/87*, 18 November 1987, p. 2.
[7] "Plenary Meeting of the CPSU Central Committee", January 27-28, 1987, *Kommunist*, no. 3, 1987, pp. 55-58.
On one-Party democratisation see M. Lewin *The Gorbachev Phenomenon - A Historical Interpretation*, University of California Press, (Berkeley, 1988)
[8] "The Yeltsin File", The Second Russian Revolution, *BBC Television, Channel 2*, 14 June 1991.
[9] See A. Brown, "The Soviet Leadership and the Struggle for Political Reform" in P. Lerner ed. *The Soviet Union-Essays From the Harriman Institute Forum-1988*, Crane Russak, (N. Y., 1989), pp. 54-56.
[10] "Plenary Session of the CPSU Central Committee - 23 May 1988", *Kommunist* no. 9, 1988, p. 5.

[11] In its resolution "On Glasnost" of 4 July 1988. "Perestroika", Chapter 4, in J. L. Black, ed., *USSR Documents Annual, 1988, Perestroika - The Second Stage*, Academic International Press, (Gulf Breeze, FL, 1989), p. 208.

[12] "Towards New Image of Socialism", *Kommunist*, no. 13, 1989.

[13] M. Gorbachev , "Socialist Ideas and Revolutionary Perestroika", *Kommunist*, no. 18, 1989, p. 18.

[14] V. Medvedev, "Towards Cognition of Socialism", *Kommunist*, no. 17, 1988, pp. 3-18.

[15] Interview with Yu. Prokofiev, member of the Central Committee, CPSU, First Secretary, Moscow State Committee, ""From "Culture" of Battle to Culture of Accord"", *Kommunist*, no. 13, 1990, pp. 3-13.

[16] R. V. Daniels, 1989, p. 97.

[17] "Political Vanguard of Society", *Kommunist*, no. 1, 1988, p. 4.

[18] "Ideology of Thought and Action", *Kommunist*, no. 5, 1988, p. 5.

[19] E. Teague, "Personnel Changes in the Politburo", *RL 233/87,* 26 June 1987, pp. 1-2. See also A. Rahr, "Ligachev Versus Gorbachev?", *RL 325/87*, 12 August 1987, pp. 2-5; E. Teague, "Gorbachev Counter Attacks in Tashkent", *RL 161/88*, 13 April 1988, p. 5 and "Ligachev's Position in Doubt", *RL 178/88*, 22 April 1988, pp. 1-2; Kevin Devlin, "Soviet Journalist Describes El'tsin's Struggle Against Party 'Mafia'", *RL 206/88,* 20 May 1988, p. 4, The Yeltsin File", The Second Russian Revolution, *BBC Television, Channel 2,* 14 June 1991.

[20] *Moscow Television Service*, 0612 GMT, 28 June 1988 in *FBIS*, 29 June 1988, pp. 13-14.

[21] *Pravda*, 29 June 1988, pp. 2-7 in *FBIS*, 1 July 1988, p. 15.

[22] *Pravda*, 30 June, 1988, pp. 3-4, in *FBIS*, 30 June 1988, pp. 4-7 and pp. 11-19.

[23] *Pravda*, 1 July 1988, p. 4-7, in *FBIS*, 5 July 1988, pp. 9-13 and 33-4.

[24] *Argumenti i fakti*, no. 27, 2-8 July, p. 2, in *FBIS*, 5 July 1988, p. 1.

[25] A. Yakovlev, *Predislovie - Obval - Posleslovie*, Novosti, (Moscow, 1992), pp. 127-128.

On Yakovlev see J. Harris, *The Public Politics of Aleksandr Nikolaevich Yakovlev, 1983-1989,* The Carl Beck Papers, no. 901, University of Pittsburgh Centre for Russian and East European Studies, December 1990.

[26] *Pravda*, 2 July 1988, pp. 10-12, in *FBIS*, 5 July 1988, p. 90 and 114.

[27] *Pravda*, 2 July 1988, p. 8, *FBIS*, 6 July 1988, pp. 23-24.

[28] *Pravda*, 29 June 1988, pp. 2-7, in *FBIS*, 1 July 1988, pp. 1-8.

[29] *Moscow Domestic Service*, 0930 GMT, 29 June 1988, in *FBIS*, 30 June 1988, p. 24.

[30] *Izvestiia*, 30 June 1988, p. 2, in *FBIS*, 1 July 1988, pp. 36-37.

[31] *Pravda*, 30 June 1988, p. 2, in *FBIS*, 1 July 1988, p. 39.

[32] *Pravda*, 1 July 1988, in *FBIS*, 1 July 1988, pp. 46-49.

[33] *Pravda*, 1 July 1988, pp. 6-7, in *FBIS*, 5 July 1988, pp. 27-32.

[34] *Pravda*, 2 July 1988, p. 9, in *FBIS*, 6 July 1988, p. 26.

[35] *Pravda*, 2 July 1988, p.10, in *FBIS*, 5 July 1988, pp. 93-94.

[36] *Pravda*, 3 July 1988, p. 2, in *FBIS*, 5 July 1988, pp. 108-109.

[37] *Pravda*, 2 July 1988, p. 6, in *FBIS*, 6 July 1988, p. 4.

[38] *Pravda*, 29 June 1988, pp. 2-7, in *FBIS*, 1 July 1988, pp. 23-24.

[39] *Pravda*, 30 June 1988, p. 7, in *FBIS*, 30 June 1988, pp. 25-27.

[40] *Pravda*, 1 July 1988, p. 2, in *FBIS*, 5 July 1988, p. 3.

[41] *Pravda*, 1 July 1988, p. 7, in *FBIS*, 5 July 1988, p. 35.
[42] *Pravda*, 2 July 1988, pp. 8-9, in *FBIS*, 5 July 1988, pp. 79-83.
[43] *Pravda*, 2 July 1988, p. 8, in *FBIS*, 6 July 1988, p. 25.
[44] *ibid.*, pp. 90-91.
[45] *Moscow Domestic Service*, 1400 GMT, 1 July 1988, in *FBIS*, 5 July 1988, pp. 101-103.
[46] *Pravda*, 24 April 1986, p. 1 in *FBIS*, 25 April, 1986, p. R2 and *Pravda*, 29 March 1986, pp. 1-2 in *FBIS*, 2 April,1986, p. I2. For example, resolutions were passed on 17 April 1986 on measures to resolve the housing problem and improving the economic management of the agro-industrial complex jointly with the USSR Council of Ministers.
[47] *Pravda*, 30 July 1986, p. 1 in *FBIS*, 6 August 1986, pp. R21-R22. An example was the resolution adopted on the question of law enforcement.The Central Committee issued basic directives "instructing" the State and government agencies and their leaders and Party organisations on this issue.
[48] *Moskovskaia Pravda*, 26 November 1986, pp. 1-2 in *FBIS*, 8 December 1986, pp. R8-R11.
[49] *Sotsialisticheskaia industriia,* 17 May 1987, p. 1 in *FBIS*, 28 May 1987, P. R7. For instance, in May 1987 the Central Committee adopted a resolution on the unsatisfactory fulfilment of a joint resolution "On the Development and Re-tooling of Ferrous Metallurgy and the Significant Improvement of the Quality of Metal Products as a Most Important Construction Material" by the Ukrainian SSR Ministry of Ferrous Metallurgy. The Collegium and the minister, Galkin, were criticised for being "intolerably slow in restructuring their work".
[50] *Pravda*, 2 June 1987, pp. 1,3 in *FBIS*, 10 June 1987, p. R2-R6. An example was the resolution passed on the question "On Progress in Fulfilling the Party Central Committee Resolutions on Overcoming Drunkenness and Alcoholism and Activating This Work". It discussed the implementation of an earlier resolution "On Measures To Overcome Drunkenness and Alcoholism" adopted on 7 May 1985. Interestingly, the production of wine and brandy products at enterprises of the USSR State Agro-Industrial Committee increased in the first quarter of 1987 in comparison with production in the previous quarter. Moonshining had increased with the tacit support of local Party organs in a large number of regions.
[51] *Pravda*, 22 July 1987, p. 1 in *FBIS*, 29 July 1987, p. S1. For example, in the case of preparing enterprises, construction sites, transport, kolkhozes and sovkhozes and municipal services for the winter and autumn in the Kuibishev oblast, the oblispolkom and its administration would pass resolutions and issue instructions instead of resolving the tasks.
[52] *Izvestiia*, 14 August 1987, p. 3 in *FBIS*, 26 August 1987, p. R 10.
[53] *Moscow Domestic Service*, 0900 GMT, 22 July 1987 in *FBIS*, 27 July 1987, pp. R7-R9. For instance, on 21 July 1987 the Central Committee and the USSR Council of Ministers passed a joint resolution on improving the supply of fruit, vegetables, and potatoes to Moscow and Leningrad.
[54] *TASS*, 1415 GMT, 14 July 1987 in *FBIS*, 15 July 1987, p. R15.
[55] From information given in *FBIS* and *Izvestiia_Tsk KPSS*.
[56] *Pravda*, 26 May 1987, p. 3 in *FBIS*, 29 May 1987 p. R1. A report on a conference of the Central Committee in May 1987 talked of devoting "enormous attention" to the working of the agro-industrial complex. It scrutinised the work in the immediate past of Party organisations in the Ukraine, Kazakhstan, Moldavia, the Central Asian republics and Voronezh and several other oblasts with regard to crop farming and stock raising. Another conference at the beginning of the year examined the work of Party, Soviet, and economic

organs in implementing the Central Committee's resolution on increasing labour productivity in agriculture.

[57] *Pravda*, 18 June 1987, p. 1 in *FBIS*, 25 June 1987, pp. R5-R8.

[58] *Izvestiia*, 1 October 1987, p. 3 in *FBIS*, 16 October 1987, pp. 49-50.

[59] "Materials of the 19th All-Union Conference of the CPSU", *Kommunist*, no. 10, 1988, p. 74.

[60] *Pravda*, 25 June 1986, p. 1 in *FBIS*, 27 June 1986, pp. R5- R6.

[61] *Pravda*, 2 January 1989, p. 2 in *FBIS*, 4 January 1989, p. 43.

[62] *Pravda*, 10 July 1989, p. 2 in *FBIS*, 31 July 1989, p. 102.

[63] *Pravda*, 10 December 1986, pp. 1,2 in *FBIS*, 24 December 1986, pp. R11-R13.

[64] *Pravda*, 18 May 1986, p.1 in *FBIS*, 19 June 1986, pp. S1-S2.

[65] Interview with Boris Kluev.

[66] Interview with A. Fillipov, former Apparatus official, Moscow, August 1992.

[67] *Pravda*, 30 June 1988, p. 4 in *FBIS*, 30 June 1988, pp. 8-9.

[68] *Pravda*, 17 June 1986, pp. 1-4 in *FBIS*, 18 June 1986, p. R1 and *Pravda*, 25 June 1986, p. 1 in *FBIS*, 27 June 1986, p. R6. For instance, at the June 1986 plenum, on "the Five Year Plan for the Economic and Social Development of the USSR for 1986-1990 and Party Organisations' Tasks To Implement It", the chief concern was to mobilise support for its implementation. The *Pravda* editorial on the plenum talked of the Party orienting its committees "toward mastering the political method of leadership" and giving up excessive administrative functions, developing the initiative of State organs and public organisations, and making them more responsible. The plenum also issued an appeal to mobilise support for its economic programme.

[69] *Izvestiia_Tsk KPSS*, no. 5, May 1989, pp. 27-29. On 31 March 1986 the Central Secretariat issued a decree in the name of the Central Committee on utilisation of labour resources in Central Asia and North Caucasus. This decree criticised the work of the Central Committees of the Communist Parties of Uzbekistan, Azerbaijan, Tajikistan, Armenia and Dagestan for not involving the population in different social fields. It "ordered" the leaderships of Uzbekistan, Kirgizhia, Turkmenistan, Azerbaijan, Armenia, Georgia, Dagestan, Kabardino-Balkaria, Northern Ossetia and Chechen-Ingushetia to correct their mistakes, work out a programme of activity and strengthen Party control. The State Committee on Social Questions and some other State organisations were asked to help them to prepare plans for social and economic developments from 1986-1990 and for the period up to the year 2000. They were to inform the Central Committee of the Party about the implementation of this decree in August 1986 and April 1987.

[70] *Pravda*, 10 December 1986, pp. 1-2 in *FBIS*, 24 December 1986, pp. R11-R13. Such as the resolution adopted on the Perm obkom's failure to fully utilise "the favourable opportunities afforded since the Congress for profound qualitative changes in economic and social life."

Moscow Domestic Service, 1400 GMT, 20 April 1987 in *FBIS*, 28 April 1987, p. R25. Another was a decision in April 1987 critically examining the organisational work of Altai kraikom on introducing financial autonomy and restructuring labour organisation in the agrarian sector. It was to eliminate shortcomings in the implemention of the Central Committee resolution on raising labour productivity in agriculture.

[71] *Pravda*, 18 June 1987, p. 1 in *FBIS*, 25 June 1987, pp. R5-R6. As in the previously discussed case of the Tashkent obkom regarding Party membership.

[72] *Pravda*, 22 September 1987, p. 1 in *FBIS*, 25 September 1987, p. 46. According to a *Pravda* editorial, this was debated broadly in Uzbekistan and other Central Asian republic Party committee plenums and meetings of Communists. It was claimed that in the course of discussions many "positive advances ... (were) outlined".

[73] *Pravda*, 20 June 1987, pp. 1-2 in *FBIS*, 29 June 1987, pp. R22-R24. The Uzbek SSR, the Tazik SSR, and the Turkmen SSR were taken to task for drawbacks in their agro-industrial complex. The question of under utilisation of the natural-economic potential of the agro-industrial complex in the Uzbek SSR, the Tadzik SSR, and the Turkmen SSR was discussed and a resolution passed asking Party, Soviet and agricultural organs to undertake corrective measures.

Pravda, 16 July 1987, pp. 1,3 in *FBIS*, 16 July 1987, pp. R19-R25. Another resolution, criticised the Kazakhstan Party organisation regarding their implementation of the nationalities policy. It laid down guidelines for the Party organisations.

[74] *Moscow Domestic Service*, 0900 GMT, 15 December 1986 in *FBIS*, 15 December 1986, pp. R3-R4.

[75] *Pravda*, 28 December 1986, p. 2 in *FBIS*, 9 January 1987, pp. R8-R9.

[76] Gorbachev's Central Committee Speech 1986, p. R-23.

[77] *Moscow World Service,* 2110 GMT, 26 January 1987 in *FBIS*, 28 January 1987, p. R1.

[78] N. Sliunkov, "Restructuring and Party Guidance on Economy", *Kommunist*, no.1, 1988, pp.15-16.

[79] A. Biriukova, "Priority Direction of Social Policy", *Kommunist*, no. 5, 1988, pp.13-14.

[80] O. Bogomolov, "The Changing Image of Socialism", *Kommunist*, no.11, 1989.

[81] *Pravda*, 11 June 1986, p. 3 in *FBIS*, 17 June 1986, p. R8. For example, a conference was held in June 1986 at which senior officials of the Central Committee, heads of ministries, departments, the AUCCTU, the Komsomol, other public organisations and representatives of the mass media, discussed work on the resolutions on tightening labour discipline and overcoming drunkenness and alcoholism. A.V. Vlasov, USSR Internal Affairs minister, G.I. Vashchenko, USSR trade minister, and L.B. Yermin, first deputy chairman of the RSFSR Council of Ministers spoke. The conference was also addressed by Ligachev and Razumovskii. It expressed satisfaction that "energetic work" was being carried out at local levels, discipline and organisation at the work place, public order and social atmosphere had improved, the number of accidents at work and crimes due to drunkenness had been reduced, and sales of alcohol had fallen by more than one-third. The alcohol industry was to be converted into satisfying the demand for confectionery, fruit juice and non-alcoholic drinks. However many ministries, departments, Party, Soviet and administrative bodies at local levels were criticised for having slackened the pace of reforms after partial results, which was symptomatic of the way they were conducted.

[82] *Moscow Domestic Service*, 1700 GMT, 6 June 1986 in *FBIS*, 9 June 1986, p. S1.

[83] *ibid.*, 1430 GMT, 5 April 1986 in *FBIS*, 7 April 1986, p. T1.

[84] *Pravda*, 2 July 1986, p. 3 in *FBIS*, 8 July 1986, pp. R13-R14. For example, in July 1986 a conference was held at the Party Central Committee which discussed the implementation of the general education and vocational school reform. It was attended by secretaries of Union-Republic Central Committees and Party kraikoms and obkoms, deputy chairmen of Union Republic Councils of Ministers, leaders of educational and vocational and technical training bodies, a number of ministries and departments, the AUCCTU, and the Komsomol Central Committee, teachers and academics.

[85] *TASS International Service,* 1520 GMT, 9 June 1987 in *FBIS*, 10 June 1987, p. R1. Such a conference was held on 8-9 June 1987 in the Central Committee and discussed "questions of fundamentally restructuring the management of the economy".
[86] From information given in *FBIS*. At least thirteen more conferences on the economy were held in the Central Committee between February 1986 and October 1988. During the same period at least eleven more conferences took place on agriculture.
[87] *Pravda*, 26 July 1991, pp. 1-2 in *FBIS*, 26 July 1991, p. 25.
[88] *Pravda*, 29 March 1986, pp. 1-2 in *FBIS*, 2 April, 1986, p. I 1.
[89] *Izvestiia*, 14 August 1987, p. 3 in *FBIS*, 26 August 1987, p. R10. For example, a joint resolution "On Measures to Ensure the Stable Operation of the National Economy in the 1987-1988 Winter Period" outlined measures to be fulfilled by a wide range of State and government bodies. Ministers and leaders were personally responsible for implementing the measures.
Pravda, 20 September 1987, p. 1 in *FBIS*, 22 September 1987, pp. 49-50. Usually these directives were quite detailed. For instance, the above joint resolution

> demanded that USSR ministries and departments, union republic councils of ministers, and local soviet and economic organs quickly eliminate shortcomings in the preparation of enterprises, construction sites, kolkhozes, sovkhozes, and other organisations for work in the winter conditions and adopt exhaustive measures to implement the planned volumes of extraction, production of energy resources and shipments of coal and petroleum products, and to create the necessary stocks of fuel, raw materials, and semi-finished goods.

[90] *Moscow Domestic Service*, 1000 GMT, 2 June 1986 in *FBIS*, 3 June 1986, p. R1. For instance, it obliged the Ministry of Radio Industry to improve the quality of domestic television sets at the Ekran Production Association at Kuibishev. In addition the Moscow Television Service on June 1986 reported the Central Committee's decision "to dismiss a television enterprise director and reprimand Soviet ministers".
[91] *Sotsialisticheskaia industriia*, 17 May 1987, p. 1 in *FBIS*, 28 May 1987, pp. R 6-R9. It adopted as a resolution "'On Progress in the Fulfilment of the Party Central Committee and USSR Council of Ministers 21 February 1985 Resolution 'On the Development and Retooling of Ferrous Metallurgy and the Significant Improvement of the Quality of Metal Products as a Most Important Construction Material' by the Ukrainian SSR Ministry of Ferrous Metallurgy'". This criticised the ministry for unsatisfactory implementation of the joint resolution. The USSR Ministry of Ferrous Metallurgy was berated for having tolerated the shortcomings of and not assisting the Union-Republic ministry. Other Republican ministries were also criticised for their inability to perform construction work effectively regarding the build-up and renewal of fixed assets at enterprises under the Ukrainian ministry. All the ministers and the State agencies' officials concerned were directed to take the necessary steps.
[92] *Pravda*, 17 June 1986, p. 1 in *FBIS*, 17 June 1986, p. R1. For example, on 16 June 1986, "a routine plenum" of the Central Committee discussed the State plan for the USSR's economic and social development for the 1986-1990 and approved its draft. It was the plenum which "deemed it expedient to forward the five-year plan to be examined by the USSR Supreme Soviet".
[93] *Pravda*, 5 May 1987, pp. 1,3 in *FBIS*,.11 May 1987, pp. R 5-R6. On 26 March 1987 the Central Committee and the USSR Council of Ministers adopted a joint resolution "On

Measures to Ensure Fulfilment of the Targets Ratified in the 12th Five-Year Plan for the Development of the Material and Technical Base of the Socio-Cultural Sphere". It criticised the USSR State Agro-Industrial Committee, the USSR Ministry of Tractor and Agricultural Machine Building, the USSR Ministry of the Coal Industry, the USSR Ministry of the Communications Equipment Industry, the USSR Ministry of Ferrous Metallurgy, the USSR Ministry of Land Reclamation and Water Resources, and the USSR Ministry of the Machine Tool and Tool Building Industry in the Georgian, Uzbek, Tajik, Kazakh, Kirgiz, and Armenian SSRs and in Pskov, Rostov, Astrakhan, Kemerovo, Chita, Murmansk, Smolensk, Riazan, Kurgan, and other RSFSR oblasts for the unsatisfactory implementation of socio-cultural projects. Leaders of the ministries, departments and Soviet organs were "warned" by the resolution of their personal responsibility for the fulfilment of the plans for housing and social construction.

[94] *Moscow Television Service*, 1530 GMT, 22 November 1986 in *FBIS*, 25 November 1986, p. R 3.

[95] *Moscow Domestic Service*, 0900 GMT, 22 July 1987 in *FBIS*, 27 July 1987, pp. R 7-R9. For example, to improve the supplies of fruit, vegetables and potatoes to Moscow and Leningrad in accordance with the joint resolution of 21 July 1986. Leaders of some of these agencies, like Zaichenko of the USSR Agroprom, Aleshin of the USSR Trade Ministry, Saikin of Moscow gorispolkom and Khodierev of Leningrad gorispolkom were individually blamed for sluggishness.

[96] *Moscow Domestic Service* , 0900 GMT, 22 July 1987 in *FBIS,* 27 July 1987, pp. R7-R9.

[97] *Pravda*, 30 July 1986, p. 1 in *FBIS*, 6 August, 1986, pp. R21-22.

[98] *Pravda*, 30 November 1986, pp. 1-2 in *FBIS*, 8 December 1986, pp. R8-R11.

[99] "Perestroika", Chapter 4, in J. L. Black, ed. *USSR Documents Annual, 1988, Perestroika - The Second Stage*, Academic International Press, (Gulf Breeze, FL, 1989), p. 183 and p. 188.

[100] *Pravda*, 1 July 1988, p.2 in *FBIS*, 5 July 1988, pp. 1-2.

[101] *ibid*., p. 6 in *FBIS*, 5 July 1988, pp. 27-28.

[102] *Pravda*, 1 July 1988, pp. 9-10 in *FBIS*, pp. 47-48.

[103] *Pravda*, 29 June 1988, pp. 2-7 in *FBIS*, 1 July 1988, p. 22.

[104] *Pravda*, 5 July 1988, pp. 1-2 in *FBIS*, pp. 143-147.

[105] *ibid*., pp. 31-32.

5 Transforming the Ideology and Shift from Political Monocentrism to Polycentrism

Introduction

By the time the Central Committee ceased to exist, its monocentric ethos had been replaced by a polycentric one. The economy had continued to worsen. Inter-ethnic conflicts became endemic. The compact and coherent organisation of the Party which had offset the centrifugal nationalist tendencies no longer existed. The principal tendencies of conservatism and reformism had differentiated into those of conservatism, centrist-reformism and radical-reformism prior to the 19th Party Conference. As the economic and political situation deteriorated, a further demarcation took place after the Conference. At least five political tendencies could now be discerned. These demonstrated on the one hand the increasing opposition of the Party and the State organs, and on the other the dissolution of the alliance between moderate conservatives and moderate reformists. By the time it ceased to exist, the Central Committee had become a fractious body having lost its earlier unity as an institution.[1]

At least five main political tendencies emerged in the Central Committee in the final phase of perestroika in 1990-91. Anti-reformists or Brezhnevites were opposed to the reforms. They argued for retaining a centrally planned economy with a one-party system and the USSR as it existed. Economic and political reforms were tantamount to a restoration of capitalism. This section represented the resistance of the most conservative sections of the Party and the State bodies. The anti-reformists were opposed to complete democratisation and called for the imposition of discipline and order in society. They were represented by the Bolshevik platform of Nina Andreeva, A.A. Sergiev of the United Workers Front and Communist Initiative Movement, V. I. Brovikov and A. P. Rubiks. Cautious reformists or Traditionalists argued for the predominance of the centrally planned economy along with limited market reforms. The market was to be regulated. They had deep reservations about the introduction of private property. For them the social class-method of analysing social and political phenomena had been abandoned in favour of pan human values and an artificial disjunction introduced between the two by the centrist-reformist leadership. This, according to them, had resulted in deideologisation and the substitution of socialist values by bourgeois ones. The reforms, in their view, had resulted in the emergence of a social basis for anti-communist political forces. They feared that such a transition would result in the destabilisation of the political and economic system. The organisational mechanism of the Party and the State was of central importance to them in the implementation of the reforms. They accepted pluralism in the political system, advocating the political hegemony of the Party. The Union was to be preserved within the existing framework of the Constitution and the laws. Reforms were to be conducted within the framework of scientific socialism. Moderate conservatives in the Party and the State apparatuses constituted this group. They were represented by Ligachev[2] and his supporters, and later by Ivan Polozkov, who inherited his mantle. Their main organisational base was in the Russian Communist Party.

Centrist-reformists or Gradualists wanted a gradual transition to a mixed economy with multiple forms of property. Equality of all forms of property was to be guaranteed. The public and private sectors were to coexist with the retention of the social welfare guarantees of socialism. A competitive multi-party political system, in which a reformed Party would play a dominant role in the foreseeable future, was to be accompanied by a renewed federation of sovereign States. They advocated a rapprochement with social-democracy, combining its best features with those of communism. These moderate-reformers within the Party and State organs argued for participatory politics of Party members and people. They were mainly represented by Gorbachev and his supporters.

Radical-reformists argued for a rapid transition to a fully-fledged market economy with the private sector playing the key role. A multi-party system was to constitute the political system. An association of politically sovereign republics with an economic union was to replace the existing Union. A confederation was to substitute the idea of a federation. They argued for the Party to abandon a vanguard role in any form and become a parliamentary party. Radical-reformists were chiefly represented by the democratic platform, which had two wings - one of a social-democratic orientation and the other liberal. The democratic platform overwhelmingly consisted of professional people, such as academics and management professionals. Syndicalists[3] were represented by the leaders of the marxist platform, which argued for the destatisation of the economy by handing property to labour collectives. They were opposed to the private ownership of the property. Syndicalism referred to destatisation through ownership and self-management of property by labour collectives which hired (and fired) a director and distributed 'power' among workers and management. The evolution and conflict of these tendencies[4] in the post-19th Party Conference period became evident in debates in plenums and other forums.

By the time the 19th Party Conference convened, Yeltsin had established his identity as a leader of the radical reformist opposition tendency within the Central Committee and the Party.[5] His election platform for the March 1989 elections was strategically in line with the Party platform, but with certain additional proposals about reform of the political system, the economy and the fight for social justice.[6] On economic issues he argued for greater rights for State enterprises, to bring them closer to the co-operatives, and supported private property in the agricultural sector, with constitutional guarantees of this right for the peasants.[7] At this stage he defended the public sector albeit with greater autonomy, accepted its primacy over the private sector favouring the latter only in agriculture. He appeared positive about the declaration of sovereignty by the Estonian parliament, and favoured the formation of a people's front, albeit on an all-Union basis. Yeltsin criticised the Estonian People's Front for moving "somewhat in the direction of a mono-national structure".[8] Thus he favoured far greater decentralisation and the emergence of opposition organisations, marking a radical shift from the consensus of the 19th Party Conference. However even the idea of a confederation was as remote from him as that of the demise of the Soviet Union. Yeltsin argued for legislative accountability of all State and non-State organisations, including the Party, to the supreme organ of power, the newly elected legislature. 20-30 per cent of deputies were to adopt "an active civic stance", to unite and involve the public and function as an opposition to the Party in the new Supreme Soviet.[9] Thus a section of the reformists within the Central Committee were breaking ranks with the coalition and consensus of the reforms and indeed with the Central Committee, intending to shift the centre of gravity of power and authority to the newly elected legislature and establish itself as the opposition. The newly constituted organs of the state like the Congress for People's Deputies and the new Supreme Soviet were emerging as the alternative forums for articulating politics and policies opposed to the Party and its leadership by some of its constituents lacking sufficient support within it. This was also encouraged by the reformist section of the Party leadership and viewed as a concrete sign of the separation of the Party and the State. The newly constituted state organs enjoyed considerable political legitimacy since they were not only a consequence of the policies of Perestroika which had popular support at this juncture but also because these were partly elective organs unlike any of their predecessors. The conservatives representing the interests of the Party and the State organs found this particularly disconcerting. If the legislature could not be controlled by the Party and the Central Committee this would undermine rather than strengthen their authority.

Ligachev, foremost spokesman of the conservatives, opposed market relations on the grounds that they would lead to deep social divisions, inequality and concentration of wealth.[10] He carried his conviction on vital issues well into 1989, arguing that the development of a market and a multi-party system would lead to the "destruction of political stability".[11] However by May 1990, Ligachev had accepted the "socialist market", which combined plan and market. The plan was to "determine the main proportions of the development of the national economy and the economic stimulators" and regulate the market.[12] He thus seemed to have revised his earlier antagonistic attitude. Yet the renewed variety of Soviet socialism he was proposing meant retention of the control and direction of the economy by Party and State bodies. However the key concern of the conservatives was the destabilising effect these policies would have politically, economically, socially and culturally on a society which had not known wide economic diversities and a basic minimum was guaranteed to each of its members through an extensive network of welfare systems. Emergence of socio-economic forces inimical to the Party and its ideology was a foregone conclusion. The political consequences of such economic reforms concerned the conservatives. Instead of renewing the political authority and the legitimacy of the Party and its leadership, the reforms had politicised its opponents and posed a real threat of a systemic transformation.

The centrist-reformists argued that the extreme concentration and centralisation of economic power, control of information, and realisation of arbitrarily taken socio-economic decisions in a command economy had led to the alienation of the working class from property as well as power. The pluralism of economic forms was seen as a way to overcome this alienation. The process of the division of power was to begin.[13] Political tendencies were to be allowed to exist within the Party, which would implement a united policy.[14] There was to be a pluralism and equality of forms of ownership and economic management.[15] Gorbachev talked of a third alternative to either preserving the earlier system in all aspects of life or reverting to capitalism.[16] The economy was to be deideologised.[17] Proponents of the third alternative, influenced by the Western social-democratic thought, believed that economic power could be devolved to people without creating conditions for the emergence of capitalism with all its contingent characteristics and class divisions. By transferring ownership rights from the state to the people through cooperatives, leaseholdings and other forms of private property, the centrist-reformists envisaged overcoming the alienation of the working class from poverty as well as power without creating a socio-economic basis for the emergence of capitalist mode of production and related vagaries of a market economy which was at this juncture in its very primitive form. The process of deideologising the economy entailed purging the theory of socialism in the argument that the state ownership of the means of production was synonymous to the social ownership of the means of production. In ideological terms the newly enunciated theory postulated that socialism could be achieved without practising such a precept, the economy should not be subject to any ideological prescriptions and the private ownership of means of production could also be a social ownership in several of its forms. Classical Marxist theory governing the Soviet political system however, considered such a proposition to be fundamentally flawed compelling the centrist-reformist to argue for deideologising the economy. The ideology of socialism, a crucial element defining the legitimacy of the Soviet political system was radically redefined.

Transforming the Ideology

Radical shift took place in the ideology of the Party and the Central Committee and the new ideology acquired shape during the course of the reforms. The Perestroika envisaged all-encompassing change in the Soviet society. Involvement of the people was identified as a key to transformation. To quote Gorbachev on this point:

> We must include the people in the process of Perestroika through democratisation of society. If I were to state wherein lay the essence of perestoika, I would simply say: we must set up such infrastructure in every worker's collective, in every Party organisations in every oblast, in every

> central administrative branch, in the entire Party so that our people felt themselves to be the master of the country.

Self-rule was the declared objective, and bureaucratism was seen as a major obstacle. The proposed involvement of the people was said to have been inspired by the October revolution, which affirmed true democracy as a means to establish a social system with the involvement of the people in governance, economy, political relations, cultural life, and so on.[18] To begin with, the necessity of reforms was realised in economy, social and moral spheres. The Party, its political and practical activities were still outside the realm of reforms. The theoretical aspects of socialism, which crystallised in the 1930s and 1940s, when the problems of the society were of a different nature, continued to have their hold on the ideology even when the nature of social problems and the society in general had undergone several important changes.[19]

> The definition of Perestroika was reasserted by Gorbachev in his speech to the January 1987 Central Committee plenum. The key element was the economy. It meant decisive overcoming of the stagnation and braking mechanism, and setting up an effective mechanism to speed up the socio-economic development of the Soviet society. The role of intensive factors were to be increased in the development of the economy, the command administrative system was to be given up and self-financing introduced in the economy. It was to develop democracy and socialist self-rule, encourage initiatives, widen glasnost and value an individual. It aimed at giving socialism completely contemporary forms of social organisations.[20]

To achieve all this, great stress was laid on 'the activation of the human factor'. In this context Gorbachev referred to Lenin who talked of maximising the democracy and of a socialist structure in which 'a person can be both a master and a creator'. Lenin was quoted as having said: "We must follow life, we must allow the masses total creative freedom".Gorbachev contended that a man would be interested in bringing his house in order if he feels like a master of the house. Such a feeling was necessary in the socio-economic field as well to activate the human factor.[21]

G. Razumovski, in an article in *Kommunist*, stressed that the higher Party educational organisations should not merely repeat 'those truths about Marxism-Leninism which are known since school days' but teach 'scientific outlook' as regards generalisations of reality. He made an interesting observation that the uniqueness of contemporary phase is that both the process of Perestroika and its theoretical comprehension are being carried out simultaneously.[22] Hence the philosphy of Perestroika was to be grounded in pragmatism. He was critical of 'dogmatic adherence to abstract theories' removed from the social realities in the training of the leading cadres.[23]

Gorbachev contended that the means and methods of bringing about the development of socialism in 1920s and 1930s did not always correspond to the socialist principles. According to him

> Forms and methods of socialist construction, forced into being by the situation, reflecting concrete historical phase of our country were canonised and ideologised and were given the status of dogmas.

The Perestroika was to be a leap in the development of socialism and the realisation of its essential characterstics. That did not mean a 'clean', doctrinated, pre-decided, and idealistic choice, though it was asserted that

> He who hopes that we shall move away from the socialist path is in for a great disappointment ... Our entire programme of Perestroika as a whole and in all its individual components is wholly based on the principle: the greater the socialism, the more the democracy.[24]

Thus the philosphy of Perestroika was to take shape and concretise as the Perestroika progressed. An element of spontaneity was introduced and reflected the pragmatic approach of the leadership. The only abstract notion floated was that of more democracy, which tied neatly with the desire of the leadership to 'activate the human factor'. The adoption of a democratic culture and habitual following of democratic norms and principles was seen as an important precondition for the formation and functioning of new thinking.[25]

The meaning of the the concept of the Party as a political vanguard seemed to be undergoing transformation. The Party was supposedly acting as an intellectual leader of society. In order to build a higher form of social organisation of the society and stimulate and direct the processes of democratisation, it attempted to take into account various interests in the society. The Party as a vanguard aimed at creating a situation whereby people could discuss social problems inside the Party, at the government and local levels.[26] Social and economic problems were to be solved by political means. One of the fundamental solutions undertaken by the Party to overcome the economic problems of the 1970s and 1980s was to develop the personality and talents of an individual.[27] The individual, his political and individual arena, talents, ability to work, his activity and position as a citizen was seen as the decisive factor for development.[28] The Perestroika was thought to open fully and clearly the humanistic potential of the society and individuality of the people.[29] The February 1988 Central Committee plenum discussed the question of renewal of the ideology. The renewed ideology was to be against scholastic dogmatism, fatalism and authoritarianism. It was to provide a moral base for the integration of creative forces of society and find 'scientific solutions' to the problems of life. Perestroika was to pass through various phases of transformation from extensive to intensive development. Perestroika was to solve the humanitarian tasks of socialism, to check social alienation, alienation from authority, means of production and results of its work and so on. Apart from the new measures for the democratisation of the social life, it was deemed important to develop the power of creativity, sound social, economic, cultural and moral prerequisites for increasing the initiatives, establishing freedom and creating responsibility in every individual. The self-financing of the enterprises, as part of democratisation, was seen to meet the interest of individuals in particular, apart from those of groups and the society. The most important task of the Party in the process of Perestroika was seen to liberalise the policies and to give more freedom to the people. The Party was meant to be creating a more favourable environment for those who worked for the betterment of the social life. The ideological education was to take steps to restore social values, remove bureaucratism and indifference to man, encourage his creative powers and work for his moral uplift.[30] Bureaucratism was seen as an hindrance to development in the process of renewal of socialism. Independent initiative, direction and actions of the people were seen as an important way of countering bureaucratism. The social meaning of Perestroika was seen as giving maximum space for free, creative and constructive energy of the individual. The highest social values were seen as full freedom for the individual and dignity of his personality.[31]

It was argued that rule by the administrative-command system and the logic of its functioning affected the basic life style. Mediocrity replaced originality and creativity. Its varied manifestations in science, ideology and culture led to the formation of monolithic thinking and unquestioned fulfillment of orders. Any 'clear' individualness amidst all this could be discerned only inspite of it or in conflict with it. In the past, a party member unquestionably following 'orders from above' was considered a good party member, whereas the one approaching the task 'creatively' would be criticised for 'different trend of thought' and lack of 'party-mindedness'. Leaders who were the 'guardians of ideological purity', speaking at the end of meetings, seminars and so on, would speak out strongly against ideas removed from their own, expressing intolerance to new ideas and views. Anything diverging from the accepted trend of thought was dubbed as 'politically harmful' or 'ideologically alien'. The present leadership talked of the rebirth of Lenin's idea of 'party-mindedness' which was simultaneously viewed as the 'condition' and the 'indicator' of political development.'Conditions' were discipline and responsibility and 'indicator' was independence, initiative and creative application to work. This was to dialectically mean - one official Party line, but allowing differences in opinion. It was deemed necessary for the Party to show tolerance for different points of view as a concrete example of democratisation.[32]

It was argued that the extreme concentration and centralisation of economic power, control of information, and realisation of arbitrarily taken socio-economic decisions in a command economy led to the alienation of the working class from property as well as power.The pluralism of economic forms was seen as the way of overcoming this alienation. Bureaucratic polycentrism was to be replaced by polycentrism of 'citizen-oriented' society.[33] A socialist governmental leviathan was created as a single, monopolistic owner of all the means of production, natural resources, working force and distribution of goods and services. Hence, society was deprived of its most important economic support in the property. Perestroika was meant to lead the regeneration of the suppressed institution of society. This was to be done by democratisation of economic, social and political life, a process which invariably raised the question of the role and position of the Party. The editorial contended that the Party could continue to maintain its monopoly over power, irrespective of the results of its policies, only under the conditions of the administrative-command system in close association with the state apparatus. This was changing in the new context with the separation of the Party and State. It argued in favour of beginning the process of the division of power and parliamentarism.[34]

Reformist arguments were for the weakening of the government. The 'government' and the 'society', according to this argument, had hitherto been identified in the 'collective consciousness' as variations of the same phenomenon. The all-encompassing 'totalitarian' government had attempted to regulate all aspects of social life. This proved counter productive. Perestroika was seen as a chance to prove in practice the possibility of the coexistence of democracy, socialism and humanism. The power, it was argued, should be gradually shifted from bureaucratic governmental power to the self rule of the people. One of the ways it could be done was by shifting the function of the government to non-governmental organisations, first and foremost to social organisations. It was thought that, as shown in the past, calls to 'work and think differently, in a new manner' would not produce any significant results without narrowing the sphere and boundaries of the government.[35]

The centrist ideology was in its formative stages as early as 1987. Gorbachev's speech to the Soviet media representatives on 10 July 1987, in which he defended his centrist position 'both against those who warn that glasnost' is out of control and against those who call for a more radical economic reform than the Party is prepared to entertain', was seen as a response to criticism aired at the June 1987 Central Committee plenum. One strand of criticisms at the plenum was summed up by Gorbachev in the following words:

> Will not the new phase turn into a negation of all that has gone before? Have we not forgotten our history? Does the present policy not amount to devaluing what was achieved by previous generations?[36]

It had acquired concrete ideological and political shape by November 1989, when Gorbachev clearly talked of a third alternative to either preserving the earlier system in all aspects of life or reverting to capitalism, in an article published in *Kommunist.* He wanted to reorganize the system, having given up the idea of rectifying or improving it.[37] He saw its roots in the Leninism of NEP. In his Lenin anniversary speech in 1990, he said:

> The most valuable thing in Lenin's ideas about socialism and his main contribution to the working-out of socialist idea are contained in his work on NEP, his policies on it, and, of course, in his testament. This is where a new stage in Lenin's work on the theory of socialism began.[38]

The new ideological underpinnings of socialism, as envisaged by the centrist reformist leadership, were succinctly explained by Vadim Medvedev, in an article entitled 'Socialism for the 21st Century', published in the *Morning Star* on 15 December 1988. In this article, he argued that socialism was lagging behind capitalism in economic development and technology, and that there was a need for a major overhaul. The new ideological basis was to be found in Lenin's ideas which had evolved 'during the transition from military Communism to the New Economic

Policy.' According to him, the Stalin period was marked by 'the diversion from Lenin's concept of the humanitarian essence of socialism.' His article was said to be an attempt to separate Leninism from what he considered to be the distortions of previous decades.

This ideology was also to be harmonized with the policy of Perestroika. In other words, this meant developing an ideological rationale legitimized by Lenin and Leninism, for the policy of Perestroika, and more significantly marking a more decisive and radical break from the past. This was to be the new ideology of reformism representing a centrist reformist position vis-a-vis those who were either still predominantly under the influence of 'the old ideology', or those who wanted to look beyond Marxism-Leninism and socialism. The role of Lenin's ideas was clear when Medvedev said 'we must grasp Lenin's ideas in the context of our present experience and current objectives.'[39]

The new socialist perspective and the new concept of socialism was to take into account 'the experience of humanity as a whole.' According to him, it was necessary not only to study other system's achievements in science and engineering, but also social organisation, economic process, including large scale and small production, cooperatives, international economic integration, and so on. Medvedev further argued for a study of 'the practice of the present-day social-democratic movement and its policies, especially the defence of the social and democratic gains of the working people'.

In the field of economy, he called for an 'overhaul' of the concept of the economic foundations of socialism. In his view, previously the development of state property was the basis for building socialism, whereas cooperatives and individual enterprise were discouraged by 'imposing artificial restrictions' and '(s)ocialisation was considered a yardstick for measuring the extent of socialism'. The new economic reforms sought to 'create and stimulate economic incentives for growth in production' and 'restructure property relations and end the alienation between people and public property'.

He talked about the renewal of the forms of the ownership of the means of production. The previous concepts of private property were to be modified. He called for a revival of the lease system and the cooperative system in all sectors of the economy and for a review of the 'concept of the relationship between goods and prices under socialism and the relationship between planning and the market. 'This was aimed at providing 'a necessary precondition for effective management based on economically sound methods.' Centralised leadership and the management of the economy, albeit modified was to remain, yet the market was 'an indispensable means of gearing production to increased demand and a major instrument of public control of quality and cost.' The central authorities were to decide 'such questions as structural changes, investment policies, the implementation of major research and development programmes and the creation of conditions ensuring the effective work of enterprises as socialist commodity producers. This marked an effective shift from what had hitherto been the unshakeable tenets of a socialist economy.

As far as the political system was concerned, a departure from the past could be seen. The presence of social, ethnic and professional groups with a diversity of interests was acknowledged for the first time in a direct antithesis of the previous interpretation. Thus Medvedev acknowledged that 'socialism must create a political system reflecting the the actual structure of society and the diversity of the interests and aspirations of all social groups and communities. 'Hence the term pluralism, until recently an anathema in the political lexicon of the Soviet Union, came into existence, albeit as 'socialist pluralism.' Yet all the reforms in the political system were envisaged within a one-Party state and there were 'no grounds for creating any alternative parties to oppose CPSU policy.' Any scaling down of the Party's role to only coordinating functions was categorically rejected. The Party's influence was to be enhanced by 'focusing efforts on a more profound and fundamental elaboration of theory and practice, rather than by methods of command-style administration.' [40]

The position of the centrist-reformers became more radical by May 1989, when they seemed in principle to have no objections to a multi-party system, though their preference was still for democratisation within a single party system. This was a major shift from their earlier position.[41] Accepting the right of tendencies to exist within the Party, Medvedev talked of its vanguard role in implementing a united policy. He acknowledged the presence of 'diametrically opposed positions' within the party.[42] This naturally found expression in the Central Committee as well.

A qualitative shift from what was enunciated as the centrist position on the economy towards the end of 1988 in *Morning Star*, by Medvedev, was discernible, when he said:

> Enterprises can be state-owned (and belong either to society as a whole or to individual republics, regions, or cities); owned by shareholders or even individuals. We firmly advocate pluralism and equality of forms of ownership and economic management...

A new concept of socialism emerged, which was a radical departure from the earlier one and indeed the one held by 'conservatives.' He saw socialism as follows:

> Socialism is a stage in the development of civilization. It inherits the best of what has been accumulated by mankind's progress..., we do not deviate from universal historical experience..., we must not reject out of hand the experience accumulated by capitalism on the sole pretext that it is a different social system. That kind of nihilism would contradict Marxist-Leninist scientific traditions... We still have to seriously study the practice of contemporary social democracy, notably in the sphere of defending the workers' social and democratic gains. This is also true of many forms of political life in bourgeois society. We do not rule out the possibility of resorting to them, especially since they are not purely capitalist creation but the result of the development of human civilization.[43]

Rapprochment with social-democracy and a shift in that direction on an ideological plane was a vital element of the centrist-reformist position. A. Yakovlev had concluded in the early phase of Perestroika that social democracy was the only way out for the country. In a private meeting with the leader of the Canadian Communist Party in 1988, Yakovlev argued that the split in the working class (between Communism and social democracy) had to be healed. According to him, there was no objective reason for them to be separate and antagonistic. The world history had shown that the way forward was through social democracy and evolution, and that the Bolshevik type of revolution was obsolete and had proven deleterious. Yakovlev was very close to Gorbachev, and probably, on matters of ideology, his main guide and mentor. His goal appeared to be that at some point a reformed CPSU would join Second International.

At the 70th anniversary of the October Revolution, a meeting was held in Moscow attended by Communist Parties and several other parties. Several social democratic parties were invited and some attended. It was the first time that such a gathering had been conceived and the meeting might have been the beginning of efforts to find other political allies. The reformist leadership of the CPSU probably had such a strategy in their mind, and were moving in that direction. Yuri Krasin, a leading Party intellectual, had worked out the theory of the necessity of healing the rift in the working class movement, and the reformist CPSU leadership seemed to accept it. Here, it has to be noted that in the context of the former Soviet Union, the meaning of social democracy was different from its western counterpart, and it did not seem to have been fully worked out. It appeared to have included democratization, glasnost, decentralization of big industries, and introduction of pluralism in the political system.

Gorbachev had managed to build up a centrist coalition not only in the Central Committee, but also in the Soviet parliament. At the fourth session of the Congress of People's Deputies in December 1990, a registration of the deputies, according to party affiliations, was undertaken. Opponents of Gorbachev had registered themselves differently. Several communist deputies, who did not want to be identified with Gorbachev, registered in different groupings, such as the Soyuz group of deputies. Yet a substantial 700 deputies or about one-third of the total deputies registered themselves with the CPSU fraction.[44]

The crisis that the system was undergoing was, it was argued not that of the socialist idea but of the form in which it was realised. Thus the reformers argued for renewing instead of negating socialism. Earlier, Lenin's statements on 'War Communism' had been stressed, having been torn out of context, as the fundamental aspect of his theory. According to Medvedev the idea of socialism was distorted under certain specific historical conditions and thus the obvious need for the renewal of the form of social life. After Lenin, the ideologisation, appraisals given seemingly from the working class point of view esentially represented barrack-like-socialism which was alienated from real life. Dogmatic models were used for suppressing progressive ideas, banishing them from the society. The most important precondition for growth, according to Medvedev, was freedom from ideological domination leading to deideologisation of political economy.[45]

The ideology was supposed to have destroyed morality and removed it from all the active regulators of social life. In politics, ideology was said to have destroyed the very essence of the Marxist theory. This distortion was the consequence of the struggle for power and attempt to retain it at all costs. It was accompanied by the hypertrophy of the place of ideology in the society.The sphere of economy too had been swallowed by the ideology. There was a set model of approach and everything new had to be judged in terms of its being socialistic or non-socialistic and only then could it be put to use. Hence, ideology was said to have captured all possible aspects of life. Society had lost its capacity to understand its own condition and had blindly succumbed to ideologising. Perestroika, glasnost and democratisation, it was contended, had brought the society out of such a state. The entire political spectrum was said to be calling for the things which common people do - like growing crops, producing machines and not associating everything with sacramental ideological slogan shouting.

Despite all the 'anti ideological allegory', ideology was seen as a necessary and constructive element of social development. It was argued that to liberate other spheres of social activity from the influence of ideology, an ideology reflecting reality was needed.

Communism was seen as an hypothesis which had failed to work in the Soviet Union. Yet it was utopia to be preserved in the intellectual arsenal of mankind. It was acknowledged as an expression of the highest form of social justice. It was believed to have played and was expected to play an important role in the moral and spiritual culture of mankind. It was an unfulfilled utopia, like the flight of Icarus, which may be realised by the creative effort of the people. The task formulated was to exorcise all things from the old ideology which could not be proved and retain 'the positive nucleus.'[46]

The 25 April 1989 Central Committee plenum was of crucial importance, since a sizeable number of members from the most conservative section of the Party retired.[47] This was an unprecedented turnover prompted by the results of the March 1989 elections, which had dealt a serious blow to the Party apparatus. Although a larger number of Party members were elected in these elections than before, a fifth of about two hundred secretaries of the Central Committees of Union-Republic Communist Parties, krai and oblast Party committees failed to gain a majority.[48] The election results were a decisive setback for the conservatives and established the reformists and radical-reformists as a political force.[49] The results produced a very negative impact on the Party bodies, which started thinking about ways and means of restoring its authority and position.[50] The elections were supported by the Party organs in the hope that the results would reinforce and legitimise its authority. However the popular mandate was clearly for reform. Despite the election of an overwhelmingly large number of Communist deputies, they were no longer a monolithic bloc and held a diversity of opinions. With the elections the differences over the pace and depth of the reforms started emerging among the reformers, with a section proposing radical reforms.[51] Thus by the time of the February plenum, the two political tendencies of reformists and conservatives had differentiated into those of conservatives, centrist-reformists and radical-reformists.

The February 1990 Plenum

The clearest conflict between these political tendencies came at the February 1990 Central Committee plenum. It was at this plenum, in the wake of the dramatic collapse of the Eastern European regimes, and where the draft platform for the 28th Party Congress was proposed, that the differentiation of political tendencies became sharply visible for the first time. The Party and the Central Committee were by now deeply divided. The conflict had reached a new peak with a conservative offensive. The draft platform, it was hoped, would provide the basis of unity. The first quarter of 1990 was a period of political turmoil. The Party was facing serious opposition from a whole range of political forces, as exemplified by mass rallies all over the USSR.[52] The grim situation for the Party was expressed by Yu. Prokofiev when he said "(we) are not just discussing the question of preparing for the next Party Congress today; the Party's political destiny is being decided".[53] A *Kommunist* editorial however took a more optimistic view, describing the plenum as a citizens' platform.[54] Sharp debates took place reflecting the reality of political pluralism in Soviet life.

The importance of a fundamental transformation of the relationship of the Party with the State and economic bodies was re-emphasised. The Party could no longer seek constitutional legitimacy and had to renounce all legal and political advantages. Thus Article Six of the Constitution had to be amended. The growth of political pluralism and emergence of public and political organisations and movements which could lead to the formation of parties at a later stage was acknowledged. The principle of democratic centralism as it existed was to be reviewed, strengthening its democratic element and the diffusion of power to the Party as distinct from the Party bodies; the centralist element of this principle was to be abandoned. The plenum was preceded by debates and discussions at various meetings. Numerous proposals were received by the Central Committee from various sections of society and the Party. Contradictions accumulated over a long period of time had surfaced. The economic situation by now had worsened. The consumer market was in disarray, there was a shortage of resources and basic commodities, and the purchasing power of the ruble had fallen. The food situation was also in crisis. Incomplete construction projects alone had consumed four-fifths of the growth in the national income in 1989. The inter-ethnic situation had deteriorated, as for example between Azerbaijan and Armenia in the Nagorno-Karabakh Autonomous Oblast.[55] It was against this background that the February 1990 plenum was held. The general crisis in society was reflected in further polarisation of the political tendencies within the Central Committee, as shown in the discussion of the key issues of the multi-party system, the economy and the national question.

Certain Central Committee members supported a multi-party system, or at least acknowledged it as a political reality. Some definitely opposed it, or gave it a qualified acceptance. The former included the centrist and radical reformers and the latter cautious-reformists and anti-reformists. Prokofiev wanted recognition of the political reality of a multi-party system.[56] Yeltsin reiterated the call of the All-Union conference of Party clubs and Party organisations held in January 1990 for a multi-party system.[57] P.K. Luchinskii, first secretary of the Moldavian Communist Party, had held similar views and suggested the formation of a commission to study countries with a two-party system, envisaging the creation of two parties based on socialist policies.[58] Ligachev supported the amendment of Article Six which constitutionally guaranteed the leading role of the Party in the Soviet political system.[59] Accepting the eventuality of a multi-party system, he later talked of the need for the Party to "earn political authority".[60] Shevardnadze,[61] Yakovlev,[62] Ryzhkov,[63] and S.S. Shatalin, acting academic secretary of the USSR Academy of Sciences Economics Department, also favoured the multi-party system,[64] as did Mironenko,[65] V.D. Kadochnikov, first secretary of the Sverdlovsk City Party committee,[66] and Boris Gidaspov, first secretary of the Leningrad obkom and gorkom.[67] V.G. Anufriev, second secretary of the Kazakh Communist Party, talked of an "era of co-operation and sensible alliances".[68] Thus by and large a consensus had emerged between moderate conservatives, centrist-reformists and radical-reformists on this issue.

Those who opposed a multi-party system included A.M. Masaliev, first secretary of the Kirgiz Communist Party, who was unhappy at the appearance of movements and organisations "directed toward the destabilisation of society and the collapse of the economy and the country's political system".[69] A.P. Miasnikov, an excavator operator at the Korshunovskii mining and enrichment combine, Irkutsk oblast, stated that "the country is not yet ready to switch to a multi-party system", although he acknowledged its inevitability.[70] N.F. Tatarchuk, first secretary of the Kalinin obkom, supported the removal of Article Six, but argued for the necessity to assess and ban organisations "destabilising the situation".[71]

Anti-reformists were opposed to economic reform, whereas cautious-reformists were sceptical and had reservations about some of its aspects, particularly the introduction of private property, though some supported them. V.I. Brovikov, USSR ambassador to Poland, was bitterly opposed to any kind of economic reform.[72] Those who were sceptical included Prokofiev,[73] N.F. Tatarchuk, first secretary of the Kalinin obkom,[74] Gidaspov, Ligachev, and V.I. Vorotnikov, member of the Politburo and chairman of the RSFSR Supreme Soviet Presidium.[75]

Centrist-reformists supporting the economic reforms included G.A. Yagodin, chairman of the USSR State Committee for Public Education,[76] Ye.P. Velikhov, vice-president of the USSR Academy of Sciences,[77] A. Yakovlev,[78] V.A. Ivashko, member of the Politburo and first secretary of the Ukrainian Communist Party,[79] N.N. Sliunkov, member of the Politburo and the secretary of the Central Committee,[80] Mironenko,[81] and M.A. Kniazuk, first secretary of the Ivanovo obkom.[82] Radical-reformists considered the economic reforms to be piecemeal and slow.

On the national question, radical reformers such as Yeltsin called for a shift "from the unitary principle of building the State ... to a voluntary alliance of the peoples".[83] Luchinskii supported the formation of a union of sovereign States on the basis of a new union treaty in which republics would decide the rights to be delegated to the centre.[84] Shevardnadze wanted "a treaty-bound union of genuinely sovereign States".[85] G.G. Gumbaridze, first secretary of Georgian Communist Party, seemed to appraise positively the national movements and advocated the participation of Union-Republic Communist Parties in them.[86] Centrist-reformists like Luchinskii, Shevardnadze and Gumbaridze appeared to advocate reforms within a federal structure although they had varying opinions on the distribution of powers between the centre and the republics. Republican leaders favoured greater sovereignty for the republics. Radical reformists like Yeltsin dramatically revised their earlier position and argued for a confederation of republics thus laying down political ground for disintegration of USSR.

In addition to the different political tendencies within the Central Committee evident from the speeches made at the plenum, the Central Committee had a larger number of "silent radical reformers". Such a claim was made by Yeltsin,[87] who voted against the draft platform, since not all his proposals were accepted.[88] The radical-reformists were preparing to part company with the Party and the Central Committee if their proposals for reforms were not fully accepted. This culminated in the dramatic departure of the leaders of the democratic platform from the Party at the 28th Party Congress.

The March 1990 Central Committee Plenum

The March 1990 plenum was a continuation of the February plenum and debated the specific ways in which Article Six ought to be amended. There was a range of opinions on this issue. Among those who favoured amendment of Article Six, and the omission of any reference to the Party, were Prokofiev, Bakatin, Mironenko, V.F. Yakovlev, the USSR Minister of Justice, I.T. Frolov, Secretary of the Central Committee and Chief Editor of *Pravda*, and V.M. Semenov, first secretary of Grodno obkom. These members represented the centrist-reformist tendency.

Yu.I. Litvintsev, first secretary of the Tula obkom, on the other hand, was in favour of including the role of the Party in some way. He represented the cautious-reformist tendency, in contrast to Brovikov and Gurenko. Brovikov was completely opposed to the reforms.[89] S.I. Gurenko, second secretary of the Ukrainian Communist Party, prophetically foresaw that the deletion of Article Six would intensify attacks on the Party aimed at removing it from the political arena.[90] Differences on other issues between present and prospective Central Committee members also emerged in the course of debate.

Around the middle of March 1990, the Congress of People's Deputies legalised the multi-party system in the Soviet Union, by amending Article Six.[91] By early 1991 eleven thousand political parties and movements existed in the Soviet Union, out of which one and a half thousand aspired to a national role.[92] Although there was a very large number of organisations claiming the status of political parties, they were a long way from being political parties in a functioning multi-party system. In effect the majority could only be described as loose groupings with ill-defined programmes and objectives. The process of alignments and realignments was just beginning to lead to the formation of fully-fledged political parties. The political system was at the threshold of a multi-party system. But the CPSU was still the largest political party with a very large organisation and resources, despite centrifugal tendencies evident within it.

The conservative section within the leadership was attempting to preserve the hegemony of the Party and the State organs, as exemplified by Ligachev's call for purging the Party ranks. His statements seemed to be directed at the members of the democratic platform, who wanted a parliamentary type of Party.[93] On the other hand, centrist-reformists were opposed to radicals and conservatives aspiring to a separate organisational base within the Party. An editorial in *Pravda* on 16 April 1990, entitled 'For Consolidation on the Basis of Principle of Perestroika', criticised those pressing for the establishment of a Russian Communist Party and the radical-reformist supporters of the democratic platform aiming at the "organisational formation of a political Party opposing the CPSU".[94] The Russian Communist Party gave political expression to the Party and State organs and to its associated social forces. In an oblique reference to the conservative section of the Central Committee, Gorbachev talked of some leading cadres who preferred the old and were refusing to integrate into the reform process. They accepted the reforms neither politically nor psychologically. They justified this non-acceptance in the interest of the people and the maintenance of ideological purity. On the other hand, with reference to the Democratic Platform, he spoke of forces in society which "are pushing us towards a bourgeois system and are linking the solution of current problems with the country's transition to capitalist tracks".[95] By now differentiation between the three political tendencies was complete. However, as the separation of the Party and the State became more effective in 1990-91 the conservatives' opposition became more and more strident in the Central Committee. This was also the period of acute economic and ethnic crises.

The Central Committee at the 28th Party Congress

The new Central Committee elected at the 28th Party Congress took into account the existence of various tendencies. Because of the single-party system, diametrically opposite points of views existed within the Central Committee and the Party. Each tendency was competing to mould the Party in its image. The decision was thus taken to allow the representatives of various political groups to participate and speak at the 28th Party Congress. It was decided that in order to reflect real life, representatives from different groups should be included in the Central Committee. This diversity was reflected in the work of the Politburo and the Central Committee.[96]

An assessment of how various political forces were ranged in the Central Committee was given by one of its members. About thirty per cent of members were acknowledged political leaders from various Party organisations in enterprises and universities who did not belong to the Party or State apparatuses. Ten to twelve of them actively opposed the latter. Some Central Committee members belonged to the social-democratic stream, whose ideas were essentially similar to Western social-democracy. Members of this group supported Gorbachev as President, but not as Party leader. It consisted of twenty to thirty members, including Latsis and Shatalin. The main leaders of the Marxist platform were Buzgalin, Prigarin and Galina Sachko. Sergiev was a representative of the Leningrad Initiative Congress of Russian Communists. There were representatives of the "young democratic coalition", a leader of the democratic platform of the CPSU from Sverdlovsk and some who were elected as representatives of regional Party organisations, but opposed the Party leadership. Gorbachev's core group consisted of forty to fifty direct supporters, some from the Central Apparatus. The other group consisted of middle-level Party functionaries, mainly secretaries of regional Party committees. They constituted about a quarter of the Central Committee and opposed the reforms. Their main slogan was the struggle for "Communism" against the "social-democratic reformist course" of Gorbachev. This group was further augmented by about one-quarter of the Central Committee members, who were from different strata of the Party or middle levels of the State apparatus. They thus altogether constituted roughly half of the Central Committee. But this was not a monolithic group and comprised about one hundred core members, who supported Ligachev. It would further increase in strength, as at the April 1991 plenum of the Central Committee.[97] Thus roughly half of the Central Committee membership, consisting of middle-level Party functionaries and other sections of the Party and the State apparatuses, was opposed to Gorbachev and the reforms. They represented anti-reformists and cautious-reformists. The rest of the Central Committee belonged to the remaining three categories, with centrist-reformists constituting a small but influential section of this body. The diverse and contradictory perspectives on reforms clashed as the old rules of the game were no longer applicable as the crisis deepened. This would be particularly evident at the January, April and July 1991 plenums.

The January 1991 Central Committee Plenum

The January 1991 plenum witnessed sharp debates on the issues of the economy, inter-ethnic relations, a multi-party system and ideology. Several members were opposed to the economic reforms and alarmed at the emergence of political forces stridently opposed to the Party, the danger to the existence of the USSR, the rapid disintegration of the Party and its plummeting political influence. This was of utmost concern to the conservative members of the Central Committee, particularly from the Party bodies, for whom the reforms aimed at reviving the Party's influence had gone awry. For them the reforms had gone too far, violating the integrity of the entire system. Political transitions are highly unpredictable and particularly those from a centralised system to a democratic one. By now, however, it was too late for the Party organs to reverse the effects of the reforms.

For M.G. Aliev, first secretary of the Dagestan Republic Party committee, the acceptance of universal human values had resulted in a process of deideologisation, replacing socialist interests with bourgeois ones. The concept of universal human values had been propagated by the centrist-reformists as an alternative to the concept of class as a basis for the new ideology of socialism as also that of analysing the social phcnomenon. Therefore the former denied any class distinctions and any antagonistic conflicts in the society based on these differences. Although the market was not incompatible with socialism according to Aliev, "the most savage and rapacious kind" was being established. His opinion seemed to reflect the cautious-reformist tendency.[98] G.P. Kazmin, first secretary of the Krasnoiarsk kraikom, seemed opposed to reforms and thought that taking "a sharp turn toward the market" was the main political mistake. He was unhappy with political pluralism.[99] A similar opinion was expressed by R. Atadzhanov, chairman of the Lenin kolkhoz in Uzbekistan, who opposed private ownership of land, which for him would split society.[100] Gurenko, member of the Politburo and first secretary of the Ukrainian Communist Party, appeared to have a cautious approach towards reforms when he supported the market, but opposed "rash privatisation", which was collectivisation "in reverse".[101] V.V. Grigoriev, first secretary of the Vitebsk obkom, also argued for the increased intervention of the Party to "counter destabilisation and unmanageability of the economy".[102] A similar opinion seemed to be held by P.M. Melnikov, the Party secretary of Karandaugol mine. P.A. Zhiganov, a fitter at the Tsentralnaia mine (Partizansk, Maritime krai) said that he was a conservative and was opposed to those who offered capitalism as an alternative to socialism.[103]

V.S. Kulikov, a milling machine operator at a production association in Nizhnii Novgorod, read an appeal from the association's communists to the plenum which accused a number of Central Committee members of issuing statements in the press opposing the aims of the Party.[104] Thus the opposition to the official line of the Central Committee was articulated publicly by its own members. Its erstwhile monocentrism had given way to political polycentrism. The Tomsk obkom first secretary, A.A. Pomorov, argued for a reconciliation of different political tendencies.[105] Polozkov, first secretary of the RSFSR Communist Party, contended that Perestroika as conceived in 1985 had not materialised. The Party, according to him, had departed from its historical mission of defending the interests of the working class, thereby allowing the development of a social base, in the class of entrepreneurs, for political parties and movements which were opposed to socialism. In his opinion, by accepting a disjunction between pan-human and class interests, "we did a disservice to the socialist idea".[106] Polozkov clearly outlined the ideological position of conservatives as distinct from that of centrist-reformers and radical-reformers.[107] The mood at the January plenum appeared to be towards restraining reforms, if not giving them up altogether. The main source of opposition in the Central Committee was from amongst Party officials, workers and peasants. The latter two categories were severely affected by the economic crisis. The Central Committee elected at the 28th Party Congress contained representatives of these two numerous sections of the society unlike those from the industrial and agricultural managements sections who represented them in this body in the previous Central Committees.

Apart from the conservative opposition, a split along national lines was evident. The Union treaty and the existence of the USSR were the most important issues for Kazmin.[108] Colonel-General N.A. Moisiev, chief of the ground forces' Political Directorate, saw the question of the existence of a renewed Union as the most crucial one.[109] They seemed to hold views close to the centrist-reformists. E.-A.A. Sillari, a Politburo member, took a radical position on the nationality question. Similarly K.I. Kommissarov, faculty head at Tallinn State Conservatory, favoured the decision of the 21st Congress of the Estonian Communist Party to constitute itself as an autonomous Party highlighting the unbridled federalisation of the Party. On the other hand M.M. Burokevicius, first secretary of the Lithuanian Communist Party, asked the leadership of the country to state publicly their attitude towards the Lithuanian problem if it was different from those who wanted Lithuania to stay within the USSR.[110] Within the highest echelons of the Party leadership, the Politburo and the Central Committee, diverse viewpoints existed and were aired by its members, underscoring the ambivalence of the leadership to an issue as politically sensitive and crucial as the division of the USSR.

The April 1991 Central Committee Plenum

The April 1991 Plenum further intensified the contradictions between reformists and conservatives in the Central Committee. Several conservatives who had earlier given a cautious welcome to reform now came out openly against it. Some continued to support limited controlled reforms if the dominance of the State sector was ensured. Few moderate reformists were now arguing for either a complete retreat from reforms or a temporary halt to them. A small proportion pressed for rapid reform. Others like those from the Marxist platform were opposed to both State control and the market, and called for a form of workers' ownership and control. Some still hoped that a orderly transition to the mixed economy was possible.

The April 1991 plenum was held against a background of serious economic crisis. In the first quarter of the year alone, there was a 10 per cent decline in the national income. Economic links were in a rapid process of collapse and the consumer market was disorganised. In the first quarter, the Union budget received a revenue of R21 billion against a projected R55 billion. Unemployment touched 2 million. Subsidies exceeded R120 billion, which was almost a quarter of the country's budget. State organs had weakened and executive power was feeble. A projection of the trends indicated a fall in industrial production and the national income by about a quarter and a drop in per capita material goods consumption by one-fifth in 1991.[111] The price rise had a considerable impact on the standard of living.[112] All this presented a scenario of a serious economic crisis, aggravating the conflict.

Gorbachev as the key architect of the reform programme was a particular target. In Shakhnazarov's view a major section under conservative influence in the Party had not accepted the programme of a democratic and socialist Party as passed by the 28th Party Congress, and there was thus the possibility of Gorbachev's resignation being proposed or of a no confidence vote at the forthcoming plenum.[113] The plenum was preceded by demands for his removal. The Tiumen obkom demanded his resignation.[114] Gidaspov, in his report to the Leningrad obkom plenum, criticised the "unforgivable passiveness and inconsistency" of the CPSU leadership and Gorbachev. Gorbachev was criticised by Gurenko, who following the Ukrainian Party plenum asked for the separation of the posts of General Secretary and President. A joint plenum of the Krasnodar kraikom and its control commission called for an extraordinary plenum to be held to hear his "account". Gorbachev was charged with having abandoned the social-class method of analysing society, of political assessment and of defining policy. The basic policy on the primacy of universal human values adopted at the 28th Party Congress was thus questioned by the plenum.[115] Direct calls for the resignation of the General Secretary were also made at the Moscow gorkom.[116] In his speech to the plenum delivered on 24 April 1991, Gorbachev spoke of several Central Committee members who were surreptitiously attempting to undermine the decisions of the 28th Party Congress and replace it with a different political line. He talked of the resolutions of various Party committees, who demanded his and the Politburo's resignation, and of several statements saying that the State and Party leadership were following an unpopular policy.[117] At the 25th April session, Gorbachev offered his resignation as General Secretary, which despite strident opposition was not accepted.[118] Among those who supported Gorbachev were Otto Latsis, first deputy editor in chief of *Kommunist*, Y.S. Krastinskii, a Leningrad Soviet deputy, V.V. Kalashnikov, Dean of the Leningrad Electro-Technical Institute, and V.V. Grigoriev, chairman of Vitebsk oblast and first secretary of the obkom.[119] Seventy two members of the Central Committee who were pro-Gorbachev or adherents of the centrist political position signed a petition in favour of Gorbachev.[120]

Prokofiev in a noticeable shift from his centrist position to a conservative one called for a temporary halt to the reforms, which in his opinion had been "subverted", and favoured protecting the interests of State enterprises and its employees.[121] He argued for the suspension of the operation of all laws adopted by the republics and the regions that contravened the USSR Constitution and laws.[122] A.A. Malofiev, first secretary of the Belorussian Central Committee, took an anti-reformist position opposing the privatisation, distribution and sale of State property and the scope for free enterprise as envisaged in the anti-crisis programme of the government. He defended the sovkhoz and kolkhoz system, and argued for a state of emergency to preserve the USSR.[123]

Polozkov supported the reform programme devised by the Communists of Russia faction of the RSFSR people's deputies, prepared under the leadership of Yu.M. Voronin, Chairman of the republic's Supreme Soviet, which talked of a two-tier economy. It proposed "'increased production to provide a 'consumer basket', using traditional, all-purpose elements of the plan system'" and "the use by producers of free capacities and resources on the basis of market relations".[124] A.N. Maltsev, first secretary of the Nizhegorodskii gorkom, proposed a reduction of prices and "destatisation by putting property in the hands of labour collectives" instead of privatisation.[125] A.V. Buzgalin, lecturer in the economics faculty of Moscow State University,[126] argued for the introduction of self-management by the labour collective, which acted "as master of the enterprise, (hired) itself a director and (distributed) powers among working people and professional managers".[127] For A.A. Prigarin the building of a mixed market economy, which had been talked about in recent months, was not socialism.[128] Maltsev, Buzgalin and Prigarin were supporters of syndicalism.

For A.M. Zaitsev, first secretary of the Kemerovo obkom, anti-communism and "the capitalisation of the economy have today become real policy in the Soviet Union".[129] A.S. Yefimov, second secretary of the Uzbekistan Communist Party, was opposed to the "privatisation of housing, the development of trade and purchase co-operatives, and price liberalisation", which in his opinion would entail negative political consequences. G.A. Khvatov, commander of the Pacific Fleet, did not favour privatisation, destatisation and the creation of multiple forms of property. A.P. Rubiks, first secretary of the Latvian Communist Party, was concerned about the "revival of a national bourgeois dictatorship and the completion of the restoration of capitalism in Latvia".[130] For Gurenko, Perestroika had destroyed the economic system, caused unemployment and poverty, and had led to violent inter-ethnic conflicts.[131] V.A. Starodubtsev, chairman of the USSR Peasants Union, believed that "the movement toward political chaos and the catastrophic collapse of the economy" had happened "with our tacit consent".[132] G.M. Abelguzina, an operator at the Meleuzovskii Chemical Plant, Bashkir ASSR, favoured a return, for at least two years, to the "planned regulation of the country's economic and social development and reliance on the basic economic structures ...".[133] The aforementioned speakers took a primarily anti-reformist position on the issues of economic reform. A similar position was expressed by A.A. Sergiev, department chief of the Academy of Labour and Social Relations, who was strongly critical of the anti-crisis programme of the government and said that it competed for "depth and consistency of capitalist changes" with the authors of the 500 days programme. For him, the economic programmes of Gorbachev and Yeltsin had not only no basic differences, but also "no differences of substance".

Bakatin defended Gorbachev and the "policy of social renewal". He considered talk of the failure of Perestroika to be "hasty". Perestroika, for Frolov, was "alive and well", although encountering new problems and difficulties. He disagreed with the view that socialist values had been betrayed. B.I. Oleinik, deputy chairman of the USSR Supreme Soviet of Nationalities, defended Gorbachev, but characterised six years of Perestroika as "going down the path of anarchist choice, admittedly with elements of socialism".[134] A.I. Volskii, President of the USSR Science and Industry Union (NPS), argued for a rapid transition to a market economy. He favoured Gorbachev's "position of political centrism". V.A. Kuptsov, secretary of the Central Committee, also supported the idea of "a political centre" mooted by Gorbachev.[135] N.A. Nazarbaev favoured pan-human values, accepted the futility of the command economy and saw the main task as organising the transition to market relations.[136] Bakatin, Oleinik, Volskii, Kuptsov and Nazarbaev seemed to hold centrist-reformist positions. Witnessing the sharp conflict at the plenum, L.A. Arutunian, head of the Yerevan State University Applied Sociology department and a member of the Central Committee, commented that the Central Committee would split because "the differences of ideas about objectives and our society are too deep".[137] A major section of Party officials, part of intelligentsia, working class and representative of the Peasants' Union opposed the reforms.

Thus before and during the April 1991 plenum, the struggle between different political tendencies intensified. On 20 June 1991, a statement published by the Marxist platform in the weekly *Glasnost* demanded the 29th Party Congress be held by the end of the year. It claimed to unite "Communist reformers", opposing both the conservative and the "liberal bourgeois wing in the Soviet Communist Party". It criticised Gorbachev and other leaders for talking of socialist choice, while in practice dismantling public property.[138] Sergiev issued an appeal in early June calling for an extraordinary CPSU Congress and decided to form an organisational committee for that purpose.[139] A section of Central Committee members, although a small one, was openly calling for a Congress to change centrist policies and remove Gorbachev and his allies from the Central Committee. A large number of the remaining gave tacit or muted support to the demand for his ouster. Those opposed to him subscribed to different political persuasions within the Party and the Central Committee. The catastrophic economic situation had resultant political fallout. The political conflict between contending ideologies and political manifestations of antagonistic socio-economic forces destabilised the political system itself and jeopardised its very existence.

The Democratic Reform Movement

On the other hand, on 1 July 1991 a statement by some prominent politicians, the majority of whom were either former or current Central Committee members, called for "the unification of democratic movements and parties". The signatories included Volskii, Yakovlev, Shevardnadze, Shatalin, I. Silaev, G. Popov, A. Sobchak, N. Petrakov and A. Rutskoi. The initiators of this movement called for the convening of a constituent conference for the "unification of the democratic forces" with the ultimate aim of forming a Party.[140] The movement was to be called the Democratic Reform Movement.[141] According to Yakovlev, the idea of forming this movement had come into existence prior to the 28th Party Congress.[142] Vital support for the movement came from Arkadi Volskii, leader of the NPS which represented the enterprises responsible for sixty-five per cent of production in the USSR. The basic principle of this organisation, according to Alexander Vladislavlev, chairman of the executive committee of NPS, was

> To consolidate all participants in material production without regard for the form of ownership in order to protect the economy from ideology and to give it the opportunity to develop in correspondence with its logic and law.[143]

This proposal to deideologise the economy was similar to the position of the erstwhile Democratic platform of the CPSU. The NPS thus provided the latter with a social and economic basis. Pavel Bunich, a member of the Central Committee, observed that the fact that Gorbachev did not mention the Democratic Reform Movement was not accidental and could be interpreted as support.[144] Bunich, a strong supporter of Gorbachev, led the Union of Leaseholders and Entrepreneurs, which by the time its first Congress began on 1 June 1990 claimed a membership of 7.5 million leaseholders and 6,000 enterprises. The Union, according to Bunich, represented "the biggest 'free' sector of the Soviet economy".[145] Hence one of the main support bases of the centrist-reformists was in the new social and economic forces that had emerged as a result of the economic reforms. On the one hand the conservatives were stepping up their campaign against the reforms, and on the other the centrist-reformists were organising a platform outside the CPSU. It seemed plausible that the Democratic Reform Movement would have provided the General Secretary and his supporters an alternative forum if they were removed from the Party or chose to leave it. However, the alliance between moderate reformists and moderate conservatives which had initiated Perestroika was irrevocably breached. Shifting power away from the Party and the Central Committee, with the Party's separation from the State, had played the crucial role in breaking this tenuous 'bond'. The Central Committee seemed on the threshold of disintegration.

The July 1991 Central Committee Plenum

The July plenum was more subdued than the April plenum, because the final conflict seemed to have been postponed to the proposed 29th Party Congress, which was expected to be held in November-December 1991.[146] This plenum discussed "putting its house in order", which meant that only groups supporting the Party platform could stay in it. Measures aimed at this were to be undertaken after the adoption of the Party Programme at the proposed 29th Party Congress.[147] However, the situation in USSR had reached a stage of deep crisis. The Party itself was passing through an unprecedented situation. Its influence in workers' collectives had weakened, with workers' organisations emerging on grass-roots initiative. So had its position amongst the scientific, technical and creative intelligentsia. By 1 July the membership of the CPSU had decreased to 15 million, the same as in 1973, falling by 4.2 million in just one and a half years. The exodus was greatest in republics where strong nationalist movements had gained power. Despite the fact that the Party was still numerically a formidable force, splits along the lines of disparate political tendencies had resulted in a situation whereby numerous 'parties' and groups existed in tenuous bondage within the larger entity, the Party, poised to separate thereby disintegrating the latter.

The economic crisis was worsening by the day, social tension was growing, the consumer market was unsettled as never before, ethnic conflicts were the order of the day, law and order problems were mounting, there was political antagonism between the Union and the republics and between the republics, as well as between the CPSU and the newly emerging parties and movements within the CPSU, where several platforms like the Bolshevik Platform, Communist Initiative Movement, Communists for Democracy Movement, Democratic Platform and Marxist Platform existed. In effect several parties existed now within the Party, which had lost its previous control of the "commanding heights".[148] The July plenum, however, witnessed neither a demand for Gorbachev's resignation nor a split in the Party.[149] None of the 38 members of the Central Committee who spoke raised the issue of Gorbachev's resignation.[150]

The adoption of the Fourth Programme of the CPSU was discussed by this plenum.[151] The draft programme was supposed to have been prepared by a special commission of 134 people, representing the diverse political currents in the Party.[152] The Party emerging out of the new programme was to be "the Party of democratic Communists that will combine the best features of social democracy and of the Communist tradition".[153] In his report to the plenum, Gorbachev outlined the crux of the document '*About The Fundamental Alteration Of Our Entire Viewpoint Regarding Socialism*'. This programme was a watershed document. The market was seen as an indivisible part of socialism. A mixed economy with multiple ownership, emphasising share-holding and lcasc-holding was to be developed. The USSR was to be integrated in the world economy. The programme called upon the Party to become "a Party of democratic reforms, political and economic freedom, social justice and values common to all mankind".[154] According to Gorbachev, the time for the dictatorship of the proletariat and class struggle was long past. The Union was to become a democratic federation of sovereign republics with guaranteed rights for all nationalities. The market economy was to be accompanied by social security and was to be integrated into a European and global economy. On the social base of the Party, the document talked of expressing and defending the interests of "the labourers". This vague formulation reflected the desire of the architects of the programme to leave open the question of the renewed Party's social base.

A diversity of opinions were expressed. A.I. Lukianov, chairman of the USSR Supreme Soviet, declared that the draft document provided "the necessary base".[155] Otto Latsis approved the draft and spoke positively of social democracy.[156] M.S. Surkov, secretary of the All-Army Party Committee took a positive view of the draft.[157] G.I. Marchuk, President of the USSR Academy of Sciences, thought that it had "a nucleus, a core that can be further worked on ...". For Abalkin it provided a good basis for debate.[158] D.A. Abdullaev, rector of the Tashkent Electrotechnical Communications Institute, favoured the draft as a basis for discussion, because in it he saw "the last chance to consolidate our ranks and prevent a decisive split in the CPSU". V.G. Anufriev, second secretary of the Kazakhstan Communist Party, said that the draft had a weak theoretical basis. He favoured reaffirming in the document "the CPSU's course of engaging in radical democratic transformations, moving to a market economy". K.M. Makhkamov, first secretary of the Tajik Communist Party organisation, considered the programme a progressive document, based on current realities but which had taken consideration of historical realities.[159] Bunich welcomed the programme, particularly its thesis about a "rapprochement with social democracy".[160]

For Gidaspov, the draft was a "deideologised manifesto".[161] According to Prokofiev, who was a member of the Programme Commission, the proposed draft programme was "neither a document giving a new vision of the Party's theoretical basis nor a programme for its action", but rather a declaration of "fine intentions" for the nineties.[162] A.N. Ilin, second secretary of the RSFSR Communist Party, wanted the programme document to reflect "the contradictions between labour and newly-emerging capital" and to reiterate "the leading role of public forms of ownership".[163] G.P. Kharchenko, second secretary of the Ukrainian Communist Party, thought that the programme was more akin to that of a liberal and social-democratic Party than of a communist party. He was unhappy that the draft did not give precedence to collective forms of ownership and management. For him, it was a retreat from the Programme Statement issued at the 28th Party Congress which talked of "private labour ownership".[164] Gennadii Ziuganov, a member of the Politburo of the Russian Communist Party, hoped that it would be substantially amended.[165] With the exception of Prokofiev, Ilin, Kharchenko, Gidaspov and Ziuganov, others welcomed in varying degrees the draft proposed by Gorbachev at least as a basis for discussion. They thus appeared to adhere to a centrist-reformist position.

Hence the opinion of the Central Committee members on the proposed draft ranged from acceptance and partial acceptance to rejection. Resistance to the reforms was increasingly evident. Again the debate reflected opposition from Party officials.

The Central Committee's Voting Pattern in the Congress of People's Deputies

Index of Dissent in the Central Committee

A study of the voting behaviour in the Congress of People's Deputies provides evidence of the differing positions of Central Committee members. 85 full and 42 candidate members of the Central Committee elected at the

27th Party Congress were in the Congress of People's Deputies. Seven issues are chosen here to analyse their voting behaviour. The position of the leadership on each issue is given in brackets. The issues were:
a. Whether the question of Article Six of the USSR Constitution be included in the agenda of the Second Congress on 12 December 1989? (Against)
b. Whether the question of the privileges of the ruling circles be included in the agenda of the Second Congress on 12 December 1989? (Against)
c. Whether the amendment to Article 95 of the Constitution to nullify Section 2[166] of the Article certifying the election of the deputies from public organisations (CPSU, AUCCTU etc.) be adopted at the Second Congress on 18 December 1989? (Against)
d. Whether deputy Akhunov's amendment to Article 6 of the Constitution deleting the words 'Communist Party' be adopted at the Third Congress on 13 March 1990? (Against)
e. Whether a referendum be undertaken on private property in land?[167] (For)
f. Whether the addendum to the declaration on sovereignty saying that 'USSR recognise the declarations of independence adopted by the parliaments of the Union republics as the freely expressed will of their people' be adopted.[168] (Against)
g. Whether a moratorium be declared on strikes in 1991?[169] (Against)

Voting Pattern of Various Occupational Categories

Occupational Categories	Total Number	Issue b	Issue c	Issue g
		F-AG-AB-NV	F-AG-AB-NV	F-AG-AB-NV
Intelligentsia	14	10-2-0-2	6-5-0-3	4-8-0-2
Party Officials	75	48-18-2-7	31-31-2-11	33-26-4-12
(1) Central	21	12-7-1-1	6-11-0-4	7-11-0-3

(2)Union Republic	13	9-2-0-2	8-1-1-3	6-2-1-4
(3) Regional	41	27-9-1-4	17-19-1-4	20-13-3-5
State Officials				
(1)Executive	24	14-5-1-4	13-9-0-2	16-4-2-2
(a) Central	12	7-3-0-2	6-4-0-2	7-3-1-1
(b)Union Republic	11	6-2-1-2	6-5-0-0	8-1-1-1
(c) Others	1	1-0-0-0	1-0-0-0	1-0-0-0
(2)Legislative	10	6-2-0-2	3-4-0-3	5-0-2-3
(a) Central	8	5-2-0-1	2-4-0-2	4-0-1-3
(b)Union Republics	2	1-0-0-1	1-0-0-1	1-0-1-0
Military	12	7-3-0-2	4-5-0-3	8-4-0-0
Mass Organisation	7	6-0-0-1	1-5-0-1	1-3-0-3
Diplomats	2	2-0-0-0	1-1-0-0	2-0-0-0
Workers	5	5-0-0-0	2-2-0-1	1-2-0-2
Peasants	3	1-2-0-0	2-1-0-0	2-0-1-0
KGB	1	0-0-1-0	0-0-0-1	0-1-0-0

Voting by members of the Central Committee is tabulated in four categories, i.e. 'For' (F), 'Against' (AG), 'Abstained' (AB) and 'Did Not Vote'

(NV). An index of dissent prepared from the table indicates the extent of dissent by Central Committee members from the official or leadership position, taken to be indicated by how Gorbachev voted on issues a, b, c and d. In the case of issues e, f and g, Yakovlev's voting is taken as the leadership's stance since Gorbachev did not vote. 3 points are given for a vote against the official position, 2 points for abstention and 1 point for not voting. Abstention is given a higher weighting than not voting and less than those voting against, since it reflected partial dissent, as the member was present and voting, as against those who did not vote owing to absence.

The highest points for dissent went to G. Arbatov and to A.T. Gonchar, writer and Secretary of the USSR Union of Writers, who was a candidate member of the Central Committee. Both received 15 points each, followed by E.P. Velikhov, Vice-President of the USSR Academy of Sciences with 13.[170] All three were members of the intelligentsia. The lowest on the index were A.I. Lukianov and V.A. Medvedev, with no points. A high proportion, 20 out of 33, of those listed belonged to non-Russian nationalities.

Among those who supported the inclusion of the issue of Article 6 on the agenda at an earlier stage, i. e. at the Second Congress on 12 December 1989, were Yeltsin, Volskii, V.N. Golubeva, who were full members of the Central Committee, and V.M. Falin, A.T. Gonchar and G.A. Metonidze, who were candidate members. T.N. Menteshashvili, a candidate member, abstained on the issue. These members may have been the earliest supporters of the deletion of Article 6. At least thirteen full and candidate members supported the adoption of deputy Akhunov's amendment to Article 6 of the Constitution, striking out the words 'Communist Party' on 13 March 1990. All the others voted against, except for nine members, including Yeltsin, who did not vote. Those voting for included Arbatov; P.G. Lushev, Commander in Chief, Group of Soviet Forces in Germany; B.K. Pugo; K.S. Salikov; G.S. Tarazevich; L.A. Gorshkov; N.E. Kruchina; V.V. Grigoriev, first secretary, Vitebsk obkom; T.N. Menteshashvili; G.A. Metonidze; M.B. Ryzhikov, secretary, AUCCTU; I.I. Skiba and E.P. Velikhov.

Seven members voted outright for the adoption of the addendum on the declaration of sovereignty, eight abstained and twenty-eight did not vote. Those who supported it included Arbatov; M.S. Mendibaev, first secretary, Alma-Ata obkom; Nazarbaev; F.A. Tabeev; M.Yu. Yusupov; M.V. Kovalev and A.T. Gonchar. Abstentions included G.S. Tarazevich; N.F. Tatarchuk, first secretary, Kalinin obkom; S.A. Shalaev, chairman, AUCCTU; V.S. Shevchenko; V.I. Kalashnikov, first secretary, Volgograd obkom; A.S. Yefimov, first secretary, Navoi obkom (Uzbekistan); V.V. Karpov, writer and Board Secretary, the USSR Union of Writers and V.V. Osipov, Commander, Kiev Military District.

The voting pattern of occupational groups represented in the Central Committee is tabulated on issues b, c and g. These issues are examined in greater detail because of their importance in demonstrating emerging political divisions. Since occupational categories were counted and not the individuals, and since several individuals held more than one position, the total number in the table exceeds the total number of Central Committee members in the Congress of People's Deputies. Split-voting was obvious in the case of all categories, as the following table indicates.

On issues b and c, members of the intelligentsia in the Central Committee voted against the leadership's position, whereas on issue g its position coincided with that of the leadership. Party officials, taken together, voted against the leadership on issues b and g, whereas on issue c votes were evenly split. In all three cases the number of those not voting was substantial. Central Party officials tended more to side with the leadership, though a substantial section of them also voted against it. Only on issue b did the majority go against the leadership. On the other two issues the majority sided with the leadership. Party officials from the union republics voted overwhelmingly against the position of the leadership in all three cases. A large number of regional Party officials voted against the leadership position on issues b and g, whereas on c there were 17 opposing the position of the leadership as against 19 supporting it. The majority of executive State officials opposed the leadership on both central and union republic categories on all three issues. In the case of the legislative category, both central and union republic, there was majority opposition to the leadership on issues b and g, but support in the case of issue c. A similar pattern was repeated in the case of the military.

The above data indicate that Central Committee members had divided positions on various issues voted on in the Congress of People's Deputies. The majority of its members from the intelligentsia took a consistent reformist position on all three issues. A substantial number of Party officials, if all the categories were counted together, took a pro-reform position. It was a similar case with State officials belonging to the executive branch, though an overwhelming majority supported a moratorium on strikes in 1991. State officials from the legislative branch seemed to be less reformist, having opposed reformist positions on two issues. The case with the military was similar. Mass organisations appeared to be greater supporters of the leadership's position, having voted with it on issues c and g.[171]

Conclusion

The Party, although overshadowed by ministerial and other interests, had been the most important political body in the Soviet Union. It incorporated a multitude of social, economic and political forces prevailing in society. Several of these were not harmonious in nature. As a consequence of state ownership of the means of production, certain forces had not existed in Soviet society until reform resulted in their emergence. These found political expression within the Party and its Central Committee. The principle of Democratic Centralism as it had been practised and the long-standing ban on factions were now under review and were no longer functional. It was the centralist element of Democratic Centralism and the organisational principle of ban on factions which had cemented the monocentric ethos. What began with the plurality of opinions resulted in multiple political tendencies within the Central Committee. These tendencies were consolidated, but could not co-exist and compete within the same institutional framework. It is difficult to surmise whether there was such a possibility, given the form in which the structure of the Central Committee had evolved and the competing interests.

The social base of the conservatives consisted of the majority of Party and State officials and Central Committee members belonging to the peasantry and the working class. Centrist-reformists were supported by a section of Party and State officials, a part of the intelligentsia, lease-holders and entrepreneurs and leaders of State enterprises. Radical-reformists had very little overt support in the Central Committee. They could be said to have been supported primarily by the intelligentsia and a small section of Party officials. Syndicalists were also supported by a small section of Party officials and the intelligentsia.

The Party and the Central Committee had been primarily involved in the day to day governance of society as a whole and managing the economy, along with State institutions. Article Six was the legal expression of this interconnection. Demands for the deletion of this article had been increasingly raised from various quarters for some time before its actual amendment. The process of separation of the Party and the State reached a qualitatively higher level with the amendment of Article Six. The constitutional instrument which had reinforced the primacy of the Party and the State bodies now no longer existed.

The emergence of an active legislature in the new Supreme Soviet and the Congress of People's Deputies, which had ceased to passively ratify the decisions of the government or follow the Party line, despite the large number of Communist deputies,[172] meant that even the reformed notion of the vanguard role of the Party was not tenable in practice. The meaning of the separation of the Party and the State as originally conceived was changing. The hope that the Party would be able to provide overall political leadership to the representative State institutions through its elected deputies, and thus retain its political hegemony with renewed legitimacy, was in doubt. The central leadership organs of the Party were unable to control the new legislature, with multiple platforms having emerged in it. The executive organs of the State and their working were now under close scrutiny.[173] The voting pattern in the Congress of People's Deputies revealed the multiple views within the Central Committee. A myriad of informal groups, popular fronts, nascent political parties representing numerous interests and increasingly politicised, frequently in opposition to and outside the influence of the Party and the State establishment, had also emerged.[174] This situation was unacceptable to the dominant section of the Party and the State apparatuses. The new circumstances of a politicised legislature and society, something quite contrary to original expectations, resulted in increased conservative opposition in the Central Committee.

Notes

[1] For the "evolving autonomy of elites" see D. Lane, "Soviet Elites, Monolithic or Polyarchic?" in D. Lane ed., *Russia in Flux, The Political and Social Consequences of Reform,* Edward Elgar, (Hants, 1992), pp. 3-23.

For plurality within the Party see R.J. Hill, "The CPSU: From Monolith to Pluralist?", *Soviet Studies*, Vol. 43, no. 2, 1991, pp. 217-35.

On the question of pluralism in the Soviet political system see S. White, "Pluralism, Civil Society, and Post-Soviet Politics", in C. R. Saivetz and A. Jones ed., *In Search of Pluralism, Soviet and Post-Soviet*, Westview Press, (Oxford, 1994), pp. 5-26 .

[2] Ligachev favoured a strategy which "better synchronised economic and political reform". See J. Surovell, "Gorbachev's Last Year: Leftist or Rightist?", *Europe-Asia Studies*, vol. 46, no. 3, 1994, pp. 465-87.

[3] For a detailed discussion see D. Lane, *Politics and Society in the USSR*, Martin Robertson, (London, 1978), pp. 272-73 and T. Bottomore, 1987, pp. 476-77.

[4] The first two tendencies could be broadly characterised as conservative and will be referred to as such in the rest of the chapter.

[5] *Sovetskaia molodezh,* 4 August 1988, pp. 1-3, in *FBIS*, 12 September 1988, pp. 55-59.
[6] *Moskovskie novosti*, no. 5, 29 January 1989, pp. 8-9, in *FBIS*, 30 January 1989, p. 52.
[7] *Sovetskaia estonia*, 19 February 1989, p. 2, in *FBIS*, 7 March 1989, pp. 54-55.
[8] *ibid.*, p. 56.
[9] *Moskovskaia Pravda*, 25 March 1989, p. 3, in *FBIS*, 7 April 1989, pp. 48-49.
[10] *Pogled* , no. 24, 12 June 1989, p. 7, in *FBIS*, 22 June 1989, pp. 56-57.
[11] *Izvestiia*, 10 September 1989, p. 2, in *FBIS*, 11 September 1989, p. 31.
[12] *Moscow Domestic Service*, 1545 GMT, 30 May 1990 in *FBIS*, 1 June 1990, p. 31.
[13] "Towards New Image of Socialism", *Kommunist*, no. 13, 1989, pp. 8-15.
[14] *Le Monde,* 25 May 1989, pp. 1-2, in *FBIS*, 2 June 1989, p. 28.
[15] *ibid.*, p. 29.
[16] M. Gorbachev, "Socialist Idea and Revolutionary Perestroika", *Kommunist*, no. 18, 1989, pp. 3-4.
[17] V. Medvedev, "A Test by History", *Kommunist*, no. 17, 1990, pp. 3-14.
[18] Editorial: 70th Anniversary of the October Revolution: The Revolution Continues. *Kommunist*, no.1, 1987, pp. 5-11.
[19] Speech of the General Secretary of the Central Committee, CPSU, M.S. Gorbachev, Plenary Meeting of the CPSU Central Committee, January 27-28, 1987, *Kommunist*, no. 3, p. 7.
[20] *ibid*,pp.12-13.
[21] *ibid*, p. 18.
[22] G. Razumovsky, To Improve the Training and Retraining of Leading Party Cadres, *Kommunist*, no. 9, 1987, p. 9.
[23] *ibid*, p. 10.
[24] Editorial - Dialectics of New Thinking, *Kommunist*, no. 1987, pp. 3-5.
[25] *ibid*, p.6.
[26] Leading Article - Political Vanguard of the Society, *Kommunist*, no. 1, January 1988, pp. 4-7.
[27] N. Sliunkov, Restructuring and Party Guidance on Economy, *Kommunist*, no. 1, January 1988, no. 1, p. 12.
[28] Speech of Gorbachev to 18 February 1988 Central Committee Plenum - Towards Revolutionary Perestroika - The Ideology of Renewal, *Kommunist*, March 1988, no. 4, p. 4.
[29] Leading Article - Ideology of Thought and Action, *Kommunist*, March 1988, no. 5, p. 3.
[30] *ibid*, pp.4-7.
[31] Editorial - Revolution, Perestroika, Humanism, *Kommunist*, no.15, October 1988, p.9-10.
[32] V. Koptyug, Democratisation of the Party - Democratisation of Society, *Kommunist*, no. 7, 1988, p. 35.
[33] Towards New Image of Socialism, *Kommunist*, no. 13, 1989, p. 8.
[34] *ibid*, p.15.
[35] Arbatov and Batalov, Political Reform and Evolution of Soviet Government, *Kommunist*, no. 4, 1989, pp. 36-43.
[36] E. Teague Gorbachev Answers His Critics, *RL280/87*, 15 July 1987, pp. 1-3.

[37] M. Gorbachev, Socialist Idea and Revolutionary Perestroika, *Kommunist*, no. 18, November 1989, pp.3-4.
[38] DR, 23 April 1990, p. 58.
[39] In an article in *Kommunist* entitled, *Towards Cognition of Socialism,* Vadim Medvedev contended Lenin's ideas evolved from War Communism to NEP and the main problem was to understand his ideas in the context of the present situation.[V.Medvedev, Towards Cognition of Socialism, *Kommunist*, no. 17, 1988, pp. 5-18.
[40] DR, 16 Dec. 1988, pp. 53-56.
[41] DR, 2 June 1989, p. 27 Vadim Medvedev in an interview to *Le Monde* published on 25 May 1989.
[42] *ibid*,p.28.
[43] *ibid*, p.29.
[44] Interview with Fred Wier, journalist in Moscow, August 1992.
[45] V. Medvedev, A Test by History, no. 17, November 1990, pp. 3-14.
[46] G. Shakhnazarov, Renewal of Ideology and Ideology of Renewal, *Kommunist*, no. 4, March 1990, pp. 46-59.
[47] *Pravda*, 26 April 1989, p. 1 in *FBIS*, 26 April 1989, p. 47.
[48] *Pravda*, 16 October 1989, p. 2 in *FBIS*, 20 October 1989, p. 37.
[49] "Revolution from Below", The Second Russian Revolution, *BBC Television, Channel 2,* 21 June 1991.
[50] Interview with Boris Kluev.
[51] *AFP,* 1940 GMT, 14 June 1989, in *FBIS*, 15 June 1989, p. 39.
[52] *Pravda*, 26 March 1990, pp. 1-2, in *FBIS*, 26 March 1990, p. 59. Between the start of the year and 23 February 1990, 1,500 rallies were held across the country with 6.4 million people participating. There were 500 pre-election rallies on 24-25 February 1990 with more than 1 million participants. On three days in March 1990, 73 rallies were held with the participation of 124,600 people. By comparison, during the whole of 1989, 5,300 rallies were held with the participation of 12.6 million people.
[53] *Pravda*, 6 February 1990, pp. 3-4 in *FBIS*, 7 February 1990, pp. 52-53.
[54] "The Party Cannot Lag Behind", *Kommunist* , no. 4, 1990, p. 5.
[55] *Pravda*, 6 February 1990, p. 1,2 in *FBIS*, 6 February 1990, p. 44-48.
[56] *ibid.*, pp. 3-4 in *FBIS*, 7 February 1990, pp. 52-53.
[57] *ibid.*, p. 5, in *FBIS*, 7 February 1990, pp. 54-56.
[58] *Pravda*, 7 February 1990, p. 2 in *FBIS*, 7 February 1990, pp. 58-60.
[59] *AFP,* 1123 GMT, 6 February 1990 in *FBIS*, 7 February 1990, p. 79.
[60] *Veteran,* no. 13, 26 March-1 April 1990, pp. 2-3 in *FBIS*, 17 April 1990, pp. 56-58.
[61] *TASS International Service*, 1216 GMT, 6 February in *FBIS*, 7 February 1990, p. 80.
[62] *Pravda*, 8 February 1990, p. 5 in *FBIS*, 8 February 1990, p. 57.
[63] *Pravda*, 7 February 1990, p. 4 in *FBIS*, 8 February 1990, p. 76-77.
[64] *Pravda*, 8 February 1990, p. 6 in *FBIS*, 9 February 1990, pp. 66-67.
[65] *Pravda*, 9 February 1990, p. 2 in *FBIS*, 12 February 1990, pp. 89-90.
[66] *Pravda*, 8 February 1990, p. 2 in *FBIS*, 15 February 1990, pp. 60-62.

[67] *Moscow Domestic Service*, 1600 GMT, 12 February 1990 in *FBIS*, 14 February 1990, p. 55.
[68] *Pravda*, 8 February 1990, pp. 2-3 in *FBIS*, 9 February 1990, pp. 78-80.
[69] *Pravda*, 9 February 1990, p. 2 in *FBIS*, 12 February 1990, pp. 92-93.
[70] *Pravda*, 8 February 1990, p. 2 in *FBIS*, 15 February 1990, pp. 62-64.
[71] *Pravda*, 6 February 1990, pp. 5-6 in *FBIS*, 12 February 1990, pp. 93-95.
[72] *Pravda*, 9 February 1990, p. 4 in *FBIS*, 12 February 1990, pp. 72-73.
[73] *Pravda*, 6 February 1990, pp. 3-4 in *FBIS*, 7 February 1990, pp. 52-53.
[74] *ibid*., pp. 5-6 in *FBIS*, 12 February 1990, pp. 93-95.
[75] *Pravda*, 7 February 1990, pp. 2-6 in *FBIS*, 8 February 1990, pp. 61-78.
[76] *Pravda*, 6 February 1990, p. 3 in *FBIS*, 7 February 1990, p. 71.
[77] *Pravda*, 7 February 1990, p. 5 in *FBIS*, 7 February 1990, pp. 84-85.
[78] *Pravda*, 8 February 1990, p. 5 in *FBIS*, 8 February 1990, p. 57.
[79] *Pravda*, 8 February 1990, p. 2 in *FBIS*, 8 February 1990, pp. 65-66.
[80] *Pravda*, 8 February 1990, pp. 4-5 in *FBIS*, 9 February 1990, pp. 64-65.
[81] *Pravda*, 9 February 1990, p. 2 in *FBIS*, 12 February 1990, pp. 89-90.
[82] *Pravda*, 7 February 1990, pp. 4-5 in *FBIS*, 9 February 1990, pp. 84-85.
[83] *Pravda*, 6 February 1990, p. 5 in *FBIS*, 7 February 1990, pp. 54-55.
[84] *Pravda*, 7 February 1990, p. 2 in *FBIS*, 7 February 1990, pp. 58-60.
[85] *TASS International Service,* 1216 GMT, 6 February 1990, in *FBIS*, 7 February 1990, p. 80.
[86] *Pravda*, 8 February 1990, p. 6 in *FBIS*, 9 February 1990, pp. 72-73.
[87] *Budapest Television Services,* 2030 GMT, 12 February 1990, in *FBIS*, 13 February 1990, p. 55.
[88] *Moscow World Service,* 1800 GMT, 17 February 1990, in *FBIS*, 20 February 1990, p. 53.
[89] *Pravda*, 17 March 1990, pp. 2-4, in *FBIS*, 20 March 1990, p. 48-58.
[90] *Pravda*, 20 March 1990, pp. 2-4, in *FBIS*, 22 March 1990, pp. 38-39.
[91] G. B. Smith, *Soviet Politics- Struggling with Change,* Macmillan, 1992, p. 94.
[92] *Moscow All-Union Network Radio Mayak Network,* 2100 GMT, 18 March 1991 in *FBIS*, 19 March 1991,
p. 33. According to Zagladin, an adviser to Gorbachev.
[93] *Moscow Domestic Service*, 1115 GMT, 1 April 1990 in *FBIS*, 2 April 1990, p. 44.
[94] *Pravda*, 16 April 1990, p. 1 in *FBIS*, 16 April 1990, pp. 46-47.
[95] *XXVII CPSU Congress*, Report by M. Gorbachev, Soviet Land Booklets, Moscow, 1990, pp. 9-10.
[96] Interview with I.I. Melnikov, former Secretary of the CPSU Central Committee, Moscow, September 1992.
[97] Interview with A.V. Buzgalin, former member of the Central Committee, Moscow, September 1992.
[98] *Pravda*, 4 February 1991, p. 4, in *FBIS*, 7 February 1991, pp. 44-45.
[99] *Pravda*, 5 February 1991, p. 3, in *FBIS*, 11 February 1991, pp. 39-40.
[100] *Pravda*, 4 February 1991, p. 4, in *FBIS*, 6 February 1991, pp. 52-53.
[101] *Pravda*, 4 February 1991, pp. 3-4, in *FBIS*, 5 February 1991, pp. 24-25.
[102] *Pravda*, 4 February 1991, p. 3, in *FBIS*, 6 February 1991, p. 51.

[103] *Pravda*, 4 February 1991, pp. 3-4, in *FBIS*, 5 February 1991, pp. 27- 28.
[104] *Pravda*, 5 February 1991, p. 4, in *FBIS*, 6 February 1991, p. 53.
[105] *Pravda*, 4 February 1991, p. 3, in *FBIS*, 8 February 1991, p. 35.
[106] *Sovetskaia rossiia*, 2 February 1991, p. 2, in *FBIS*, 4 February 1991, pp. 29-30.
[107] *Moscow Domestic Service*, 1400 GMT, 4 February 1991, in *FBIS*, 5 February 1991, p. 29.
[108] *Pravda*, 5 February 1991, p. 3, in *FBIS*, 11 February 1991, pp. 39-40.
[109] *Krasnaia zvezda*, 6 February 1991, p. 1, in *FBIS*, 8 February 1991, p. 33.
[110] *Pravda*, 5 February 1991, pp. 3-4, in *FBIS*, 7 February 1991, pp. 41-44.
[111] *Pravda*, 26 April 1991, pp. 1-2 in *FBIS*, 26 April 1991, pp. 19-22.
[112] A. McAuley, "Poverty and Underprivileged Groups", in D. Lane ed. *Russia in Flux*, Edward Elgar, (Hants, 1992) pp. 204-5.
[113] *L'Unita*, 14 April 1991, p. 13, in *FBIS*, 17 April 1991, pp. 24-25.
[114] *Komsomolskaia Pravda*, 12 April 1991, p. 2, in *FBIS*, 17 April 1991, p. 27.
[115] *Izvestiia*, 24 April 1991, p. 1, in *FBIS*, 24 April 1991, p. 27.
[116] *Pravda*, 26 April 1991, p. 3 in *FBIS*, 26 April 1991, p. 31.
[117] *Pravda*, 24 April 1991, pp. 1-2, in *FBIS*, 25 April 1991, p. 24.
[118] *TASS*, 1847 GMT, 25 April 1991, in *FBIS*, 26 April 1991, p. 16.
[119] *Moscow Central Television* , 1800 GMT, 25 April 1991, in *FBIS*, 26 April 1991, pp. 16-17.
[120] *ibid.*, 1842 GMT, 3 July 1991, in *FBIS*, 5 July 1991, p. 42.
[121] *Pravda*, 26 April 1991, p. 3 in *FBIS*, 26 April 1991, p. 31.
[122] *Moskovskaia Pravda*, 27 April 1991, p. 2 in *FBIS*, 3 May 1991, p. 21.
[123] *Pravda*, 26 April 1991, p. 3 in *FBIS*, 29 April 1991, pp. 2-3.
[124] *Sovetskaia rossiia*, 27 April 1991, p. 2 in *FBIS*, 29 April 1991, pp. 3-4.
[125] *Pravda*, 27 April 1991, p. 3 in *FBIS*, 29 April 1991, p. 11.
[126] He said at the plenum that he had been elected as a representative of the minority trend in the Party.
[127] *Pravda*, 29 April 1991, pp. 3-4 in *FBIS*, 29 April 1991, pp. 32-33.
[128] *Pravda*, 27 April 1991, p. 4 in *FBIS*, 29 April 1991, pp. 12-13.
[129] *Pravda*, 29 April 1991, p. 3 in *FBIS*, 29 April 1991, pp. 18-19.
[130] *Pravda*, 27 April 1991, pp. 3-4 in *FBIS*, 29 April 1991, pp. 20-26.
[131] *Pravda*, 26 April 1991, p. 3 in *FBIS*, 29 April 1991, p. 1.
[132] *Pravda*, 29 April 1991, p. 4 in *FBIS*, 29 April 1991, p. 31-33.
[133] *Pravda*, 27 April 1991, p. 3 in *FBIS*, 29 April 1991, p. 29.
[134] *Pravda*, 29 April 1991, pp. 3-4 in *FBIS*, 29 April 1991, pp. 5-31.
[135] *Pravda*, 29 April 1991, pp. 3- 5 in *FBIS*, 29 April 1991, p. 14-18.
[136] *Pravda*, 27 April 1991, p. 4 in *FBIS*, 29 April 1991, pp. 27-29.
[137] *Pravda*, 29 April 1991, p. 4 in *FBIS*, 29 April 1991, p. 33.
[138] *TASS*, 1151 GMT, 20 June 1991, in *FBIS*, 21 June 1991, p. 31.
[139] *TASS*, 1928 GMT, 10 June 1991, in *FBIS*, 11 June 1991, p. 46.
[140] *Izvestiia*, 4 July 1991, p. 1, in *FBIS*, 9 July 1991, p. 41.
[141] *Komsomolskaia Pravda*, 5 July 1991, p. 1, in *FBIS*, 5 July 1991, p. 40.
[142] *Sovetskaia rossiia*, 3 August 1991, p. 1 in *FBIS*, 6 August 1991, p. 29.

[143] *Interfax*, 1230 GMT, 2 July 1991 in *FBIS*, 3 July 1991, p. 37
[144] *TASS*, 1215 GMT, 25 July 1991 in *FBIS*, 26 July 1991, p. 32.
[145] *Moscow Television Centre*, 1700 GMT, 1 June 1990 in *FBIS*, 12 June 1990, pp. 61-62
[146] Gorbachev Addresses Plenum, *Pravda*, 26 July 1991, pp. 1-2 in *FBIS*, 26 July 1991, p.
[147] Interview with I. I. Melnikov, former Secretary of the Central Committee of the CPSU, Moscow, September 1992.
[148] *ibid.*, pp. 24-31.
[149] *Rossiiskaia gazeta*, 27 July 1991, p.1 in *FBIS*, 30 July 1991, p. 43.
[150] *Pravda*, 27 July 1991, p. 2 in *FBIS*, 30 July 1991, p. 45.
[151] *Moscow Central Television*, 1800 GMT, 26 July 1991, *FBIS*, 30 July 1991, p. 46.
[152] *ibid.*, 2021 GMT, 24 July 1991 in *FBIS*, 25 July 1991, p. 37.
[153] *L'Unita,* 22 July 1991, p. 4 in *FBIS*, 24 July 1991,pp. 30-31.
[154] This did not seem very different from the manifesto of the Democratic Reform Movement.
[155] Rabochaia tribuna, 27 July 1991, p. 2 in *FBIS*, 29 July 1991, p. 42.
[156] *ibid.*, pp. 44-45.
[157] *Pravda*, 27 July 1991, p. 5 in *FBIS*, 29 July 1991, p. 46.
[158] *Pravda*, 29 July 1991, p. 3 and 5 in *FBIS*, 1 August 1991, p. 3 and pp. 6-7.
[159] *Pravda*, 27 July 1991, pp. 4-5 in *FBIS*, 1 August 1991, pp. 7-18.
[160] *TASS*, 26 July 1991, 1215 GMT in *FBIS*, 26 July 1991, p. 32.
[161] *Sovetskaia rossiia*, 27 July 1991, p. 2 in *FBIS*, 1 August 1991, p. 13.
[162] *ibid.*, p. 49.
[163] *Pravda*, 27 July 1991, p. 4 in *FBIS*, 1 August 1991, pp. 1-2.
[164] *Pravda*, 29 July 1991, p. 4 in *FBIS*, 1 August 1991, pp. 15-16.
[165] *Interfax*, 1500 GMT, 25 July 1991 in *FBIS*, 26 July 1991, p. 32.
[166] Section 2 stated: 'A part of the People's Deputies of the USSR and other republics may be elected by public organisations.'
[167] The issue was discussed at the Fourth Congress on 24 December 1990.
[168] The issue was discussed at the Fourth Congress on 25 December 1990.
[169] It was discussed at the Fourth Congress on 24 December 1990.
[170] Several others too received higher points in the index.
[171] Calculated from *Indem Data Base*, Moscow; *RL 145/86,* 1 April 1986, pp. 1-23 and *RL 151/86*, 9 April 1986, pp. 1-14.
[172] S. White, G. Gill and D. Slider , *The Politics of Transition, Shaping a Post-Soviet Future,* (hereafter S. White, G. Gill and D. Slider, 1993), Cambridge University Press, (Cambridge, 1993), p. 127.
[173] *ibid.*, see Chapter Three.
[174] *ibid.*, see Chapter Eight.

6 Transforming the Political Leadership after the 19th Party Conference

Introduction

The changes in the composition of the Central Committee[1] were integral to the process of reforms. These took place at two levels, viz institutional representation and in the individual membership. Institutional reforms changed the nature of the institutions, particularly those of the State, represented in the Central Committee. New institutions and social forces, both economic and social, came to be represented. The generation which ascended to the positions of power in the 1930s started leaving the political stage for reasons of illness, infirmity and incompatibilty with the new politically reformist thinking and policy-orientation. To become a viable leadership organ, the Central Committee had to become more representative of those sections of society whose politics and policies were benign to them, it proposed to articulate since economic reforms resulted in the birth of newer socio-economic forces. However, it could not possibly have incorporated all the emergent ones since many were fundamentally antagonistic to each other. This could only have been undertaken if the political leadership developed an arbitrating mechanism, a necessary condition for an as yet hypothetical one-party democratisation.

The reformist leadership had initially hoped that the Central Committee would be able to provide political leadership by formulating policies and laying down a central political line under which State institutions would operate in the new circumstances of one-party democratisation. The Party would be able to represent a wide array of socio-economic forces and could become a forum where different political and policy-orientations could be articulated and arbitrated, thus maintaining its vanguard role. These were to be those of different sections of society rather than primarily of the ministries, State committees, Party and State apparatuses, military and the KGB, as in the past. Ministerial interests had long been predominant because of the vital position of the ministries in a centrally planned economy. Ministries continued to be represented during Perestroika, although in drastically reduced numbers. However, those directly concerned with economy and agriculture were excluded. The ministries now represented were mainly concerned with the administrative arm of the State and with social affairs.

The Central Committee no longer provided the forum for the resolution of conflicts of competing intra-ministerial interests. The newly defined vanguard role was to be different from that hitherto practised, based not on coercion but on consent and consensus, thus attempting to maintain the political equilibrium of the system. The concept of consent was to be active rather than passive. The former implied an active citizenry participating in the political process through parliamentary and extra-parliamentary means such as informal groups. The Party as a whole, and not the Party and the State organs, were to exercise the vanguard role. However, with the emerging contours of a multi-party system, the meaning of the separation of the Party and State was changing. The emergence of a multi-party system was both a consequence of the separation of the Party and State and a cause which further propelled this process. In accordance with the 19th Party Conference, the Party was to implement its political course through the Party members working in the organs of State power[2].But if a multi-party system was accepted then either all the other parties had the same rights or none at all. Elective organs of State power could be open for political competition, but not the permanent ones such as the State committees. One fundamental shortcoming was that the separation was incomplete because of the continued representation of several State institutions. It seems, however, that the leaders of State institutions now primarily derived their authority and power from the State institutions themselves rather than the Central Committee unlike in the past.

With the possibility of other political parties emerging, the vanguard role and monopoly of political power by the Party and the Central Committee were in doubt and logically untenable. A new State system with separation of powers and parliamentarism was evolving. In both conditions, its separation from the State institutions was imperative, although more so in the latter case. A single party could no longer exercise monopoly over State institutions either directly or indirectly. In both cases it was a necessary precondition for the revival of the Party as a political organism. This also entailed federalisation of the Central Committee and granting greater rights to the lower Party bodies in its election, particularly in view of resurgent nationalist sentiments. Lower tiers of Party and mass organisations had to be better represented to ensure that the problems of the population were better articulated in this body. Changes in the composition of the Central Committee, and the long-standing principles governing it, were thus necessary for its transformation. However since the system itself was in transition, the separation of the Central Committee from State institutions, although substantial, was not taken to its logical culmination. The duality of the system of the Party and the State bodies continued to be reflected in its composition. Yet, on the whole, it can be argued that the changes in the composition of the Central Committee stemmed from the fundamental reform of the separation of the Party and the State and had gone a significant way. The dynamics that culminated in the changes in the composition of the Central Committee as a part of the process of separation of the Party and the State was effectively set in motion at the 25th April 1989 Central Committee plenum.

The 25th April 1989 CPSU Central Committee Plenum

The General Secretary, after assuming office, would initiate the process of change in the Central Committee's composition to consolidate his position. He would inherit the Central Committee and the Politburo and would then have to contend with the institutions and the members represented in them. Under Brezhnev, these institutions had acquired relative autonomy because of their institutionalisation. Thus the Central Committee had their representatives with strong institutional loyalties. These institutions and the majority of their leading personnel were conservatives. Although a major turnover took place at the 27th Party Congress prompted by a generational change, within three years the Central Committee had 58 "dead souls" - members who had died, retired or who were removed from posts which entitled them to membership. This constituted about 19 per cent of the full membership.[3] These members could easily have left the Central Committee at the 27th Party Congress. Partly because of the system of the representation of posts some individuals remained. Yet another factor which seemed more crucial was that they represented the most conservative sections which were still significantly strong within the Party and the State organs. No changes took place in the composition of the Central Committee at the 19th Party Conference.[4] Rule 34 of the Party rules stated that vacancies could only be filled from the candidate membership,[5] but this was more conservative than reformist.[6] In accordance with the old Party rules they would have remained in the Central Committee until the next Party Congress. The rules were changed only at the 28th Party Congress so that up to one-third of the membership could be replaced between the Congresses. Conferences held between the Party congresses could make these changes.[7] The adoption of "Instruction on the Conduct of Elections to Leading Party Organs" in August 1988 provided for recall of inactive members and the renewal of Party committees, including the Central Committee, up to 20 per cent at five yearly Party conferences.[8]

The major inter-Congress reshuffle came at the 25th April 1989 Central Committee plenum in which 98 members resigned en masse. These included 74 full and 24 candidate members.[9] The March 1989 elections had the most important bearing on these mass resignations. Although a large number of Party members returned victorious[10] after the elections, several senior Party officials suffered humiliating defeats in a number of places. For example, in Leningrad all six Party and Soviet leaders of the city and the oblast failed to get elected.[11] The election resulted in an increased political polarisation between the reformists and conservatives. Soviet sources at the time expected an offensive against Gorbachev's reform programme at the special plenary session of the Central Committee. Reforms were blamed as the chief reason for the defeat and for other problems. The Leningrad Party organisation, considered a bastion of the conservatives, had officially asked earlier that month to discuss the "work of the Party" at the forthcoming plenum.[12] This could have resulted in the reconsideration of the reforms but the reformists won this round. The election results gave an opportunity to remove an influential section of the Central Committee.[13] This was a serious blow to the Party organs, essentially the conservatives, and weakened their position considerably. The reformist section of the Party had gained in the elections, thus strengthening its position vis-a-vis the conservatives. The results were deemed to be a vote for reforms.[14] The election results gave a major opportunity to renew the Party bodies, particularly the leading ones.

The conservative section of the Party did not seem to be reconciled to reforms, particularly that of a multi-candidate electoral system, which threatened their position of power. Resistance to the resignations at the April 1989 plenum was part of the general opposition to the reformist course. However, the base of conservatives within the Party seemed to have been eroded.[15] Representation of the Party and State apparatuses and military fell. The intelligentsia, mass organisations, workers and peasants and the diplomatic services were better represented.[16] This pattern of changes in the representation of various occupational categories was followed when the new Central Committee was elected at the 28th Party Congress, with the exception of the diplomatic corps, whose representation fell drastically. The number of State and government officials registered a much steeper decline at the 28th Party Congress than at the April 1989 Plenum.[17] In the case of the intelligentsia, mass organisations and workers and peasants, the upward trend of representation continued at the 28th Party Congress. The retirees included most of the Soviet officials who had left the posts qualifying them for membership.[18] Although several leading officials of the Party were outside the Central Committee, including six out of 14 first secretaries of the Union-Republics and 88 out of 150 first secretaries of the krai and oblast Party committees,[19] only 24 new members were elected. The occupational breakdown[20] reveals that although the number of Party officials was quite high among the new entrants, the number of workers, peasants and intelligentsia elected to the Central Committee was proportionately very high compared to the past,[21] a trend continued at the 28th Party Congress.

The resignations were seen as opening the way to bring in reformist members and "to regroup forces". The departure of a generation which was responsible for the era of stagnation however was not smooth, as was hinted in the speech of A.P. Nochevkin. He was unhappy with the way resignations were taking place, and wanted an open vote or consultation with Party members in the primary Party organisations on the appeal to resign.[22] His speech gave some idea of the resistance to the resignations.

This change was also preceded by a major reshuffle of personnel in lower Party bodies through Party elections. In the election campaign, 37 per cent or 160,000 secretaries were replaced, and 1,433 new regional and city Party committee secretaries were elected.[23] In addition, between 1986 and 1989 all the 14 republican Party secretaries had been replaced, some more than once. Two-thirds of the secretaries of regional, territorial and Union-Republic Party organisations, and about 70 per cent at the district and city level, had been replaced towards the end of 1988.[24] Thus the elections themselves had been preceded by a major 'cleansing' of the lower Party organisations. Such a turnover weakened the support of the most conservative sections within the Party apparatus.[25] This plenum was preceded by the report back and election meetings, conferences and plenums which were held in the Party organisations at various levels.[26] These changes undermined the support base of the conservative sections, prepared the ground for the resignations and facilitated the reshuffle.

The Central Committee Elected at the 28th Party Congress

Major changes in the composition of the Central Committee came at the 28th Party Congress. They were necessitated by the separation of the Party and the State and had far-reaching consequences. The Congress elected a new Central Committee with 412 full and no candidate members by a secret ballot on 13 July 1990. The category of candidate members was abolished in accordance with the new rules.[27] 54 members received more than 500 votes against.[28] Most of them were proposed on the central list. A. Bessmertnikh represented Party organisations of Soviet institutions abroad.[29]

Only 58 members elected in 1981 and 1986 were left in 1990. The new Central Committee included 354 new members who had not been members of either of the Central Committees elected at the 26th or the 27th Party Congresses.[30] Only 38 or 9.22 per cent of the previous Central Committee members continued in 1990. Only 20 of the 170 candidate members or 11.4 per cent elected at the 27th Party Congress were promoted to full membership of the Central Committee at the 28th Party Congress. For comparison, the numbers promoted from previous Central Committees is much lower in 1956 and 1961 (the Khrushchev era) than between 1966 and 1981 (the Brezhnev era). The case was similar with those promoted from candidate membership or the CAC. In both cases the figures were very low in 1961, much lower even compared to 1956, indicating the high period of Khrushchevian reforms, before rising phenomenally in 1966, the period when Brezhnev's era of 'stability of cadres' began. The similarity between 1961 and 1990, which represent the peak of Gorbachevian reforms is striking, although the fall was much more drastic in 1990. This suggested a continuity of approach in the two periods. In both cases changes in the composition were seen as an important instrument of reforms.

The number of members re-elected to the 1990 Central Committee from 1986 was particularly high, indicating the continuation of some members of the initial reformist team into the new body. The 20 promoted members included five from the Central Party category, five obkom officials, three from the State and government category, two from the Soviets, and one each from the media, mass organisations, industry and intelligentsia. Thus the largest number of those promoted were from the Party, i.e. eleven.[31] The degree of renewal could be gauged from the fact that 157 out of 412 members of the Central Committee were not in 22,000 names listed as "active" in the SOVT computerised register.[32] This indicated "not only a generational change in the political elite, but also a profound transformation of its outlook".[33]

The abolition of the 'reserve pool' or candidate members who were promoted to full membership between Congresses, and from amongst whom a sizeable section was usually recruited to full membership at a Congress, was a major departure from the principle of the organisation of the Central Committee. It meant opening up the membership to a wider field of recruitment of reform-minded individuals rather than restricting it to a limited pool of candidate members. This appeared to be a logical culmination of the practice which had began at the 27th Party Congress, when a very large number of the new membership (97) had not previously been part of the higher leadership echelons. Such a big turnover represented a major purging of those remaining from the Brezhnev era, with relatively more reform-oriented members joining the Central Committee.

The Party, State and government representation in the Central Committee, according to geographical area, was reduced considerably, particularly in bigger republics like the RSFSR and Ukraine. In other republics, the variations were less marked.[34] This seemed to result from the process of federalisation, particularly in the case of the Party representation. In the case of the RSFSR it fell drastically from 87 to 48, in the Ukraine from 25 to 14, and in Kazakhstan from 16 to 12. For Belorussia the reduction was marginal, from seven to six. The dominance of larger republics, particularly Russia, had been a contributing factor in the resurgence of the nationalist sentiments. A system of proportional representation within the Central Committee now restored the equilibrium. In the case of Lithuania, Latvia and Estonia it rose from two each to five, four and four respectively. State and government representation on the whole fell dramatically overall from 124 to 36 in the case of the central category. For the RSFSR it fell from 18 to 15 and for the Ukraine from seven to four. For Kazhakhstan it increased from three to four, whereas for Belorussia it dropped from four to two. Lithuania, Armenia and Estonia had no representation in the State and the government category, as against two each previously. The reason may have been that these republics had non-Communist governments. Moldavia and Latvia with opposition governments had a reduced representation of one as against two each previously. A noticeable feature was the increased Party representation from the Baltic republics, with the highest increase from Lithuania, perhaps to bolster support in the rebellious republics.[35]

The system of electing the Central Committee was completely transformed at the 28th Party Congress. This issue had been raised prior to the 19th Party Conference. It was asked why Party members and the people should not know why and by whom members were elected to the Central Committee, what was said about each candidate and what was the distribution of votes. Making Central Committee membership some sort of "honorary addendum to an official post" was undemocratic. It was suggested that the highest Party bodies be elected in open sessions at the Congress and according to personal merit and not official posts.[36] Such a system allowed for the indirect election of Central Committee members. This could have shaped it as a parliament of the Party; Party organisations could choose their representatives. Although this did not make the system of elections necessarily democratic, it was certainly more so than before. The election of the Central Committee at the 28th Party Congress was a step in that direction. Yet until its stabilisation such a system was more likely to accentuate cleavages in the Central Committee along national-territorial lines and those of social, economic and other interests.

The basic principles for the formation of the Central Committee were discussed and approved at a meeting of the council of delegations' representatives. A quota system was established for the Union-Republic Communist Parties, and the territory and province Party committees. Each republic was guaranteed a minimum of five seats. The total number of members was calculated on the basis of the number of Party members in those Party organisations, including those in the autonomous provinces. 100,000 Party members were represented by one member in the Central Committee. On the basis of this norm a total number of 311 members were initially proposed in the first list presented to the Congress. Another list, a central list, included 85 names of the officials of Central agencies, scientific and cultural figures, workers enjoying authority in the Party organisations and secretaries of primary Party organisations. This list included the nominees of the leadership. Thus the initial list of new members proposed was 398, including the General Secretary and the deputy General Secretary.[37] The final number of members elected (i. e. 412 compared with the initial proposed number of 398) was because 14 more individuals with divergent opinions were added later on to the central list. According to Prokofiev "... had (they) not been elected this would have demonstrated a lack of tolerance of dissent",[38] something unimaginable in the past.[39] For the first time, nominations came from lower Party organisations. Candidates on the first list were nominated by the republican, krai and oblast Party organisations, by the Party organisations in the Soviet army, the navy, the border troops, the internal troops of the USSR Ministry of Internal Affairs, and Soviet establishments abroad. The elections were conducted by secret ballot in which 4,459 out of 4,683 delegates voted.[40] In the past, the composition of the Central Committee was essentially determined by the proposals made by the central apparatus. These proposals were considered by the Politburo and presented to the Congress for election. At the 28th Party Congress the proposals for the Central Committee came from 'below' or from the regions, because of the new quota system. For example, during the election campaign of delegates to the Congress, 84 candidates were nominated from Moscow. This number fell to 78 at the Moscow city conference by excluding the members of the then Central Committee on the initial list until the Central Committee had given its report. Out of these 11 were finally selected to be nominated by the Moscow Party organisation at a secret ballot in which 278 people attending the conference of the Moscow group of delegates to the 28th Congress participated. All of these eleven nominees were finally elected. They included four workers, three secretaries of the local Party organisations, the first secretary of the gorkom, and three prominent members of the Moscow intelligentsia: P. Bunich, Latsis and Shatalin.[41] This would have been inconceivable at the 27th Party Congress or earlier. Gorbachev, in his report to the 19th Party Conference, had mooted the proposal that during elections to all Party committees up to the Central Committee more candidates than the number to be elected be proposed, and that nominations were "to be guided in this not by what post is held by a person but by his stance on restructuring".[42]

Hence the system of constituting the Central Committee was completely reformed. The previous practice of constituting it from the 'top' in a carefully controlled selection process was overturned at this Congress. The lower echelons of the Party organisations now determined who was going to represent them in the highest organ of the leadership. Of the two lists proposed at the Congress, the first could be characterised as a representative list and the other a non-representative list. However the system of election was much more democratic than in the past. It gave Party organisations the right to elect their representatives in the Central Committee. This meant a devolution of power and authority to lower levels. The hierarchical system of the transmission of power and authority was diminished and lateral linkages became more significant. On the one hand it made the Central Committee more responsive to the interests of subordinate tiers, but on the other hand it undermined its previous integrity. Such a devolution, however, seemed to be the only way to democratise it as a body, and allow it to play a significant role in contemporary conditions by incorporating newly emerging and unrepresented interests. This was a step in the direction of adjusting the composition of the Central Committee to contemporary conditions.

Most of the smaller republican parties gained in terms of the increased representation of provincial officials in the Central Committee, breaking the earlier pattern.[43] Larger republican Party organisations, particularly in the RSFSR, Ukraine, Kazakhstan and Belorussia, were losers with the introduction of the system of "proportional representation". The decrease in the dominant role of the larger republican Party organisations, particularly the RSFSR in the Central Committee may have been a direct consequence of the aspiration of smaller republican Party organisations, particularly in the Baltics, to acquire independence from the CPSU. Some of them had no representation in this body in the past. However, inherent in such a system of organisation was a potential split along national lines, something which became increasingly evident. Soviet leaders in the past had always claimed that the national question had been resolved, something which the events unfolding under Perestroika showed to be otherwise. The Party leadership seemed to be taking belated steps to accomodate such an intense manifestation of nationalism. But it was a case of too little, too late. With centrifugal national forces spinning out of control in the entire political system and the CPSU, the various national contingents in the Central Committee coexisted tenuously.

All the Union-Republics had representation, unlike in the past. (For example, the Azerbaijan Party organisation had no representation for several years.[44]) This system of representation gave it a federalist character. Previously, the Central Committee had an unitary character, and the representation of various nationalities was not a factor in determining the composition of the Central Committee. But during the period under study, the resurgence of nationalism in the country was reflected in the Party, and played an important role in giving the Central Committee elected at the 28th Party Congress a federalist character. Federalism entailed the redistribution and decentralisation of power and authority within the Party. The Central Committee became both a platform for debating diverse points of views and an institution formulating overall policies with the participation and the direct input of the lower Party committees represented in it. In the past their interests may have been taken into account, but they were subordinated to other dominant interests, chiefly those of the ministries. Expression of interests based on local specifications which had threatened the integrity of the centralised political and economic system was discouraged, to say the least. The Central Committee now became a forum for the frequent airing of, for instance, nationalist aspirations and grievances. Lower Party committees including PPOs could put forward their opinions and positions on various issues. This federalism was similar to the conception of federalism in the State system, in that it sought to integrate the myriad Party organisations and interests in a common political space while granting them autonomy. However, federalism entails compromise and consensus, and it was precisely this that seemed to be lacking, hence the centrifugal tendency within this body. On the one hand, this was a consequence of the external political environment impinging on it; on the other, the problem of transition from a centralised body to a democratic one.

Important State institutions like the Army, the Navy, the KGB and MVD continued to be represented, although at considerably reduced strength, in contradiction to the declared aim of the separation of the Party and State.[45] A high number of members, i.e. eleven, were from the Army and Navy and one each from the KGB and MVD. Six of the military members were associated with either the political wing of the military or the Party committees in it. Now the political arm of the military instead of military commands represented their interests. The Central Committee clearly wanted to retain control over the military. However this was consistent with the approach of the reformist section of the leadership, which viewed this period as one of transition. It was also in accordance with the conception of the separation of the Party and State formulated at the 28th Party Congress. The major difference was that intra-military interests were no longer brokered within this body. And the military as a bloc of various commands was no longer present.

Major reforms took place in the system of occupational representation in the Central Committee. The proportion of the 'central Party' was reduced drastically to 5.1 per cent in 1990. The representation of the 'regional Party' category fell as well. By contrast, that of the 'local Party' category rose sharply, to 10 per cent in 1990. The role of the lowest echelons of the Party, which interacted more closely with the population, became more significant in the conditions of political competition. Likewise, the share of the 'mass representative' category increased greatly, to 31.6 per cent. Thus those tiers of the Party and mass organisations which could potentially mobilise political support in an emerging multi-party system were to become important. The hierarchical system of organisation of the Party leadership was abandoned in favour of a system in which horizontal linkages were crucial. The nature of the mass organisations represented, however, completely changed, as discussed later. Traditional mass organisations were no longer represented. Several did not even seem to exist any longer.

Representation of the 'central State' category went down dramatically to 6.6 per cent. Similarly the representation of the 'regional State' category decreased to 4.9 per cent in 1990. That of other State institutions like the military and the diplomatic corps was reduced as well. In the case of the 'military' category, it fell to 2.7 per cent. For the diplomatic corps, only 0.5 per cent were left.[46] The separation of the Party and State, which had started at the lower levels, thus reached the highest echelons.

A high number of obkom and primary Party officials were represented.[47] The executive agencies of State and government, including the military and KGB, had a much higher representation, i.e. 63 out of 87, than the representative institutions like Soviets which accounted for the rest.[48] This, indeed, was contrary to the declared intentions of separation. However they no longer derived their power and authority from the Central Committee. The sizeable increase in the proportion of industrial and agricultural workers in the Central Committee elected at the 28th Party Congress points to an attempt to draw support from the working class and the peasantry. Their representation rose sharply to 104.[49] Previously the working class and peasantry had only a token representation in the Central Committee. The emergence of independent trade unions outside the influence of the Party may have been a compelling reason for the increased inclusion of workers, though this would not prove successful in enhancing the influence of the Party on the working class. The representation of the 'intelligentsia' more than doubled, to 57 in 1990.[50] The increased representation of this important section of the society was commensurate with its crucial role in Perestroika. All the increases in the representation of the 'intelligentsia' and the 'mass representative' categories took place at the expense of State institutions.

In its age structure, the Central Committee grew much younger, with an almost four-fold increase in the number of members below 50 years of age and a sharp drop in those above 60. The percentage of members above 60 dropped to an all time low of 15.1 per cent. The lowest fluctuation was recorded in the age-group 50-59, which changed to 44.4 per cent.[51] This was "Gorbachev's age-group" and constituted the single largest 'bloc' in the Central Committee. Members in the 40-50 age group were joining the Central Committee under Brezhnev[52]; now it became the dominant group.

Social and Economic Composition of the Central Committee

The Central Committee elected at the 27th Party Congress, and indeed before, had included ministers directly concerned with the economy and agriculture.[53] In the new Central Committee ministers directly concerned with the economy and agriculture were conspicuously absent. The social composition of the Central Committee changed to a large extent. However key leaders of ministries, military and security agencies, State committees, the USSR Security Council, the USSR Defence Council, Chairman of the USSR Supreme Soviet, USSR Military-Industrial Commission, Chairman of the USSR State Bank, the USSR State Arbitration Court, the USSR President and Vice-President and the Prime Minister continued to be represented. They derived their power and authority, however, from these State institutions rather than from the Central Committee.

The most important social forces represented were the intelligentsia, the working class and the peasantry.[54] Members of the Academic Intelligentsia represented those from the Higher Education Category. This category included leading academicians from the most prestigious academic institutions, like the Academy of Sciences and their republican branches; directors of the most important institutes, like the Economics Institute; rectors of some State universities; some scientists from important scientific institutions, like the Tallinn State Conservatory, the "V. Fanardzhan" Oncological Scientific Centre, the Poltava Medical Institute and so on. There were 31 members from this category. The Lower Education Category mainly included those from secondary education. They were represented by three directors of secondary schools.

Sixty six members belonged to the Skilled Workers category. They were the workers with specialised knowledge in their respective trades: a caster in a telephone factory; a repair mechanic in a production association; a lathe operator in a machine factory; a driver in a transport association; a chauffeur at a forestry enterprise; a bus driver; a miner; a metal worker; a tractor driver from the Gorkii Sovkhoz; a combine harvester operator from the Uralkalii production association etc. Three of the members were Peasants.

Thirteen members belonged to the Higher Industrial Management Category. These mainly included powerful chiefs of state-owned enterprises. They included the General Director of the Leningrad Association of Industrial Enterprises; the President of the Kalmyk Enterprise Association; the General Director of the Svenigorod Production Association in Moscow, etc. A similar number belonged to the Lower

Industrial Management Category. These were chiefly lower-rung supervisors in the management hierarchy. Examples were the head of an equipment-building brigade from Azerbaijan, the head of a construction brigade, the brigade leader of a ship repair yard, etc.

Fourteen members belonged to the Higher Agricultural Management Category. These were the leaders of collective and state farms. They included the chairman of the Gorkii Kolkhoz, Moscow; the chairwoman of the Kirov Kolkhoz Administration, Turkmenia; the director of a sovkhoz from Georgia. Ten members belonged to the Lower Agricultural Management Category. They included members of the lower management cadres in the state and collective farms. This category included a group leader from the Shoro-Bashat sovkhoz, Kirghizia; the head of a cotton growing brigade in Tajikistan; the head of a cattle-breeding brigade in the Gorno-Altay AO, etc.

Other categories represented were the Scientific Intelligentsia which included a senior oncologist from Leningrad; the Artistic Intelligentsia included a playwright, a cinema and theatre director from the Turkmenfilm cinema studio, and an actor in a dramatic theatre from Ternopol; and the Technical Intelligentsia, including the chief designer at the Illyushin machine-building factory in Moscow.

Economic interests[55] were represented by leaders of the enterprises, state farm and collective farms, production associations, the Union of Entrepreneurs and Leaseholders, and the Scientific-Industrial Union. The chairman of a co-operative association at the Rossiia kolkhoz and a leaseholder were also included. Among the mass organisations represented were the USSR and RSFSR Writers' Unions, the Soviet Women's Committee, the USSR Association of Cinematographers, the All-Union Council of War and Labour veterans, the USSR Union of Architects, the USSR Artists' Union, the USSR Farmers' Soviet, the RSFSR Trade Union of Stage Designers and the All-Union Komsomol. A new organisation called the USSR Foreign Policy Association was represented by Shevardnadze. A notable omission was that of the AUCCTU. Sergiev represented the Shvernik Trade Union Institute of Moscow.

Three of the youngest members had been born in 1962. They were F.A. Avazov, a lathe operator from Tajikistan, N.V. Kolesnikova, head of a cattle-breeding brigade, and I.V. Kornichuk, a fitter in a radio-technical factory in the Ukraine. Among the oldest members were Marshal N.V. Ogarkov representing All-Union Council of War and Labour Veterans, and B.V. Paton, President of the Ukrainian Academy of Sciences. Important academic institutions represented were the USSR Academy of Sciences, the

Moldovan Academy of Sciences, the Tajik Academy of Sciences, the Uzbek Academy of Sciences, the Ukrainian Academy of Sciences, Tbilisi State University, the Belorussian State University, Yerevan State University, the Tallin State Conservatory, the Academy of the National Economy, the Economics Institute of the USSR Academy of Sciences, the Institute for the World Economy and International Relations, the Centre for Political Analysis and Forecasting, and the Europe Institute of the USSR Academy of Sciences.[56]

Conclusion

Between the two congresses, then, the composition of the Central Committee underwent major transformations. The separation of the State institutions and its leadership from the Central Committee was extensive. The new composition represented the increased influence of the intelligentsia, the working class and peasantry, and Party officials, compared with that of the leaders of State institutions. However, the working class was mainly represented by skilled workers and the peasantry by representatives of the agricultural management category. The major section of the working class, the blue collar or non-skilled workers, was not represented directly. This section constituted the bulk of the Soviet work force. This seems to have deprived the Central Committee of a major constituency which was to be most affected by the reforms.[57] The economic reforms were most visible in this section.

The most significant difference from earlier Central Committees was that different kinds of social and economic forces came to be represented in the Central Committee. Previous Central Committees had predominantly represented the interests of the ministries, State committees, the military and so on. The representation of other social and economic forces was mediated through them. In the new Central Committee not only did these get directly represented, but some new ones, like those of leaseholders, co-operators and entrepreneurs, were included. The nature of the Central Committee thus seems to have changed considerably.[58] It was evolving into the leadership of a Party preparing to function in a parliamentary system, in which the newly formed State would represent the general interests of the society and the Party would represent specific social and economic interests.[59]

Paradoxically, the strength of this transformation was its weakness. A sizeable number of its members did not seem to be political personalities of much consequence, although they might have been recognised leaders in their respective localities. (A. V. Buzgalin confirms this when he says that the rank and file members of the Central Committee hardly had any powers. It was the membership of the Central Committee that gave them political recognition.[60]) The Party itself was in disarray and decline in a hostile political environment.[61] The State institutions themselves were transitional in nature. Hence the changes hastened the Party's dissolution. This only heightened the resistance of the Party and State apparatuses. The separation of Party and State itself was not complete, and major State institutions continued to be represented in the Central Committee so that the two apparatuses continued to have an important platform in this body. The reformist section of the Party leadership saw changes in personnel as an important step towards this separation. But personnel and institutional changes, though important, were not a sufficient condition. Such a separation had to be accompanied by change in the old precepts, organisation and working of the Central Committee, replacing them with new ones.

Notes

[1] For the changes in the composition of the Party, see B. Harasymiw, "Changes in the Party's Composition: The 'Destroyka' of the CPSU", *The Journal of Communist Studies*, vol. 7, June 1991, no. 2, pp. 133-60.

For the membership of the CPSU and its social composition between 1952-91, its membership in the republics in 1989 and ethnic composition in 1989, see A. Brown, M. Kaser and G. S. Smith ed., *The Cambridge Encyclopaedia of Russia and the former Soviet Union,* Cambridge University Press, (Cambridge, 1994),
pp. 341-2.

For the composition of the Central Committee see E. Mawdsley, The Central Committees of the CPSU since 1917, Lorton Papers, 1991.

[2] *Pravda* Carries Gorbachev's Report, *Pravda*, 29 June 1988, pp. 2-7 in *FBIS*, 1 July 1988, p. 32.

[3] A. Rahr, "Turnover in the Soviet Nomenklatura?" *RL 238/88,* 5 June 1988, pp. 1-3. 22 or 38 per cent of these "dead souls" were Party officials such as the former republican leaders of Azerbaijan, Armenia, Kazakhstan and Uzbekistan. Another 10 per cent were retired military men. A further 17 or 30 per cent were former ministers.

[4] E. Teague, "Gorbachev Says Ligachev's Position is Secure", *RL 233/88*, 1 June 1988, pp. 3-4.

[5] D. Lane, *Politics and Society in the USSR*, Martin Robertson, (London, 1978), p. 522.

[6] However a major reshuffle had taken place at lower levels. By the middle of 1988, Gorbachev had replaced 10 out of 14 republican first secretaries (except from Ukraine, Moldavia, Latvia and Estonia). 93 or 59. 2 per cent of the 157 regional Party first secretaries (31 in 1985; 23 in 1986; 29 in 1987 and 10 in 1988) were removed. 33 or 10 per cent had been replaced under Andropov and Chernenko. 31 or 19. 7 per cent were still holding over from Brezhnev era. Also only 7 candidate members of the Central Committee had been promoted to full membership in about two years preceding the 19th Party Conference. [A. Rahr, "Turnover in the Soviet Nomenklatura?", *RL 238/88,* 5 June 1988, pp. 3-4].

[7] S. White, "Reformulating the Programme and Rules" in Profile, The Twenty-Eighth CPSU Congress, *The Journal of Communist Studies,* vol. 7, March 1991, p. 110.

[8] G. Gill, 1994, p. 69.

[9] *Pravda*, 26 April 1989, p. 1 in *FBIS*, 26 April 1989, p. 47.

[10] *Moscow Domestic Service*, 1800 GMT, 25 April 1989 in *FBIS*, 26 April 1989, p. 51.

[11] *Pravda*, 27 April 1989, p. 4 in *FBIS*, 27 April 1989, p. 46.

[12] AFP, 1744 GMT, 24 April 1989 in *FBIS*, 25 April 1989, p. 40.

[13] *Moscow in English to North America,* 2300 GMT, 28 April 1989 in *FBIS*, 1 May 1989, p. 65.

[14] *Moscow Domestic Service*, 1800 GMT, 25 April 1989 in *FBIS*, 26 April 1989, p. 51.

[15] E. Teague, "Fall in Representation of the Party Apparatus in CPSU Central Committee", *Report on the USSR,* 12 May 1989, p. 4. Table 3.4 in Chapter Three demonstrates the extent of changes from the 26th Party Congress to the April 1989 Plenum.

[16] Calculated from J. F. Hough, 1982, Table 2. 2, p. 46. For comparison, the percentage breakdown of the professional representation of the full members of the Central Committee elected in 1976 is shown in table 3.5 in Chapter Three.

[17] E. Mawdsley, Table 4.

[18] D. Mann, A. Rahr, and E. Teague, "Gorbachev Cleans Out Central Committee", *Report on the USSR*, 5 May, 1989, p. 8.

[19] *Moscow Domestic Service*, 1630 GMT, 25 April 1989 in *FBIS*, 26 April 1989, p. 48. Such a massive turnover is reminiscent of that undertaken by Khrushchev in the first two and a half years of his assuming the office of First Secretary. M. Fainsod, 1963, p. 200.

[20] In table 3.6 in Chapter Three.

[21] On the basis of the information available in *Moscow Domestic Service*, 1700 GMT, 25 April 1989 in *FBIS*, 26 April 1989, p. 44.

[22] *Pravda*, 27 April 1989, p. 3 in *FBIS*, 27 April 1989, p. 48-50.

[23] G. Razumovski, "To Lead the Perestroika Effort, to Generate the Energy of Renewal", *Kommunist*, no. 4, 1989, pp. 10-11.

[24] S. White, *Gorbachev in Power,* Cambridge University Press, (Cambridge, 1990), pp. 20-21.

[25] E. Teague, "Gorbachev Consolidating His Position", *RL 201/85*, 20 June 1985, p. 3-4, E. Teague, "Pockets of Opposition to Kremlin Policies?", *RL 39/86,* 22 January 1986, p. 1 and Dawn Mann, "Party Report and Election Campaign Winds Down", *RL 59/88,* 27 January 1988, pp. 1-2.

[26] *Moscow Radio Domestic Service,* 1630 GMT, 25 April 1989 in *FBIS*, 26 April 1989, p. 48.

[27] *TASS*, 1758 GMT, 13 July 1990, p. 33 in *FBIS*, 16 July 1990, p. 33.

[28] Names and votes cast against are as follows: P. Bunich (1088), B. Gidaspov (632), O. Latsis (1139), I. Polozkov (606), Yu. Prokofiev (624), S. Shatalin (1100), G. Gumbaridze (653), M. Moiseev (543), L. Abalkin (1681), L. Arutunian (651), V.S. Babichev (825), V. Bakatin (757), O.D. Baklanov (995), N. Bikkenin (562), V. Boldin (1186), A. Buzgalin (875), A.V. Vlasov (1418), A. Volski (1187), V. Vylegzhanin (604), A. Gelman (1109), A. Girenko (680), A. Grachev (707), N. Gubenko (817), Guseletov (1026), A. Degtiarev (703), M. Yefimov (598), V. Ziukin (1537), Kalpopov (563), N. Kruchina (2000), A. Lukianov (544), Yu. Manaenko (823), G. Marchuk (538), Masliukov (901), A. Medvedev (1875), Yu. Mkrtumian (522), M. Nenashev (1128), G. Novozhilov (900), N. Ogarkov (641), B.I. Oleinik (576), T. Sarkisian (663), G. Sachko (1435, A. Sergiev (660), I. Silaev (543), S. Sitarian (909), V. Starodubtsev (530), Ye. Stroev (667), M. Ulianov (1768), V. Falin (1110), I. Frolov (1045), L. Shvetsova (646), E. Shevardnadze (872), G. Yagodin (1186), V. Yakovlev (551), and G. Yanaev (531).

[29] *Moscow Television Service*, 1722 GMT, 13 July 1990 in *FBIS*, 16 July 1990, pp. 7-9.

[30] E. Mawdsley, Table 2.

[31] Calculated from *RL151/86,* 9 April 1986, pp. 1-14 and Ulrich-Joachim Schulz-Torge, ed. *Who was Who in the Soviet Union*, K. G. Saur, (London, 1992), (hereafter K.G. Saur, 1992), pp. 61-69. Tables 3.8, 3.9 and 3.10 in Chapter Three demonstrate the extent of changes that took place in the composition of the Central Committee at the 28th Party Congress.

[32] According to Michel Tatu.

[33] Giulietto Chiesa, "The 28th Congress of the CPSU", *Problems of Communism*, July-August 1990, p. 37.

[34] As table 3.10 in Chapter Three indicates.

[35] See Tables given in Chapter Three. The figures for 1981 and 1986 are only of the Government representation and are taken from R.V. Daniels, 1989, Table 4. 3, p. 103.

The figures for State/Government category for 1990 include all individuals connected with state and government agencies, including members and leaders of Soviets of all levels, members of the Congress for People's Deputies apart from Council of Ministers, state committees, Presidency etc. Despite that, the change in the representation is drastic, particularly in the Central category. This data has been taken from K.G. Saur, 1992, pp. 61-69.

[36] *Moscow News,* no. 20, 22-29 May 1988, p. 13 in *FBIS*, 17 June 1988, pp. 52-53.

[37] *CDSP,* Vol. XLII, No. 35 (1990), PP. 19-20.

[38] *Moskovskaia Pravda*, 24 July 1990, p. 2 in *FBIS*, 15 August 1990, p. 35.

[39] A.V. Buzgalin also talks of a "third list" prepared during and proposed from the floor of the 28th Party Congress. He and Galina Sachko were elected on this list. A.V. Buzgalin, *Belaia Vorona, Poslednii God Zhizhni Tsk KPSS: Vzgliad Iznutri,* Znanie, (Moscow, 1993) (hereafter A.V. Buzgalin, 1993), pp. 73-4.

[40] *Moscow Television Service*, 1722 GMT, 13 July 1990 in *FBIS*, 16 July 1990, p. 7.

[41] *Moskovskaia Pravda*, 24 July 1990, p. 2 in *FBIS*, 15 August 1990, p. 34.

[42] *Moscow Television Service*, 0612 GMT, 28 June 1988 in *FBIS*, 29 June 1988, p. 31.

[43] The representation of various republican Communist parties and other Party organisations in the first list of 311 members is shown in table 3.11 in Chapter Three. The percentages do not include Central Committee members of different nationalities who were elected either in the Central list or from the list of representation of 'other party organisations' as given below. The list basically gives a break down of the percentage of 'provincial officials.'

the Central list or from the list of representation of 'other party organisations' as given below. The list basically gives a break down of the percentage of 'provincial officials.'
Moscow Television Service, 1722 GMT, 13 July 1990 in *FBIS*, 16 July 1990, pp. 7-9 and J.F. Hough, 1982, Table 2. 4, p. 49.

[44] *Pravda*, 27 April 1989, p. 6 in *FBIS*, 28 April, 1989, p. 44.

[45] Representation of other Party organisations is shown in table 3.12 in Chapter Three.

[46] E. Mawdsley, Table 4.

[47] Table 3.13 in Chapter Three gives the breakdown of Party officials in the Central Committee elected in 1990.

[48] Calculated from K.G. Saur, 1992, pp. 61-69. Table 3.14 in Chapter Three gives the breakdown of the State and government category in the Central Committee.

[49] E. Mawdsley, Table 6.

[50] *ibid*., Table 7.

[51] *ibid*., Table 12.

[52] J.F. Hough, 1982, p. 39.

[53] S. Belitsky, V. Konovalov and H. Kraus, *RL 145/86,* 1 April 1986 and *RL 151/86,* 9 April, 1986. For example, the minister for Heavy and Transport Machine-Building, minister of Installation and Special Construction work, ministers for Ship-Building, the Fish Industry, Ferrous Metallurgy, Tractor and Agricultural Machine-Building, Grain Products.

[54] For the composition of the members and candidate members of the CPSU up to 19th Party Conference in accordance to the social classification see, *Materiali Delegatu XIX Vsesouiznoi Konferentsii KPSS,* (Moskva, 1988), p. 227.

[55] On emerging economic interests during this period see "The Politics of Economic Interests", Chapter 9 in S. White et al, 1993. For social and economic interests during Perestroika and their attitude towards reforms, see T. I. Zaslavskaia, "Friends or Foes? Social forces working for and against Perestroika" in A. Aganbegian, ed., *Perestroika Annual,* Futura, (London, 1988), pp. 255-278.

[56] K.G. Saur, 1992, pp. 61-69.

[57] See E. Teague, "Manual Workers and the Workforce" in D. Lane ed., *Russia in Flux,* Edward Elgar, (Hants, 1992), p.114.

[58] In view of G. Gill the Central Committee was "being turned into a representative parliament of the Party". See G. Gill,1994, p. 140.

[59] Shevardnadze believed that new social forces that could provide the requisite base for a "bolder programme" were neglected. E. Shevardnadze, 1991, p. xviii.

[60] A.V. Buzgalin, 1993, p. 76.

[61] For a detailed analysis of the disintegration of the Party, see G. Gill, 1994.

7 Remodelling the Institution of the Central Committee: the Central Secretariat, the Apparatus and the Commissions

Introduction

The changing nature of the relationship between the Party and the State under perestroika affected the Central Secretariat and the central apparatus - the key executive institutions of the Central Committee. The two institutions constituted an integrated set, the former was composed of the leaders of the Central Committee, some of whom would be the members of the Politburo, and the latter of appointed officials. Thus they stood at the apex of the Party organisation. In conditions of one-party democratisation, the Party was to reinforce its political role and give up direct participation in general administration and the management of the economy. Therefore, these two bodies had to engage in the dual task of policy-making to outline the broad guidelines under which State institutions were to operate, and provide leadership to Party organisations. Both functions were also legitimate under the emerging multi-party system, as long as the CPSU was the ruling party. However, in both conditions its partnership with state agencies was not unassailable. It was at the 19th Party Conference that the decision was taken to reorganise the central apparatus. The Party was to implement its policies, verify its decisions and lead the lower Party organs assisted by the central apparatus. Thus emphasis on the role of the apparatus shifted more and more to inner-Party affairs.

The functions of the Party committees and state and economic bodies were to be demarcated, parallelism and duplication eliminated, and the apparatus was to be reorganised, its quality improved and made subordinate and accountable to the elected Party bodies. The resolution of the July 1988 plenum underlined the crux of the problem which the Party encountered. The structures of the leadership as they had historically evolved were a part of this problem which had been raised ritually in the past but left unattended. If the Party and the State agencies functioned as a set of integrated institutions, the Party would be deeply involved in resolving day to day economic issues and running the administration. Power would gravitate to the Party and State apparatuses. The parallelism and duplication would continue to exist since the Party's main function was not political. The apparatus would become bureaucratised, and in an inverted relationship would come to dominate the Party bodies. The changes were intended to be implemented before the end of 1988 and were expected to result in a major reduction in the number of apparatus officials. The Party's withdrawal from its traditional administrative and economic role meant that the apparatus required fewer officials.[1]

Over a period of time narrow departmental interests had become institutionalised. To eliminate such a situation the sector departments were abolished in the central apparatus. This had been preceded by a similar process in lower Party organs. As an experiment several Party committees in Moscow raikoms and in several other cities and raions had been working without sector departments. An example was that of the apparatus of the Leninskii raikom in Omsk. This was meant to have made the organisation of the apparatus "non-compartmentalised". This highlighted another problem that the Party faced at all levels. The existence of sector departments limited the view and the approach of the Party committees in comprehending the problems of society. The raikoms depended on these departments which in turn "viewed life and its problems from a narrow sectoral standpoint". Thus exclusion of sector departments was seen as helping to enhance the individual role of the Party worker and change the working of the apparatus from "excessive speechmaking, paperwork and telephone leadership" to "real life political work with people ...".[2] It can be a fair assumption that such circumstances existed in the central apparatus.

The historical evolution of the organisation of the apparatus at all levels and its primary involvement with the administration and the economy resulted in circumscribing its 'vision' to limited departmental interests. The central leadership organs like the Central Committee, Politburo and Central Secretariat were dependent on the departments, which in turn relied on the sector departments. The latter tended to promote the interests of the ministries they were associated with. Thus the central leadership organs would virtually be formulating policies on the basis of the input of information coming from them. This not only limited the scope of decision-making but also resulted in a selectivity of the kind of interests represented, promoting some and rejecting others. This situation had developed its contradictions, and a separation of the State and the Party along with one-party democratisation was seen as the solution. Thus extrapolating from the example of the Leninskii raikom, it can be assumed that the new organisation of the central apparatus was to become non-compartmentalised. The Central Committee like other Party committees in circumstances of the complete separation of Party and State would comprise primarily of political leaders representing a wide array of interests. It would be assisted by the renewed apparatus which could function under a multi-party system.[3]

The new departments of the Central Committee were to be reorganised parallel to the new Central Committee Commissions, which were being set up. The number of departments and the apparatus officials were to be reduced by up to fifty per cent. The redundant officials were to get jobs in other sectors like the State and economic management apparatus, teaching and so on.[4] The prospect of being retrained and shifted to other jobs was another reason for opposition from within the apparatus. The commissions formed were to rely on the assistance of the Party Structure and Cadre Policy department, the Ideology department, the Economic and Social Policy department, the State and Legal Policy department, the Agricultural Policy department and the International Policy department.[5]

Reduction in the number of departments and their personnel meant severe weakening of the apparatus. This weakened the base of resistance to the reforms yet increased its intensity. It was around this time in October 1988 that the Central Secretariat, according to Ligachev, who took the leading role in the Secretariat, stopped meeting and did not function for a long time. The cessation of work by the Secretariat, which was the statutory body on "questions of cadre policy and monitoring the fulfilment of Central Committee decisions",[6] meant that a major change in the Central Committee was under way. The functions of various departments and their organisation showed that they would be mainly concerned with policy-making and intra-party affairs. For example, a 'consultants' group was to be created in the ideology department "to prepare analytical materials and study key problems of the ideological process, and the theory and practice of restructuring".[7]

Regional committees were controlled by the central apparatus. The lower committees had always reinterpreted the directives of the Central Committee and modified them to suit local interests during their implementation. These committees were in the command structure led by the Central Secretariat and the central apparatus. It was this chain of command that constituted the Party apparatus. The entire apparatus, however, shared common interests. The Party apparatus, as already discussed, was the main constituency of conservative forces within the Party. The link between the highest Party leadership and the Party organisations was mediated by the Party apparatus. Thus reformist measures would be effective only in so far as they did not come in contradiction with the interests of the Party apparatus. Hence it was necessary for the reformist section of the leadership to reorganise the apparatus. This, it was hoped, would undermine the source of resistance to the reforms, and revitalise and involve Party organisations, as distinct from Party committees, and Party members in the activities of the Party. To democratise the political system, the Party had to be democratised first. Both in a one-party democratisation or a multi-party system such a reorganisation was necessary to restore the political character of the Party and separate it from the State. However, it resulted in the virtual rebellion of several lower Party committees which no longer accepted the authority of the Central Committee, its Secretariat and the apparatus. Thus despite being reformed to a large extent, the Central Secretariat and the central apparatus could not re-establish their authority as the leadership structures over the lower Party committees. The traditional organisational set-up and chain of command, through which their power and authority had been exercised, were dissolved.[8] The growing autonomy of the regional Party committees, at least in theory, was consistent with the devolution of power and authority to lower levels. Again in theory, this would have reasserted the political authority of the Central Committee over them, with a renewed legitimacy in contemporary conditions as the reformist leadership envisaged. However, in practice, this autonomy reflected the growing opposition of conservative sections of the Party apparatus.

After its enforced decline in the latter period of 1988, there seemed to be a revival of the Central Secretariat which met 34 times in 1989.[9] Its role shifted to policy-making. For instance, in October 1989 it was asked to work out a concrete programme based on the main points of the Party's nationality policy. Its activities appeared to be more concerned with questions pertaining to the Party. In October 1989 it considered a number of questions connected with the ideological life of the Party, decided to analyse the activities of Universities of Marxism-Leninism and supported the proposal to create a central publishing house called 'Druzba Narodov'.[10]

The Central Secretariat continued with its role of reviewing the implementation of the decisions of the Central Committee in the Party.[11] In 1989 and 1990 the Central Secretariat was giving up its traditional role and was more concerned with the activities of Party and policy-making. The central apparatus did not seem to have adjusted to its new role. It was criticised for serious shortcomings by V.I. Melnikov, first secretary of the Komi obkom, at the 25th April 1989 plenum of the Central Committee. It was unable to comprehend and ignored the situation in the localities. He said,

> ... The Central Committee apparatus has little interest in our practice, in our opinion. We have every reason to believe that some of the information from below that we prepare sometimes does not reach Politburo members, or reaches them in a toned down, soothing form. The Central Committee apparatus is clearly shielding the General Secretary from the acuteness of the situation prevailing at the grassroots ... Here to some extent I see the Central Committee apparatus as out of touch with grassroots Party links.[12]

This testified to the fact that the despite the reorganisation, the reforms were challenged within the central apparatus at this stage. It reflected both the continued dependence of the lower Party committees on the centre, and, inconsistently, a certain degree of independence. The dependency was reflected in the tendency to look for guidance from the centre on local matters, and growing independence in the withering criticism of a central body hitherto out of bounds for questioning. The earlier chain of command seems to have been effectively broken. Yet the very fact that such criticisms could be voiced testified to the success of reforms. The latter also seem to have succeeded to the extent that at least some Party committees were attempting to break out of the complacency and inertia. This revealed the isolation of the central apparatus from the severity of the political situation in the society. In the new found spirit of glasnost within the Party, the mediating link between the highest leadership and the lower Party committees was facing a vote of no-confidence for its ineptitude.

The question now was whether an apparatus was at all necessary. This issue was debated both inside and outside the Party. Those who accepted the need for the existence of the apparatus, but wanted to reform it, saw it as an "echelon of managerial technology" which was to be reorganised. Many thought that it was a structure that could be dispensed with as it had done more harm than good. Those arguing against retaining the apparatus did not think it could be reformed. The reformist section of the leadership, however, believed that it could be.[13] Highly qualified members specialising in different areas were brought in. In February 1990 it included 71 doctors of science and 343 candidates of science, constituting one-third of the entire apparatus. They had a 96 per cent wage increase, apparently in a bid to attract better talents.[14] Thus attempts were made to reform the apparatus into an organ of highly qualified personnel to analyse the complex political and socio-economic situation of the USSR and assist the Party leadership organs in an era of political competition.

The new apparatus being formed had at least two distinct groups of new officials. It consisted of young people with higher education and Party officials from the provinces.[15] There was evidence of a major turnover in these departments with new members often taken from a Moscow-based think tank. According to one estimate three-quarters of the International department was renewed in the previous three years (1987, 1988 and 1989). Their influence on government bodies was deemed to have decreased. They were getting more and more involved in inner Party matters and in collecting information. A Central Committee department chief predicted in the middle of 1989 that these departments would be substituted by Supreme Soviet standing committees "as major originators of policy",[16] confirming that they were to be mainly concerned with the Party and its activities. Despite major changes in the apparatus, in an acknowledgement of resistance within the apparatus to the changes inside and outside the Party, several Party and other officials were still said to feel 'psychological barriers' in adapting to the new political situation.[17]

In the third quarter of 1990, another major restructuring of the central apparatus took place. An organisational department was formed to replace that of Party Construction and Personnel Work department to work with all Party organisations and deal with the "problems of the renewal of Party life". It was to co-ordinate between the central apparatus and local Party organisations, and support Party-wide activities. The formation of this department may have been the outcome of criticisms like that of Melnikov and an attempt to resurrect the broken links between the centre and lower levels, albeit in a renewed form. A department for 'Ties With Public-Political Organisations' was created which seemed to be the forerunner of the Socio-Political department. This department also dealt with questions related to worker and youth movements and was to find coalition partners sharing closer political perspective.

The State and Law department was replaced by the department on

Legislative Initiatives and Legal Questions. Since the Party was being attacked by its opponents this department was to organise the legal defence. It was to formulate legislative proposals to be presented in the Supreme Soviet and organise the work of Party deputies in the Supreme Soviet. This department seemed to be preparing the Party for its parliamentary role. The department of Nationality Relations was renamed the department of Nationalities Policy whereby the policy-making role would replace any direct involvement in this issue.

A department of Social and Economic Policy was to replace the Social and Economic department, again signifying a withdrawal from socio-economic management. The Defence department was to be abolished and the Agrarian department to be renamed as the Agrarian Policy department. The abolition of the Defence department and the conversion of all the departments into policy-making bodies was a significant step in the process of separation of Party and State. The General department and the Administrative Office of the central apparatus were to be retained.[18] Thus the basic nature of the central apparatus was fundamentally changing. It was being prepared for the impending multi-party system and political competition, and with the gradual separation of the Party and State which was now reaching the highest echelons of the Party, the role of the Central apparatus was being transformed into becoming the apparatus of a political Party no longer supervising and directing State institutions.

Its strength was further reduced to 40.4 per cent or 603 out of a total of 1,493 officials. This had been preceded by another major reduction of 536 officials in 1989.[19] Since the apparatus was no longer involved in administration of the affairs of State agencies and managing the economy, a bloated apparatus was no longer necessary. The representation of the central apparatus in the Central Committee was reduced drastically, further indicating the loss of its erstwhile position of importance. In the Central Committee elected at the 28th Party Congress the share of the Central apparatus dropped to seven.[20] The change may also have been due to the reduced number of departments. The figures however also indicate their diminished position. The trend of reduction in its representation showed that its presence in the Central Committee was transient. It was no longer the centre of real power as in the past, but resembled more that of a 'secretarial assistant' to the elective bodies. Despite resisting its loss of power, it was continuously losing it under the impact of the reforms and a rapidly transforming external political environment.

The Role of the Central Committee Departments

The departments continued to play an important role in monitoring the implementation of the decrees of the Central Committee well into 1989.[21] Local Party committees were at this juncture very much dependent on the departments and part of the chain of authority within the Party apparatus. The importance of the departments within the Party could be judged from the fact that they prepared recommendations for the Central Committee members.[22] Representatives of departments who visited the regions and investigated the situation provided the analysis, as in the case of the decree on utilisation of labour resources in Central Asia and the Northern Caucasus. It was through them that the central apparatus monitored the execution of the decrees. However, such inspections in the absence of other means, like active representative local organs, were very limited. Assuming that such inspectors were genuinely interested in understanding the prevailing conditions, there always existed the possibility that they might not be allowed to probe further than local entrenched interests wanted them to. Thus the result of such investigations might be very superficial. There also existed a possibility of defending the lower Party organisations. In this case they concluded that the local Party organisations did not do anything about the situation regarding the utilisation of labour resources in these regions, and depended on the Central Committee for help. Weakness of Party control in these regions was criticised. This report also highlighted the limitations of the exercise of Party control in economic affairs and the lack of expertise to be able to do so as indicated by the dependence on the Central Committee.[23]

The implementation of the decrees that had been issued would be reviewed and recommendations given. They would be virtually the same indicating that the same problems remained unresolved and the same solutions were re-emphasised. The cardinal problem lay with this system of inspection as such. The same agencies would be exhorted to work better and produce better results. The mechanism of implementation was also faulty. Traditional channels of implementation, the Party and State organisations, the trade unions, the Soviets were proving inadequate. Absence of representative bodies at all levels, the inadequacy of the technical expertise of the Party and the State organisations, ideological constraints and the conventional approach and practices which became established during the Brezhnev era played an important role. This highlighted the malaise of the system of administration itself.

The information regarding the fulfilment of the above decree was issued by the departments of Economy and Party Work on 30 June 1986, which mentioned the visit of several departments to these regions. Some positive assessment was followed with criticisms of the Central Committees of the republics for not including measures for the fulfilment of the decree by these departments in their respective plans. It gave concrete and varied recommendations like paying special attention to building kindergartens, strengthening Party control, taking serious measures to strengthen political work among the population and to organise meetings with workers in this connection.[24] Another decree issued by the Central Secretariat on the fulfilment of the above decree on 8 September 1987 was based on the report of the Economic department and the department of Organisational-Party Work issued on 4 September 1987.[25] The departments of the Economy and Organisational-Party Work issued yet another report on the fulfilment of these decrees on 4 June 1988. In this report they criticised the Central Committees of these republics for not taking measures to change a situation in which unemployment continued to increase. Some recommendations, namely that the local Party organisations should strengthen organisational work and control the activity of their Central Committees, clearly sought the solution to the problems of implementation in decentralisation.[26] At least nine more decrees based on the notes of the departments were issued between August 1989 and October 1990.[27]

Departments would issue notes elaborating and detailing the decrees of the Central Secretariat.[28] They would review the implementation of a particular decree and another one would be issued by the Central Secretariat on the basis of the note of that department. An example was the decree issued on measures to develop a technical base in the socio-cultural sphere.[29] The departments were expected to carry out the instructions of the Politburo and play an important role in reforming the institutions as they existed, in fact they were seen as the key to implementing the reforms by the reformist section of the leadership.[30] The issues entrusted to the departments were quite important.[31] There seemed to be efforts to build up a new organisational structure within the Party linking the Politburo, and the commissions of the Central Committee to the lower Party organisations. This was a distinct organisational linkage which had not hitherto existed. The new 'chain of command' seemed to be from the Politburo through the elective organs of the commissions of the Central Committee led by the Central Secretariat, elected from the heads of the commissions, down to lower Party organisations. Thus the mediating link of the Party apparatus headed by the central apparatus and old type Central Secretariat would no longer exist. Some departments were asked to prepare proposals in this area.[32] However, the leading Party bodies were to continue to rely on the departments in developing proposals on various issues. The revamped departments were to continue to formulate policies and proposals. In the Politburo's decree on the results of the September 1989 plenum issued on 11 October 1989, the departments were asked to make proposals on political, ideological and organisational questions concerning future elections in local Party organisations.[33] Likewise the Central Secretariat would issue instructions to the departments in relation to compliance with its decrees.[34] Usually these notes were detailed.[35] Thus as late as early 1990, the Central Committee departments played an important role in preparing recommendations for the State agencies. It was only around this period that the separation of Party and State was reaching a qualitatively higher stage. The notes issued by the departments could also be discussed by the Central Secretariat without necessarily issuing a decree on it.[36]

A new pattern of functioning was emerging which could be thought to underscore the growing importance of State institutions. It also showed that until the Presidential apparatus was in place and functioning properly, Gorbachev continued to rely on the central apparatus. This showed the weakness of the newly established executive arm of the State during the period of transition. It further highlighted the problems of the transfer of power and the functions of the government to the new executive and representative organs of the State. The Central Secretariat issued a decree based on the note of the Ideology and Socio-Economic department issued on 11 September 1990, which in turn was based on a note by an individual minister. The decree on measures regarding the cultural sphere under conditions of a transfer to a market economy was based on the note of the Minister of Culture, N. Gubenko, addressed to Gorbachev, who sent it to the aforementioned departments. The decree was based precisely on the recommendation of these departments. This reflected the link between the departments and the government, and the continued importance of the former. Perhaps the departments were indispensable because they contained members with relevant expertise.[37] It also showed a new pattern of functioning by the departments and the Central Secretariat.

The Central Committee was preparing to function through the State organs, as in the case of legislative initiatives, which the departments played an important role in drafting. The Ideology, Social-Economic and State-Legal departments were to prepare a statement from the Central

Committee to the Supreme Soviet of the USSR on the necessity to work out and accept key laws on culture in the Soviet Union and the republics in 1991. They were asked to make proposals for formulating the legislative initiatives for the Supreme Soviet. Recommendations were made to the Central Committees of the republican Party organisations to ask their Supreme Soviets to protect culture under market conditions. In a new way of functioning through elected deputies of the Supreme Soviet of the USSR, they were to ask the Scientific-Industrial Council of the USSR, the Peasants' Council of the USSR and the Council of Co-operators to take necessary measures in order to provide financial support to enterprises, banks and other organisations.[38]

In another variant of their role, they provided analysis without making recommendations. This seemed to be the beginning of a new pattern whereby the impression that the departments were the main power which did everything, with the Secretariat just rubber-stamping their decisions, was to be abandoned. Until now, everything including recommendations had basically seemed to be formulated by them. A decree of the Central Secretariat "On the Strengthening Tendencies of Cultural Commercialisation and on the Measures to Overcome Them" was issued on 11 July 1990 and was based on the note the Ideology department issued on 28 June 1990. The latter had contained an analysis of the issue, whereas the decree had the recommendations.[39]

The departments were emerging as the 'secretariat' of the commissions. An example of their relationship was the meeting of the Socio-Economic Policy commission held on 8 December 1989 which discussed the problems of improving economic reforms. The meeting of the commission was based on a note by the department of Socio-Economic Policy on a more effective use of investments and on improving the economic structure in the construction industry. The basic agenda, direction and recommendations for the meeting of the commission were prepared by this department. This note was more or less accepted by the commission at its meeting.[40]

Departments would also be asked to make proposals on a decree of the Central Committee.[41] Central Committee decrees were also based on the notes of departments.[42] At least 17 decrees were issued by the Central Secretariat between October 1990 and July 1991, most of them based on the research and analysis done by the departments of the Central Committee. A few were based on the notes of commissions.[43] Most of these decrees, particularly in 1990-1991, were political in nature and were concerned with the Party and Party organisations. Some were on internal Party questions. They did not issue directives or instruct State and government bodies as in the past. There was a distinct shift in the nature of decrees which no longer dealt with economics specifically or ones which involved giving directives to the State and the government bodies. These decrees, even for Party organisations, at most may have had a recommendatory nature. They were analytical in nature, confirming that the role of the departments would be confined to research and analysis. As the Central Secretariat and Central Committee lost their directive power over State and government institutions, so did these departments.

The Commissions

Gorbachev in his speech to the 27 January 1987 Central Committee plenum talked of the Central Committee being merely a rubber stamp. Its meetings were "brief and formal" with low participation in debates and putting forward proposals.[44] The commissions were intended to remedy such a situation. Involvement of the Central Committee members in the commissions was to curtail the monopoly of the apparatus on information and policy-making. They were to improve the activity of the Central Committee by developing new forms of its work to ensure the participation of all its members in the discussion of important political decisions. The Central Committee, the Politburo and the Central Secretariat were to rely on them to resolve important questions.[45] It was through them that the increased participation of Central Committee members in the working of the Politburo was envisaged.[46] They were to draft proposals for the Party organisations, analyse the work and the results achieved, prepare documents and analytical material for the Politburo.[47] These functions had traditionally been in the purview of the central apparatus. The commissions appeared to be inspired by the sub-committee system of the Supreme Soviet,[48] which seemed to have functioned actively in the past. Two sets of commissions existed during perestroika. Primary questions remained as to whether they emerged as intended? What were the issues discussed by them and did they signify a radical departure from the past consensus? How did their composition affect them? In the final analysis did their deliberations result in any concrete changes in the Party and the Central Committee, their organisation, working and ethos?

The 29 July 1988 Central Committee plenum passed the resolution

"On Fundamental Guidelines for the Restructuring of the Party apparatus" to remodel its structure in accordance with the reforms. The Central Committee plenum of 30 September 1988 took the decision to form the following six commissions:

(a) Party Building and Cadre Policy Commission (under the chairmanship of Razumovskii).

(b) Ideology Commission (Medvedev).

(c) Socio-Economic Policy Commission (Sliunkov).

(d) Agrarian Policy Commission (Ligachev).

(e) International Policy Commission (Yakovlev).

(f) Legal Policy Commission (Chebrikov) .

They were established in the most important areas of the reforms.[49] Their formation signalled the beginning of the process of the reduction in the role and the authority of the Central Committee departments.[50] However, a symbiotic relationship between the latter and the commissions was envisaged. The November plenum affirmed their personnel composition.[51]

The significant features of the composition of the commissions were as follows:

1. They were constituted from the Central Committee elected at the 27th Party Congress. All the commissions had a high number of provincial Party and State officials, who constituted the dominant group within them. With the Central Party and government officials they formed an overwhelming majority. The reason for this lay in the composition of the Central Committee, with its dominant representation of these groups. Thus in effect the commissions were miniature Central Committees largely composed of Party and State/government officials.

2. The Party Issues and Personnel Policy Commission had a high number of members from the central apparatus and provincial Party and State officials, accounting for 18 out of 25 members. The Party and State officials were thus to have the greatest say in the issues relating to the Party and its personnel.

3. The Ideology commission had a significant number of members from the intelligentsia, writers and artists, the media and scientific workers who were to participate in formulating the new ideology. However the commission had a total of 13 members out of 25 from among Party and State/government officials, reflecting their preponderance.

4. The Social and Economic Policy commission had a high number of provincial Party and State/government officials accounting for 16 out of a total of 21 members. They were thus to play a key role in formulating social and economic policies.

5. The Agrarian Policy commission headed by Ligachev had 20 out of 23 members from the Party and State/government categories, highlighting their dominance.
6. The International Policy and Legal Question commissions were similarly constituted.

The composition of the commissions thus signified that although they were meant to curtail the influence of the central apparatus in particular and the Party apparatus in general, the latter predominated. This, however, reflected the existing composition of the Central Committee. The commissions were to be particularly concerned with improvement in the functioning of Party organisations, and implementation of the political line of the Party and the decisions of its congresses and conferences. They were to analyse different aspects of Party life and "weigh up the various options". Party activists, leading academics, specialists, public figures and other guests were to participate. They were to submit "draft documents and analytical materials" to the Politburo and Central Committee plenums. The Politburo could seek the opinion of the commissions on the drafts of decisions and documents, and ask them to organise referenda within the Party or in the country on these and other basic issues of socio-economic and social development. The commissions could make recommendations for Party organisations and committees regarding functional, organisational and ideological matters, and with the permission of the Politburo place them before Party organisations.

Pertinent issues were to be discussed collectively at their sessions. Each member had the right to raise an issue. Sessions of the commissions were to be held as and when required, but not less than once in three months. The commissions could form working groups and instruct its individual members. The Central Committee departments and Party scientific and training establishments were to assist them in their work. The General Department and the Department of the Administration of Affairs of the CPSU Central Committee were to provide "the organisational and technical conditions"[52] for the functioning of the commissions.

The resolution provided for the involvement of the commissions in a very wide area of decision-making and decision-implementing processes on issues concerning the Party and its activities. It was to carry out this role not merely at the level of the highest leadership organs, but also in the lower echelons of the Party. Provision was made for the representation of union and autonomous republics and other "national formations". The regulations regarding their work had "not been firmly established"[53], confirming their experimental nature and flexibility in their scope and role.

Table 7.1 Background of members of the Central Committee Commissions elected in 1988

Background of Members:	Commissions (1)	(2)	(3)	(4)	(5)	(6)
Provincial Party and State Officials	13	6	9	15	8	7
Central Party apparatus	5	3	1	3	3	1
Govt. officials	1	4	6	2	4	4
Military	--	--	--	--	1	1
KGB	--	--	--	--	1	1
Trade Unions	1	--	1	1	--	1
Komsomol	1	--	--	--	--	--
Mass Media	1	1	1	--	1	1
Writers and Artists	--	6	--	--	1	--
Prosecutors Office	--	--	--	--	--	1
Scientific Workers	--	3	1	--	3	1
Workers	3	2	2	2	1	3
Total Membership	25	25	21	23	23	21

Source: A. Rahr, "Gorbachev Changes Party Structure", RL 519/88, 30 November 1988, p. 3.

The political reforms introduced at the 19th Party Conference made a review and redrawing of the approach to all aspects of society imperative. Hence the crucial role of the commissions in the spheres of ideology, the economy, the legal system, agriculture, international relations and the Party itself. Because the Party still constituted the core of the political system, society and the economy, these commissions remained powerful, unlike those formed at the 28th Party Congress. These commissions dealt with vital issues. Paradoxically, their emergence was part and parcel of the process of disengagement of the Party from the State and the economy. Given the transitional nature of the political system, however, they combined the 'aura' of the past and the unsure evolution of the future.

The Working of Various Commissions

In 1989, a high total of 21 meetings of the commissions took place.[54] Ideology had been the key cementing factor holding the Party and the political system together. The new reformed ideology was to play a similar role. All changes in the entire gamut of policies were to flow from this new ideological framework, hence the importance of the Ideology Commission. In its first session, held in January 1989, it discussed the shaping of the ideological sphere in relation to the practical tasks of perestroika, namely the fulfilment of the economic and political reform programmes. Developing "a modern concept of socialism" was deemed to be a task of "special significance". It discussed the draft laws on the press and the mass media[55] and "On Freedom of Conscience and Religious Organisations".[56] The commission decided to send the material from this meeting to the Politburo.[57] The Central Committee members were, for the first time, afforded the opportunity to decide on the reorganisation of the Central Apparatus, as in the case of the Ideology department.[58] One of the sessions prepared for the forthcoming Central Committee plenum on inter-ethnic relations to "develop a new strategy for nationality policy". Recognition of the nationality problem and a fundamental inquiry into the shortcomings of the existing approach was undertaken with the participation of Central Committee members and others. Lenin's legacy, a question which was gaining central importance in the discussion about the reforms, was reviewed.

Commission members had regular "working meetings" with representatives of the media. A proposal of some commission members working on a permanent basis[59] for fixed periods found a place in the draft platform of the Central Committee for the 28th Party Congress.[60] The commissions thus seemed to be developing their own apparatus separate from their respective departments. This may have been an attempt to be less dependent on the existing departments which were still undergoing reform.

The Legal Policy Commission was to prepare proposals to renew existing legislation, elaborate the political concepts governing them, help the Central Committee in exercising legislative initiative, prioritise legislative work and formulate proposals for laws requiring immediate promulgation. This commission was to help in the parliamentary work of the Central Committee by identifying issues and drafting legislation, thus emerging as its standing committee on parliamentary affairs. There were proposals to curtail arbitrariness in the administration of justice and revamp the entire legal system. It stressed the need to enhance the legal education of the people and improve the legal standards of the activities of the State, social organisations and leaders at various levels. Questions pertaining to the entire Soviet legal system, such as restructuring the forms and methods of the activities of the procuracy and improvement in the Soviet legal services, were examined.

A proposal to devolve and decentralise power to the republican levels was discussed. Issues relating to the forthcoming plenum of the Central Committee on improving inter-ethnic relations in the USSR, the concept proposed by the working group "for legal regulation of inter-ethnic relations" and legislation on it were discussed. The commission planned to formulate legislation to amend the USSR Constitution to redefine the distribution of powers between the Union and the republics, granting the latter more autonomy in political and socio-economic spheres.[61] Commissions became forums to raise hitherto prohibited issues. For example, A. Brazauskas, first secretary of the Lithuanian CP CC, proposed reconsideration of the pact between the Soviet Union and Germany in 1939. Several important proposals, including a list of new bills to be proposed in 1989, were discussed. The meeting decided to form working groups in the commission to help the Central Committee to influence the work of the local Party organisations and the activity of the Soviets.[62] The separation of the judiciary was discussed in one of its sessions, which approved proposals to strengthen the independence and prestige of the law courts and the introduction of strict accountability for interference in their work.[63] The Soviet judicial system had no institutionalised checks against arbitrariness. The absence of an independent status prevented the courts from overturning arbitrary acts of the State. Such a measure, however modest, was thus a step in the direction of the separation of powers.

The commissions had considerable powers in examining an issue. They could hear reports from the ministers and officials concerned, criticise their shortcomings and 'instruct' them on what should be done. Reports from A. Ya. Sukharev, the USSR Procurator General, and V. V. Bakatin, the USSR Interior Minister, were heard on the question of the fight against crime. The commission was critical of the law and order situation and expressed concern at the growth of crime and its changing nature. The USSR Ministry of Internal Affairs, the USSR Procuracy, and the USSR Ministry of Justice were asked to take urgent measures in line with the directives of the April 1989 Central Committee plenum.[64]

The main task of the Socio-Economic Policy Commission was to work out political methods for the implementation of social, economic, scientific and technical policies and facilitate orienting the economy towards social needs. The Party's withdrawal from direct management of the economy and society in one-Party democratisation necessitated a new mechanism to implement its policies in a non-administrative way. It was to monitor the fulfilment of the decisions of the Central Committee on the entire range of socio-economic problems, replacing the central apparatus. Important social questions like those regarding pension provisions were discussed by the Commission. The pensions of old people were to be increased, a new bill prepared and the experiences of other countries studied. The social effect of the increase in the prices was discussed and the pensions of Afghan war veterans increased.

Since the commissions were composed predominantly of Party and State officials, they could exercise executive authority, instructing various State and Party agencies to study different options and proposals. However this contradicted the quest for a 'political approach'. The environment was on the commission's agenda as a result of Chernobyl, as was "the rational utilisation of natural resources" prompted by the wasteful nature of the economy.[65] The construction industry, the fulfilment of foreign agreements, Central Committee decisions on the economy, the recovery of the national economy and the reorganisation of economic relations in the countryside were all in its purview.[66] Proposals were submitted by participants to its sessions, for example, regarding the reduction of material-intensiveness, the cost of the construction industry and improving quality. Academic institutions were involved, as in this case, in which the Academy of Sciences was to prepare a draft resolution for the government on the basis of the discussions.[67]

The proposals of the commissions were to be generalised by the related Central Committee departments, and the opinions of lower Party organisations were to be taken into account, as in the case of the reform package to upgrade scientific and technological management. These proposals could also be further discussed at a national conference.[68] Thus the attempt seemed to be to take policy-making out of the narrow confines of the apparatus and broaden the issues involved as well as the participation. However this endeavour was severely limited because of the presence of a large number of Party and State officials which could constrain such an exercise in accordance with ideological, political and governmental imperatives and priorities. Although the realm of policy-making was broadened, it was not completely entrusted to professionals.

The commissions' relationship with the government was also undergoing change. By the end of 1989, the government's autonomy was considerable and the commissions could discuss and approve government documents, as in the case of the government's report presented to the Second Congress of People's Deputies, on the improvement of economic reforms.[69]

Although the commissions were replacing the central apparatus, they relied on old structures and methods of working at this stage. The commissions would review the implementation of the resolutions. Thus the basic problem remained unresolved. The Agricultural Policy Commission, for example, discussed the joint resolution on the programme of social development in villages, the reorganisation of economic relations in agriculture, improving technical facilities for socio-economic development[70] and the state prices for the agricultural produce.[71] It further studied the organisational work of the leaders of various State and government agencies and enterprises to reduce the losses of agricultural products during production, transportation, storage and processing. Commission members also visited sites to study the problems. Government and State leaders and Party members were criticised for their failure to implement Party and government decisions.[72] Here the commission members were practically functioning in the way the apparatus would.

A reformed Party was expected to play an important role in one-Party democratisation and give a political lead. The Party-Building and Cadre-Policy Commission was to revive the functioning of Party organisations as distinct from the apparatus. It was to study problems and prepare for the Central Committee proposals on the activity of Party organisations and indicate whether they fulfilled the decisions of the Party, its congresses and conferences. Commissions, instead of the apparatus, were to form the link between the Central Committee and lower Party organs. Party life was to be democratised, and its functioning reorganised in accordance with the separation of the Party and the Soviet and economic organs. It was to determine the parameters of personnel policy and generalise on the basis of the election campaign within the Party. This commission was to prepare for the 28th Party Congress.[73] All the above activities had been undertaken by the central apparatus in the past.

The Commission discussed certain questions to be raised at the 28th Party Congress.[74] It debated changes in the Party programme, the role of local Party organisations and their reorganisation. The importance of the role of local Party organisations was reflected in the fact that they were discussed in the very first session. The status of the local Party organisation, which hitherto had no effective role vis a vis Party committees, was becoming important. The beginning of the devolution of functional responsibility to the lowest levels of the Party, however insignificant, was a step to revitalise the former. A good number were still steeped in the organisational culture of passivity which had embedded itself from the pre-perestroika period. In other words, a fresh infusion of membership was to shake up the fossilised Party structure at its lowest levels. Granting independence to lower Party organisations over questions of membership freed them from supervision by the higher bodies. Recruitment was not to be done on sociological or other criteria as before, but on political ones. This in itself meant a shift from the Party being at the core of a system to a political Party with open recruitment on a political-ideological basis. Party programmes had provided the theoretical underpinnings of any Communist Party, whether ruling or otherwise. With reforms in general and those initiated by the 19th Party Conference in particular, the inadequacy of the Party programme, its inability to provide a theoretical basis for the new developments and the need to change it were acknowledged. The commissions were to develop lateral links as well, owing to the overlapping of competence, as exemplified by the decision of the Party-Building and Cadre-Policy commission to work with others.[75]

It was thought that the enhanced independence and the responsibility of primary Party organisations would result in increased Party membership.[76] The decline in Party membership seemed to have prompted the Party leadership to take up this issue, and PPOs, functioning at the grassroots, were to fulfil this task. Devolution of independence was also an attempt to revitalise them. Abolition of candidate membership meant opening a wider field of recruitment by eliminating the probationary period. The significance of the candidate membership stage lay in that it had acted as a filter and a stage in the political socialisation of the individual in the norms of the Party. Its abolition meant opening Party ranks to wider recruitment.[77] On the basis of its work, the commission adopted and submitted a draft document ,"on the progress of recruitment to the CPSU and measures to reinforce the Party's ranks", to the Central Committee for its consideration.[78] Local Party organisations were to decide the number of members to be admitted and all other related questions.[79] The Party's lack of sociological services to analyse various social processes, something other organisations had, was studied by the commission. The analytical and informational backup needed by the Party was unavailable, putting it in a disadvantageous position vis a vis other organisations.

Preparing itself for a political role required a continual process of understanding society and social processes, something in which it proved to be woefully lacking, given the absence of a political mechanism and inadequacies of the Partya apparatus. The lack of such a system also affected the issue of recruitment to Party membership, and absence of a more complete understanding limited the Party's political role. Hence the inadequacies of the policies framed.

Another important issue discussed was practical measures to dismantle the *nomenklatura* system of cadre policy. The multi-candidate principle was to be further improved when filling vacancies.[80] The *nomenklatura* system[81] was the mainstay of political and administrative superintendence of the Party over the Soviet system, hence its removal effectively meant abdicating a key mechanism of control. However, if the reforms were to have any impact it was important to do so, because the system had resulted in the arbitrary selection of personnel with less emphasis on capability and performance and more on political and possibly personal loyalties, which became a key cause of stagnation and declining performance. Moreover, the nature of political loyalties was changing given the reforms, so that the existing *nomenklatura* system was more of a liability than an asset. It was also redundant in a situation where the Party was surrendering its control over the economy and State.

In November 1989, the Central Committee adopted a resolution "On Party Organisations' Work To Consolidate Their Ranks and Renew the CPSU's Composition in Conditions of Deepening Perestroika and Political Reform". This was based on the recommendations made by the commission. It changed the approach towards the criteria for Party membership. This seemed to be an attempt to harmonise it with and reflect society and newly created, as well as the existing but unrepresented, social interests.[82] However it also meant abandoning the policy of deliberately recruiting proletarian elements to the Party which had prevailed under Brezhnev.[83] The basis of Party membership thus shifted to a new political criterion abandoning the earlier one, rather than an attempt to balance membership on the basis of class, sex, nationality etc. The Party statutes were to be changed to match the new requirements.[84]

The Party programme[85] and fundamental conceptual provisions of the draft Party Statutes for the 28th Party Congress, its framework and the proposals for electing delegates which were to be submitted to the February plenum of the Central Committee were discussed in other sessions. Another significant question examined was that of the Party functioning at places of residence.[86] A switch in the Party functioning from the work place to the place of residence on the one hand meant preparing the Party for a parliamentary role, but on the other, renunciation of the Party's traditional constituency in the workplace. This commission also suggested the inversion of the process of election of the central Party leaders. Oblast and krai Party conferences and Union-republican Communist Party Congresses were to send proposals on candidates for central Party organs to the 28th Party Congress, on the basis of the opinion of Party organisations.[87] The 28th Congress approved this proposal.

The entire range of foreign policy was studied and generalised by the International Policy Commission. The issue of a common European home was discussed. Two meetings of the Commission of International Policy [88] discussed matters pertaining to Soviet foreign policy. It decided to prepare for the future meetings of Gorbachev and Reagan, and discussed Soviet relations with China, India and Vietnam and the conflict in Kampuchea. It accepted the necessity of reorganising foreign relations, decided to prepare a report on foreign economic relations, the issue of celebrating the anniversary of the Second World War and the events of 1939. These reports were to be given to the Central Committee.[89] The new Soviet foreign policy was to pave the way to an era of co-operation, a logical culmination of the period of détente in international relations.

The Politburo and the Commissions

The intention of the reformist section of the leadership to substitute the central apparatus as the key component and to return the leadership role to the Central Committee was evident when the commissions were instructed by the Politburo to play an active role in the Party and society. The traditional mediating link between the Politburo and the lower Party organisations, i.e. the Central Secretariat and the central apparatus, was being replaced by that of a reorganised Central Secretariat and the commissions.[90] Thus the commissions were to make the channels of upward vertical communication to the highest levels more effective.

The CPSU Central Committee draft platform approved by the plenum held in February 1990 proposed the inclusion of Party members from various sections of society, namely the working class, peasantry and intellectuals, in the commissions on a permanent basis. The commissions were to be headed by Central Committee secretaries.[91] Perhaps for the first time a proposal allowing non-Central Committee members of the Party to work on a permanent basis in a central leadership organ was mooted. This would have provided greater expertise to the commissions and facilitated their functioning. The draft Party statutes gave a categorical decision-making right to the commissions. The right to execute its decisions was vested in the Central Committee Secretariat, which was to be formed "from the leaders of the commissions". It was to co-ordinate the activities of the commissions and organise the execution of their decisions in the Party. This, however, meant that as a co-ordinating body it would lack its previous cohesiveness, and thus would be unlikely to become a source of resistance to reforms.[92] The commissions, which were in existence at the time this proposal was made, did not have the right to adopt decisions on issues within their competence.[93] A growing role for the commissions was thus envisaged in the future. But in the final version of the Statutes as ratified, direct references to the decision-making power of the commission, the execution of its decisions by the Secretariat, and the election of the leaders of the commission preceding that of the Secretariat were dropped, perhaps as a concession to the conservatives.[94] They were to continue playing mainly an advisory role to the Central Committee. However the "regulatory documents" on the CPSU Statutes approved by the 28th Party Congress were finalised in the Commissions with the participation of representatives of the Central Control Commission, advisers and academics.[95]

The Central Committee Commissions after the 28th Party Congress

The Central Committee plenum of 9 October 1990 decided to establish the following eight permanent Commissions in accordance with paragraph 29 of the CPSU rules: (a) Ideology; (b) Socio-political; (c) Social and Economic; (d) Agrarian policy; (e) Women and Family Questions; (f) Nationalities policy; (g) International policy; and (h) Renewal of the Primary Party Organisations' Activities. Three more Commissions were formed in accordance with the resolutions passed by the 28th Party Congress. They were: (i) Science, Education and Culture; (j) Youth policy; and (k) Military policy.

These commissions were seen as forums for the functioning of Central Committee members, developing coherent Party policy and linking the central Party organs with the lower levels. A Central Committee member could be a member of only one commission. Members could be allowed to transfer from one commission to the other. This intra-commission mobility was perhaps designed to prevent compartmentalisation, which had resulted in departmentalism in the earlier organisation of the apparatus. It also allowed Central Committee members to familiarise themselves with different areas of work. Commissions could recommend advisers whose appointment would then be approved by a Central Committee plenum. These commissions were to prepare and approve the work plans for 1991. The Secretariat was to collate and send them to individual Central Committee members and Party organisations at all levels.[96] Thus in this scheme the Secretariat would lose its role as the authoritative centre of power.

The Ideology Commission had a high number of obkom officials and none from government and State institutions. The representation from intelligentsia was also low. This perhaps signified the pre-eminence of the middle ranks of the Party in both the formulation and the dissemination of ideology. No representation of any Central Committee member elected at the 27th Party Congress meant that the influence of the old ideological formulations was to be decidedly diminished.

Similarly the Socio-Political Commission had a high number of Party officials, especially from the obkoms. Thus they were to define the ideological-political orientation of the Party. It may also indicate the importance of the middle ranks of the Party which were acquiring greater independence and were more responsible for Party activities. This commission had a high number of academics, workers and peasants representing key sections of society. Most of them were elected at the 28th Party Congress and might be expected to have been more actively in touch with social-political processes.

The importance of the Socio-Economic Commission was shown by the fact that half of its members were Party officials, of which two-thirds were from the central category; policy-making in this area was thus to be kept under the close supervision of Central Party officials.

The Agrarian Policy Commission again had a high number of Party officials, particularly from the Central Party category. All the members of commission on Women and Family Questions were elected at the 28th Party Congress, perhaps signifying a major break from the past approach, or lack of it, to this issue. The formation of such a commission in itself constituted a significant step in addressing this question.

The Nationality Commission had a high number of Party officials, half of them from the republics, given the crucial importance of this issue. All except one were elected after the 27th Party Congress.

The International Policy Commission also had a high proportion of Party officials, the largest section belonging to the Central Party category. Academics were also well represented, and most of the members of the commission were elected at the 28th Party Congress.

Table 7.2 Background of members of the Central Committee Commissions elected in 1990

Professional Category	Commissions									
	a	b	c	d	f	g	h	i	j	k
Central Party officials	1	3	5	5	1	2	5	2	1	1
Republican "	-	1	2	2	-	4	1	-	-	
Obkom "	4	6	1	1	-	2	3	1	5	
Raikom "	-	1	-	-	-	-	-	-	1	
P. P. O. 's	-	1	-	-	1	-	-	5	2	
2-Ministers (Union and Republican)	1	-	3	1	-	-	-	-	2	
3-Government and State officials	-	3	-	-	-	-	2	-	-	
4-Soviets (Central, Republican, oblast, City)	1	3	-	-	-	1	2	-	1	
5-Academicians	2	4	1	-	-	2	4	-	12	
6-Media	1	-	1	-	-	-	-	-	2	
7-Industry	-	4	2	-	2	-	2	-	-	
8-Workers and Peasants	-	10	-	-	2	4	3	2	1	
9-Kolkhoz Officials	-	-	-	2	-	-	-	-	-	
10-Mass Organisations	-	1	-	1	-	1	1	-	3	
11-Military	-	1	-	-	-	1	1	-	-	
12-KGB	-	-	-	-	-	-	1	-	-	
13-Congress of People's Deputies	-	-	-	1	-	-	-	-	-	
14-Diplomats	-	-	-	-	-	-	2	-	-	
15-Retired and Unknown	1	-	1	2	-	2	-	-	1	1
T0TAL	11	38	16	14	6	19	26	10	33	2
Elected to the Central Committee at or before 27th Party Congress	-	4	3	6	-	1	1	2	4	
Elected in 1988 and 1989	4	1	2	-	-	2	1	-	-	
Elected at 28th Party Congress	7	33	*	*	6	16	16 *	8 *	29	1 *

The breakdown of the representation of the Military Policy Commission was as follows:
(1) Sub-committee on 'Questions on Implementing Reform and the Further Development of the USSR Armed Forces through the Party':
Armed Forces -- 1.
Air Force -- 3.
Minister -- 1.
The head of the sub-committee was M. A. Moiseev, Chief of the General Staff, USSR Armed Forces.
(2) Sub-committee on 'Problems of Social Welfare and Legal Protection of Soldiers and their Families':
Armed Forces -- 2.
Navy -- 2.
Industry -- 1.
The head of the sub-committee was N. I. Shliaga, Head of the Main Military-Political Directorate, USSR Armed Forces.
(3) Sub-committee on 'Questions on Securing Military Technology and Conversion Through the Party':
P. P. O. -- 1.
Industry -- 7.
Worker -- 1.
The head of the sub-committee was L. L. Nikiforov, General Director, 'S. P. Kovalev' Production Association, Kiev.
(4) Sub-committee on 'Ties with State and Social Organisations and Movements and with the Mass Media':
Party Officials-
Obkom -- 2.
P. P. O. -- 1.
Minister -- 1.
Industry -- 1.
Worker -- 2.
The head of the subcommittee was A. I. Gromoglasov, First Secretary, Arkhangelsk obkom.
The chairman of the Commission was O. D. Baklanov, first Deputy Chairman of the USSR Defence Council. Apart for two members, all were elected to the Central Committee at the 28th Party Congress.

Source: Prepared from K.G. Saur, 1992, pp. 46-53.

Eight out of ten members of the Primary Party Organisation Renewal

Commission were Party officials, with five from PPOs for obvious reasons. This commission was of particular significance given that PPOs were to function as political units of a Party competing for power, rather than primarily as the implementing arm.

The Commission on Science, Education and Culture not surprisingly had a high number of academics, and 29 out of 33 of its members were elected at the 28th Party Congress.

The three important general characteristics of the composition of these commissions were the presence of a high number of Party officials, particularly from the regions, the presence of members who were more directly related to the areas of the commissions, and the fact that overwhelming majority were elected at the 28th Party Congress.[97] The high number of regional officials seemed to indicate the growing importance of the middle-ranking Party officials. However, this was also the largest potential source of opposition to the reforms. That the composition in the main was new was a result of the overwhelmingly new Central Committee itself.

The Ideology Commission was to deal with information problems apart from that of ideology and propaganda. It seemed that the flow of information to the highest level of leadership was problematic, given the absence of sufficient institutions in society to collate and articulate information. The Socio-Political Commission was evidently to analyse the socio-political situation, the work of Communist deputies, and the process of state-building, and to establish relations with other organisations. The Party was in the course of learning the art of parliamentarism and parliamentary activities. The contemporary political situation required a politics of coalition, finding allies outside the Party. Since the Soviets at all levels were elected in competitive elections and included members opposed to the Party and various shades of opinions existing within the Communist deputies, there was a need to analyse their work. With the separation of the Party and State, the issue of rebuilding the State came to the fore. This meant developing representative institutions and an independent judiciary, and establishing an executive Presidency with an organisation independent of the Party in an institutional sense. The existing representation of State institutions in the Central Committee seemed to be an intermediary stage towards the complete separation of the two, once the State institutions were up and running. Such an intermediary stage was necessary given the peculiarity of a Soviet political system with a single-Party system. The Socio-Economic and Agrarian Policy Commissions were to work towards the transition to market relations. The Nationalities Policy Commission was to conduct discussions on problems related to the Union treaty. The Commission on Women and Family Issues was to involve women in the new economic conditions, develop their political role and mould Communist women leaders.

The Commission on the Renewal of Primary Party Organisations' Activity was to reorganise the local levels of the Party organisation. Councils of secretaries of Party organisations were to be organised. It seemed to be a preparation for an ever increasing number of PPOs to be organised on a territorial basis in the new political environment in which the political arena was shifting from the workplace to the territories. This was also meant to curtail mediation of the apparatus in inter-Party organisation relations. Such lateral linkages could develop co-ordination and co-operation among the PPOs in common areas of interests, and bring them out of their existence as isolated units by breaking the compartmentalisation that existed between them. Thus they could share common problems and tasks, develop a common understanding and work out collective responses as vital grassroots components of the Party.

The commissions varied in size. The number of members of the Socio-Economic Policy Commission was 54 and that of the Agrarian Policy Commission 47, whereas those of Youth Policy and Military Policy Commissions were 25 and 24 respectively,[98] and that of the commission on the Renewal of the Activity of the Primary Party Organisations 37.[99]

The Working of New Commissions

These commissions were of a different nature to their predecessors, since they emerged in the final phase of perestroika when the Party had effectively lost its political monopoly and was in a situation of full-blown crisis. Political pluralism had emerged and a multi-party system was taking shape. Thus these commissions lacked any authority. They functioned for less than a year as organs of a Party convulsed with internal strife and in a hostile external environment. Hence they never had an opportunity to consolidate themselves.

The Commission on Women and Family Questions discussed the political activities of women and their social security during the transition to a market economy,[100] their work in local Party committees, the situation in different regions and their role in the political campaign for the referendum on the Union.[101]

The Science, Education and Culture Commission was to devise Party policy in the field of science.[102] Scientific collectives, creative councils and Party committees were to be involved in this work. Its programme included spheres such as scientific-technical progress, ecology, the improvement of personnel and in the activity of Party organisations of cultural, educational and scientific associations.[103] The question of the legal regulation of the cultural processes in the country was discussed and proposals made.[104] Its working group was to draft a document on human policy.[105]

The Socio-Political Commission was to study the socio-political situation[106] and the Party's relationship with other political formations. A social and political club was formed in the Central Committee to play the "role of a centre for contacts with representatives of the new parties, movements, fronts, civic initiatives and the press".[107] It issued a document entitled "On Relations of the CPSU with Other Political Parties, Social Movements and Other Organisations".[108] The work of Party deputies in the Soviets was a key area of competence.[109] Previously, Party deputies were under strict Party discipline. With the emergence of a heterogeneous corps of deputies from the Party, the task of implementing the political line became a complex one requiring all the art of coalition-building. With the emergence of independent working-class movements in the country, one of the key issues faced by the commission was to work out the approach of Party organisations towards them.[110]

The purpose of the Commission for the Renewal of Primary Party Organisations was to collect the positive experiences gathered in the primary Party organisations and provide them with feedback.[111] The question of their functioning in the prevailing situation, the expansion of their rights, an increase in their responsibility for implementing Party policy and the drafts of Party documents were within its purview.[112] The strengthening of the Party was an obvious issue confronting it.[113] The last session discussed the proposals of Party organisations concerning the rules of the CPSU and proposed to convoke a plenum of the Central Committee.[114]

The Military Policy Commission prepared material to be given to the Supreme Soviet for legislative initiatives to be considered.[115] The commission discussed the negotiations on disarmament and military security[116] and the work of the Urdmurtskaia Republic Party organisation on the conversion of the military enterprises of the republic and the results of military service in 1990.[117]

The Ideology Commission was to develop and defend the new ideology, to analyse and forecast the political situation, influence public opinion, and generalise and disseminate the experiences of the Party organisations. Further, the Commission was to make recommendations for the Party media, develop contacts with the non-Party media and promote political co-operation with other parties and socio-political organisations inside and outside the country. [118]

The Nationalities Policy Commission's proposals on the Union treaty were to be taken into account during the preparations for the Central Committee plenum on this matter.[119] The legislative acts of the republics on measures for the provision of the rights of the individual, the legal protection of national minorities and their representation in the governmental organs at all levels were discussed.[120] The International Policy Commission was concerned with the role of CPSU in the current situation[121] and the relations of the USSR with foreign countries.[122]

The Youth Policy Commission was naturally concerned with affairs of youth.[123] Its main task seemed to be to restore a collaborative relationship between the Party and the Komsomol.[124] One of its sessions considered the questions of interaction between Party committees, Komsomol organisations, youth associations and State organs on resolving the social problems of youth.[125]

The Socio-Economic Policy Commission studied the preparation for the plenum of the Central Committee on the work of Communists in Soviets at all levels.[126] The formation, fulfilment and control of the Party budget and expenditure of the central Party organisations for 1991 was within its scope.[127] It studied the question of the formation of a multi-structured economy[128] and prepared a document "On the Fulfilment of Communist Party Policy in the Sphere of Denationalisation of Property". Lower Party organisations and those of the ministries and organisations were asked to strengthen political influence on the process of denationalisation of enterprises. The commission was to prepare necessary materials on this issue for local Party committees. The working group of the commission was asked to prepare proposals to strengthen the control of Soviet laws on property and give them to the Supreme Soviet and Cabinet of Ministers of the USSR.[129]

The Agricultural Policy Commission studied the socio-economic position of the peasantry. It worked out recommendations for Party committees, in which they were told to support legislative acts on the reform of land relations and the role of Party organisations in implementing them.[130] It discussed the functioning of the agricultural complex in market conditions[131] and the problems of resources and provisions for agriculture in gathering that year's harvest.[132]

Joint Sessions of the Commissions

The commissions also held joint sessions. A joint session of the Commission for the Renewal of the Activity of Primary Party Organisations and the Socio-Political Commission discussed final drafts on the status of secretaries of PPOs, the financial and economic activity of the Party and the role of Party organisations in the army. The two commissions also discussed ways to improve the work of Party members and deputies in the organs of State power.[133] Such joint meetings were necessitated by the overlap in the areas of competence of various commissions.

The Central Secretariat and the Commissions

There were a few examples of the reliance of the Central Secretariat on the proposals of the commissions, as in the case of the 26 March 1991 decree on the work of the Party with women and women's organisations. It was based on the analysis and recommendation contained in the note of the commission.[134] Another decree relied on the note of the Military Policy Commission dealing with the role of the Udmurtskaia Republic Party Organisation in the conversion of regional military enterprises and the social protection of workers. The decree agreed with the recommendations of the commission and decided to send this note to the republican central committees and local Party organisations.[135]

Conclusion

By the time the Central Committee was in decline, the role, nature and composition of the departments had substantially altered. They were very different from those Gorbachev had inherited when he became General Secretary. An example of the reformed role and composition of Central

Committee departments was that of the International department. The earlier tasks of monitoring and implementation of decrees no longer existed by 1991. The conversion of the department into a 'think tank' was confirmed by its composition. It consisted of 100 members who were specialists in international affairs. 29 of them had high qualifications, 16 knew one foreign language, and 17 knew two or more.[136]

The earlier organisation revolved around the Central Secretariat and central apparatus as the mainstays of effective power. During the course of Perestroika, these virtually surrendered their power. In the latter stages of Perestroika the Central Secretariat was no longer an independent centre of power. This was a part of the general decline in the authority of the Party and its organs. Gorbachev made several decisions without consulting either the Party or the leading decision-making bodies, and then asked the Central Secretariat to carry them out, realising that despite the steep decline, the Party had considerable resources and a large organisational network.[137]

Thus the Central Committee's organisation changed considerably during the course of perestroika. The political influence of the Central apparatus was reduced to a great extent, although not eliminated. The apparatus continued to play an important role but changed qualitatively. During the entire period it was progressively curtailed, and the commissions emerged. The central apparatus was reduced to the status of an 'assistant', albeit still an important one, to the Central Committee and its commissions.

The Party apparatus in general had played an integrative role in the political system in the past. The Central Secretariat and central apparatus were at the apex of this integrative mechanism. However, it was precisely this function that contributed to the inability of this institution to respond adequately to the realities of a complex society. Their responses had been limited to the traditional socio-economic forces represented in the system. During perestroika not only did new interests emerge, a systemic transition was taking place. This rendered the integrative function obsolete. One of the central sources of the power of these two institutions, that is, power to influence selection to key positions in the society, became non-existent. The economic and administrative functions of the two changed to policy-making on various issues. Hence by the time the Party ceased to exist, these were changed institutions primarily concerned with intra-Party matters and broad policy-making functions.

The commissions seem to have played an important role in formulating major documents. They appear to have had a wide sweep of issues in their competence, confirming their intended importance. Although the final drafts of statutes watered down their role, in practice the reformist section of the Party leadership seemed intent on developing them as an important form of organising the work of the Central Committee. In contrast with the previous commissions, they were no longer instructing or listening to reports from the State and government officials and the agencies. Their key role now was to work out legislation, concretise the basic policy directions of the Party, work out the role of the Party organs in carrying out these directives, deal with internal Party questions, and determine the Party's position on various issues and its role in conditions of a multi-party system.

These commissions functioned as sub-committees of the Central Committee in important areas. Despite their limitations, they deliberated issues which questioned the very foundation and integrity of the Soviet system as it had existed for more than seven decades. In a certain sense, parallelism with State institutions continued, although with the key difference that these bodies were only a part of the policy-making process and no longer directly involved in executing policy. The first set of commissions was dominated by Party and State officials but State officials were conspicuous absentees in the second set. On the one hand this was consistent with the separation of Party and the State, but on the other it explained the ineffectiveness of these commissions.

The effects of different commissions varied. In general, they had limited success, one reason being that they existed only for a brief period. The Commission for Youth Policy, led by Melnikov, had good contacts with the State structures working in this sphere, including the Supreme Soviet and the government. The main outcome of its work was the document "On Youth Policy in the USSR", which was adopted by the Supreme Soviet, and measures were undertaken to implement this document throughout the country. This example suggested that individual commissions functioned through their own individual resources, and that institutional channels were lacking, for instance, for the implementation of the Commission's policies by the State institutions. This indicated the rupturing of the relationship between the Party and the State by this period. The Socio-Political Commission, headed by V. Kuptsov, worked very actively. Kuptsov was in communication with all important leaders of social and political movements in the country. This was a new experience, since the commissions had not existed in the past. Apart from the Central Committee members, they also included scientists, experts, representatives of the local Party committees. The meetings of these commissions were open, and scientists, journalists and representatives of various parties and organisations were invited to attend these sessions. Their main work was analytical.[138]

The purpose of the commissions was to make the working of the Central Committee more efficient. The role of the apparatus continued to be important. The Central Committee and its members and the plenary sessions were supposed to play a decisive role, but in practice this had not been the case for a long time. The step of forming the commissions was precisely a step in the direction of increasing their direct involvement. Another raison d'être for the commissions was to develop closer contacts and links between the Central Committee and lower Party committees and Party organisations. Their formation had the underlying idea that members of the Central Committee should be real leaders and that the apparatus should function as an assistant to the members of the Central Committee in the commissions. However they were not without limitations.[139] Commissions functioned as instruments for formulating policies. They acted mainly as policy-drafting bodies or 'think-tanks' to generate new ideas. The Commissions were an 'unfinished story' and short-lived. Nevertheless during their brief existence, despite their limitations, they were involved in debating vital issues.

Notes

[1] "Perestroika", Chapter 4, in J.L. Black, ed., *USSR Documents Annual, 1988, Perestroika - The Second Stage*, Academic International Press, (Gulf Breeze, FL, 1989), p. 196.

[2] *Pravda*, 11 August, 1988, p. 1 in *FBIS*, 11 August 1988, p. 26.

[3] For changes in the Party Apparatus, see also, D. Lane and C. Ross, "The CPSU Ruling Elite 1981-1991: Commonalities and Divisions" (Unpublished Paper) and A. Rahr, "The CPSU in the 1980s: Changes in the Party Apparatus", *The Journal of Communist Studies,* vol. 7, June 1991, no. 2, pp. 161-69.

[4] *Argumenti i fakti*, no. 41, 8-14 October 1988, pp. 1-2 in *FBIS*, 7 October 1988, p. 29.

[5] *Rude pravo*, 14 October 1988, p. 7 in *FBIS*, 21 October 1988, p. 54.

[6] *Sovetskaia rossiia*, 6 February 1991, p. 3 in *FBIS*, 7 February 1991, p. 30.

[7] *Pravda*, 20 February 1989, p. 2 in *FBIS*, 21 February 1989, pp. 72-73.

[8] Interview with Boris Kluev.

[9] *Izvestiia Tsk KPSS*, no. 1, January 1990, pp. 3-5.

On the Secretariat between 1919-91 see S. White, The Soviet Leadership: the Politburo, Orgburo and Secretariat of the CPSU, 1919-1991, Lorton Papers, 1994.

[10] *ibid.*, no. 11, November 1989, pp. 3-6.

[11] *ibid.*, no. 5, May 1990, pp. 3-6.

[12] *Pravda*, 27 April 1989, p. 7 in *FBIS*, 28 April 1989, p. 51.

[13] This was accompanied by drastic changes at the lower levels as well. G. Razumovskii, "To Lead the Perestroika Effort, to Generate the Energy of Renewal", *Kommunist*, no. 4, 1989, pp. 12-13.
[14] *Pravda*, 12 February 1990, pp. 1-2 in *FBIS*, 13 February 1990, p. 64.
[15] *Pravda*, 3 April 1990, p. 2 in *FBIS*, 17 April 1990, p. 66.
[16] J.P. Willerton, Jr., "The Political Leadership", in S. White, et al, eds.1990, p. 60.
[17] *TASS*, 0643 GMT, 2 August 1990 in *FBIS*, 2 August 1990, p. 24.
[18] *CDSP*, Vol. XL11, no. 41 (1990), pp. 7-8.
[19] *ibid.*, p. 8.
[20] Calculated from K. G. Saur, 1992, pp. 61-69.
[21] *Izvestiia Tsk KPSS*, no. 3, March 1989, pp. 62-65. For instance, the Ideology department reviewed the implementation of the decree on the reorganisation of secondary and higher education addressed to the Grodnieskii Party committee and issued statement on the same. Similarly, a note from some departments on the reorganisation of political and economic education of workers contained information about the help rendered by the departments to 50 local Party committees. It criticised the Latvian CP CC for paying no attention to Central Committee recommendations.
[22] *ibid.*, pp. 66-68. For example asking them to teach workers the main ideas of perestroika and pay special attention to the political lectures given by them.
[23] *ibid.*, no. 5, May 1989, pp. 29-32.
[24] *ibid.*, pp. 32-35.
[25] *ibid.*, pp. 38-40.
[26] *ibid.*, pp. 40-44.
[27] From the information given in the issues of *Izvestiia_Tsk KPSS* in this period.
[28] *Izvestiia Tsk KPSS*, no. 7, July 1989, pp. 14-17. For instance, the Central Secretariat issued a decree on the shortcomings in implementation of another one on the improvement of living conditions of invalids. They made extensive criticisms of different ministries, local Party organisations and trade unions for not taking sufficient measures in fulfilling the decree. Detailed criticisms of various Party and governmental agencies were made.
[29] *ibid.*, no. 8, August 1989, pp. 28-30.
[30] An example was their role in implementing the key points of a speech by Gorbachev to a meeting of first secretaries of republican and local Party organisations. Important educational institutions, Party media and other organisations were to be reformed. The department of Party Building was told to take some measures on the improvement of the personnel system in the Academy of Social Sciences and Higher Party School. The Ideology department was asked to hold a meeting of directors and secretaries of Party organisations of Academic institutes. They were asked to prepare and hold a conference called 'Perestroika: Theoretical and Practical Problems' and a meeting of the editors of Party journals on the question of reorganisation of their activity. The Ideology department was to make proposals about the reorganisation of the Soviet House of Political Education in the Central Committee and about the Houses of Political Education of the Party Committees. It was also charged with formulating proposals on the reorganisation of the activities of the Party organisations of academic establishments.
[31] For example, the State-Legal department was to formulate a political conception of the State programme on the fight against crime and forward it to the Central Committee. It was

also told to prepare proposals on the improvement of legal education and on the organisation of legal studies in the country. The existing relationship between the Party and its mass organisations was being re-evaluated. The Ideology, State-Legal and Party-Building departments were told to study the problems of relations between Party organs and social organisations and to formulate practical proposals to be considered by the Central Committee.

[32] *ibid.*, no. 9, September 1989, pp. 9-11.

[33] *ibid.*, no. 11, November 1989, pp. 7-9.

[34] *ibid.*, no. 9, September 1989, pp. 12-13. An example was the decree on developing the statistical department of the Academy of Social Sciences and Higher Party schools. In the decree, the Party-Building and Ideology departments were ordered to consider the proposals of the Academy of Social Sciences on the structure and financial provisions of the activity of the centre of statistical work.

[35] *ibid.*, no. 4, April 1990, pp. 7-10. For example, one on preparing young people for military service discussed the lack of an effective system of preparation for youths in the military services. The leaders of the political committee of the military were criticised for not paying attention to their spiritual life. The lack of improvement in the activities of the Soviet and Party organs in order to settle their problems was questioned. It criticised the non-fulfilment of the provisions of resolutions such as the establishment of military sports camps and the organisation of special sport-technical sections. The departments pointed out the shortcomings to the Central Committees of the republic Party organisations, the Ministry of Defence and the Central Committee of Komsomol. Ministers Yazov, Yagodin, Chazov, Ruusak and Kotolovtev were told to prepare proposals for the Council of Ministers on military studies. They recommended that this note be sent to the Central Committees of the republican Party organisations, Central Committee of Komsomol, Committee of State Education, State Sports Committee, Ministry of Health Protection and to the Office of the Public Prosecutor.

[36] *ibid.*, no. 4, April 1990, pp. 3-6.

[37] One such example was the International Department. The link however was a fluctuating one. See M. Kramer, "The Role of the CPSU International Department in Soviet Foreign Relations and National Security Policy", *Soviet Studies*, vol. 42, no. 3, July 1990, pp. 429-446.

[38] *Izvestiia_Tsk KPSS*, no. 10, October 1990, pp. 19-23.

[39] *ibid.*, pp. 23-26.

[40] *ibid.*, pp. 18-23.

[41] *ibid.*, no. 9, September 1990, p. 9. For instance, on the decree issued on 7 August 1990, entitled "On the Organisation and Conditions of the Subscription to Party Newspapers and Journals for 1991", the Ideology and General departments were asked to make proposals concerning the quantities of periodical newspapers and journals of the *Pravda* group. The Ideology department was to work out measures to make the ideological work of local Party organisations more active and to provide financial credits to the Party press.

[42] An example was the decree "On Organisation of the Meeting of the Citizens with the Members of the Central Committee in the General Department" issued on 20 August 1990. The practice of citizens visiting the department to meet leaders of the Central Committee had started in February 1990. Between February and June 1990, 98 members and candidate members of the Central Committee received citizens. In this period they had met 907 people

out of whom 427 were Party members. A time-table for the members of the Politburo, Central Secretariat and Central Committee as to when they would receive citizens was prepared by the General department. Some examples from the time-table are as follows-

For members of the Politburo and the Central Secretariat from September to December 1990-
September 1990-1-G.V. Semenova. 2- A.N. Girenko.
October 1990- 1-O.D. Baklanov. 2-A.I. Teplenichev.
November 1990- 1-A.S. Dzasokhov. 2-V.A. Kuptsov.
December 1990- 1-O.S. Shenin. 2-I.I. Melnikov.
For members of the Central Committee-
September 1990-
4 September- A.A. Malofeev.
11 September- G.V. Novazhilov.
25 September-A.V. Vlasov.
October 1990-
2 October-A.Ya. Diagterev.
4 October-B.N. Makarov.
9 October-I.N. Denisov.
November 1990-
12 November-V.A. Achalov.
28-29 November-V.A. Proskurin.
December 1990-
4 December-A.A. Sergiev.
5 December-L.V. Galkin.
11 December-E.I. Kalinina.

43 From the information given in issues of *Izvestiia_Tsk KPSS* in this period.

44 E. Teague, "Gorbachev Discusses Personnel Policy", *RL 38/87*, 28 January 1987, p. 4.

45 *Izvestiia_Tsk KPSS*, no. 1, 1989, pp. 93-94.

46 "Materials of the 19th All-Union Conference of the Central Committee of the CPSU", *Kommunist*, no. 10, 1988, p. 48.

47 G. Razumovskii, "To Lead the Perestroika Effort, To Generate the Energy of Renewal", *Kommunist*, no. 4, 1989.

48 R.J. Hill, *Soviet Union, Politics, Economics and Society*, Frances Pinter, (London, 1985), p. 105.

49 *Moscow Television Service*, 1340 GMT, 30 September 1988 in *FBIS*, 30 September 1988, pp. 28-29.

50 *Rude pravo*, 14 October 1988, p. 7 in *FBIS*, 21 October 1988, p. 54.

51 The Commissions are numbered as follows: (1) Party Issues and Personnel Policy, (2) Ideology, (3) Social and Economic Policy, (4) Agrarian Policy, (5) International Policy, and (6) Legal Questions.
A. Rahr, "Gorbachev Changes Party Structure", *RL 519/88*, 30 November 1988, p. 3.

52 *ibid.*, p. 57.

53 *Argumenti i fakti*, no. 49, 3-9 December 1988, pp. 1-2 in *FBIS*, 2 December 1988, pp. 55-56.

54 *Izvestiia_Tsk KPSS*, no. 1, January 1990, p. 3.

55 *Pravda*, 28 January 1989, p. 2 in *FBIS*, 30 January 1989, pp. 51-52.

56 *Pravda*, 8 May 1989, p. 2 in *FBIS*, 8 May 1989, pp. 36-37.

[57] *Izvestiia_Tsk KPSS*, no. 6, June 1989, pp. 75-77.
[58] *ibid.*, no. 3, March 1989, pp. 42-43.
[59] *Pravda*, 1 February 1990, pp. 1-2 in *FBIS*, 22 February 1990, pp. 59-67.
[60] *Pravda*, 13 February 1990, pp. 1-2 in *FBIS*, 14 February 1990, p. 52.
[61] *Pravda*, 14 March 1989, p. 4 in *FBIS*, 21 March 1989, pp. 86-88.
[62] *Izvestiia_Tsk KPSS*, no. 4, April 1989, pp. 31-33.
[63] *Pravda*, 15 April 1989, p. 2 in *FBIS*, 17 April 1989, pp. 63-64.
[64] *Pravda*, 17 May 1989, p. 2 in *FBIS*, 17 May 1989, pp. 50-51.
[65] *Pravda*, 19 March 1989, p. 2 in *FBIS*, 22 March 1989, pp. 69-70 and *Izvestiia_Tsk KPSS*, no. 4, 1989,
pp. 34-36.
[66] *Izvestiia_Tsk KPSS*, no. 4, April 1989, pp. 34-36.
[67] *Pravda*, 25 April 1989, p. 2 in *FBIS*, 26 April 1989, pp. 81-82.
[68] *TASS*, 1824 GMT, 1 September 1989 in *FBIS*, 5 September 1989, p. 81.
[69] *Izvestiia_Tsk KPSS*, no. 1, January 1990, pp. 3-5.
[70] *ibid.*, no. 3, March 1989, p. 4.
[71] *ibid.*, no. 10, October 1989, pp. 29-35.
[72] *Pravda*, 10 October 1989, p. 2 in *FBIS*, 12 October 1989, pp. 90-91.
Izvestiia_Tsk KPSS, no. 12, December 1989, pp. 24-27.
[73] G. Razumovskii, "To Lead the Perestroika Effort, to Generate the Energy of Renewal", *Kommunist*, no. 4, 1989, pp. 13-14.
[74] *Izvestiia_Tsk KPSS*, no. 3, March 1989, p. 4.
[75] *ibid.*, pp. 44-45.
[76] *Pravda*, 4 June 1989, p. 6 in *FBIS*, 8 June 1989, p. 29.
[77] *Izvestiia_Tsk KPSS*, no. 8, August 1989, pp. 46-55.
[78] *Pravda*, 4 June 1989, p. 6 in *FBIS*, 8 June 1989, p. 29.
[79] *Izvestiia_Tsk KPSS*, no. 8, August 1989, pp. 46-55.
[80] *Pravda*, 16 October 1989, p. 2 in *FBIS*, 20 October 1989, p. 37.
[81] For a detailed study of *nomenklatura* see M. Voslensky, *Nomenklatura-Anatomy of the Soviet Ruling Class,* The Bodley Head, (London, 1984).
[82] *Pravda*, 12 November 1989, p. 2 in *FBIS*, 16 November 1989, p. 95.
[83] T. H. Rigby cited in R.J. Hill and P. Frank, *The Soviet Communist Party*, George Allen & Unwin, London, 1981,
p. 37.
[84] *ibid.*, p. 99.
[85] *Izvestiia_Tsk KPSS*, no. 11, November 1989, p. 3.
[86] *Pravda*, 4 February 1990, p. 2 in *FBIS*, 2 March 1990, pp. 53-54.
[87] *Pravda*, 14 February 1990, p. 1 in *FBIS*, 27 February 1990, pp. 53-54.
[88] *Izvestiia_Tsk KPSS*, no. 4, April 1989, pp. 3-6.
[89] *ibid.*, no. 5, May 1989, pp. 54-56.
[90] *ibid.*, no. 9, September 1989, p. 3.
[91] *Pravda*, 13 February 1990, pp. 1-2 in *FBIS*, 14 February 1990, p. 52.
[92] *Pravda*, 28 March 1990, p. 2 in *FBIS*, 28 March 1990, p. 59.

[93] *Pravda*, 12 March 1990, pp. 1-2 in *FBIS*, 12 March 1990, p. 61.
[94] *Pravda*, 18 July 1990, pp. 1-2 in *FBIS*, 19 July 1990, p. 43.
[95] *Pravda*, 2 February 1991, pp. 2-3 in *FBIS*, 4 February 1991, p. 27.
[96] *TASS International Service*, 2042 GMT, 9 October 1990 in *FBIS*, 10 October 1990, pp. 59-60.
[97] Calculated from K.G. Saur, 1992, pp. 46-53. * Complete figures not available.
[98] *Pravda*, 10 October 1990, p. 2 in *FBIS*, 11 October 1990, pp. 36-37.
[99] *Rabochaia tribuna*, 3 November 1990, pp. 1-2 in *FBIS*, 13 November 1990, p. 50.
[100] *Izvestiia_Tsk KPSS*, no. 11, November 1990, p. 27.
[101] *ibid.*, no. 2, February 1991, p. 12.
[102] *ibid.*, no. 4, April 1991, p. 7.
[103] *ibid.*, no. 11, November 1990, pp. 29-30.
[104] *ibid.*, no. 7, July 1991, p. 10.
[105] *ibid.*, no. 8, August 1991, pp. 33-38.
[106] *Pravda*, 26 October 1990, p. 2 in *FBIS*, 1 November 1990, p. 34.
[107] *Selskaia zhizn*, 27 October 1990, p. 3 in *FBIS*, 6 November 1990, p. 49.
[108] *Izvestiia_Tsk KPSS*, no. 11, November 1990, pp. 27-28.
[109] *ibid.*, no. 6, June 1991, pp. 11-12.
[110] *ibid.*, no. 7, July 1991, p. 10.
[111] *Moscow Television Service*, 1625 GMT, 5 November 1990 in *FBIS*, 6 November 1990, pp. 37-38.
[112] *Sovetskaia rossiia*, 27 October 1990, p. 2 in *FBIS*, 1 November 1990, p. 34.
[113] *Izvestiia_Tsk KPSS*, no. 5, May 1991, pp. 10-13.
[114] *ibid.*, no. 8, August 1991, p. 9.
[115] *ibid.*, no. 11, November 1990, p. 30.
[116] *ibid.*, no. 4, April 1991, p. 7.
[117] *ibid.*, no. 6, June 1991, pp. 11-12.
[118] *Pravda* (Complete details not given) in *FBIS*, 27 November 1990, pp. 54-55.
[119] *Rabochaia tribuna*, 6 December 1990, p. 2 in *FBIS*, 10 December 1990, p. 55.
[120] *Izvestiia_Tsk KPSS*, no. 6, June 1991, pp. 11-12.
[121] *ibid.*, no. 12, December 1990, p. 10.
[122] *ibid.*, no. 6, June 1991, pp. 11-12
[123] *ibid.*, no. 12, December 1990, p. 10.
[124] *ibid.*, no. 4, April 1991, p. 7.
[125] *ibid.*, no. 6, June 1991, pp. 11-12.
[126] *ibid.*, no. 2, February 1991, p. 12.
[127] *ibid.*, no. 6, June 1991, pp. 11-12.
[128] *ibid.*, no. 7, July 1991, p. 10.
[129] *ibid.*, no. 8, August 1991, p. 18-29.
[130] *ibid.*, no. 5, May 1991, pp. 10-13.
[131] *ibid.*, no. 7, July 1991, p. 10.
[132] *ibid.*, no. 8, August 1991, p. 9.

[133] *Moscow Domestic Service* 1200 GMT, 9 December 1990 in *FBIS*, 10 December 1990, p. 56.
[134] *Izvestiia_Tsk KPSS*, no. 6, June 1991, pp. 25-31.
[135] *ibid.*, no. 8, August 1991, pp. 53-55.
ibid., pp. 12-15.
[136] *Izvestiia_Tsk KPSS*, no. 7, July 1991, pp. 57-59.
[137] Interview with I. I. Melnikov.
[138] *Ibid.*
[139] The International department, for instance, performed the major bulk of the task of preparing the necessary documents and information for the commission. Although there were 35 to 40 members of the International Commission, only 14 to 15 of them attended the meetings. Not more than fifty per cent of members would attend. Meetings of these commissions always coincided with plenary sessions of the Central Committee and were never held separately. Around the time of a plenum, usually four to five hours would be reserved for the meetings of the commissions. Generally the sessions were held after the plenum, and most Central Committee members would be tired or in a hurry to go back, thus affecting the quality of the sessions. Only once did all the commissions have their sessions before the Central Committee plenum, and that was on the eve of the Central Committee plenum which discussed the draft of the new Party programme. The sessions were organised to get the opinions and remarks of the Central Committee members on the draft programme, and since it was not possible to do so during the plenum itself, commission meetings were held two days before the plenum. It was in these sessions that a large number of members got an opportunity to express their opinions, which were collected and presented to the Programme Commission. This was the only instance, in view of Fillipov, when the meetings of the commissions were organised in a proper way. Given time, the commissions could have consolidated and become effective, but in the event the Party was banned and the commissions ceased to exist.
Interview with A. V. Fillipov, Moscow, August 1992.

8 The Working of the Central Committee after the 19th Party Conference

Introduction

The working of the Central Committee too started reforming after the 19th Party Conference. Previously its activities had been primarily oriented towards administering society and the economy. The 19th Party Conference initiated the process of transforming this body to enable it to play a political role.

Participation of the Central Committee Members in Accordance with Occupational Background and Geographical Area

The major activities of the Central Committee were increasingly routed through special commissions of the Central Committee instead of the central apparatus. An example was the decision of the plenum held on 29 July 1988 to examine the question "On Practical Work To Implement the Decisions of the 19th All-Union Party Conference".[1] Instead of the task being given to the apparatus, a Commission, with broader involvement, was charged with drafting additions and amendments to the Constitution, electoral law and other legislative acts, and submitting them to the forthcoming USSR Supreme Soviet session.[2] This trend culminated in the formation of permanent commissions of the Central Committee, as discussed earlier.

A study of participation in the plenums revealed that Party officials, followed by those from the State, were the major participants in the debates. The overwhelming majority constituted republican and regional Party officials. No participation of lower Party officials was evident in 1988-89, but in 1990-91 their participation grew. This was consistent with the policy of growing autonomy and increased participation of the lower Party committees. Among State officials, those belonging to the central executive category, such as ministers and the **heads of state** committees, were the main participants. Their participation showed a decline after 1990, a result of the drastic reduction in their numbers in the Central Committee. The involvement of the intelligentsia was quite low until 1990. It increased in 1991, particularly at the last two plenums. The April plenum was the one which witnessed the sharpest conflict, and the July plenum discussed the Party programme, explaining the increased participation. Working-class participation was very low, but registered an increase in 1991, resulting from the large number of workers in the Central Committee. No peasant member of the Central Committee spoke. A negligible number of members from the industrial or agricultural management categories spoke. Russian was the largest nationality participating in the plenums, reflecting the fact that most Party and State officials belonged to this nationality. On the whole, the participation of other nationalities increased in 1990-91, particularly in 1991, not only because of increasing national awareness, but also because of the increased autonomy of republican organisations, which had largely come to represent national interests. However the participation of Georgia, Azerbaijan, Kirgizia, Moldavia and Tajikistan was either nil or negligible in the 1990-91 plenums. Some of these republics had a strong nationalist movement. In any case, most of the smaller republics did not participate in 1988-89, except for the September 1989 plenum on nationalities, when all the republics were represented.[3]

The contrast between the pre-Perestroika and Perestroika era was marked. The highly selective nature of participation under Brezhnev, for example, was noted by Ligachev when he reminisced that in 17 years of his first secretaryship of Tomsk obkom, he never had an opportunity to speak at a Central Committee plenum or a meeting. It was only under Andropov, that in a meeting on agriculture he asked for the floor and was given it for the first time.[4] During Perestroika the debates at the Central Committee plenums were reminiscent of the initial years of the revolution. Like the Commissions, the plenums became a more frequent method of the Central Committee's functioning. Twenty-two plenums were held between the 27th and 28th Party Congresses, double the number required by the rules for a five year period.[5]

Despite being participatory, the plenums became forums for conflict of diverging opinions and interests. This resulted in the absence of "reasonable compromises", and a lack of decisions and guidelines for Party organisations which disoriented them. Alternatives would be suggested by the "oppositions" like the Marxist platform, although these were never incorporated in the resolutions.[6] Critical debates became an important part of the plenums. The functioning of the Central Committee came under strong criticism by participants of the 25th April 1989 plenum. The Central Committee and its activities itself came under serious scrutiny. It was criticised for being ill-equipped to match the task required.[7] It was criticised for its inability to keep up with changes owing to inertia in approaches, style and methods of work and "in understanding the processes at work".[8]

Table 8.1 Participation of Central Committee Members in the Plenums in accordance with occupational background (A) and geographical area (B)

A.	July 1988	Nov. 1988	Apr 1989	Sept. 1989	Mar 1990	June 1990	Jan 1991	Apr 1991	July 1991
Party officials	12	6	11	26	24	3	16	11	19
State officials	4	2	2	8	3	3	2	3	3
Intell.*		1	2	1	1		2	7	10
Ind. Man.		1						1	
Agri. Man.							1	1	1
Working class	1		1	1			3	2	3
Peasantry									
Military/ KGB					1		1	1	
Mass org/ Pensioner		1	/6	1	2	1/1		2	1
Diplomat					1	1			
Total	17	11	20	37	32	9	25	28	37
B. Central@	4	2	1	7	4	5	3	6	6
RSFSR	7	4	10	13	20	3	12	14	16
Ukraine	2	1		2	1		1	1	3
Kazakh.	2	1	1	2	2		1	1	1
Belorussia	1	1		1	1		2		1
Georgia				1					
Azer.		1	1	1					
Latvia	1			1			1	1	1
Kirgizia				1	1				
Moldavia				1					1

Lithuania			1	2		2	1	2
Tajikistan			1					1
Armenia			1				1	1
Turkmenia			1	1			1	1
Estonia	1		1			2		1
Uzbek.			1			1	1	1
Unknown/ Pensioner		1/6	1		1			

Source: Compiled from_FBIS and CDSP.
The table illustrates the participation of the speakers at plenums of the Central Committee on the basis of occupational breakdown (A) and geographical area (B).
* Includes Academicians, Scientific and Cultural intelligentsia and Media.
@ Includes Ministers, heads of State Committees, mass organisations, representative State institutions, diplomats and functionaries such as advisers to the USSR President.

Altogether eight plenums of the Central Committee took place in 1989[9] and four in 1990.[10] The most noticeable feature of the 15 plenums held between 1989 and August 1991, apart from the large-scale participation in the debates, was that they were mainly concerned with Party policies and positions on various issues, internal Party political and organisational questions, and analysis of the situation in the country, and not with specific issues of the State and government. Different political tendencies contested their positions at these plenums. This conflict became particularly sharp from the February 1990 plenum, which witnessed "keen arguments and clashes of views".[11] Since the Party was losing its erstwhile position of power, opposition to the reforms from the Party and State apparatuses was reflected in the conservative offensive at several subsequent plenums.

Important resolutions were passed at these plenums.[12] Central Committee members were consulted and documents relating to the agenda were distributed to them.[13] Gradually the character of plenums became more meaningful. In an attempt to make the participation of members more effective, a 'selection of letters' from the public to the Central Committee was given to them regularly.[14] Participants in the March 1989 plenum were provided with draft documents on the Party's agrarian policy prepared by the Politburo with a similar purpose.[15]

The first ever Election Commission of the Central Committee for the election of deputies from the Party was organised with 13 members led by Valentin Koptyug, Vice-President of the USSR Academy of Sciences, in

December 1988.[16] The candidate deputies were given 'mandates' at election campaign meetings on political, socio-economic, defence and foreign policy. The March 1989 plenum passed a resolution on these 'mandates'.[17]

Resolutions

The practice of passing resolutions continued in the latter stages of Perestroika. One passed was "On the Restructuring of the System of Working People's Political and Economic Study" and on the shortcomings of the Ulianov oblast.[18] Another was "On Progress in Fulfilling Party Central Committee Resolutions on Questions of Intensifying the Campaign Against Drunkenness and Alcoholism". A noticeable feature of this resolution was that although the Party, mass organisations, State and government agencies were criticised and asked to improve their performances, the tone of the resolution was no longer 'directive'. It was more recommendatory in nature, particularly in the case of State and government agencies.[19]

The nature of resolutions changed in the post-19th Party Conference period. A study of 64 resolutions passed between October 1988 and July 1991 revealed a drastic fall in the number of resolutions on the economy. The trend of issuing direct resolutions on these issues declined, and resolutions on political and social issues took precedence. A sizeable number, at least 38 out of 64, were directly concerned with the Party and its members, particularly in 1990-1991.[20] 30 more resolutions were passed by the Central Committee, apart from those which have been mentioned earlier between July 1988 and July 1991.[21]

A decree issued by the Central Secretariat on the political education of Party committees was concerned that the decisions of the Central Committee were fulfilled very slowly, and that several first secretaries did not appreciate the importance of such studies and did not deeply analyse various activities.[22] Another decree recommended in October 1989 that the media should give coverage to women's issues and activities. A new magazine for Russian women was to be introduced. The activity of women's councils were to be introduced. The Academy of Social Sciences was to organise a special course on the improvement of the qualifications of the leaders of these councils, and publication of a special women's magazine was to be organised. This decree was based on an article by L. Vasilieva published in *Pravda* in June 1989.[23]

A decree of the Central Secretariat was issued in February 1989 on the illegal use of child labour in the country. It criticised the employment of young students in agricultural work, for example, in the Marisk region in Turkmenia, and in many collective farms in Uzbekistan, Tajikistan, Kirgizia and Moldavia. According to the decree, child labour was extensively used, and they were even made to work in their spare time. In certain places, for instance in the collective farm "Birnintza" in the Lazovskii region of Moldavia, children as young as 7 or 8 years were made to work.[24] A decree was issued in November 1990 on efforts to disband Party organisations in Moscow institutes, like the Moscow Architectural Institute and Moscow Technological Institute. The Central Committees of the republics and local Party organisations were asked to protect their Party structures and defend the rights of Communists. Similarly, another decree was issued on the persecution of Communists in the Western region of the Ukraine, and it was decided to give the necessary materials on this question to the Supreme Soviet.[25]

Conferences

Conferences continued to take place at the Central Committee. Experts, academics, leaders of the government and State agencies along with Party leaders participated in them. One such meeting took place on the question of hydro-electric power in September 1988.[26] These conferences monitored the fulfilment of decisions, such as that examining "progress in fulfilling the decisions of the Party and government to improve the supply of foodstuffs to the population and accelerate the socio-economic development and scientific-technical progress in the national agro-industrial complex".[27] A round-table at the Party Central Committee's Institute of Marxism-Leninism formulated recommendations and proposals for the plenum on nationality questions. This discussion was attended by academics and Party, Soviet and Komsomol personnel.[28]

More than 31 conferences took place in the Central Committee between January 1989 and May 1991.[29] Some were held in the localities with the participation of Central Committee members and took decisions there. For example, at one held in Orlovskii oblast, the Central Committee decided to give local organisations rights to organise trade and services, and also gave them some buildings. A decision to allow citizens to buy their flats, which would become their private property, was also taken.[30] This conference revealed the process of decentralisation and the role of the Central Committee in implementing economic reforms at this time.

A conference of members of the Central Committee with workers on 14 February 1989 considered problems of the social and economic development of the national economy. More conferences with workers took place. Some Central Committee members visited collective farms, factories, plants, hospitals, schools and institutes, and held discussions.[31] This may have reflected an attempt to reach out to various sections of the population specifically in view of the forthcoming elections.

At least 14 conferences out of a total of 20 held between January 1990 and May 1991 were with the leaders of Party organisations at various levels, possibly highlighting the discussions of Party problems.[32] These appeared to be in contrast with those of previous years which were mainly on socio-economic and agricultural issues. Between September 1988 and November 1989, eight conferences took place on socio-economic issues, four on agricultural issues, two on Party affairs and six on political-ideological issues.[33]

According to a former apparatus official, A. Fillipov, conferences were meant to gather the opinions of experts with regard to particular issues. The frequency of specialised conferences, seminars and round table discussions did not decline greatly at any stage during Perestroika. Usually the results of these conferences were important for the work of the Central Committee and its apparatus. The expert opinions, recommendations and concrete suggestions of these conferences, seminars and round-table discussions acquired greater significance during Perestroika.[34]

The Central Committee and Lower Party Organisations

Lower Party organisations, essentially their committees, had been accustomed to detailed central directions. In his memoirs, Shevardnadze recollects how centralisation had stifled the autonomy of lower Party organisations, up to and including the republican ones, on important issues. A district Party Secretary would be impeded in the resolution of problems by "numerous restrictions" and would have to go to higher authorities. The latter would be dependent on still higher ones, thus concentrating the final authority at the highest levels. He encountered a similar problem, on a larger scale, as leader of the Georgian Party organisation, despite being a candidate member of the Politburo. No issue, whether the allocation of electric power to open a preparatory school for Georgian youth joining higher military academies, replenishing tea industries' stocks or building major public works could be undertaken without "the knowledge and permission of Moscow". This was not only contrary to the spirit of sovereignty of the republic in the Soviet Constitution,[35] it nurtured *the culture of dependence* of the lower Party organisation on higher ones.

An attempt was made to change this situation during Perestroika by increasing the autonomy of lower Party organisations. S. A. Niazov, a member of the Central Committee and first secretary of the Turkmen Party organisation, claimed:

> We had grown accustomed to being told from above what to do and how and to having everything assigned for us. As of 1986 we began to notice that no one from the Central Committee was giving us orders as to how to work and what to do. I think that all the country's Party organisations felt that they must find for themselves effective methods and forms of work, taking local conditions into account.[36]

However, in the early post-19th Party Conference period the Central Committee continued to direct lower Party committees. A conference of secretaries of Union-republic Communist Party Central Committees, kraikoms and obkoms was held on 5-6 September 1988 in Ulianovsk. It discussed the implementation of the Central Committee resolution on reorganising the work of the Ulianovsk Party organisations regarding the political and economic education of workers. Members of the central apparatus delivered reports to these conferences.[37] Similarly, the Central Committee adopted resolutions on the work of the Kiev Party organisations, the Norilsk gorkom, and Leningrad's Viborgskii raikom asking them to "radically ... (improve) political and organisational work and set an example of democratic conduct, collective spirit and high exactness".[38] Central Committee commissions would investigate the activities of leaders of lower Party organisations, and where necessary issue punitive decrees against them.[39]

Decrees on regional Party organisation were passed, like that on the Kiev Party organisation, asking it to fulfil the decisions of the 27th Party Congress. This decree and the subsequent plenum showed how the provisions of the Congress were not fulfilled by regional Party organisations.[40] The February 1988 plenum of the Central Committee issued a decree 'About the Reorganisation of Secondary and Higher School Education and About the Aims of the Party on its Fulfilment', addressed to the Grodnieskii Party committee in Belorussia. After a year the Ideology Department analysed the implementation of the decree and issued a statement. The Grodnienskii Party committee had looked into the education system in the light of the decree and found that the process of reorganisation was proceeding too slowly.[41] The practice of issuing decrees on an individual Party organisation continued in 1991. The difference now was that they would be addressed to the Party committee instead to state agencies.[42]

In a new method of working, a decree would order the secretaries of the Central Committee to speak to the first secretaries of the Central Committees of the Communist Parties of the republics. An example was the Central Secretariat decree issued on 28 August 1990 on the grave situation resulting from acute problems in the supply of foodstuffs and consumer goods to the population. As late as the third quarter of 1990, the central leadership was involved in resolving issues of an economic nature. It seemed that in the existing crisis situation and under conservative pressure there was an attempt to rely on traditional economic measures. However, the important thing was that Party organisations and not State agencies were made responsible for such measures. In this decree, the secretaries of the Central Committee were asked to talk to first secretaries of the republican Central Committees and local Party committees on the fulfilment of concrete measures for the improvement of the social and political situation in each region and labour collective.[43]

The Central Committee decrees were becoming more recommendatory to the lower Party organisations. In a decree issued on 11 September 1990 the Central Committees of republican and local Party organisations were recommended to ask the Supreme Soviets of republics to protect culture under conditions of a market economy.[44] A similar decree concerned the role of the Party organisations in livestock farming in winter and preparing for spring. Both testified that the Party was to continue playing an important role in social, cultural, economic and agricultural issues, although indirectly.[45] Such a system of recommendations to the Party committees continued well into 1991.[46] The Central Committee seemed to rely on older methods of functioning until new methods were consolidated. Old and new methods coexisted, but with decreasing emphasis on the former.

The issue of devolution of power to the lower echelons, which was part of the political and economic programme of reforms, was debated. The process of shifting power to local levels and granting greater independence to republics, local bodies and economic organisations followed.[47] Lower Party committees were becoming more autonomous. In a novel method of the Central Committee's functioning, at the suggestions of the Krasnoiarsk kraikom, Vitebsk, Voronezh, Tashkent and several other obkoms, primary Party organisations in these regions were given the right to decide by themselves questions of admission or expulsion of candidate Party members on an experimental basis.[48] This was a modest initiative in the direction of granting greater autonomy to lower Party organisations.

In unprecedented developments, in the latter years of Perestroika, the Central Committee faced criticism from lower Party committees on various issues and proposals submitted to it. For example, the joint plenum resolution of the Leningrad obkom and gorkom issued on 21 November 1989 criticised its work. Such a criticism was generally either from conservative sections of the Party, as in this case, or from radical reformists.[49] By early 1991 the autonomy of the primary, oblast, city, and republican Party organisations had reached a state where they had become 'uncoordinated', to the extent that Prokofiev, at the January 1991 Central Committee plenum, said that the Party did not act as "a single co-ordinated political mechanism".[50] Raion and primary Party organisations were openly critical of the Central Committee. This was acknowledged by the leadership of the Central Committee.[51] Such autonomy was particularly a matter of concern for conservative elements in the Party leadership.[52]

Fillipov, an apparatus official, asserted that in the last years of Perestroika, in 1989-91, lower Party organisations became more autonomous and more independent, and had more rights and more possibilities of acting on their own and taking initiatives. This process of independence for local Party organisations had started in 1989 when they were given formal rights. On the one hand, the relationship between the Central Committee and republican Party organisations reflected closer contacts than in the past, with members of the Central Committee from the republics visiting Moscow more frequently and meeting the Party leadership. On the other hand, the control of the Central Committee over lower Party organisations was loosened to a great degree in comparison with the past. One of the purposes of the commissions of the Central Committee was to have closer political contacts with them. Full-time workers from Central Committee departments would go to lower Party committees and attempt to reach the lowest echelons such as factories, sovkhozes and kolkhozes in an attempt to collect more accurate information.[53]

Implementation of Central Committee Decisions

The implementation of decisions was as usual facing difficulties in the fourth year of Perestroika. In Lithuania, the measures from the centre were ignored. Decisions of the Central Committee were not even brought to the knowledge of Party members and committees.[54] Although this may have been a specific case, it was not markedly different in other places. People were losing faith because of the non-fulfilment or partial fulfilment of decisions.[55]

A study conducted by the Central Control Commission and Central Committee organisational department revealed that Party members were not even familiar with several decisions of direct concern to them. This was true of gorkoms, raikoms, and primary Party organisations as well as of obkom and kraikom bureau members. For example, in Volgograd obkom, only eight out of 15 members of the bureau were familiar with the Central Committee resolution "On the Self-Disbandment of Moscow City Educational Establishment Party Organisations". Similarly at the Volgograd gorkom, the city's Tsentralnii raikom and higher educational establishment Party organisations, nobody at all was aware of this resolution.[56]

The general method of implementation of Central Committee decisions did not change very radically even under Perestroika. After a decision was adopted, each Party organisation was expected to work out a plan of realisation of such decisions and allocate individual responsibilities. In the case of specific decisions, only the Party organisations involved were obliged to have such a working plan; for instance, a decision on agriculture would not be relevant to the Party committee at the Institute of Psychology or at a Medical Institute, hence they would not need to have a working plan. Sometimes the working plans were not realistic, resulting in only partial implementation of the Central Committee decisions. The change under Perestroika was perhaps that more concrete and realistic working plans were adopted. They were more manageable and coincided with the particular characteristics of each Party organisation, and were more acceptable to it.[57]

The mechanism of implementation of decisions had broken down by 1990. The traditional mechanism of a well regulated and hierarchical system of implementation from the Central Committee to the grassroots organisations had become disorganised. Previously, this system comprised formal structures as well as a system of informal interpersonal relations known as the "telephone rule" which ensured a minimum credible implementation. The motives which had kept the system going, like career, material well-being, compliance with the routine, etc. no longer existed. The external function of the Party, that of executing the decisions pertaining to the functioning of State and government machinery no longer worked.[58]

Election of CPSU Deputies

Another example of the newly emergent style of operation was the process of election to the Congress of People's Deputies. The election commission set up by the Central Committee called for the submission of proposals for the Party's candidates to the posts of deputies through the press, Party organisations and Central Committee members. According to the procedures set by the commission, proposals about the Party members working at local levels were to be considered in primary Party organisations, then in higher ones right up to the Union-Republics. The candidacies of political, State and public figures, and those from workers, peasants, academics and cultural figures working or living in other republics, territories and regions were to be sent directly to the Central Committee.

In the course of nominations, 105,000 primary Party organisations participated, proposing 31,500 candidates for consideration by city and district committees. There the number was scaled down to 3,500. After discussions in regional and territorial Party committees and the Central Committees of Union-republic Party organisations, a list of 207 candidates was finally submitted to the Party Central Committee. Several direct proposals from Party organisations, work collectives and individuals were received by the Central Committee in 12,000 telegrams, letters etc. Most proposed the candidatures of Politburo and Central Secretariat members. The number of candidacies proposed in this way was 382.[59] In the past, such a list would essentially have been drawn up by the Central Secretariat and the central apparatus, with or without feedback from lower levels.

The final election of these 100 deputies took place at a Central Committee plenum on 15-16 March 1989. Apart from the members, who had the decisive votes at the plenums, a wider section of leading Party cadres were to be allowed to vote. This latter category was to include candidate members, members of the Central Auditing Commission, first and second secretaries of the Union-republic organisations, leaders of the regional Party committees, presidents of the presidiums and chairmen of the governments of the Union-republics, ministers and heads of central State agencies and organisations and commanders of military districts.[60] The list also included candidates to the Congress of People's Deputies from the Party who were not members of the central leadership organs.[61]

Opinion Polls and Public Relations

The Central Committee was adopting hitherto unknown methods of functioning such as opinion polls to assess the popular mood. These polls were initiated by the Central Committee on the most topical problems of Perestroika, the development of democratic processes, and Party organisations' activity. One such example was the All-Union public opinion poll on "Party Committees and the Renewal of Political Life" prior to the conference on questions of Party work.[62] In addition a Press Centre was started at the Oktiabrskaia Hotel in Moscow. Soviet and foreign journalists were to be given information "about the most important events in the life of the Party" at least once a week.[63]

Participation of Central Committee Members in its Work

The problems of the active participation of members in the Central Committee's work were revealing. Central Committee members from the working class and peasantry did not have a place to work were they could meet people, there was lack of transport facilities, and lack of information to those working in localities which left them ill-equipped for debates on important questions. The status of the members was ill-defined. There was a persisting tendency of members to look towards the centre.[64] The problem of the lack of authority of members when it came to dealing with the Party apparatus, thus impairing their functioning, was explained succinctly by V.M. Malikhin, leader of a team of electricians at the Volga Automobile Plant and a member of the Central Committee, when he said:

> At present little depends on our position, for we cannot call a negligent Party official really to account at the local level. Our rights, the rights of the Central Committee members from the localities, are not clearly defined in the Party Statutes or in any instructions. For instance, can we demand

> that a particular gorkom or raikom secretary be dismissed for failings in his work? I personally do not know. At best, if people respect you, they somehow heed your opinion. No more. Maybe we are the only ones in this position? I don't think other people have it any better.[65]

Popular expectations of members of the Central Committee were quite high. They were expected to actively implement the Party's policy and its line and not just participate in their elaboration.[66] However in the period of transition, with strident opposition outside the Party and from the Party and the State apparatuses, these were the tasks in which they evidently failed.

Conclusion

The separation of the Party and State meant that the Central Committee as an institution was no longer the centre for the aggregation of interests and decision-making in the way it used to be. It certainly was a forum for the articulation of numerous political, social and economic interests, both represented and unrepresented. Policy-making was its key function, in keeping with its proclaimed political role. It seemed to have become the parliament of the Party, with contending political tendencies. Its activities were geared towards intra-Party affairs and what the policies of the Party should be in various spheres. Plenums, which were held quite often, were marked by critical debates, which reflected both the strength and the weakness of this body. The strength was that the speeches were political in nature, highlighted many different points of views, and discussed the problems and prospects of Perestroika from diverse positions. Its weakness was that this platform was used in the political conflict of various political tendencies, and could not reach consensus and compromise on outstanding issues of the day. It did not consolidate itself as the Party's parliament. Although its work was still conducted through the numerous resolutions passed and conferences held, their nature and content had undergone major change.

The 19th Party Conference inaugurated a series of important political reforms. In the ensuing period the activity of the Central Committee became more participatory, both in numbers and substance as far as plenums were concerned. However, individual participation in the activities of the Central Committee was still problematic, particularly for those members who did not represent the Party and State apparatuses, such as the workers and peasants, at least until 1989. This was as a consequence of a Central Committee which was still a collective of institutions rather than a political body. Such a situation seemed to have continued throughout Perestroika because of the continuing opposition from within the Party and the State apparatuses to the reforms. However, Central Committee members were better informed by contrast with the situation in the past, as the debates suggested. The practice of bargaining between various interests such as those of ministries and other agencies, which was conducted behind the scenes in the past, was no longer evident after the 28th Party Congress; by then most of them were not represented in the Central Committee.

The working of the central bodies were deemed to be deficient and unable, in its old form, to match the magnitude of the task unfolding; hence the need to make it an open and participatory body. Its relationship with lower Party organisations changed in keeping with federalisation within the Party. If the Party was not to participate in affairs of the State, manage the economy, and play a political role, then the command system was structurally redundant. Decentralisation within the Party was imperative, allowing the lower levels to formulate their political approach in keeping with local specificities within the overall framework of national policy, which itself could be decided with their participation. Thus these lower Party organisations would operate within a common political space, with the centre providing a forum for the articulation of local interests and the input into policy-making.

However, it was becoming evident that lower Party organisations were either unwilling or unable to reform themselves. Most were proving resilient to the changes required to adjust the organisation and their work to the prevailing political environment. The decrees of the Central Committee on their activities, ranging from reorganising their own political and organisational methods of work to their role in implementing reform measures, seemed to be a catalogue of failures. The reason, as discussed previously appeared to lie in that the Party structures and methods of work which had evolved over a long period of time had been primarily geared towards administrative tasks. As a result, a series of decrees were issued from the Central Committee criticising them. This also highlighted the problems of its functioning in a new way during the period of transition.

Similarly, such decrees underscored the problems of the separation of Party and State. The implementation of the decrees of the Central Committee was as problematic as before. In several cases, they were completely ignored and not even publicised, particularly in the case of republics like Lithuania. Worse still was that Party members and leaders of

Party committees were not even familiar with various Central Committee resolutions. This meant that most either did not find these resolutions of any practical significance or did not agree with the reforms, as in the case of conservative and radical Party committees, or that autonomy went to the extent of complete independence. It is also doubtful if several committees existed as working Party committees, reformed or otherwise. Possibly these were only concerned with their own localised matters.

The Central Committee departments and their officials continued to play an important role, particularly in the earlier years. However, the suggestions of lower Party organisations on the process of their own autonomy were taken into account and implemented. At a later stage, with the growing independence of lower Party organisations, the decrees of the Central Committee would be generally ignored by them, compelling the central secretaries to personally attempt to persuade their leaders to implement them. This emphasised the lack of authority of the central leadership. One of the reasons for this was the opposition resulting from the conservatism or radical-reformism of various Party committees. Several Party committees used their autonomy to criticise the reforms and the leadership. Instead of changing themselves and grappling with the problems that surfaced, they turned inwards and held Perestroika and the reformist sections of the leadership responsible for the problems. Such opposition came from the lowest levels of Party organisations as well. Apart from the fact that the earlier hierarchical system of organisation was no longer operating, another key factor for the 'rebellion' at the lower levels seemed to be that the activities of the Central Committee fell short of the requirements of the contemporary situation. In the absence of adequately functioning State organs, the Central Committee as the leadership of the ruling Party was criticised by grassroots Party organisations which were in direct contact with the prevailing conditions. Most importantly, the middle level of the Party's organisational structure, that is the regional and district level, most of which consisted of conservative constituencies, continued the practice of conveying selective information to higher leadership organs. Hence the inadequacy of the decisions taken and the resultant 'rebellion' of the lower Party organisations. Despite the drawbacks and variations which inevitably accompany transitions of such magnitude, the working of the Central Committee had been transformed as never before.

Notes

[1] *Pravda*, 30 July 1988, p. 1 in *FBIS*, 1 August 1988, p. 35.
[2] *Pravda*, 1 August 1988, p. 1 in *FBIS*, 2 August 1988, p. 44.
[3] Compiled from *FBIS* and *CDSP*. The table illustrates the participation of the speakers at the plenums of the Central Committee on the basis of occupational breakdown (A) and geographical area (B).
[4] E. Ligachev, "Iz Vospominanii", *Argumenti i fakti*, no. 3, 1991, p. 5.
[5] *Pravda*, 3 July 1990, pp. 2-4 in *FBIS*, 3 July 1990, p.19.
[6] A.V. Buzgalin, 1993, pp. 80-3. An example of ignoring the suggestions of the "opposition" was cited by Buzgalin. According to him, at the second plenum of the Central Committee after the 28th Party Congress, he as part of the Drafting Committee, thought that a particular resolution required redrafting. He told the Chairman of the Committee, V.A. Ivashko, that the proposed draft could not be taken as a basis for the resolution. Ivashko replied that it was already late in the evening and the resolution had to be adopted the next morning which was the last day of the plenum. Buzgalin took the responsibility of drafting the resolution. Next day he brought the draft prepared by him and Andrei Kolganov. The members of the committee read the draft, as they later stated, with interest and rejected it. However Dzasokhov promised to discuss the draft at the Secretariat meeting. When a disappointed Buzgalin asked for the draft to be handed back, he was refused. Most committee members wanted to keep it. This example showed the difference of interests which hindered the decision-making process.
[7] *Izvestiia*, 27 April 1989, pp. 1-2 in *FBIS*, 27 April 1989, p. 35.
[8] *ibid.*, p. 41.
[9] *Izvestiia_Tsk KPSS*, no. 1, January 1990, pp. 3-5.
[10] Calculated from *Izvestiia_Tsk KPSS*.
[11] Leningradskaia *Pravda*, 23 February 1990, pp. 1-2 in *FBIS*, 4 April 1990, p. 79.
[12] *Pravda*, 31 July 1988, pp. 1-2 in *FBIS*, 1 August, 1988, pp. 50-54. For example, resolutions 'On Practical Work To Implement the 19th Party Conference Decisions', 'On Reports and Elections in Party Organisations' and 'On Basic Guidelines for Restructuring the Party apparatus', were passed after the 19th Party Conference at the July 1988 plenum.
[13] *Moscow Television Service*, 0612 GMT, 28 June 1988, in *FBIS*, 29 June 1988, p. 30.
[14] *Pravda*, 2 December 1988, p. 4 in *FBIS*, 6 December 1988, p. 115.
[15] *Pravda*, 16 March 1989, p. 1 in *FBIS*, 16 March 1989, p. 50.
[16] *TASS*, 2003 GMT, 8 December 1988 in *FBIS*, 9 December,1988, pp. 74-75.
[17] *Pravda*, 19 March 1989, pp. 1-2 in *FBIS*, 20 March 1989, pp. 54-57.
[18] *Pravda*, 5 October 1988, p. 1 in *FBIS*, 6 October 1988, pp. 42-43.
[19] *Pravda*, 26 October 1988, p. 1 in *FBIS*, 1 November 1988, pp. 74-75.
[20] Calculated from the list of resolutions given earlier and from all the issues of *Izvestiia_Tsk KPSS*.
[21] From the information in *Izvestiia_Tsk KPSS*.
[22] *Izvestiia_Tsk KPSS*, no. 11, 1989, pp. 13-17.
[23] *ibid.*, no. 12, 1989, pp. 12-14.
[24] *ibid.*, no. 2, 1990, pp. 23-24.

[25] *ibid.*, no. 12, 1990, pp. 15-17.
[26] *Moscow Television Service*, 1800 GMT, 26 September 1988 in *FBIS*, 27 September 1988, pp. 44-45.
[27] *Moscow Domestic Service*,1630GMT, 2 November1988 in *FBIS*, 3 November1988, p. 32.
[28] *Pravda*, 7 July 1989, p. 4 in *FBIS*, 15 August 1989, p. 63.
[29] Calculated from *Izvestiia_Tsk KPSS*.
[30] *Izvestiia_Tsk KPSS*, no. 1, January 1989, p. 36.
[31] *ibid.*, no. 3, March 1989, p. 4.
[32] Calculated from information in *Izvestiia_Tsk KPSS* 1989-1991.
[33] Calculated from information in *FBIS*.
[34] Interview with A. Fillipov.
[35] E. Shevardnadze, 1991, p. 27.
[36] *Pravda*, 20 March 1990, pp. 2-4, in *FBIS*, 22 March 1990, p. 53.
[37] *Pravda*, 7 September 1988, p. 2 in *FBIS*, 9 September 1988, p. 69.
[38] *Pravda*, 15 November 1988, p. 1 in *FBIS*, 5 December 1988, p. 114.
[39] *Izvestiia_Tsk KPSS*, no. 3, March 1989, pp. 10-11.
[40] *ibid.*, pp. 57-60.
[41] *ibid.*, pp. 62-65.
[42] *ibid.*, no. 5, May 1991, pp. 23-26.
[43] *ibid.*, no. 10, October 1990, pp. 13-15.
[44] *ibid.*, pp. 19-21.
[45] *ibid.*, no. 4, April 1991, pp. 26-28.
[46] *ibid.*, no. 8, August 1991, pp. 38-41.
[47] *Izvestiia*, 27 April 1989, pp. 1-2 in *FBIS*, 27 April 1989, p. 35.
[48] *Pravda*, 31 August 1989, p. 1 in *FBIS*, 6 September 1989, p. 77.
[49] *Leningradskaia Pravda*, 29 November 1989, p. 1 in *FBIS*, 21 December 1989, p. 76.
[50] *Pravda*, 4 February 1991, p. 3 in *FBIS*, 5 February 1991, p. 24.
[51] *Pravda*, 2 February 1991, pp. 2-3 in *FBIS*, 4 February 1991, p. 28.
[52] *Sovetskaia rossiia*, 27 April 1991, p. 2 in *FBIS*, 29 April 1991, p. 5.
[53] Interview with A. Fillipov.
[54] *Moscow Domestic Service*,0600 GMT,-26December1989in *FBIS*,26December 1989, p. 45.
[55] *Pravda*, 8 February 1990, p. 3 in *FBIS*, 9 February 1990, p. 69.
[56] *Pravda*, 2 February 1991, pp. 2-3 in *FBIS*, 4 February 1991, p. 28.
[57] Interview with A. Fillipov, Moscow, August 1992.
[58] A. V. Buzgalin, 1993, pp. 84-85.
[59] *Pravda*, 11 January 1989, pp. 1-2 in *FBIS*, 11 January 1989, pp. 39-40.
[60] *TASS*, 1455 GMT, 10 January 1989 in *FBIS*, 11 January 1989, p. 41.
[61] *TASS*, 0758 GMT, 15 March 1989 in *FBIS*, 15 March 1989, pp. 34-35.
[62] *Krasnaia zvezda*, 5 August 1989, p. 2 in *FBIS*, 22 August 1989, p. 68.
[63] *Moscow Television Service*, 1730 GMT, 25 July 1990 in *FBIS*, 26 July 1990, p. 37.
[64] *Pravda*, 25 September 1989, pp. 1-2 in *FBIS*, 25 September 1989, pp. 52-54.
[65] *ibid* in *FBIS*, 26 September 1989, p. 55.
[66] *Pravda*, 8 December 1989, p. 1 in *FBIS*, 11 December 1989, p. 79.

9 The Separation of the Party and the State

Introduction

Although the integration of the Party and the State had been formally acknowledged by the Soviet leadership to be a central political problem for a long time, it was only during Perestroika that serious attempts were made to address it, beginning at the lower levels and gradually reaching the Central Committee itself. This chapter traces the process of separation of the Party and State with particular reference to the Central Committee.

At the outset of Perestroika, the central apparatus was deeply involved in the personnel turnover in the government and in administration in general. There were numerous such examples. Ligachev claimed that under his leadership, the Organisational department was responsible for changing roughly 22 per cent of the members of the Council of Ministers.[1] In his memoirs, he reminisced about the severe winters of 1984-85, when the transport system was particularly badly effected. Fears existed that the economy might be brought to a standstill. An emergency headquarters to deal with the situation and to co-ordinate economic activities was established. Ligachev was put in charge of this headquarters by the Politburo, with Ryzhkov periodically participating in its activities.[2] Shevardnadze's appointment as Foreign Minister was endorsed by the Central Committee secretaries.[3] Ryzhkov recalled in an interview that when he became Prime Minister, the government was not independent of the Central Committee. During his tenure, he claimed to have widened its responsibilities.

Prior to the Perestroika, vital areas like the military-industrial complex, agriculture and foreign trade were only formally controlled by the respective ministries and the Council of Ministers. The practical responsibility of management lay with the Central Committee, the Secretaries and the members of the Politburo who were in charge of these sectors. Issues of foreign trade were directly decided by the General Secretary and the ministry. However during Perestroika, the government started influencing these areas, although this did not mean that complete responsibility had devolved on it. Ryzhkov would only become aware of decisions in these areas, prepared by the respective ministries and the Central Committee, during the meetings of the Politburo. Decisions in the foreign policy area would be taken by the foreign ministry and the General Secretary.[5] He claimed that four ministers in his Council of Ministers - the Minister for Defence, the Minister of the Interior, the Minister of Foreign Affairs and the Minister for the Defence Industry - did not obey him. They took their orders from Gorbachev as General Secretary, when he was not yet President.[6]

On the process of selection, Ryzhkov would prepare suggestions with his aides and discuss them with the Central Secretaries concerned, for example, with V. Dolgikh in the case of key industrial ministries, and with N. Sliunkov, in the case of economic ministries, and get their approval. These proposals would then be finalised in consultation with Gorbachev. If the two of them concurred, the Politburo would approve them. These would then be presented to parliament for final approval.[7] A similar opinion was expressed by V.V. Bakatin, Minister for Internal affairs.[8]

Razumovskii contended that the separation of the Party and the Soviets was undertaken in a number of Party organisations after the 19th Party Conference. It led to the reorganisation of the Party and Soviet apparatuses, creation of new structures of economic management and the transition of enterprises to new economic conditions. He admitted that very often Party committees only spoke of reorganisation but did not do anything.[9] In practice, the involvement of the Central Committee in state structures continued in 1988-89. This was despite a clear declaration that in the new context, the Party was preparing to refrain from a part of its earlier function and distance itself from a number of structures of power.[10] For instance, the Commission on the Reorganisation of the Central Economic Structures of USSR was ordered to consider the question of improving the activity of the banking system. It was also decided to rename this as the Commission for the Improvement of Economic Structures. A report on this commission was presented by N. Ryzhkov, N. Talizin, L. Zaikov and N. Sliunkov to the Central Committee plenum of 23 November 1988.[11] A joint decree was issued on the question of the social welfare for the members who were made redundant from the central apparatus.[12] Decrees continued to be issued in 1988-89, although with much reduced frequency. The ministers and leaders of various other State and governmental agencies continued to participate in sessions of different commissions.[13]

A Central Secretariat decree, issued in the name of the Central Committee, could still order State agencies and the Council of Ministers to undertake a particular activity. One of the decrees on the role of the Party and State organs in improving food production in the Ternobolskii region ordered the State Agricultural Committee of the USSR and the Council of Ministers of the Ukraine to help in the preservation of food products purchased from the population.[14] However, in general a process of refraining from a direct involvement was under way. A decree on the shortcomings in fulfilling a joint decree on providing the technical basis for the development of the socio-cultural sphere was addressed only to certain Party organisations such as the Central Committees of various republics.[15]

With the emergence of an active parliament, the process of separation acquired momentum. The clearest and most authoritative hint that the separation of the Party and State, particularly the Central Committee and State, had started working, came when Ryzhkov elaborated on the experiences of the first few months of the operation of the new Soviet parliament. In his view, the Congress and its proceedings showed that the Central Committee had proved inadequate to function in the new system comprising the Central Committee, the Supreme Soviet, and the USSR Council of Ministers. He further said:

> Under the conditions of a USSR Supreme Soviet constantly in session and with constitutional powers, the functions previously exercised by the Party Central Committee plenum and the Party Central Committee Politburo with regard to the elaboration of concepts for the country's economic development, the formation of the five-year and annual plans, and the adoption of the decisions on State programmes and so on are becoming unclear. Direct recommendations on questions of economic building, economic reform, scientific and technical policy, and many other things can no longer be made solely at the Party level. The practice of the past few months has shown that neither the USSR Supreme Soviet, nor its commissions and committees, will accept such recommendations. In short, a real and mighty power has appeared in the shape of the Congress of People's Deputies and the USSR Supreme Soviet. We cannot fail to take this into consideration. If the Party does not find a way out of this situation, it could lose its influence on State government.[16]

A mechanism of interaction between the Party and State organs in which the former would be "society's political vanguard" and the latter, particularly the Soviets, would exercise power and administer, was being put in place. The Party was to formulate policy and the Soviets would implement them. Communist deputies were to "adopt the same stance as the Central Committee on questions arising from the Party's political strategy."[17] This however was resulting in a power vacuum in many places,[18] not surprisingly given the traditional involvement of Party committees and their leaders directly in issues as diverse as the building of a concert hall or an Academy of Sciences research institute in Tomsk, and developing infrastructural facilities like road construction. First secretaries of obkoms, for instance, would liaise between various agencies for important projects. They would be directly involved as important links between the Council of Ministers and their regions in organising the latter's development.[19]

Competitive elections for the Congress of People's Deputies, reorganisation of the central parliamentary system, and revamping the local bodies, the Soviets, were a quantum leap in the transfer of power and authority. The legislature was to be strengthened at the expense of the executive. Representative State institutions were to take decisions for Soviet society instead of the Party.[20] In 1989 the Supreme Soviet was becoming more active and influential and the Central Committee was losing its "*political primacy*". Vital questions which were once upon a time within the exclusive domain of the Central Committee were debated in the sessions of the Congress of People's Deputies. These included important policy issues such as laws on agricultural leasing arrangements, taxation of co-operatives, limited economic autonomy for the Baltic republics and so on.[21] The Supreme Soviet also asserted its independence by rejecting two nominees of Prime Minister Ryzhkov, while six were not forwarded for approval by the Standing Committees responsible for reviewing their credentials.[22] Thus the representative arm of State had emerged as an autonomous, democratic body.

Towards the end of 1988, amendments made to the Soviet Constitution of 1977 transferred several functions hitherto exercised by the Central Committee to the Congress of People's Deputies and the Supreme Soviet.[23] The Supreme Soviet, having acquired some of the functions undertaken earlier by the Central Committee, acted through 22 permanent commissions and committees, preparing legislation for it and exercising "some degree of public control over key areas of national life."[24] That the Supreme Soviet[25] had acquired some autonomy of its own and Party control been loosened was also reflected by the relatively greater independence of Party deputies vis-à-vis the Party line as suggested by their voting pattern. Central Committee members no longer dominated the Supreme Soviet. The number of members of higher Party organs in the Supreme Soviet had decreased. The fact that only 100 Central Committee members were elected on its slate to the Congress demonstrated the intention to limit the number of Central Committee members in it.[26]

In 1990 there were a few instances of the direct involvement of the Central Committee with State or government agencies. In January 1990, a joint statement of the Central Committee and the Presidium of the Supreme Soviet and the Council of Ministers of the USSR entitled "For the Peoples of Azerbaijan and Armenia" was reported.[27] A decree of the Central Secretariat issued on 11 July 1990 to counter growing cultural commercialisation decided to create a State Committee on Social and Cultural Questions. It asked the Union Council of Ministers to tell ministers and organisations to consider proposals of the Ministry of Culture, creative councils and social organisations to protect the arts, paintings and different groups of the population from the negative results of the commercialisation of the culture.[28] Another decree of the Central Secretariat issued on 2 October 1990 regarding the depoliticisation of education ordered the leaders of the State Committee on Education of the USSR to implement actively the resolutions of the 28th Party Congress on Youth policy and policy in the sphere of education, science and culture of the Party.[29] Such instances, however, were few and scattered.

Article 6 had become the constitutional means of the Party's integration with the State, and with the process of separation of the Party and State its amendment became imperative.[30] This in turn gave an impetus to the process of separation.[31] In March 1990, it was amended. In an almost simultaneous process, the nature of the relationship between the Party and State also changed. Decrees were no longer compulsory directives and were addressed to political agencies in these bodies or individual leaders. This process became particularly evident towards the end of 1990. A decree on the persecution of the Communists in western Ukraine decided to inform the Supreme Soviet, and to send it the note by A. Girenko on which it was based. The departments of Nationality policy and Social-Political organisations and the Organisational department were ordered to provide the Supreme Soviet with the necessary material on this question.[32] Party organisations, for instance that of Rostovskii region, were to assist in establishing a multi-structured agricultural economy. A decree issued in this connection on 8 January 1991 asked Chernoivanov, head of the State Committee of the Council of Ministers on Foodstuffs; Mostvoi, the head of the State Committee on Supply; Orlov, the head of the Ministry of Finance; Pugin, the head of the Ministry of Agricultural Machines; Obuzintsev, head of the Agricultural Bank; and Federko, head of the Central Union to consider questions on the improvement in 1991 of the resource provisions of all the structures of the agricultural complex.[33] The decision of the socio-economic commission on the Party's policy on the denationalisation of the economy asked Party committees of ministries and organisations to pay attention to the strengthening of political influence on the process of denationalisation of enterprises.[34]

The Presidency

The institution of the executive Presidency was an important step in the direction of the separation of the Party and State. According to Yakovlev

> Today, when authority is being passed from the Party to constitutional bodies, one should be prepared for organic changes in the structure of the political power...[35]

V.N. Kudriavtsev, vice-president of the USSR Academy of Sciences and a participant in the working group of the Presidium of the USSR Supreme Soviet on the issue of Presidency, clearly connected the two in a statement on the matter on behalf of the Presidium.[36] According to F. Burlatskii, the process of transfer of power was well advanced and the central organs of the Party were directing their attention to questions of political strategy, ideology and cadres.[37] However, the question as to how well prepared State institutions were for the exercise of power remained.

N.F. Tatarchuk, first secretary of the Kalinin obkom, complained at the February 1990 Central Committee plenum that although several questions had been transferred to the competence of the Soviets, and presumably since they were not working effectively, Party committees were "blamed for virtually everything, for the unrest, the shortcomings in trade, medical services, and transport operations, and even the unloading of railcars".[38] This may well have been true in the highest echelons of power, with the Central Committee gradually shedding its past executive involvement and the inability of nascent institutions of State to exercise the power being vested in them. This notion was strengthened by the lack of authority of the legislative acts of the Soviet parliament and later of the executive Presidency.

Primakov cited the emergence of a multi-party system as another major factor calling for the institution of the Presidency and the further separation of the Central Committee and State. According to him, the "transition to a multi-party system ... will require appropriate changes to the country's State structure".[39] In a situation in which a decision to give up the former role played by the Central Committee and the Party had been taken, the establishment of an executive Presidency was imperative.[40] The arguments in favour of the Presidency indicated that the process of the separation of the Party and State was effective in the sense that power had started shifting away from the Party, although the newly formed State and the government agencies had not come to the point of having effectively acquired and exercised it. The institution of the Presidency was to fill up the resultant power vacuum.

This was also seen as Gorbachev's drift away from the Party as the only ruling institution, giving him "greater personal security by providing him with an institutional power base outside the Party".[41] Discussing the history of the institution of an executive Presidency, Burlatskii revealed that this proposal had been mooted by a working group, of which he was a member, in 1964, but that it had "met with derision from Party leader Nikita Khrushchev."[42] Had an executive Presidency been established then, perhaps the Soviet history would have been different.

Vadim Medvedev speaking at the Third Congress of the Congress of People's Deputies on 12 March 1990 identified the process of transfer of power from the Party to the State as "a pivotal policy of the Party leadership" linking it to the Presidency and the amendments to Articles 6 and 7.[43] At the same Congress, a similar opinion was expressed by V.I. Vorotnikov, chairman of the USSR Supreme Soviet Presidium.[44]

The problems of the transfer of power were manifested strongly in 1990. N.I. Ryzhkov highlighted the problems of this transition. He said :

> As a matter of fact, what the current situation boils down to is that one form of government has weakened, and the other hasn't gained strength. This explains why we are in such a predicament today. We know only too well who used to make all the decisions before. The Party did, or rather its headquarters. It so happened that since the thirties the Party dealt with all problems. Today the Party is saying: all power should be given to the Soviets. Other government bodies should also acquire executive powers. This process is now underway. No power vacuum should be permitted ... Now that the regrouping of the power is in progress, all power institutions are to be set up to avoid anarchy.[45]

However, by the middle of 1990 the growing autonomy of the government from the Central Committee was reflected in a statement by the first secretary of the Saratov Party organisation, Vladimir Golovachev. At the Russian Communist Party conference he noted: "The government has ideas of a market-run economy; the Central Committee does not. A bridge must be found between the two".[46]

The 28th Party Congress and the Separation of the Central Committee and the State

The 28th Party Congress, according to Yakovlev, completed the process of the separation of the Party and the Central Committee from the State. He considered this to be the main result of the Congress. According to him:

> The Party leadership now contains no one who holds any State post. That is the fundamental point. The Party leadership is now formed in such a way that it is directly concerned with questions of the Party's development. At the same time the Party leadership will certainly be concerned with those socio-economic problems that directly effect the people.

The structure of the Party in his view was built into the State-administrative system. Hence in a certain sense the Party was being transformed into one which would manage its own affairs. Its withdrawal from direct participation in State and legislative power had created the pre-conditions for it to become the ideological leader in society.[47]

At a meeting with the Moscow City Party aktiv, Prokofiev noted that the Central Committee elected at the 28th Party Congress had a fundamentally new composition, not only in terms of personal and social composition, but also in terms of positions. The formation of the Politburo and the "distribution of the duties" among the Central Committee secretaries was different from past practice, indicating a shift from the "State-Party" concept and the process of the completion of the transfer of power from the central Party organs to the State.[48]

The Post- 28th Party Congress Situation

By April 1991 the separation of Central Committee and State seemed substantially advanced. Correspondingly advanced was Gorbachev's alienation from the Party. A.M. Anipkin, first secretary of the Volgograd obkom, said in his speech to the April 1991 joint-plenum of the Central Committee and Central Control Commission that the Party was neither performing its "external function" of supporting the measures of the President and defending him from the opposition, nor its "internal function" of adjusting the President's course. He said further that Gorbachev had not been consulting the Party, thus creating the opinion that he did not lead it.[49] According to Gurenko, first secretary of the Ukrainian Communist Party, the Party had practically no role in the implementation of the reforms. It had been "deprived of the means" to influence social processes at all levels. The plenums, in his view, were by and large fruitless and he urged Gorbachev to rely on the Party both as General Secretary and the President. He further said:

> Only today is the Central Committee discussing the Cabinet of Ministers' anti-crisis programme, yet it is a Communist government, and if it fails responsibility will again fall on the Communist Party. [50]

A.S. Efimov, the second secretary of the Uzbek Party committee, gave a more concrete understanding of the decimated hold of the Party and by implication, its Central Committee, on the Congress of People's Deputies, when he said that

> Communists have no steady majority or deciding influence among the body of USSR People's deputies, we no longer have the requisite levers for government today. [51]

N.N. Korablev, chairman of the Leningrad obkom Control and Auditing Commission said that the plenums did not influence Gorbachev's policies.[52] The autonomy was further confirmed when Prokofiev complained in this plenum that the anti-crisis programme of the government had been adopted a day before the plenum, that is on 23 April 1991, by the Supreme Soviet, thus presenting the Central Committee with 'a fait accompli'. It exhibited "the extent to which the Party (was) isolated from the solutions of the most important questions of the State's present life".[53] Ligachev, in an article published in *Sovetskaia Rossiia* in August 1991, complained that the principle of collective leadership had been abandoned and that the Politburo had become non-functional.[54] This indicated that Gorbachev had ignored the leadership bodies of the Party and took an independent stance on crucial issues.

The representation of State and government leaders in the Central Committee diminished drastically compared to previous ones, including that formed at the 27th Party Congress. The representation of the central State category was reduced from 25.1 per cent and 24.7 per cent in the years 1981 and 1986 respectively, to 6.6 per cent in 1990. Similarly, the representation of the regional State category also declined from 8.5 per cent and 7.85 per cent in the Central Committees elected at the 26th and the 27th Party Congresses respectively, to 4.95 per cent in 1990. That of other State institutions like the military and the diplomatic corps were reduced as well. In the case of the military it fell from 7.7 per cent in 1981 and 7.65 per cent in 1986 to 2.7 per cent in 1990. The diplomatic corp representation was only 0.55 per cent in 1990, as compared to 4.75 per cent in 1981 and 4.8 per cent in 1986.[55] 88 per cent of the voting members were members of the Supreme Soviet in 1976,[56] whereas only 85 full members and 42 candidate members elected at the 27th Party Congress and 105 elected at 28th Party Congress were members of the Congress of People's Deputies.[57]

In August 1991, seven out of a total of 17 members of the Federation Council were members of the Central Committee, if the USSR President and Vice-President are not counted. Only four out of a total of nine members of the USSR Cabinet of Ministers (if we only include the Prime Minister, first deputy Prime Ministers and deputy Prime Ministers) were members of the Central Committee. One out of three first deputy Prime Ministers and 2 out of 5 deputy Prime Ministers were members of the Central Committee.

Out of a total of 28 leading officials in the Presidential apparatus, only two were members of the Central Committee: Boldin, the head of the apparatus, and Baklanov, head of the Department for Questions of Defence and State Security. Only two of the 33 leading officials of the USSR Supreme Soviet were members of the Central Committee, which included chairmen of the important permanent commissions and committees of the USSR Supreme Soviet. No chairmen of the Permanent Commissions of the Supreme Soviet were included in the Central Committee. Only one of the 20 chairmen of the USSR Supreme Soviet Committees was included in the Central Committee.[58]

Thus towards the end of the 1980s and the beginning of the 1990s more concrete changes started taking place in the direction of separation. The process was certainly uneven as several documents at the

Constitutional Court showed. A significant role was played by interpersonal relations in maintaining linkages between Party and State institutions at an informal level, since the people in both knew each other well having worked together for many years. Until Article 6 was amended, there was no example of rejection of the Central Committee proposals in the Supreme Soviet. Only after this did the struggle for separation take a qualitatively higher form, with the Yeltsin's decree on the de-Partisation of the Army, the KGB and so on.[59] But separation changed the ethos and functioning of most State institutions substantially.[60]

Conclusion

The nature and content of the proposals made by the Central Committee differed radically from those in the past, indicating the trend of adjustment to the new requirements. The Central Committee helped deputies from the Party faction to propose laws in the Supreme Soviet and discuss them. However, many of its proposals were amended - a far cry from the unanimity of the past. Painstaking preparation and expert involvement went into the formulation of legislation, given the presence of vocal and active opposition in the legislature. The work of the Central Committee with the government was also on approximately similar lines. The process of separation gave rise to its contradictions. The integrated system of the exercise of power fell apart with the withdrawal of the Party and the inability of nascent State institutions to start functioning immediately. According to Melnikov, the Party did actually transfer power, although this process should have taken place in a phased manner.[61]

The separation did not become immediately effective since the whole system was accustomed to the old structure of power. With the amendment of Article 6 and the acceptance of a multi-party system, however it became inevitable. The negative aspect of the separation was the way it came about, dissolving the existing structure of power rather than transferring it to various spheres. Thus the decline in the authority of the Party coincided with the decline in the authority of the entire State structure. A kind of simultaneous collapse of the entire system took place. One of the reasons for this was that the separation was not done in a systematic manner or with sufficient forethought as to how to bring about such a transfer to the proper sphere.[62]

Until 1988-89, the Central Committee and its apparatus, and those members of the Central Committee who were regional Party leaders and leaders of State apparatus, were the real centres of power in the country. In 1990s the distinction between the Party and State was increasing, yet close interpersonal linkages existed between the members of the Central Committee, the Party committees and State organs.[62]

The process of separation of the Party from the State was initiated on an experimental basis in the early years of Perestroika, and gathered momentum from the 19th Party Conference.[63] It was a conscious exercise in the transfer of power to State institutions.[64] The separation of the Central Committee and the State was at an advanced stage by the 28th Party Congress. This process did not proceed either smoothly or uniformly. It started from the lower levels of the Party and State structure, and had reached the Central Committee and the highest State and government agencies by the time the Party ceased to exist. Thus the Central Committee was not only deprived of its earlier partnership in the exercise of power along with the State, but contributed to the dissolution of the existing structures of power and authority.

Notes

1 E. Ligachev, "Iz Vospominanii", *Argumenti i fakti*, no. 5, 1991, p. 5.
2 E. Ligachev, 1992, pp. 49-50.
3 E. Shevardnadze, 1991, p. 39.
4 M. Nenashev, *Posledenoe Pravitelstvo SSSR, Lichnosti Svidetelstva Diialogi,* (Moskva, AO <KROM>, 1993), pp. 11-13.
5 Interview with Prof. V. S. Lel'chuk, Institute of Russian History , Moscow, August 1992.
6 *ibid.*, p. 21.
7 *ibid.*, p. 76.
8 G. Razumovskii, "To Lead the Perestroika Effort, to Generate the Energy of Renewal", *Kommunist*, no. 4, 1989, pp. 9-10.
9 "Towards New Image of Socialism", *Kommunist*, no. 13, 1989, p. 15..
10 *Izvestiia_Tsk KPSS*, no. 1, January 1989, pp. 69-73.
11 *ibid.*, pp. 93-94.
12 *ibid.*, pp. 90-94.
13 *ibid.*, no. 7, July 1989, pp. 18-19.
14 *ibid.*, no. 8, August 1989, pp. 28-30.
15 *Pravda*, 21 July 1989, pp. 1-4 in *FBIS*, 21 July 1989, pp. 66-67.
16 *Pravda*, 8 August 1989, p. 1 in *FBIS*, 18 August 1989, p. 62.
17 *Izvestiia*, 5 February 1990, p. 2 in *FBIS*, 6 February 1990, pp. 93-94.
18 E. Ligachev, "Iz Vospominanii", *Argumenti i fakti,* nos. 4 and 5, 1991, pp. 5-6.
19 Jeffrey W. Hahn, "The Soviet State System", in S. White et al, 1990, p. 103.

[20] John P. Willerton, Jr. , "The Political Leadership", in *ibid.*, p. 62.
[21] Jeffrey W. Hahn, "The Soviet State System", in *ibid.*, p. 102.
[22] E. Teague and D. Mann, "Gorbachev's Dual Role", *Problems of Communism,* January - February 1990, p. 3.
[23] *ibid.*, p. 4.
[24] For a detailed analysis of the Supreme Soviet during Perestroika see D. Lane and C. Ross, "The Social Background and Political Allegiance of the Political Elite of the Supreme Soviet of the USSR: The Terminal Stage, 1984 to 1991", *Europe-Asia Studies*, vol. 46, no. 3, 1994, pp. 437-463.
[25] *ibid.*, p. 5.
[26] *Izvestiia_Tsk KPSS*, no. 2, February 1990, p. 3.
[27] *ibid.*, no. 10, October 1990, pp. 23-24.
[28] *ibid.*, no. 11, November 1990, pp. 12-13.
[29] *Sovetskaia estoniia*, 26 November 1989, p. 6 in *FBIS*, 22 December 1989, p. 66.
[30] This however has also been seen as a non-event. See Neil Robinson, "Gorbachev and the Place of the Party in Soviet Reform, 1985-91", *Soviet Studies*, vol. 44, no. 3, 1992, (hereafter Neil Robinson, 1992), p. 439.
[31] *Izvestiia_Tsk KPSS*, no. 12, December 1990, pp. 15-17.
[32] *ibid.*, no. 4, April 1991, pp. 17-19.
[33] *ibid.*, no. 8, August 1991, pp. 19-20.
[34] *TASS*, 1357 GMT, 27 February 1990 in *FBIS*, 28 February, 1990, p. 40.
[35] *Moscow Television Service*, 1600 GMT, 27 February 1990 in *FBIS*, 28 February 1990, pp. 41-42.
[36] *Izvestiia*, 11 February 1990, p. 3 in *FBIS*, 14 February 1990, pp. 65-66.
[37] *Pravda*, 6 February 1990, pp. 5-6 in *FBIS*, 12 February 1990, pp. 93-94.
[38] *Selskaia zhizn*, 27 February 1990, pp. 1-3 in *FBIS*, 27 February 1990, p. 48.
[39] *ibid.*, p. 49.
[40] E. Teague and D. Mann, "Gorbachev's Dual Role", *Problems of Communism*, January-February 1990, p. 1.
[41] *ibid.*, p. 3.
[42] *Moscow Television Service*, 2041 GMT, 12 March 1990 in *FBIS*, 13 March 1990, pp. 54-55.
[43] *Moscow Television Service*, 1929 GMT, 12 March 1990 in *FBIS*, 13 March 1990, pp. 58-59.
[44] *New Times*, no. 11, 13-19 March 1990, pp. 5-6 in *FBIS*, 27 March 1990, p. 58.
[45] *Moscow Television Service*, 1945 GMT, 19 June 1990 in *FBIS*, 20 June 1990, pp. 84-85.
[46] *Izvestiia*, 27 July 1990, p. 3 in *FBIS*, 27 July 1990, pp. 39-40.
[47] *Moskovskaia Pravda*, 26 July 1990, p. 1 in *FBIS*, 14 August 1990, pp. 66-67.
[48] *Pravda*, 26 April 1991, p. 3 in *FBIS*, 26 April 1991, p. 18.
[49] *ibid* in *FBIS*, 29 April 1991, p. 1.
[50] *Pravda*, 27 April 1991, p. 4 in *FBIS*, 29 April 1991, p. 21.
[51] *Pravda*, 27 April 1991, p. 3 in *FBIS*, 29 April 1991, p. 23.
[52] *Moskovskaia Pravda*, 27 April 1991, p. 2 in *FBIS*, 3 May 1991, p. 22.
[53] *Sovetskaia rossiia*, 3 August 1991, p. 4 in *FBIS*, 8 August, 1991, p. 42.

[54] E. Mawdsley, Table 4.

[55] J. F. Hough and M. Fainsod, 1979, p. 456.

[56] Calculated from *INDEM Data Base*, Moscow; "CPSU Central Committee Full Members Elected by the Twenty-Seventh Party Congress in March 1986", Compiled by S. Belitsky, V. Konovalov and H. Kraus, *RL 145/86*, 1 April 1986; "CPSU Central Committee Candidate Members Elected By The Twenty-Seventh Party Congress in March, 1986", *RL 151/86*, 9 April 1986 and K. G. Saur, 1992, pp. 61-69.

[57] Calculated from A. Rahr, "The Soviet Leadership on the Eve of the Coup", *Report on the USSR*, 23 August 1991, pp. 3-6 and K. G. Saur, 1992, pp. 61-69.

[58] Interview with Prof. V. S. Lel'chuk.

[59] An example was the State Radio and Television. Yevgeni Nikitenko, deputy-director of the Moscow Radio World Service, described his experience of the relaxation of the Central Committee's control over the media. He said that when he joined the institution 14 years earlier, there was a rigid system of control and censorship. The Chairman of the Radio and Television would be a member of the Central Committee, it was not possible for him and his subordinates to deviate from the Central Committee's decisions and reporting had to be done accordingly. Reporters and other personnel were expected to observe the demands and the recommendations of the Central Committee while writing the stories and covering the attitudes on this particular issue. Before Perestroika, journalists were required to fulfil the line of the Central Committee. It was a normal phenomenon that in the morning conferences addressed by the editor-in-chief of the department, the journalists would be told that someone from the Central Committee wanted them to do some thing in particular. In the early years of Perestroika there would be instructions in the form of advice from the Central Committee. Hence there was an informal system of instructions from the Central Committee in practice. The Central Committee followed the work of the institution. There were instructors from the local Party committee who would constantly have meetings with the editors-in-chief of the various departments, and discuss important issues with them.

The directives of the Central Committee were scrupulously implemented by a special department. On reports concerning issues which were deemed sensitive, a journalist had to get a 'red pencil' approval from this department. This was the censorship department, controlled directly by the Central Committee. With the coming of Gorbachev, the rigid control loosened, particularly with the initiation of the policy of glasnost. Media personnel were granted a freer hand and were expected to mirror real life situations. Subsequently, as glasnost developed, the very mentality started changing rapidly, and the Central Committee benefited from the feedback from the practical activities of the journalists. Leonid Kravchenko, though a Central Committee member, said that he was mandated to fulfil the will of the President and that the job of the institution was to reflect the ideas of Perestroika. The Chairman of the Radio and Television was made a member of the Presidential Council and would report to the President, who was still the General Secretary of the Party. Hence a duality existed and the link was not completely broken. The major difference was that now he would not have to report to the Central Committee or its departments as in the past. The Central Committee could express an opinion on his activities but could not order him to do any particular thing. He took his orders from Gorbachev as President. Another indication of the Central Committee practically losing all its control over this institution was that several people stayed in their jobs even after resigning from the Party, saying whatever they wanted to, but not being penalised, as in the past.

The Central Committee could still request that a particular campaign be organised, but it would not have to be treated as an order to the Chairman and the journalists as before. The institution acquired considerable independence, although the Party committee existed with greatly diminished influence. The Chairman would insist on following the Central Committee line, but he would not demand that every reporter do the same. There were instances when decisions in which the Central Committee and the Chairman of the institution were interested could not be implemented because of opposition from the personnel of the radio and television. It was abolished during Perestroika. The system changed considerably in the first years of Perestroika and almost completely changed in the final years. Direct control almost vanished although informal influence continued to exist. Party leaders might ring up the Chairman to express their opinions on some programme or the other. [Interview with Yevgeni Nikitenko, deputy-director, Moscow Radio World Service, Moscow, August 1992.]

[60] Interview with I.I. Melnikov.

[61] Interview with Dev Murarka, Moscow, August 1992.

[62] Interview with A.V. Buzgalin.

[63] On the relationship of Party and state under Gorbachev, see also, C. Ross, "Party-State Relations" in E. Huskey ed. *Executive Power and Soviet Politics-The Rise and Decline of the Soviet State*, M.E. Sharpe Inc., (London, 1992), pp. 49-82.

On the CPSU and the Soviet State see also G.B. Smith, *Soviet Politics, Struggling with Change*, Macmillan, (Basingstoke, 1992), pp. 94-154.

[64] In view of N. Robinson it was not "a fully conscious attempt by Gorbachev to shift power away from the CPSU to other bodies". See N. Robinson, 1992, p. 423.

10 Political and Social Pluralism in the Post-Soviet Era

Introduction

The central reform entailing the separation of the Party and the State during the Perestroika, particularly in its later phase, resulted not only in de-institutionalising and dismantling the formidable Soviet political system but also in the political and social manifestations and resurgence of the subalteran and subterranean forces, for example, nationalisms and sub-nationalisms, hitherto lying dormant. The political transformation and mutation accompanied a disintegrating economy and socio-cultural entropy, a lethal combination for any political society and political system. The nationalism and sub-nationalism that coloured the political complexion of the fifteen independent nation-states emerging from the debris of the former Soviet Union provided the basis for the distinctive political and socio-cultural identities and the nature of the conflicts thereof. The seeds of transformation and the shape of politico-economic and socio-cultural systems that emerged in successor states were laid down during the Soviet era - in particular during the Perestroika itself. The carrier of these transformations has been, in several cases, Soviet era political leadership which has continued to determine the destiny of these nascent nation-states. Many of them have been key members of the Central Committee itself, thus underlining the continuity with the Soviet past. Changes, however, too had been crystallising during the Soviet era, more distinctly during Perestroika, under the impact of the competing forces of conservatism and reformism. Thus, although it was the separation of the Party and the State during Perestroika that culminated in the disintegration of the Soviet political system, the successor States and their politico-economic and socio-cultural systems are evolving within the paradigm laid during Perestroika with erstwhile political leadership playing the crucial role. The continuity, therefore, is as striking, if not more as the change is.

Political Pluralism in Post-Soviet States

Multiplicity of political forces was obvious in post Soviet Russia. Most of these merged during the latter phase of Perestroika in some form or the other. The ideological persuasion informing these political parties and groups not only existed but campaigned openly during this period. Former CPSU re-emerged in the form of different communist and socialist parties and groups representing different nuances of left-wing politics in Russia. [1]

Democratic Russia Movement was reported to have a membership of 150,000, DPR (50,000), NPSR (70,000), SPT (60,000), RKRP (100,000), RPK (3,000), RKhDD(1,000-1,500). The Democratic Russia Movement included RPRF, PKD, RPST, RKhDP, SvDPR. The Democratic Choice Movement included 30 organisations like Democratic Russia, NPP, RPRF, RKhDP and PKD. Civic Union bloc included DPR, NPSR, VSO and the Smena-New Policy faction of the Supreme Soviet of the Russian Federation. The New Russia bloc included the NPR, SDPR, RSLP, KPR, KhDS etc.[2]

From the wreckage of the Communist Party of the Soviet Union, several left oriented parties and groups started emerging within four months of its demise. The economic, social and political circumstances created by 'shock therapy', the liberalisation and privatisation drive resulting in poverty, acute economic and social differentiation and unemployment, resulted in the revival of at least five parties of socialist and communist orientation by the end of 1992. Four of them registered with the Ministry of Justice of the Russian Federation whereas the fifth considered itself to be an All-Union party and therefore did not register with the Russian authorities. The Socialist Workers Party had many members active in the Russia, Agrarian Union and Fatherland factions of the parliament. The party laid primary emphasis on the parliamentary forms and organised a Congress of Democratic Forces of the Left. The Russian Communist Workers Party on the other hand emphasised extra-parliamentary methods like meetings, demonstrations, picketing etc. Its Congress adopted a resolution to revive the Soviet power based on the political dominance of the working class. The Russian Communist Party advocated a centrist line opposing both 'liberalism' and 'Stalinism'. It sponsored different associations of communists and other sections of the left and aimed at unifying different left forces. The Union of Communists endeavoured to unite communists in the former republics of the Soviet Union and revive the CPSU. It held the 20th Party Conference and was preparing for the 29th Party Congress to restore and unify the CPSU. The All-Union Communist Party of Bolsheviks supported a 'neo-Stalinist' programme and organisational structure harking to the ideals of the 1930s-1940s. The era of 'Stalinism' was seen by them as the high point of socialism. According to them the restoration of capitalism began with Khrushchev and culminated with Yeltsin. All these parties are post-Soviet Union phenomenon. A body incorporating the leaders of the new parties and groups of communists who appeared before the Constitutional Court - the Roskomsovet - was formed, which subsequently formed an organising committee to convene a 'restoration-unification' congress of the Communist Party of Russia in February-March 1993. Except for the Russian Communist Workers Party, all other parties joined the process of unification to form a new united Communist Party of Russia. The common basis for such an unity was seen as opposition to the capitalisation of society, reorienting societal development towards socialism, creating a new Union and the transnational unity.[3] From a single platform within the former CPSU - the Marxist Platform, three tendencies emerged in post Soviet Russia. One led to the formation of the organisaiton committee of the party named "Union of Communists" led by a former Central Committee member Alexei Prigarin. Another tendency resulted in the formation of a new communist party called the "party of communists" led by Anatoli Kriuchkov. The Party argued for adherance to the erstwhile Marxist Platform in the CPSU as the basis of the programme fo the new party. The third tendency was led by the Central Committee member Alexander Buzgalin and Andrei Kolganov. The new party formed on its basis was called the Party of Labour claiming to be the successor of the former CPSU. The "Democratic Movement of the CPSU" and the parliamentary faction "Communists for Democracy" led by A. Rutskoi and V. Lipitski, led to the formation of the Democratic Party of Russia's Communists providing another instance of splinter parties emerging from the disintegrating CPSU. The forerunner of "Yedinstvo" (Unity) and the All-Union Communist Party of Bolsheviks was the Bolshevik platform in the CPSU. The "Communist Initiative" organisation emerged from the erstwhile United Front of the Working People and the Leningrad Initiative Congress of Russia's Communists, which represented the conservative sections of the erstwhile CPSU and its leadership.[4]

At least 13 major electoral blocs and political parties existed in Russia in December 1993. They included Russia's Choice, Russian Movement for Democratic Reforms, Yavlinski-Boldyrev-Lukin bloc, Russian Unity and Accord Party, Dignity and Charity, CEDAR, Women of Russia, Russia's future-New Names, Civic Union in the Name of Stability, Justice and Progress, Democratic Party of Russia, Agrarian Party of Russia, Communist Party of Russian Federation and Liberal-Democratic Party. Russia's Choice was the party of the government which included government ministers, advisers and officials like A. Chubais, A. Kozyrev,

M. Poltoranin, D. Volkogonov, S. Filatov, V. Danilov-Danilian, Yu. Yarov, A. Pochinok etc. The Russian Movement for Democratic Reforms included parties like the Free Labour Party and factions like Reform of the Army, Accord for Progress and the Reform Coalition. It included representatives of the regional management structures of the Council of ministers, leaders of soviets and administrations and former people's deputies of the USSR and Russian Federation. For example, I.Kh. Khiveldi was chairman of the Council for the Development of Entrepreneurship of the Russian Federation Council of Ministers, N.P. Shmelev, member of the Consultative Council of the Russian Federation President and Ye.M. Kozhokin was the deputy chairman of the State Committee on Federation and Nationality Affairs. The Yavlinski-Boldirev-Lukin bloc included parties such as the Republican Party, The Social-Democratic Party and the Republican-Democratic Party of Adigeia. It included leading members like V.L. Sheinis, a well-known reformist and one of the authors of the Statute on Elections to the State Duma, N.Ya. Petrakov, former economic adviser to the USSR President, A.L. Adamishin, deputy foreign minister of the USSR and the Russian Federation, V.N. Shostakovskii, former Rector of the Higher Party School of the CPSU Central Committee and chairman of the Policy Council of the Republican Party of the Russian Federation, Ye.M. Ambartsumov, former member of the Presidium of the Russian Federation Supreme Soviet, chairman of the Committee of the Supreme Soviet for International Issues, K.V. Yankov of the Social-Democratic Party and Yu.M. Bliagoz, enterpreneur and chairman of the Republican-Democratic Party of Adigeia. The Russian Unity and Accord Party included the Smena-New Policy faction represented by V.A. Kirpichnikov, President of the Union of Russian Cities and the Socialist Party represented by V.A. Lepekhin. Government members like G.G. Melikian, Minister of Labour, S.B. Stankevich, Adviser to the President for Political Issues and A.Ye. Sebentsov, first deputy chief of the Council of Ministers Staff, were other important constituents. The electoral bloc Dignity and Charity included chairmen of all-Union and large regional organisations of war and labour veterans, the handicapped, victims of Chernobyl, officials of administrations working on issues of the handicapped and veterans etc. The CEDAR claimed to be an ecological association. The top leadership of the movement however comprised of high officials of state hygiene control and medical establishment. Women of Russia consisted of the trade union leaders and those from the executive and legislative organs. The bloc included leaders like N.D. Malkhakina, Chairperson of "Childhood, Society, Charity", and deputy chairperson of the Federation of Independent

Trade Unions (formerly AUCCTU), F.Sh. Arshianova, from the Agrarian Union faction, T.E. Chupasova, chief of the territorial administration of the State Committee for anti-Monopoly Policy and Support of New Economic Structures and R.I. Skripitsina, deputy mayor of the city of Obninsk. Russia's Future-New Names include successors of former trade union and Komsomol organisations. This bloc included the Free Russia faction (the Rutskoi Party) and the Smena-New Policy faction. One of its members N.L. Gen was the former deputy chairman of a Supreme Soviet committee. Civic Union in the name of Stability, Justice and Progress included powerful blocs like the former Civic Union members who were on the list of Travkin's Democratic Party, Russia's Future-New Names, Women of Russia and S. Shakhrai's Russian Unity and Accord Party. The Civic Union list includes key leaders of the industry, trade union officials, state-commercial structures, people's deputies and leaders of krai and oblast soviets. It includes I.Yu. Yurgens, first deputy chairman of the General Trade Union Confederation (formerly AUCCTU), O.G. Rumiantsev, formerly Secretary of the Russian Constitutional Commission, T.V. Novikova, President of the Young People for the Russian Foundation and secretary of the Russian Youth Union (formerly Komsomol), M.L. Goriachev, one of the 20 richest person in Russia, V.O. Ispravnikov, former chairman of the Supreme Economic Council, V.I. Sergienko, president of the Union of Merchandise Producers and Entrepreneurs of Krasnioarsk Krai. The Democratic Party of Russia supported A. Rutskoi and Khasbulatov during the October 1993 crisis. The Agrarian Party of Russia included the Agrarian Union faction in the Supreme Soviet, the Agro-Industrial Union, the Federation of Independent Trade Unions of Russia, leaders of the Communists of Russia faction and that of the National Salvation Front. The Party included officials of the organisations of the ministry of Agriculture, various associations of rural commodity producers, heads of administrations, chairmen of oblast and city soviets, and general directors of plants and factories.[5]

Political Personalities and Parties in Post-Soviet Russia and Central Asia

Several electoral blocs emerged in December 1993 with many of those leaders who had played important political role in the former Soviet Union, particularly under Perestroika. They were important leaders of the erstwhile political society. Russia's Choice included Pavel Bunich, a former Central Committee member who was Corresponding member of the Russian

Academy of Sciences (RAN). The Russian Movement for Democratic Reforms included A.N. Yakovlev, former member of the Politburo and presently the Chairman of the Commission of the Russian Federation President for the Rehabilitation of Victims of Political Repression and formerly the Chairman of the Commission of the CPSU Central Committee Politburo for the study of records associated with repression in the 1930s, 1940s and 1950s and Ye.I. Shaposhnikov, Marshal of the Air Force, former commander of the united CIS forces. The Yavlinsky-Boldirev-Lukin bloc of course included Grigory Yavlinsky and N.Ya. Petrakov, economists and former advisers to Gorbachev, A.L. Adamishin, diplomat and deputy foreign minister of the USSR and the Russian Federation, V.N. Shostavaskii, former Rector of the Higher Party School of the CPSU Central Committee and Ye.A. Ambartsumov, former member of the Presidium of the Russian Federation Supreme Soviet and Chairman of the Committee of the Supreme Soviet for International Issues. Abdulatipov, former Chairman of the Soviet of Nationalities of the Russian Federation Supreme Soviet played the central role in the formation of the bloc Russian Unity and Accord Party. Another important leader of the Party was Yu.Kh. Kalmikov, deputy chairman of the USSR Supreme Soviet Committee for Issues of the Rule of Law, Legal Order and Combating Crime. The Agrarian Party of Russia included A.G. Nazarchuk, former first deputy chairman of Altai Krai Executive Committee, M.M. Abdulbasirov, former first deputy chairman of the Council of Ministers of the Dagestan Soviet Socialist Republic, I.Ye. Klochkov, former second secretary for propaganda of the Moscow Oblast CPSU and deputy chairman of AUCCTU and I.P. Ribkin, former first secretary of a CPSU raion committee in the city of Volgograd. Most of the leaders of the Communist Party of the Russian Federation included former CPSU, Komsomol, AUCCTU and oblast and city committee secretaries and journalists associated with the Party press. These included V.V. Chikin, Editor in Chief of the Sovetskaia rossia, G.N. Seleznev, former Editor in Chief of Pravda, A.I. Lukianiov, former chirman of the USSR Supreme Soviet, V.I. Zorkaltsev, former first secretary of the Tomsk CPSU Oblast Committee, V.A. Bekov, former Chairman of the Novosibirsk Oblast Executive Committee, A.A. Ponamarev, former department chief with the Tambov Oblast CPSU Committee and S.N. Reshulski, former Secretary of the Dagestan Oblast CPSU Committee.[6]

Two hundred and forty three religious and public associations existed in Kazakstan according to the list of organisations registered by the Kazakstan Ministry of Justice. These alongwith 15 smaller groups and factions merged in early 1992 to form an opposition platform called Social

Defence Coalition. Several of these which stood opposed to one another in the past joined forces to oppose the existing leadership of the Kazakhstan. This front constituted of as diverse parties and political organisations as radical national party 'Alash', 'Yedinstvo' (Unity), a movement representing the sizeable Russian population, Kazakh nationalist 'Azat' movement, Kazhakhstani People's Congress Party (NKK), 'Zheltoksan' Party, Kazakhstani Independent Trade Union Centre, Kazakhstani Helsinki Group, the Workers Movement, the 'Adilet' society and the Kazakhstani 'Memorial'. Several of these parties and groups were of the opinion whilst discussing the draft Kazakhstan Constitution that the type of presidential republic being sought to be introduced will in practise be an authoritarian "presidential administration" replacing the "*administrative apparat*" previously led by the Communist Party in Kazakhstan. Although some recognised the necessity of a "presidential republic" because of a weak party system, the general fear was that of an authoritarian political system replacing the old one. In short the critics in opposition movement argued that the same set of ruling elite led by the erstwhile First Secretary of the Kazakhstan Central Committee now functioning as the President of the republic would continue to rule with the quasi-authoritarian political ethos of the previous years. This combination however was constituted of political forces with nationalist, ethnicity-based orientation, those advocating a form of ethnic minorityism, independent working class movements, human rights activists and anti-Stalinists etc. who had made a common cause in opposing the regime of Nursultan Nazarbaev representing the ruling political leadership.[7]

In October of 1992 at a congress held in Alma-Ata the "Azat" movement and the "Zheltoqsan" Party merged forming a Kazakhstan republic "Azat" Party. Its chairman was a member of Kazakh intelligentsia, Kamal Sarwaruli Ormantiev, corresponding member of the Kazhakhstan National Academy. The key task outlined was to ensure rapid development of the republic and especially the Kazakh people while claiming equality with other nationalities. The Party strived to organise the 'natives' in true nationalist spirit exhorting the Kazhakh intelligentsia to unite and help the new nation to ".stand on its own two feet.". Other organisations with Kazakh nationalists approach were 'Qazaq tili society' and 'Nevada-Semei' Movement. The forerunner of these nationalist parties and groups during the Soviet era was an "Alash" Party in Kazakhstan. One of the important symbolic acts of the nationalist movements was celebrating and remembering those associated with the nationalist movements of the past. Nationalist parties like these favoured a controlled market economy to curb commercialism and speculation. In a markedly nationalist stance, they argued for certain privileges for the Kazakhs in the process of privatisation over other nationalities apart from arguing for the preservation, development of the Kazakh language and culture and ensuring that no language other than Kazakh gets the status of official language.[8]

Kirgizstan was no exception to the prevailing newly-discovered open political pluralism in this part of the globe. By the end of 1993 eight political parties had registered themselves with the Ministry of Justice, the latest being the Agrarian Party. The other parties are the Republican People's Party, Party of Communists of Kirgizstan, "DDK" Party,"Ata-Meken" Party, "Erkin Kirgizstan" Party, "Asaba" Party and Social-Democratic Party. In a survey conducted in November 1993 by a group of sociologists, interesting trends were revealed regarding the ratings of various political parties according to the region, nationalities, age and that of their leaders. Party of Communists of Kirgizstan got the highest votes in the total (16.63 per cent) and led in all the oblasts (Osh, Dzhalal-abad, Issik-Kula, Narin and Chuiak) and in Bishkek except in Talas oblast. They were followed by the Republican People's Party (9.00) and "DDK" Party (5.86). The number of respondents who decided not to vote was substantial at 14.56 per cent. The Party of Communists of Kirgizstan received the maximum support from all the nationalities including Kirgiz, Russians, Uzbeks, Kazakhs, Germans and others followed again by the Republican People's Party in all cases, except Russias and Kazakhs in whose case the second runner was the "DDK" Party. In the case of voting by age, too, the Party of Communists of Kirgizstan lead the polls followed by the Republican People's Party except in the age group of over 60, in which the "DDK" Party was the runner up. In the case of the rating of the leaders of the political parties by the regions in the republic on a five point scale, the winner was Zhumgalbek Amanbaev, leader of the Party of Communists (1.51 points) followed by Topchubek Turgunaliev, leader of the "Erkin Kirgizstan Party (1.17). The former won the highest popularity rating except in Narin Oblast were he lost to the latter. In Bishkek, Chuisk and Talas oblast, the latter was a close second whereas in Issik-Kula oblast he was far behind. The most obvious reason for the popularity of the communists was a nostalgia amongst people for the certainties of the bygone era in the face of bleak prospects because of the economic decline.[9]

The Communist Party of the Workers of Uzbekistan was created in 1992. The Secretary of the Organising Committee was V.Ioffe. The Party advocated equality and friendship of all nationalities and religions, complete separation of religion from the state and the school from religion whilst acknowledging freedom of conscience. It argued for the restoration of the socialist path of development, planned market economy, social protection of the working class and preventing growth of social inequality and the division of the society. The party argued for a 'creatively developed Marxism' as its theoretical and methodological base. The Party talked of only constructive criticism of the ruling People's Democratic Party of Uzbekistan and did not consider itself to be an opponent of the latter. It accused 'right-wing bourgeoise nationalist parties of an extreme nationalist bent' and 'the forces of extreme reaction primarily from among the Islamic fundamentalists' of destabilising the political situation. The party critically evaluated the role of Yeltsin and declared its sympathy with the left opposition in Russia. It supported the Commonwealth of Independent States (CIS). It aimed at creating 'a renewed commonwealth (union, community) of the people's of the former USSR or in other words a more defined confederal union replacing the CIS on the lines of the European Union. Discounting the possibilities of revival of the CPSU, the party favoured the formation of a political association or the union of the communist and left oriented socialist parties and groups in different republics of the former USSR with the constituent parties completely independent organisationally and politically.[10]

A list of 100 most influential politicians in Russia published in February 1993 in *Nezavisimaia gazeta* included leading politicians of the Soviet era. Heading the list were Yeltsin, President of the Russian Federation, R.I. Khasbulatov, the then chairman of the Supreme Soviet, Chernomirdin, the Prime Minister and A.V. Rutskoi, the then Vice-President. These were the top four names awarded highest points on a scale ranging from 10(highest) to 1(lowest) and each of them were amongst the first hundred politicians of the Soviet era preceding the demise of the former Soviet Union. Other such leading politicians included O.G. Rumiantsev, R.G. Abdulatipov, A.I. Volskii, V.V. Gerashchenko, G.K. Popov, Y.A. Ambartsumov, Yu. M. Voronin, V.N. Lysenko, S.N. Fedorov, V.S. Lipitski, G.G. Melikian, G.A. Ziuganov, A.P. Vladislavlev, A.N. Yakovlev, Yu. D. Chernichenko, I. Ye. Klochkov, V.I. Anpilov, V.N. Shostakovskii, S.Z. Umalatova, V.F. Yakovlev, Yu. M. Vorontsov, N.A. Andrieva and R.A. Medvedev. Among them Rumiantsev lead the Social-Democratic Centre; Popov, Russian Democratic Reform Movement; Fedorov, Economic Freedom Party; Lysenko, Republican Party; Lipitski, Free Russia People's Party; Ziuganov, Council of Popular and Patriotic Forces; Vladislavlev, All-Russian Renewal Union; Yakovlev, Democratic Reform Movement; Chernichenko, Peasant Party; Klochkov, Federation of

Independent Trade Unions; Anpilov, Russian Communist Worker's Party; Shostakovskii, Republican Party; Umalatova, National Salvation Front; Andrieva, All-Union Communist Party (Bolshevik); and Medvedev, Socialist Party of the Labouring People.[11]

Divergent Factions and Blocs in the Russian Parliament

The Sixth Congress of Russian Federation People's Deputies revealed the presence of 13 factions and 3 blocs. A deputy may however belong to a single faction or bloc or to many of them at the same time. The Russian Unity bloc with 311 deputies constitued of the Communists of Russia, Russia, Fatherland, and Agrarian Union factions. The Bloc of Constructive Forces included 165 deputies from the Industrial Union, Workers Union of Russia and Rising Generation factions. 248 deputies belonged to the Bloc of Democratic Factions which included the Radical Democrats, Left-Centre, Democratic Russia and Free Russia factions. 44 deputies from the Nonparty Deputies and 53 from Sovereignty and Equality factions did not belong to any bloc. An interesting study employing the method of indexing the parties and blocs as pro-government, pro-western and pro-current state-building process or against them underscored the political positions of different factions and blocs. The Voting pattern of various deputies was analysed on a scale ranging from +100 to -100. results of the following motions voted upon at the Congress were analysed:

(1) Deputy Isakov's motion of no-confidence in the government. (A)
(+100 = all supporting the motion, whereas -100 = all opposing the motion).
(2) Deputy Slobodkin's amendment on protecting the ruble vis-à-vis the dollar. (B)
(+100 = "Total Patriotism", -100 = "Liberalism" or "Westernism").
(3) Deputy Fedotov's proposal to include on the agenda the question of whether the creation of CIS was in keeping with the constitution and the results of the all-Union referendum of 17 March 1991. (C)
(+100 = completely opposed to the President and the policy of state-building, -100 = completely supporting the President).

The results were as follows:[12]

Bloc/Faction/ Party	A	B	C
Communists of Russia	+80	+36	+69

Agrarian Union	+72	-5	+55
Fatherland	+62	+43	+66
Russia	+52	+2	+46
Industrial Union	+1	-46	-3
Sovereignty and Equality	-13	-36	-10
Rising Generation	-20	-53	-7
Worker's Union of Russia	-22	-62	-64
Free Russia	-61	-84	-52
Nonparty Deputies	-68	-79	-77
Left-Centre	-71	-94	-76
Democratic Russia	-74	-86	-91
Radical Democrats	-86	-89	-79

Multi-nationalism in Post-Soviet Nation States

According to the State Committee of Russia for Interethnic Relations and the State Committee for Statistics, 26.29 million or 17.68 per cent of the population of Russia reside in 31 autonomous republics, okrugs and oblasts belonging to Russia spread over 9106 million square kilometres or 63.33 percent of the entire territory of the federation. Dual citizenship laws exist in republics like Yakutia by which an individual is both a citizen of Russia as well as that of Yakutia. This may but be a step towards the sovereignty of the republic. In the Republic of Adigeia, the parliament was to decide on the draft law on languages by which both the languages Adig and Russian would be made official languages. It was being speculated that at a later stage the Russian language may be stripped of its official status despite the fact that Adigs constitute only thirty per cent of the population. The shaping of the relationship between the centre and the periphery, the conflict between their legislations and divisions of administrative powers like in the case of law enforcement agencies, between the two are some other issues of contention like in the case of proposed and conducted debates in the legislatures of Tuva, Tatarstan, Khakassia and Buriatia.

Table 10.1 Territorial and demographic situation in the autonomous entities of Russia as of the first half of 1992[13]

Autonom. Entity	Territory (1000 square km.)	Population (1000 people)	Russians (1000 people)	Percentage of Russians
Bashkor.	143.6	1,008.3	1,548.291	39.3
Buriatia	351.3	1,059.4	726.165	70.0
Altai	92.6	198.1	115.188	60.4
Dagestan	50.3	1,890.2	165.940	9.2
Kabardo-Balkaria	12.5	784.3	240.750	32.0
Kalmikia	76.1	326.9	121.531	37.7
Karacheievo-	14.1	430.5	175.931	42.4
Karelia	172.4	800.5	581.571	73.6
Komi	415.9	1,225.0	721.780	57.7
Mari El	23.2	761.9	355.973	47.55
Mordovia	26.2	963.3	586.147	60.8
North Ossetia	8.0	695.3	189.159	29.9
Adigeia	7.6	442.0	293.640	68.0
Tatarstan	68.0	3,695.9	1,575.361	43.3
Tuva	170.5	306.3	98.831	32.0
Udmurtia	42.1	1,637.1	945.216	58.9
Khakassia	61.9	581.1	450.430	79.5
Chechenia and Ingushetia	19.3	1,308.0	293.771	23.1
Chuvashia	18.3	1,353.1	357.120	26.7
Sakha (Yakutia)/ Yamal	3,103.2	1,092.5	550.263	50.3
Nenets	750.3	479.0	292.808	59.2
Kariak	301.5	39.4	24.773	62.0
Nenets	176.7	53.9	35.489	65.8
Chukotka	737.7	145.7	108.297	66.1
Jewish Auton.	36.0	221.5	178.087	83.2
Evenk	767.6	24.7	16.718	67.5
Achinsk Buriat	19.0	78.9	31.473	67.1
Komi-Permiak	32.9	60.0	57.272	36.1
Taimir	862.1	52.6	37.438	67.1
Ust-Ordinsk	22.4	140.0	76.827	56.5
Khanti-Mansi	523.1	1,304.9	850.297	66.3

Source: Kommersant Daily, 23 December 1992, p. 11.

The nationality question was central to the formation of Russian statehood because of the multiplicity of cultures and languages. Therefore 'self-recognition' and 'self assertion' were crucial to its federal statehood. Functioning and effective state authority, which had historically been the distinguishing feature of Russia and a part of its collective and individual consciousness, had been missing in contemporary Russia where the statehood is only a means to implement economic reforms and not an end in itself. Russia has been a state-centric political system rather than social centric system. The core of Russian statehood historically had been multinationalism and multiculturalism and therefore the preservation of this national cultural diversity. A section of Russian politicians like G. Popov, O. Rumiantsev, S. Baburin, M. Salie etc. argued for a policy of unifying Russian statehood and replacing existing national-state formations with gubernias or territorial-administrative units for the sake of governability. The Federal Treaty of the constitution as in 1993 proposed to preserve 'historically formed statehood' taking into account the existing 'status of national-state, national-territorial and territorial-administrative subjects of the Federation' according to Ramazan Abdulatipov, Chairman of the Russian Supreme Soviet's Council of Nationalities.[14]

The ethno-social tensions in Central Asia have been continuing for a long time and have particularly acquired greater proportions in post-Soviet era. National divisions of Central Asia has been a more modern 20th Century phenomenon. In 1921, in keeping with the centuries old tradition not recognising the division on ethnic lines, the local population listed their nationality as "Muslim". In 1924 the Third Special Session of the Central Executive Committee of Turkestan ASSR issued an edict on national divisions in Central Asia. Currently at least ten 'disputed' zones, some potential sites and some where inter-ethnic conflicts have already taken place, exist in Central Asia. In Kirgizstan, the conflict between Uzbeks and Kirgiz in Osh Oblast turned violent. Fergana Valley had been divided into Uzbekistan, Tajikistan and Kirgizstan. The Osh Oblast, part of Fergana Valley, had been home to Uzbeks. Kirgiz residing in the mountains moved there resulting in short supply of arable land, overcrowding and unemployment resulting in discontent leading to bloody clashes on ethnic lines. Another consequence of such division is that the historical centres of Tazik national culture, Bukhara and Samarkand are territorially a part of Uzbekistan. Regional conflicts in Tazikistan apparently an essential dimension of the conflict between the communists and the democrats. The conflict is also seen as that between the 'pure persian speaking' tribes and those under Turkic and Mongol influences as in Leninabad and Kuliab. In

Tazikistan, the inter-ethnic conflicts have caused an estimated loss of 90 billion rubles by 1992. In Kirgizstan the regional conflict is between the dominant north and the 'rebellious' south or the 'southern opposition'. Askar Akaev, the President represents the dominant north. He separated the Dzhalal-Abad oblast from the Osh oblast in order to weaken Southerners and his supporters removed Bekmamat Osmonov as head of the administration in the former to subdue "southern opposition" resulting in destabilising the political situation to the extent that Akaev had to issue an statement that: "We must do everything within our power to prevent the repetition of the Tajik story in our republic". In Turkemenistan tribal divisions exist in form of Tekin, Salir, Sarik, Goklen, Chaudor and Iomut. According to Nikolai Petrov and Leonid Smirniagin in the anthology "The Geography and Anatomy of Parliamentary Elections":

> The sharply diverging political views of even such closely related people as the Azeris and Turkmens are well known: In Azerbaijan the 'relocation' of rayon first secretaries-their appointment to 'foreign' rayons-was widely practised, but in Turkmenia this was absolutely impossible, because the Tekins would never listen to an Iomut secretary, and the Iomuts would never have paid any attention to a Tekin.

Thus the potentiality of regional conflicts. The President, Saparmurad Niazov, a Tekin by birth, emphasised his stay at an orphanage as indicative of his supra-tribal credentials in appealing against regionalism. Uzbekistan has not shown open inter-ethnic divisions. However an interesting action of 200 parliamentary deputies in October 1991, led ostensibly under the indirect leadership of the then Vice-President Shukrullo Mirsaidov, who subsequently relinquished his post and came out in open opposition to the President Islam Karimov, may be indicative of subterranean regionalism.

These deputies criticised the policies of the President in an open letter and the striking feature was that virtually all of them came from Tashkent Oblast! The ruling elite of Uzbekistan has been from the the Samarkand oblast for many years, a fact overlooked by the opposition with a stronger base in Fergana Valley.

Minority nationalities were organising themselves on the community-basis, something unknown during the Soviet era, under the circumstances of the resurgence of nationalism. Nationalism gave rise to the reactive nationalism of the minority communities which felt that their socio-cultural identity was in danger. For instance, the Russian community, which was seven million strong in Kazakhstan organised its association with branches in 14 oblasts of the republic and all the raions of Alma-Ata with a population of 600,000 Russians, and registered its charter with the republic's Ministry of Justice. It can be considered as a response to the emergence of Kazakh nationalist parties like Alash and Azat. The leader of the community was Yuri Bunakov.[15]

Table 10.2 Index of ethnic conflicts, nature of political institutions and influence of religion in Central Asian Republics

Indicators	Kirgizstan	Uzbekistan	Turkmen
Probability of national-territorial conflict	Strong	Strong	Slight
Probability of regional conflicts	Strong	Slight	Strong
Probability of Islamisation	None	Strong	None
Probability of autonomous emergence from crisis	Negligible	Strong	Strong
Political aims of republic leadership	Democracy	Authoritaria -nism	Authoritaria -nism
Per Capita Land (in hectares)	0.29	0.20	0.33

Source: Nezavisimaia gazeta, 21 January 1993, p. 5.

An index of ethnic conflicts, nature of political institutions and influence of religion in Central Asian republics of Kirgizstan, Uzbekistan and Turkmenistan is as in Table 10.2:[16]

Ethnic composition in independent nation states underwent changes. For instance, in Kazakhstan, birth rates particularly fell for the Russians, Ukrainians, Belorussians and Germans between 1991-93. Since 1990s the total number of Russians had been decreasing because of the fall in natural increase like the birth rate, emigration and nationality changes with many nationalities reclaiming them. Between 1989-91, 282,000 people emigrated from Kazakhstan an excess of those arriving. Table 10.3 gives the net migration from Kazakhstan between these years:[17]

In January 1992 a radically nationalist Tatar party, an Organisational Committee comprising of parties like the Tatar National Independence Party gave a call that a Milli Medzhlis (National Assembly) be elected at a Kurultai (All-Tatar Congress) . It was to be a supra-assembly representing 7 million members of the Tatar nationality residing in

Tatarstan, superior to the Tatarstan Supreme Soviet, with powers to repeal the laws and ban political parties. The two in the proposed scheme of things would work in tandem to revive the ethos of the Tatar nation with Medzhlis being recognised as a state structure. The Kurultai and the Milli Medzhlis were proposed to have higher legal and political status than the Tatar parliament. Although officially the leadership of Tatarstan, which included President Shaimiev, initially took an unsympathetic view, particularly with the signing of the Tatarstan-Russia economic treaty, later on they seemed to have softened their political attitude towards the convening of a Kurultai and the formation of a Milli Medzhlis and towards its initiators.

Table 10.3 Net migration from Kazakhstan between 1989-91

Net Migration of Major Kazakhstan Nationalities (1989-91)

Ethnic Group	Total Natural Increase 1989-91	1 January 1992 estimated population (without migration)	Migration
Total Population	709868	17174332	-282719
Kazakhs	480744	7015360	+57712
Russians	107236	6334785	-77701
Ukrainians	13030	909270	-19475
Belorussians	4339	186940	-3228
Uzbeks	26392	358402	-1994
Tatars	9158	337140	-541
Others	68969	2032435	-237492

Source: Ana tili, 7 January 1993, p. 4 in FBIS-USR-051, 24 April 1993, pp. 80-83.

In Kirgizstan, a department for International Affairs and Relations with Public Associations and Religions was incorporated in the Presidential apparatus to deal with the issues of multi-nationalism, movements and parties. In January 1993 about 200 public formations were registered in Kirgizstan. The most representative were the ethnic cultural based and other political parties like Asaba, Erkin Kirgizstan, Atameken, the Republican Party, the Communist Party of Kirgizstan, the Private Builders Movement, the Kirgizstan Democratic Movement currently facing a split with the liberal wing supporting the President and the radical wing opposing him. The Communist Party of Kirgizstan was lead by the former CPSU

Politbureau member Absambat Masaliev. The Private Builder's Union consisted of private home owners living in communities around Bishkek. It was a mono-ethnic formation constituting of Kirgiz nationals.[18]

In March 1993, a nationalist organisation "Union for the Rebirth of Russia" organised a Congress of Russian Communities which called for the principle of "enlightened patriotism". The majority of the delegates were from the former constituent republics of USSR facing ethnicity based alienation in their respective new nation-states. For them, two hitherto united concepts -Native Land (Rodina), the republic of birth and Fatherland (Otechestvo), and Russia had been separated. A very high number of Russians, 25 million, lived outside the boundaries of the Russian Federation. Other sections of the delegates which were constituted by those from 'far abroad' and Russian social organisations from former autonomous constituents of the Russian Federation were disturbed at the growth of national and regional separatism. The Congress argued for direct or indirect intervention, of the Russian state, to ensure the redress of the grievances of the Russian diaspora in the newly-formed nation-states like offering custom privileges to the countries that protected the rights of the Russian population, ensuring that a part of the credit offered to them was invested in the population of Russian origin by for example, giving them employment. The argument in support of the latter proposal was that attempts were being made to 'overcrowd' the Russian nationals by inviting the indigeneous people living abroad and giving them the jobs in the state sector, particularly were the knowledge of the native language was required. An International League of Russian Entrepreneurs was formed at the Congress to help the Russian diaspora engage in private enterprise. A Russian Institute was established by the Congress to help the Russian communities with the exchange of information and provide higher education whereas the International Legal Defense Service was to render legal aid to the Russian diaspora. The Congress of Russian Communities was to function as a permanently functioning body with committees and deliberate on the political aspects of the problems faced by the Russians, particularly from 'near abroad'.[19]

The Congress of Russian Communities of the former USSR republics which concluded on 30 March 1993 decided to create "a diversified network" of Russian communities living in 'near abroad' to undertake steps to protect and promote their interests, particularly by lobbying with the Russian government. 25 million Russians living in the 'near abroad, were distributed as follows :[20]

Table 10.4 Number of Russians within territory of the former USSR

Country	Population (in thousands)	Russian (in thousands)	Percentage (of Russians in thousands)
Azebaijan	7,021	392	5.6
Armenia	3,305	52	1.6
Belarus	10,152	1,342	13.2
Georgia	5,401	341	6.3
Kazakhstan	16,464	6,226	37.8
Kirgizstan	4,258	917	21.5
Latvia	2,667	906	34.0
Lithuania	3,675	344	9.4
Moldova	4,335	562	13.0
Tazikistan	5,093	388	7.6
Turkmenistan	3,523	334	9.5
Uzbekistan	19,810	1,653	8.3
Ukraine	51,452	11,356	22.1
Estonia	1,565	475	30.3

Source: Kommersant daily, 31 March 1993, p. 10.

Within Russia, regional assertions of varying degrees - from independent decisions to acts verging on separatism have plagued the Russian political scene in the post-Soviet era, thereby keeping the issue of federalism and multi-nationalism very high on the political agenda. On the one hand were the explosive issues of separatism as exemplified by the conflict in Chechenia, on the other were independent agreements like the one on trade, economic, scientific, technical and cultural cooperation signed by Krasnodar Krai and Nizhni Novgorod oblast in January 1993 bypassing the centre and establishing horizontal regional ties.[21] On the one hand these actions were a consequence of the incapability of the central authorities to be able to provide for the regions as in the past, on the other, they were a significant byproduct of the liberal economic reforms and legitimate yearnings of the constituent regions for greater decentralisation and political and economic power. In many cases these were driven by the ethnic, religion, language and other cultural manifestations getting politicised in or not always healthy political reflection.

State Institutions in Russia and Central Asian Republics

The Russian Federation was constituted as a republic with federal structure of the state and a new constitution adopted on 12 December 1993. The Russian parliament has two houses, the State Duma, the lower house with 450 deputies elected on the basis of territorial constituencies, 225 elected on the basis of first past the post system and the remaining half from the party list, and the Federation Council, the upper house, with 178 deputies representing Russia's 89 republics and regions and consisting of the chiefs of the regional Parliaments and executive bodies. However the real power resides with the executive Presidency through powers invested by the Russian Constitution drafted in the aftermath of the October 1993 crisis, which ended in a bloody showdown between the Parliament and the President, decisively changing the balance of forces in favour of the latter, a correlation of power which reflected starkly in the newly drafted Constitution vesting the President with overwhelming powers vis-à-vis the Parliament. These powers have been flaunted by the President in an attempt to cow down a recalcitrant parliament from time to time. The second source of power for the President has been his prerogative to appoint the government of the day.

One of the key problems the Russian Federation, composed of 89 republics and regions and 120 nationalities and ethnic groups, faced in the post-Soviet era was that of the threat of disintegration on the lines of the former Soviet Union with rebellious republics and regions refusing to pay central taxes and preventing movement of resources. Some were resolved through treaties like the one between the Russian Federation and the Republic of Tatarstan in February 1994, subsequently concluded with most of the ethnic republics, accepting Tatarstan as a 'sovereign state', devolving major powers and underscoring the association based on the two constitutions. The unresolved ones resulted in massive military showdowns at a huge human and material cost, as with Chechenia pursuing the aim of total secession from the Russian Federation, towards the end of 1994. Subsequently an agreement was signed in August 1996 granting overwhelming sovereignty to Chechenia, a clause which had been interpreted in accordance with the political convenience both by the nationalist Chechens and the Russian authorities.

Other major threats to Russian society and the State are rampant crime and corruption. Russian Interior Ministry sources accepted the presence of 9000 organised criminal gangs controlling 40,000 organisations and 450 banks. These dangers are further accentuated by an economy struggling to recover from the crippling effects of unbridled economic reforms and a bankrupt state, unable to cushion the effects of the reforms through reasonable welfare measures, resulting in social tensions threatening the social stability.

Turkmenistan became an independent republic in December 1991 and its new President-centric Constitution came into effect in May 1992. On 21 June 1992, Saparmurad Niazov, the sole Presidential candidate was elected as President. The representative body Khalq Maslakhti (the People's Council) meets once a year and the Majlis (the National Assembly) is the legislative body. Although the Council of Elders and Cabinet Ministers were subordinate to the former, the real power was vested in the President. The republic of Tazikistan became an independent entity in September 1991. The executive Presidency was abolished in November 1992, and a parliamentary republic created only to restore the Presidency in November 1994 and Imamali Rakhmanov was elected the President. The civil war was brought to an end in March 1997 and an interim government constituting of a 27 member National Reconciliation Council (NRC) was formed until replaced by a new administration. Kirgiz Republic came into existence in August 1991 with the new Constitution being promulgated on 5 May 1993. A referendum in February 1996 strengthened the Presidency. A 105 member Bicameral legislature replaced the earlier 313 member Jogorku Kenesh. Askar Akaev was elected unopposed in October 1991 and further re-elected in December 1995 with 71.6 per cent of the votes. It is the President who appoints the Prime Minister, who in turn appoints the Cabinet. The republic of Uzbekistan declared its sovereignty in 1990, its independence on 31 August 1991 in a referendum and adopted a new Constitution on 8 December 1992. Uzbekistan was declared to be a multi-party democracy with a Presidential system and a 150 member unicameral, Ali Majlis (the Parliament).Islam Karimov was elected President in December 1991 with 86 per cent of the votes. The President nominates the Prime Minister and a Council of Ministers although he exercises unrivalled power through the appointed Hakims (regional governors) with unlimited powers. The Parliament is controlled by President Karimov's party, the Popular Democratic Party (PDP; the reincarnation of the former Communist Party), thereby giving him virtually absolute control over the reins of power.[22] The Republic of Kazakhstan came into existence on 16 December 1991 and its new Constitution was approved in a referendum on 30 August 1995. The Executive Presidency was greatly strengthened undermining the Bicameral legislature which consisted of a 67 seat lower house (the Majlis) and 47 seat upper house (the Senate). Nursultan Nazarbaev was elected the

President in December 1991 with 95 per cent votes in an election in which he was the only candidate. The President names the Prime Minister and the Council of Ministers exercising virtual control over them.[23]

In Tashkent and Ashgabat the state machinery was used to suppress political opposition. Organised opposition no longer exists in Uzbekistan. Some sections of the opposition supported the domestic policies of Islam Karimov out of fear that the violent inter-ethnic turmoil of Tazikistan may be repeated in Uzbekistan and gave the regime a convenient excuse to suppress democracy and replace it with an authoritarian regime. Similarly in Turkmenistan, activists of political parties for example poet Shirali Nurmiradov of the Agzibirlik movement and Durdimurad Khodzhanepesov of the Party for Democratic Development of Turkmenistan faced persecution.[24]

Conclusion

The plurality in the polity and society within the geographical boundaries of the former Soviet Union was the logical consequence of the process unravelling the political system set in motion in the later phase of Perestroika. The basis of pluralism was laid down during Perestroika by officially accepting pluralism within the Party, its leadership and the society. The pluralism then manifested itself in organised, semi-organised and disparate forms - moderate and extremist, democratic and undemocratic, radical and revolutionary or revivalist, disruptive and constructive, status-quoist or reformist - thereby making the single-party political system something of an anachronism. The latter disintegrated and with it the Soviet state and its socio-political-economic-geographical identity and the political party, the CPSU which was at its core.

However the new political systems that emerged in the fifteen independent nation-states were not all that different and displayed remarkable continuity with the past especially with the period under Perestroika. The basis of the economic and political systems had been laid during this period. During the Soviet period, the 'quasi-authoritarianism' of the political system emerged from the political fact of the existence of a single political party and the integration of the Party with the Soviet state. The 'quasi-authoritarianism' of the post - Soviet phase, despite the elected parliaments and presence of numerous parties, emerged from the executive Presidencies invested with immense powers concentrated in the hands of a President and his/her small coterie of functionaries at the expense of popularly elected Parliaments and in the absence of a proper system of checks and balances. The reasons given for such political dispensations were many, ranging from the necessity to build 'democracy' under the benign guidance of a 'strong' President who could keep 'anti-democratic' forces at bay! thus extending a peculiar thesis of building democratic institutions by a fusion of democratic and authoritarian means; to ensure rapid economic transformations from a 'statist' economy to a 'free market' one so as to resuscicate a decaying and dying economy; to curb the menace of numerous sub-nationalisms and tribal resurgence threatening the harmony and stability of the newly-liberated nation-states and their societies; and prevent inter-state conflicts in a situation of serious socio-political and economic crises engulfing them. The obvious fact however remains that most of these newly formed nation-states are under authoritarian political dispensations with the best and most democratic ones displaying at best 'quasi-democratic' characterstics. Political democracy, even in a liberal-democratic sense has a long road to travel before it finally arrives in terms of institutions and practices.

Notes

[1] Following political parties and groups were present in Russia in January 1993:

1. All Russian Renewal Union (VSO)
2. Democratic Russia Movement (DR)
3. Democratic Party of Russia (DPR)
4. Peasant Party of Russia (KPR)
5. People's Patriotic Party (NPP)
6. People's Party of Russia (NPR)
7. People's Party of Free Russia (NPSR)
8. Party of Constitutional Democrats (PKD)
9. Party of Economic Freedom (PES)
10. Russian Movement for Democratic Reform (RDDR)
11. Russian Communist Workers Party (RKRP)
12. Russian Party of Democratic Transformation (RPDP)
13. Russian Party of Communists (RPK)
14. Republican Party of Russia (RPRF)
15. Russian Party of Free Labour (RPST)
16. Russian Social-Liberal Party (RSLP)
17. Russian Christian Democratic Movement (RKhDD)
18. Russian Christian Democratic Party (RKhDP)
19. Free Democratic Party of Russia (SvDPR)
20. Social Democratic Party of Russia (SDPR)
21. Socialist Party of Workers (SPT)
22. Christian Democratic Union of Russia (KhDS)

[2] *Rossiskie vesti*, 28 January 1993, p. 2.
[3] *Pravda*, 25 December 1992, pp. 1-2.
[4] *Left and Workers Movement in the ex-USSR, materials of the information agency "Economy and Democracy"*, 1992, Moscow, pp. 3-6.
[5] The most important political parties and groups in Russia and other Central Asian republics in 1997 were as follows:
Russia
The Communist Party of the Russian Federation (CPRF)
Our Home is Russia (OHR)
Liberal-Democratic Party (LDP)
Yabloko
Agrarian Party of Russia (APR)
Russia's Democratic Choice (RDC)
The Women of Russia
Congress of Russian Communities
Turkmenistan
Democratic Party of Turkmenistan (formerly the Communist Party)
Peasant Justice Party (a government sponsored party)
All other political parties are banned. Two opposition groups from Ashgabat, the Democrat Party and Agzybirlik (Unity) groups are politically active.
Tazikistan
Socialist Party (former Communist Party)
Islamic Rennaisance Party
Democratic Party
Rastokhez (Rennaisance) Party
Party of People's Unity and Accord
United Tazik Opposition (UTO)
National Revival Party
Kirgiz Republic
Communist Party of Kirgizstan
Ata Meken
Erkin Kirgizstan
Civic Movement of Kirgizstan
Kazakhstan
Party of National Unity (PNU)
Cooperative Party
Democratic Party
People's Congress of Kazakhstan
Rebirth Party
Socialist Party
Lad (Harmony), ethnic Russian party
Communist Party.
Uzbekistan
Popular Democratic Party (PDP), (former Communist Party)
Adolat
Social-democratic Party of Uzbekistan, government sponsored opposition party
Istiklol Yoli, government sponsored opposition party

Birlik (Unity), the party is banned
Erk (Will), the party is banned
Islamic Rennaisance Party , the party is banned.

[6] *Rossiskie vesti* 10 December 1993 in *FBIS*-USR-93-162, 22 December 1993, p. 2.

[7]*Nezavisimaia gazeta*, 23 January 1993, p. 3.

[8] *Qazaq adebieti*, 4 December 1992, p. 14-15 in *FBIS*-USR-93-033, 20 March 1993, pp. 96-99

[9] *Slovo kirgizstana*, 25 December, 1993, p. 10.

[10] *Glasnost*, 19-25 November 1992, p. 2.

[11] *Nezavisimaia gazeta*, 3 February,1993, pp. 1-2.

[12] *Nezavisimaia gazeta*, 24 April 1992, p. 4.

[13] *Kommersant daily*, 23 December 1992, p. 11.

[14] *Rossiiskaia gazeta*, 19 January 1993, pp. 1,4.

[15] *Rossiskaia gazeta*, 12 January 1993, p. 7.

[16] *Nezavisimaia gazeta*, 21 January 1993, p. 5.

[17] *Ana tili*, 7 January 1993, p. 4 in *FBIS*-USR-051, 24 April 1993, pp. 80-83.

[18] *Slovo kirgizstana*, 23 January 1993, p.6 in *FBIS*-USR-93-025, 5 March 1993, pp. 84-86.

[19] *Rabochaia tribuna*, 6 April 1993, p. 3.

[20] *Kommersant daily*, 31 March 1993, p. 10.

[21] *Rossiskaia gazeta*, 30 June 1993, p. 4.

[22] *EIU Country Report*, 3rd Quarter 1997.

[23] *EIU Country Report*, 1st Quarter, 1997.

[24] *Nezavisimaia gazeta*, 21 January 1993, p. 5.

11 The State of the Economy in the Post-Soviet Era

Introduction

The economic crisis played a vital role in the political drama enacted towards the end of Perestroika and the socio-political instability that became a vexed problem for the post Soviet nation-states. Free-fall in the standards of living, burgeoning unemployment, galloping inflation, nose-diving production, obsolete technology, depreciating ruble, dismantling of the welfare system, a bankrupt state unable to pay its employees and collect revenues, unbridled privatisation, reign of economic mafia not governed by any laws, rapid emergence of social and class differentiation thereby disturbing the societal harmony, a conflict between the existing public sector and emerging private sector and absence of any redistributive mechanism to ensure a more equitable distribution of resources and wealth contributed to a state of social, political and cultural entropy. The basis for all these was laid during the Soviet era and every foregoing element was as true for the last phase of Perestroika as for the post-Soviet era, albeit in a more severe form.

The State of the Economy in Post-Soviet Russia

According to a report by the Russian State Committee on Statistics entitled "The Socio-Economic Situation and Development of Economic Reforms in the Russian Federation in 1992", the production and the standards of living of the people continued to decline as indicated by Table 11.1.

During 1992, more than 46,000 enterprises from different sectors of the economy were either partially or wholly privatised 82 per cent of these were however small enterprises with four-fifths of them from trade and communal services sphere.[1]

The changing economic-class orientation, newly emerging stratification of the society, emergence of new sections of the society as a result of the reforms during Perestroika providing a social base to numerous political formations was evident from the data (Table 11.2) released by the

USSR State Statistics Committee on the distribution of the population's employment in various spheres of the economy.

Table 11.1 Percentage decline in the production and the standards of living

	1992	1992/1991 Percentage (in comparable prices)
Gross Domestic Product	15.0	81.0
National Income generated	13.1	80.0
Industrial Production	16,135.0	81.2
Agricultural Production	3.0	92.0
Capital investments, all sources of financing (by actual cost)	2,445.0	55.0
Housing put into operation, all sources of financing, millions of square metres of total area	38.0	77.0
Shipment (dispatch)of freight overgeneral-use transportation, billions tonnes	5.0	78.0
Passenger turnover, general use transportation, billions of passenger-kms	583.0	88.0
Monthly monetary wage of a singleworker/ employee, rubles average for the year	6,158.0	11.2 fold
in December	16,132.0	12.3 fold
Monthly pay in Kolkhozes, rubles average for the year	3,444.0	8.0 fold
in December	11,400.0	9.7 fold
Retail Trade Turnover	3,562.4	61.0
Paid services	340.0	64.0

Source: Ekonomika i zhizn, no. 4, January 1993, pp. 13-15.

Unemployment

According to the data of RF Goskomstat (State Committee for Statistics), unemployment was upto one per cent of the population of workable age in January 1993. However the real state of unemployment could have been much worse as revealed by a survey conducted by state statistical agencies in several thousand state enterprises. Length of the work week had been reduced in most, it was not known as to how many unemployed had approached employment services or registered at unemployment agencies. A survey conducted by the Institute for Integrated Social Studies in Tomsk oblast in the Fall of 1992 revealed trends which were instructive of and

Table 11.2 The distribution of the populations employment in various spheres of the economy

	January-September			
	1990		1991	
Category	People (in million)	% employed	People (in million)	% employed
Total employed	138.2	100	135.7	100
State Enterprises and Organisations	108.8	78.7	98.9	72.9
Leased enterprises			9.0	6.6
Joint-Stock Companies	3.8	2.7	1.0	0.7
Economic Associations (Concerns etc.)			0.7	0.5
Public Organisations (foundations)	1.8	1.3	1.8	1.3
Joint Enterprises	0.1	0.1	0.2	0.2
The Collective Farm and Cooperative Sector of the Economy	18.8	13.6	17.6	13.0
Cooperatives involved in the Production of the Goods and Services	4.0	2.9	3.2	2.4
The sphere of Private and Individual Enterprise (private farms, personal auxillary farming operations, individual labour activity, contract workers etc.)	4.9	3.6	6.5	4.8

Source: Argumenti i fakti, no. 43, November 1991, p. 5.

representative of trends in the whole of Russia. The study was conducted amongst a large number of workers working at several enterprises from different sectors of the economy chosen to adequately represent the main social-professional and demographic groups proportionately of the employed population, economic managers, unemployed people, students in higher studies and educational institutions. The majority of those working at the enterprises were concerned about losing their job with a section hoping that things may become better. Similar were the observations of the three all-Russian Surveys conducted in April, June and December of 1992. An overwhelming majority of economic managers confirmed that the layoffs of workers would continue. Many enterprises had already done that and most foresaw this possibility in 1993. Similar fears were expressed by the workers with only a miniscule number hopeful of a turnaround. The possibility of getting a suitable alternative job was deemed remote by an overwhelming majority of economic managers and workers. The reason for unemployment was seen not to lie in the market transformations, or the structural reorganisation of production or the technical progress but that of the decline and disintegration of production. There may be shortage of workers in one sector of the economy whilst another sector may experience the presence of an idle labour force at the same time. Small businesses which were expected to provide alternative employment did not do well compounding the problems of unemployment. Rigours of unemployment had been accompanied with a massive decline in the standard of living with hyperinflation resulting in wiping out the savings of the workers and other sections of society. Social or community support to the unemployed was absent since everybody sailed in the same boat. The majority of those surveyed either survived from one paycheque to the next(58 per cent) or found it difficult to make both ends meet (24 per cent), whereas only one per cent lived comfortably and 15 per cent fairly well. A sharp decline in the standard of living had been the inevitable and most painful consequence, along with the loss of their previous social status, experienced by the unemployed. A majority of the respondents believed that the unemployment situation would create social tensions and result in social conflicts. An overwhelming majority of people attributed the reasons for unemployment to the disruption of the economic links between the enterprises and the general nation-wide economic crisis. Very few attributed it to the conversion of the defence industry and reduction in the army and a miniscule number to the introduction of such modern scientific technology which reduces the need for manpower. Financial difficulties of the enterprises and reducing production as a result of non-economic factors were seen as the key reasons for unemployment followed by structural reorganisation of production, privatisation and technical progress. The main brunt of unemployment was borne by the women and inexperienced young people. The majority of students in their final years at school, in vocational technical schools, technical schools and institutions of higher education (VUZs) were not sure if they would be able to find jobs after completing their studies. They were the ones who were primarily and indeed ironically required to assimilate modern science and technology and the new methods of economic management unleashed by the mutating economic system. These social groups were followed by skilled workers in the basic production sectors as potential victims of job-cuts. Most people expected the state to intervene and minimize the impact of unemployment by creating new jobs and retraining the jobless to be absorbed in newer sectors of production like services and entrepreneurial activities. This seemed to be a difficult proposition since these required a massive infusion of capital which the state simply did not have. Neither did the enterprises suffering from inflation and a declining trend in productivity or the banks meant to provide credit to the enterprises had. Another factor that compounded the problem further was if the unemployed were retrained what professions should they be trained in be since there was a general unemployment scenario and secondly they would certainly effect the prospects of new graduates. It was propagated and expected that the sphere of services would develop to the extent that it would absorb the losses of employment in primary sectors like mining, defense etc. The State had withdrawn from its responsibilities in the social sector and enterprises had lost their former resource base to finance them in an environment of unbridled privatisation and commercialisation. Budgetary expenditure by the federal government on education, science, art and culture reduced 2 to 3 times in 1992. Privatisation and commercialisation in circumstances where the vast majority of the population was nearing insolvency, the demand for manpower in the social sector was automatically bound to decrease. The study revealed that the largest unemployed group in Tomsk oblast (constituting 35 per cent of the whole) was from those working in the field of trade, public catering, public health, education, science and culture.[2]

In 1992, the number of the registered unemployed was 2.4 million which was approximately 1.6 times more than in 1991. Sixty per cent of these were women, 2.6 per cent were students, 2.2 per cent were pensioners and 3.3 per cent wanted to change their job as against 91.3 per cent who were not working at the time. 29.7 per cent found a job with the help of the employment services. The employment services helped create 12,000 jobs which was 6 times more than in 1991. In 1992, the job vacancies reduced to nine-fourteenths of the 1991 level totalling 314,500 jobs of which 88.3 per cent were blue- and 11.7 per cent white-collared jobs. In 1992, unemploment rose from 61,900 people to 577,700, that is, by a factor of 9.3. The highest levels of unemployment were in Yaroslavl oblast (2.8 per cent), Pskoc oblast (2.4 per cent), Dagestan and Kostroma and Ivanovo oblast (2.2 per cent) and Murmansk, Sakhalin, and Arkhangelsk oblasts, Mordivinia, Udmurtia, Adigeia, and the city of St. Petersburg (from 1.3 per cent to 1.7 per cent).[3]

On 1 February 1993, unemployment stood at 1,028,808. An estimated 2 million Russians were partially employed. The official number of those unemployed increased by 8.8 per cent in the month of January. The availability of jobs to the employment services had been falling from 840,000 on 1 January 1992, to 450,000 on 1 April 1992 to 300,000 in February 1993. Only 12 per cent were white-collared jobs with the rest being blue-collared. The rate of providing jobs for those who applied to the employment services had been increasingly falling.[4]

Standards of Living

One of the consequences of economic reforms in Russia was the rapid stratification of the population based on income levels which continued well into 1993. Income of the wealthiest 10 per cent was 11 times as high as the income of the bottom 10 per cent in 1993 and the differential was burgeoning. It had increased substantially from a correlation of 7.5-8.0 per cent in 1992 and 4.5 times in 1991, in accordance to the statistics provided by the State Committee for Statistics (Goskomstat). In accordance to the "Genie coefficient" which is an index of income concentration ranging from 0(level of absolute equality) up to 1(the level at which everything is owned by a single individual), the coefficient in Russia was 0.346 at the end of 1993, 0.327 and 0.256 at the end of 1992 and 1991 respectively. In 1993, per capita income of every one in three Russians was below the minimum subsistence level 13 per cent had only enough to provide minimum food allowance and 5 per cent were below that required for sheer physical survival. The economic and therefore social stratification is indicated by Table 11.3.

Average per capita income in November 1993 was 37,908 rubles. Which could be further classified as 42,799 for physically fit adults, 26,705 for pensioners and 37,896 for children according to the specifications laid down by the Russian Federation Ministry of Labour. This was based on the expenditure of the lowest 10 per cent section on food, non-food items and services, taxes and other obligatory payments. However social stratification does not have a one to one correlation with the income stratification since there was a more equitable distribution of 'social means' like housing, transportation and medicine which to some extent were being financed by the state budget thereby reducing the magnitude of the income differential to a certain extent.[5]

Table 11.3 Distribution of Russian population according to per capita monetary income in November 1993

Income(in Rubles)	Millions of People	Percentage
Total	148.7	100.0
Under 10,000	0.6	0.4
10,001-20,000	9.0	6.1
20,001-30,000	20.2	13.5
30,001-40,000	24.5	16.5
40,001-50,000	23.6	15.8
50,001-60,000	20.4	13.7
60,001-70,000	16.7	11.2
70,001-80,000	13.3	9.0
80,001-90,000	10.5	7.1
Over 90,000	9.9	6.7

Source: Izvestia, 17 February 1994, p. 4.

Unmitigated price rises as a result of inflation had become a consistent trend. Production declined at an alarming pace. In January 1992 it declined by 15-16 per cent, in January 1993 by 17-18 per cent and in January 1994 by 23 per cent. Inflation in the background of an economy in tailspin with solvency crunch and economic chaos had a more severe impact on the standards of living. Arrears of labour remuneration in industry, construction and agriculture, a not so human method employed by the state to control inflation, was Ruble 766 billion on 1 January 1994. The largest wage arrears were in Tiumen oblast (R60 billion), Krasnoiarsk Krai(R39 billion), Tatarstan(R35 billion) and Cheliabinsk oblast(R32 billion). Other places with high arrears were Kemerovo, Saratov, Irkutsk, Sverdlovsk, Magadan, Volgograd and Altai Krai. A three week or more delay in payment of wages accounted for two-thirds of the total amount. In Central and Far Eastern regions was the highest rate of non-payment of wages was for two months. 24,000 enterprises, which included 5,000 in industry, 4,000 in construction and 15,000 in agriculture(the state's indebtedness to agriculture was highest) where debtors had not payed the back wages. By the end of 1993 the differentiation in the average wages of the highest and lowest paid 10 per cent worker, measured by a factor of 27, with some being paid R 1 million per month and 1 million Russians getting less than the minimum wage, which at that time stood at R 14,620, pointed towards serious income disparities. Regional income disparities were indicated by the differences in the average per capita income which was as low as R57,000 in Ivanovo oblast and as high in Tiumen oblast as R245,000. Among gas industry workers in Krasnoiarsk Krai in December 1993 it was R2.4 million.[6]

In January 1994 production declined by 23.1 per cent in comparison to the same month in 1993 and by 17.2 per cent when compared with December 1993. Foodstuff and consumer prices as well as consumer services continued to rise. Consumer prices rose by an overall 21.4 per cent, including foodstuff by 21.1 per cent, non-food items by 12.5 per cent and consumer services by 73.8 per cent. The average monthly cost of a consumer basket comprising of 19 vital food items was R39,100 in February 1994. In Moscow it was R43,800 and in St. Petersburg, R39,900.[7]

Real monetary income in Russia was R96.4 per capita per month in 1992 based on 1983 prices. In the third quarter of 1993 real monetary income was less than forty per cent of that in the fourth quarter of 1991 in accordance with a study conducted by the All-Russian Centre for the Standard of Living(VTsUZH) of the Russian Federation Ministry of Labour. The minimum levels for wages, pensions, stipends, subsidies and social outlays etc. had lagged behind price rises. Galloping inflation had contributed to a rise in poverty levels. The decline in per capita real income basically effected less well-off sections of the society whereas new stratas like entrepreneurs and those engaged in shadow economy, speculative activities etc emerged with disproportionately high monetary incomes. Most people relied on more than one job or private plots to supplement their meagre incomes. Gross output from private plots between 1985 to 1991 on 1983 prices rose by a factor of 1.4. Their proportionate share in the entire nation's agricultural output increased by 23-33 per cent over the same period. The decline in real income is reflected in the decreasing consumption levels of the population from 1990 upto 1992 as the following table illustrates:

Table 11.4 Decline in the consumption levels of the population from 1990 to 1992

Consumption Item	1990	1992
Meat and Meat Products	68 Kg./year	58Kg./year
Meat and Dairy Products	386 Kg./year	295Kg./year
Eggs	296	256
Sugar	47.2 Kg.	33.6 Kg.
Vegetable Oil	10.0 Kg.	6.5 Kg.
Vegetables/Melons/ Gourds	89 Kg.	83 Kg.
Fruits and Berries	35 Kg.	33 Kg.
Potatoes and Grain Products	119 Kg.	122Kg.
Fabric Consumption	39.14 square metres	22.0 square metres
Shoes	3.27 pairs	2.16 pairs

Source: Ekonomika i zhizn, no. 7, February 1994, p. 16.

Regional differentiation was quite varied in case of real incomes and personal consumption from one region to another. Severest effected were Severo-Kavkazski, Tsentralni and Severo-Zapadni regions. Tsentralno-Chernozemnii and Povolzhskii regions were customarily better off with better provisions of consumer goods alongwith Uralski and Volga-Viatski regions were defence complexes existed. Dalnevostochnii region was first in per capita consumption followed by Tsentralnii region. Per capita consumption for Povolzhoskii and Severnii regions had showed some improvement whereas that in Zapadno-Sibirskii and Vostochno-Sibirski regions where the per capita consumption levels corresponded to the All-Russian average had started showing some decline. To assess the regional differentiation, concepts of "Minimum Consumption Budget"(MPB) and "Minimum Subsistence Budget"(BPM) were employed. The former refers to the provision of complete satisfaction of reasonable personal needs whereas the latter refers to the provision of basic needs, to ensure the health and working capabilities of the population. The BPM envisage a basket for per capita consumption consisting of food items and a basic calorific intake. It also includes expenditures on non-food goods, services, taxes and other compulsory outlays. This varied on a regional basis. For instance, it was highest in Dalnevostochnii region (R58,237 in October 1993), KhantaMansiskii Autonomous Okrug (R87, 244) and in Amurskaiia oblast (R69,126) and lowest in the Tsentralno-Chernozemnii regions of Russia(R18,864), the Republic of Tatarstan(R15,815), the Republic of Karelia(R10,970) and Rostovskaiia oblast(R17,123). Between July and October 1993, the minimum cost of living went down in comparison to the Russian average in Sever-Zapadnii, Volga-Viatskii, Tsentralno-Chernozemnii, Povolozhskii and Uralskii regions, but increased quite noticeably in Vostochno-Sibirskii, Zapadno-Sibirskii and Dalnevostochnii regions with the correlation remaining almost the same in other regions.

The average per capita money income of 10 per cent better off in October 1993 doubled by a factor of 6 in comparison to that of the 10 per cent worse off. The former shared 19.3 per cent of the total income fund whereas the latter about 3.2 per cent. The VTsUZH gave the following classification of the different stratas of the population and the per centage constituting these groups in accordance to the level of income and consumption in relation to consumption budgets:

a. Group 1 - Poor families with incomes less than or equal to the estimated minimum subsistence budget. (32)

b. Group 2 - Low-income families with per capita incomes between the estimates of minimum subsistence budget and minimum consumption budget. (41)

c. Group 3 - Middle-income families with per capita incomes between one and two MPBs or close to the average budget. (20)

d. Group 4 - Well-off families with per capita incomes between twice the MPB or the average budget and the reasonable consumption budget of the rich. (5.5)

e. Group 5 - Rich families whose per capita incomes are higher than the reasonable consumption budget or the income conventionally characterizing rich, which was over R150,000 per family member in July 1993. (1.5)

In 1993, the per capita income of the rich families was in excess of that of poor families by a factor of 30 underscoring the wide divergence.[8] The social consequences of the poverty and income differentials have been that the number of deaths exceeded the number of births in 68 regions of Russia and the life-expectancy fell to 65.8 years in comparison to 69.3 years in 1986. 77 per cent of the population had an income less than double that of the minimum subsistence level and 30 per cent below the subsistence levels in 1993. The poorest include those with large families and single pensioners and the disabled despite the indexation. The 'new poor' which emerged in Russia in 1993 includes the section of population eligible for work living below the subsistence levels including the unemployed (more than one million in 1993), workers from loss-making enterprises sent on leave (more than 4 million officially) and the youth. In 1993, more than 10 per cent of high school passouts, 70 per cent graduates of elementary vocational schools, more than 60 per cent of intermediate vocational schools and about 50 per cent college graduates could not find employment. The highest level of unemployment with 11 to 33 contenders for each job existed in republics of Mari El, Dagestan, Chuvashia, Adigei, Mordivinia, and Pskov, Yaroslavl and Ivanovo oblasts. Employment in the non-state sector of the economy comprised of 40 per cent whereas it was shrinking in state enterprises. The average wage increase generally lagged behind the increase in prices. The divergence in wages in 1993 was as high as by the factor of 27. In State enterprises the income differential between the salaries of the top managers and regular workers was a factor of 12-15. Wages were meant to ensure normal production by the labour force and give incentives for effective labour in normal circumstances. In contemporary Russia however, they are not linked with the results of labour but with the increase in prices.[9]

During the period of December 1991 and January 1992 the jump in the prices was drastic so as to reduce the real incomes of the population by a whopping 35-40 per cent. In January 1993, a consumer basket consisting of 28 food items, 148 non-food items and 30 services cost an individual between the age group 30-59, R14,606; a married couple, R26,219; a single-child (7-12 years) family, R31,712; a family with two children (7-12 and 13-17 years), R39,940. This was 4-5 times more than in January 1992.[10] According to January 1994 data, 52.6 million Russians had an average per capita income below the subsistence level and 26.3 million (or one in five) were semi-starved. Their income was less than the cost of food barely necessary for survival. An example of the State's insensitivity to the subject was the proposal of the Ministry of Labour (Mintrud) to increase the minimum wage from R14,620 to R20,500 from 1 March 1994 when according to the Russia's Goskomstat the minimum subsistence wage for an able-bodied Russian in January 1994 was R58,000 and was expected to increase substantially by March. The money required for merely buying the meagre food products for mere survival was R39,44 in January and estimated R53,000 in March. Thus the minimum wages have always trailed the price rises.[11]

Regional Dimensions of the Economy in Russia:

The Goskomstat (State Committee for Statistics) data for the development of economic reforms for 1992 indicates the diversity of the vast country such as the Russian Federation. The profitability growth of Russian enterprises and organisations were as follows:

Table 11.5 Regional variations in the profitability growth of Russian enterprises and organisations

Region	By a Factor of
Murmansk oblast	26.1
Leningrad oblast	25.2
Lipetsk oblast	24.5

Eastern region of Russia (the Urals,Western Siberian, Eastern Siberian and Far Eastern Regions) :

Republic of Bashkortostan	22.8
Perm oblast	19.7
Irkutsk oblast	18.0
Kemerovo oblast	18.3
Kamchatka oblast	2.5
Republic of Sakha(Yakutia)	5.0
Republic of Tuva	5.5
Republic of Khakassia	5.6
Magadan oblast	6.7

European part of Russia:

Industrial St. Petersburg	8.7
Ivanovo oblast	7.2
Kaluga oblast	8.7

Profits in Gross Ruble terms (in billion):

Moscow	R261.4
Tiumen oblast	R217.6
Sverdlovsk oblast	R185.1
Samara oblast	R132.1
Republic of Bashkortostan	R130.7
Krasnoiarsk Krai	R125.5

Republic of Tuva	R0.3
Republic of Altai	R0.5
Kamchatka oblast	R2.3
Republic of Adigeia	R4.1
Republic of Dagestan	R4.8

The proportional share of unprofitable enterprises in all types of economic activity (in per cent):

Magadan oblast	39.6
Republic of Tuva	38.6
Republic of Sakha	37.3
Sakhalin oblast	30.6
Murmansk oblast	31.3
Astrakhan oblast	23.5
Arkhangelsk oblast	23.0
Republic of Komi	22.7
Krasnioarsk Krai	9.6
Sverdlovsk oblast	11.6
Cheliabinsk oblast	12.1

Figures for average monthly wages of workers and office-workers in industry in 1992 (in fold increase):

Russia	11.3	R5,996

(The consumer price index in December 1992 was 26.1 times higher than in December 1991)

Average monthly wages in the national economy as a whole R10,576

Eastern Siberia	14.0	R9,839
Northwestern region	8.9	R4,151
Chukotka	17.3	R22,941
Magadan oblast	17.5	R21,579
Yamal-Nenets	17.9	R21,981
Taimur Autonomous okrug	18.2	R20,447
Kemerovo	14.5	R11,128
Novosibirsk	8.9	R4,708
Kabardino-Balkaria	7.2	R2,426
Republic of Kalmikia, Khalmg-Tangch	7.3	R3,215
Republic of Mari El	8.0	R3,398

Penza oblast	8.7	R3,431
Karachai-Cherkassia	8.6	R3,483
Moscow	9.7	R5,044
St. Petersburg	8.3	R4,151

Source: Federatsia, 23 February 1993 p. 5.

The economic diversity increased with the progress of the reforms. Areas close to the capital city of Moscow gained. Northern Caucasus lost its economic supremacy.[12]

The State of the Economy in Central Asia and Other Members of the Commonwealth of Independent States

Central Asian economy is predominantly an agrarian economy. In 1988, 50 per cent people in Uzbekistan, 55 percent in Tazikistan, 53.4 per cent in Turkmenistan and 44.6 per cent in Kirgizstan were engaged in agriculture. Agriculture was dominated by the indigeneous population, whereas in the industry the proportion of Russian to indigeneous people was in a proportion of three to one. Apart from working in Kolkhozes and Sovkhozes, the peasantry tilled their small subsidiary plots. Land has perpetually been in short supply and so has water. In the past century, although the population increased by 11.5 times the irrigated land only increased by 2.5 per cent. The traditional way of life in Central Asia conflicts with the modern industrial lifestyle. Thus the economic reason of the paucity of land and the socio-cultural factor of the conflict between the traditional lifestyles and the pressures of modern industrial way of life are twin attributes causing inter-ethnic tensions. Kirgiz-erstwhile nomadic herdsmen are in a minority in the republic. Such factors have created additional inter-ethnic tensions in the region when the primary inhabitants find themselves deprived of its fertile land.[13]

Individual farming gathered momentum in CIS. In 1992 there were 470,000 farms with 12 million hectares of land. Following is the number and size of the farms (Table 11.6).

Very few individual farms were established in Tazikistan. The agrarian reforms in CIS countries included redistribution of land, privatisation and reorganisation of collective and state farms. In Russia one in five individual farms had less than five hectares of land. Individual farms in Russia accounted for 3 per cent of the agricultural crops and 4 per cent of the arable land. Sown areas of agicultural farms belonging to private farmers in Russia increased from 321,000 hectares in 1991 to 2.4 million hectares in 1992. More than one million people were working on individual farms in 1992-93. The individual farmers rarely employed hired labour, the farms were ill-equipped, had a shortage of livestock and livestock raising infrastructures, lacked electric supply, link roads, infrastructure, lacked technology, seeds, fertilizers, credits at high interest rates, faced managerial problems, the negative attitude of the population, lack of State support and absence of other resources. 5000 individual farms went out of business in 1992 owing to these problems.[14]

Table 11.6 Number and size of the farms in the Commonwealth of Independent States

Member States	Size of the Farms
Russia	183,700 (43 hectares per farm)
Ukraine	14,400 (20 hectares)
Kirgizstan	8,600 (43 hectares)
Kazakhstan	8,500 (400 hectares)
Uzbekistan	6,000 (8 hectares)
Belarus	2,000 (19 hectares)
Armenia	243,000 (2 hectares)
Turkemenistan	100 (10 hectares)
Moldova	500 (3 hectares)

Source: Izvestia, 2 February 1993, p. 2.

The standards of living nose-dived in almost all the member states. Table 11.7 indicates the changes in the major economic indicators between January-October 1992 in comparison to the corresponding period in 1991:

Table 11.8 is illustrative of the fall in the rate of commissioning of the facilities of social and cultural importance in CIS (January-October 1992 as a percentage of January-October 1991).

The average rise in the prices for consumer goods in the retail trade were colossal as illustrated in Table 11.9.

The CIS exports fell by 29 per cent in January-October 1992, in comparison to January-October 1991, to $ 36 billion. Barter operations replaced currency deals owing to declining hard currency revenues in the Commonwealth countries. In Russia barter deals were up to 8 per cent. The

Table 11.7 Changes in the major economic indicators between January-October 1992 and the corresponding period in 1991

Member State	National Income Produced	Total volume of Industrial Prod.	Industrial Enter. Wholesale Industrial Prod.	Pop. Monetary Income	Pop.Monetary Expend. on Purchase of Goods and Payments for Services	Retail Turnover in Current Prices	Retail Turnover in Compar. Prices
Azerbaijan	74.5	75.0	--	--	--	392	40.0
Armenia	58.4	47.7	1,022	227.3	215.0	198	26.6
Belarus	85.5	87.0	1,936	682.6	694.8	725	68.0
Kazakh.	82.6	83.8	2,179	567.0	428.8	502	59.8
Kirgizstan	75.2	75.8	1,740	371.4	324.4	340	34.1
Moldova	75.9	73.7	1,199	446.4	413.8	446	48.9
Russia	80.0	81.9	1,811	619.7	624.7	662	60.8
Tajikistan	--	78.0	1,408	--	--	273	30.0
Turkmen.	82.4	78.6	0991	551.0	389.5	438	54.5
Uzbek.	78.2	91.6	1,140	402.1	387.9	395	66.5
Ukraine	84.0	90.3	2,120	8.73 fold	7.3 fold	833	79.0
CIS as a whole	80.7	82.2	18.5 fold	7.1 fold	6.0 fold	656	62.8

Source: Delovoi mir, 15 December 1992, p. 8.

Table 11.10 Changes in the number of unemployed (in thousand people)

Month	Azerbaijan	Armenia	Belarus	Kazak hstan	Kirgiz stan	Moldova	Russia	Tajiki stan	Turkm enistan	Uzbeki stan	Ukraine
Jan	4.9	--	2.6	4.5	0.2	--	69.2	--	--	--	--
Feb	5.5	--	3.4	6.7	0.3	0.2	93.1	--	--	--	--
Mar	7.0	--	4.2	9.2	0.5	0.3	118.4	--	--	--	--
Apr	7.9	6.1	5.1	11.8	0.7	0.4	151.0	0.5	--	--	--
May	7.2	8.9	5.8	13.6	0.8	0.4	176.5	1.3	--	--	--
Jun	7.2	14.5	7.1	15.8	0.8	0.6	202.9	3.5	--	--	--
Jul	6.8	20.8	9.7	19.6	1.1	0.9	248.0	3.6	--	1.4	--
Aug	6.6	29.3	12.2	22.4	1.2	1.2	294.2	5.5	--	2.1	--
Sept	6.2	35.6	14.9	25.0	1.4	1.6	367.5	7.2	--	3.6	60.7
Oct	6.3	41.8	17.8	28.2	1.5	1.9	442.4	--	--	5.7	63.9

Source: Delovoi mir, 15 December 1992, p. 8.

Table 11.8 Fall in the rate of commissioning of the facilities of social and cultural importance

Member States	Housing	General Education School	Pre-school facilities	Hospitals	Outpatients and Polyclinic facilities
Armenia	17	19	17	84	--
Belarus	70	90	78	43	54
Kazakhstan	70	70	44	67	51
Russia	73	63	72	43	60
Uzbekistan	50	64	59	90	95
Ukraine(Jan. -Sept.)	104	82	105	36	51

Source: Delovoi mir, 15 December 1992, p. 8.

energy resource situation was unsatisfactory as well. Electricity generation fell in all CIS states. The production of consumer goods including textiles, fell substantially. Similarly the production of food products including that of animal products declined. The volume of capital construction continued to show a downward trend. Between January-October 1991 and the corresponding period in 1991, housing reduced by 26 per cent; general education schools - 33 per cent; hospitals - 47 per cent; and outpatient and polyclinic facilities - 39 per cent. The consumer market was characterised by an increase in prices of consumer goods and food products. The number of unemployed increased. Table (11.10) indicates the changes in the number of unemployed (in thousand people):[15]

Privatisation

The overall process of privatisation was undertaken at a very rapid pace. Out of 652,000 trade and consumer service enterprises more than 433,000 were owned by the state when the process of privatisation began. By November 1993, 37 per cent of the retail turnover and 36 per cent of consumer services was by private and non-state enterprises as against 8 and 23 per cent respectively compared to the previous year.[16] According to the chief of the Main Administration for Privatisation of the Russian Federation State Committee for the management of State Property, in the first two months of the 1993, the number of privatised enterprises in Russia increased from 47,000 to 58,000 and was 23.8 per cent of the total number of state enterprises subject to privatisation. Over these two months 7,000

Table 11.9 The average rise in the prices for consumer goods in the retail trade

Member States	January-October 1992 in relation to January-October 1991	October 1992 in relation to October 1991	October 1992 in relation to September 1992	For Reference: Average Monthly Price Increases Over March-September 1992
Azerbaijan	987	1,397	116.0	112.0
Armenia	743	905	122.2	111.7
Belarus	1,018	1,388	114.6	112.4
Kazakhstan	841	1,233	116.9	114.0
Kirgizstan	984	1,508	123.7	110.2
Moldova	935	1,109	119.2	107.3
Russia	1,078	1,314	120.8	112.5
Tazikistan	933	1,295	108.0	110.9
Turkmenistan	803	908	104.2	108.5
Uzbekistan	637	666	112.9	108.4
Ukraine	1,028	1,600	120.0	115.1
CIS as a whole	1,025	1,332	119.7	113.1

Source: Delovoi mir, 15 December 1992, p. 8.

small enterprises were privatised constituting a quarter of the total number privatised during the entire 1992. This despite the rate having slowed down for the months of November-December 1992. By March 1993, 35,000 or 45.5 per cent of the total of 76,884 small enterprises marked for privatisation were in private hands. This included 19,000 trade enterprises (45.6 per cent), more than 4,500 public catering enterprises (38.6 per cent) and over 11,000 consumer services enterprises (48 per cent). 7,462 enterprises were to be converted into joint-sector enterprises by 1 March 1993. 3,757 were converted into joint-stock enterprises (with 1,381 just over two months of 1993). Thus a 40 per cent conversion had taken place since July 1992.[17]

In the agricultural sector the pace of privatisation in 1992 was revealed by the figures mentioned in Table 11.11.[18]

In the beginning of 1993 the total number of peasant (private farmer) farms was estimated at 185,000 encompassing an area of 8.2 million hectares of land with an average of 42 hectares per farm.[19] By January 1993, 18 million families were given 5 million hectares of land to undertake private subsidiary farming. 800,000 families were allocated 100,000 hectares of land. 29 million families owned 2.1 million hectares of collective gardens and orchards. 11,000 kolkhozes and sovkhozes were converted into 800 associations of peasant farms, 3,800 joint-stock companies, 1,100 agricultural cooperatives.[20]

The data released by the Russian Federation State Committee on Economic Cooperation with Member States of the Commonwealth of Independent States revealed the extent of the percentage decrease in the economic indicators of the CIS States in 1992 when compared with 1991:[21]

In Russia, the real GDP growth remained negative (1992, -14.5; 1994, -12; 1995, -4.0 and 1996, -5.0). The consumer price inflation,

Table 11.11 Number of peasant (Private Farmer) farms in Russia

	Number of Peasant (Private Farmer) Farms in Russia
1 January 1992	49,000
1st Quarter	92,500
2nd Quarter	129,200
3rd Quarter	150,100
4th Quarter	183,700

Source: Vek, no. 6, 12-19 February 1993, p. 1.

Table 11.12 Percentage decrease in the economic indicators of the CIS states in 1992 when compared with 1991

National Income

Member State	Percentage Decrease
Russian Federation	20
Lesser Decrease than in Russia:	
Kazakhstan	14

Uzbekistan	13
Turkmenistan	15
Ukraine	15
Greater Decrease than in Russia:	
Armenia	43
Azerbaijan	28
Kirgizstan	26
Tajikistan	31
Moldova	21

Industrial Production

Russian Federation	19
Lesser decrease than in Russia:	
Belarus	10
Kazakhstan	15
Uzbekistan	6
Turkmenistan	17
Ukraine	9
Greater decrease than in Russia:	
Armenia	53
Azerbaijan	24
Kirgizstan	27
Moldova	22
Tajikistan	24

Retail Trade Turnover

Russian Federation	39
Lesser Decrease than in Russia:	
Ukraine	23
Belarus	26
Uzbekistan	31
Turkmenistan	38
Greater decrease than in Russia:	
Armenia	73
Azerbaijan	63
Kirgizstan	67
Moldova	49
Tajikistan	72

Kazakhstan	39

Retail Prices (Factoral Increase Over December 1991)

Russian Federation	17.5
Lesser increase than in Russia:	
Uzbekistan	8.4
Armenia	13.3
Kazakhstan	15.4
Moldova	14.6
Tajikistan	14.5
Turkmenistan	9.8
Greater increase than in Russia:	
Azerbaijan	22.8
Belarus	20.5
Kirgizstan	17.6
Ukraine	21.8

Source: Moskovskie novosti, no. 8, 21 February 1993, MN Business, p. 11B.

however, came down from a very high percentage of 1,353 and 874.7 in 1992 and 1993 to 197.4 and 47.6 in 1995 and 1996 respectively. Average wages largely lagged behind the consumer price rise. They changed from 994.0 and 878.5 per cent in 1992 and 1993 to 123.6 and 51.9 per cent in 1995 and 1996 respectively. They were only marginally higher in 1993 and

Table 11.13 The percentages of real GDP growth (a) and average consumer price inflation (b), employment in the industry (c) and registered unemployed (d) between 1992-96

Country	Eco. Ind.	1992	1993	1994	1995	1996
Kirgizstan	a	-15.8	-16.3	-20.1	-6.3	5.6
	b	855	1209	278	42.6	34.5
	c	--	--	219,000	201,000	180,000
	d	--	--	118,00	46600	77900

Kazakhstan	a	-13.0	-15.7	-25.0	-8.9	1.1
	b	1,513	1,571	1,880	176	39
	c			Not Applicable		
	d			Not Applicable		
Uzbekistan	a	-10.6	-2.3	-4.2	-0.9	1.6
	b	645	534	1,568	305	64
	c			Not Applicable		
	d			Not Applicable		
Turkmenistan	a	-5.3	-10.0	-18.8	-8.2	-3.0
	b	493	3,102	1,748	1,005	992
	c	--	--	144,000	162,000	155,000
	d	-	--	--	--	--
Tajikistan	a	-30.0	-27.6	-15.0	-12.4	-16.7
	b	1,157	2,195	452	635	65
	c	--	--	184,000	190,000	172,000
	d	--	--	30900	34200	50700

Source: Compiled from EIU Country Reports, 1997 for Kirgiz Republic, Kazakhstan, Uzbekistan, Turkmenistan and Tajikistan.

1996 than the percentage change in the consumer prices. The rate of unemployment as a percentage of the labour force grew from 4.9(1992 and 5.5 (1993) up to 8.8 (1995) and 9.3 (1996). Industrial Production (1990=100) fell from 75 (1992) and 65 (1993) to 49 (1995) and 46 (1996). By 1996, it was less than half of what it was in 1990. Similarly agriculture production (including animal sector), particularly that of grain, meat, milk, eggs and wool fell by a considerable degree.[22]

Conclusion

The reforms under Perestroika primarily started as economic reforms. These were meant to be intra-systemic and essentially controlled in the initial years of Perestroika. However, these reforms created such new social classes and stratas which clamoured for deeper economic reforms oriented towards the emergence of a fully-fledged market economy. This induced the struggle for political reforms because of the perception that economic reforms cannot proceed any further unless the political system is suitably modified. The strategies obviously differed with some arguing for an incremental political and economic reform, others opposing any reforms, yet others insisting on rapid economic and political reforms to ensure a full blown market economy and a liberal-democratic multi-party system. Therefore the economic imperatives and political and social consequences of economic reforms during Perestroika defined to a considerable extent the contours of the Soviet political system as well as the newly emerging nation-states within its politico-geographical boundaries. The social forces, the new social classes and groups, generated during the course of economic reforms during Perestroika played a decisive role in the social and political transformation of the formidable Soviet political system, its disintegration and demise.

Notes

[1] *Ekonomika i zhizn*, no. 4, January 1993, pp. 13-15.

[2] *Delovoi mir*, 14 January 1993, p. 3.

[3] *Rossiskie vesti*, 6 March 1993, p. 5.

[4] *Trud*, 24 February 1993, pp.1-2.

[5] *Izvestia*, 17 February 1994, p. 4.

[6] *Trud*, 12 February 1994, p.2.

[7] *Segodnia*, 16 February 1994, p. 3.

[8] *Ekonomika i zhizn*, no. 7, February 1994, p. 16.

[9] *Obshchaia gazeta*, no. 7, 18 February 1994, p. 15.

[10] *New Times International*, no. 11, March 1993, pp. 18-21.

[11] *Trud*, 22 February 1994, p. 1.

[12] *Federatsia*, 23 February 1993 p. 5.

[13] *Nezavisimaia gazeta*, 21 January 1993, p. 5.

[14] *Izvestia*, 2 February 1993, p. 2.

[15] *Delovoi mir*, 15 December 1992, p. 8.

[16] *Delovoi mir*, 24 November 1993, p. 4 in *FBIS*-USR-93-163, 23 December 1993 p. 21.

[17] *Ekonomika i zhizn*, no. 16, April 1993, p. 1.

[18] *Vek*, no. 6, 12-19 February 1993, p. 1.

[19] *Lesnaia gazeta*, 6 February 1993, p.3.
[20] *Krestianskaia rossia*, no. 3, 30 January 1993, p.2 in *FBIS*-USR-93-022, 27 January 1993, p. 35.
[21] *Moskovskie novosti*, no. 8, 21 February 1993, MN Business, p. 11B.
[22] *EIU Country Profile 1997-98*, Russia Reference Tables, pp. 41-49 and *EIU Country Report*, Third Quarter, 1997, p.5.

12 Conclusion

During Perestroika the Central Committee became a parliament of interests and political tendencies. This was in contrast to its previous role as a body composed of political-administrative institutions. The traditional "job-slot system" of representation was no longer applicable. Although the ministries representing the administrative arm of the State and those concerned with social matters were still represented, their centre of activity lay in the realm of the State. The latter was no longer influenced by this body. The upsurge in nationalist sentiments resulted in a proportionate representation of different nationalities. This was meant to provide the Central Committee with a pan-national equilibrium. Paradoxically, this contributed to increased centrifugal tendencies.

Several mass organisations were no longer represented in the Central Committee. The key absentee was the official trade unions. This reflected first the emergence of independent trade unions, causing the official trade unions to lose their central position, and second the desire of the reformist leadership to represent the interests of the working class through its actual members (the Central Committee contained a large number of skilled workers). This was significant because the long-standing practice of the Party's direct control of the trade unions was transformed. It was as a result of the inability of the official trade unions to adequately represent the interests of the working class. Trade unions by themselves could better articulate its interests, with the Party supporting them as a ruling Party in a one-party or a multi-party system. This however meant that the Party and the Central Committee could no longer directly influence the priorities of the trade unions. They could exercise their right to bargain, e.g. through strikes which were legalised, independently of the Party. The Party's guiding role over the proletariat in both theory and practice had come to an end. This perhaps heralded an era of "pure and simple trade unionism". It reflected the acceptance by the Party of the reformist position that the two "had complementary but distinct spheres of competence". The trade unions were no longer to be Lenin's "school of communism" with the Party playing a decisive role.[1] Also striking was the fact that unskilled workers were not included in the Central Committee, a substantial section of society which was extensively affected by the reforms. However certain new interests like leaseholders, co-operators and entrepreneurs were included!

The lower echelons of the Party organisations now determined their representation in this organ as opposed to a process of selection from the top. Varied and conflicting opinions could be expressed in it. It was not monocentric, and horizontal channels of communication replaced vertical ones. Horizontal communication prevented the previous atomisation of its membership. It was no longer the centre of political legitimation and authority. Expertise and experience were not the criteria for representation. Imputed status and importance of individuals and institutions did not determine the membership. Requirements of the State no longer regulated its organisation. The Central Committee was now an elected organ rather than a selected one. The norms of election became rational; the circular flow of power, which characterised the previous Central Committees, ceased. Its unitary organisation was federalised. All this led to its marginalisation in Soviet politics. The arena of political struggle had shifted to state bodies to the extent that in August 1991 the leaders of the State Committee for the State of Emergency, despite being members of the Central Committee, did not even bother to consult this body.

In the early years of Perestroika, the reformers did not envisage a systemic or radical change. The coalition between moderate reformists and moderate conservatives, although inherently unstable, could thus be forged. This alliance was largely comprised of members whose political education had taken place in the era of Khrushchevian reformism. It was this coalition which initiated reforms in three key areas: the economy, the nationalities and the democratisation of the political system. One of the main arguments of the proponents of reforms was that the command economy and the corresponding political system had resulted in the alienation of the working class both from property and power. Conservatives later accused the reformists of having abandoned the social class method of analysing the situation in society and defining policy. The strains in this coalition were increasingly manifested. By the time of the March 1989 elections, the consensus was already breaking up, with radical-reformists taking an independent line and conservatives taking a more revivalist position. For them the changes could destabilise the situation and result in unintended consequences. The two contending trends had existed within the same institutional boundary which lacked a democratic mechanism to provide a regulatory framework to fix the norms of such a contest. With the features of a new system emerging, the coalition started disintegrating. The common institutional framework was unable to contain the conflict since a politically active society was now involved in the debate for the future of the Soviet Union.

The organisation of the Central Committee underwent significant changes. The Central Apparatus had been known to be selective about the information reaching the higher leadership and defending the lower committees. This was openly claimed by Gorbachev at the beginning of Perestroika, making its reorganisation an important priority. Regional Party committees provided an important base for the Central Secretariat and the Central Apparatus, giving the latter effective control over the Party organisation to the detriment of the Politburo and the Central Committee. They had been deeply involved in matters of the economy and the administration. During Perestroika, the Central Secretariat and the Central Apparatus became primarily involved in the task of policy-making. Inner-Party matters acquired greater priority. The ensuing reorganisation resulted in the disintegration of the traditional chain of command undermining their authority as leadership organisations, something which could not be re-established. The lower Party organisations gained autonomy and the Central Apparatus faced severe criticism from them. On the whole, both the Central Secretariat and Apparatus continued playing an important role in formulating and implementing the resolutions of the Central Committee. However, it became increasingly obvious that both the system of resolutions and their implementation were not working in practice.

Permanent commissions emerged as sub-committees of the Central Committee. This provided an opportunity for direct participation in the process of policy-making to members of the Central Committee. Non-members were also included for the first time on a permanent basis. The issues discussed by these commissions were a radical departure from the past. But a new consensus commensurate with the reforms was yet to emerge. The majority of those in the Party and State organisations resisted this process. The first set of commissions had a sizeable representation from them. Hence they could exercise administrative authority. The new consensus would have undermined this. But the second set of commissions appeared in the final years of Perestroika, and therefore lacked any authority and could not be consolidated.

The debates at plenums increasingly reflected issues of the day. They were sharp and critical. The plenums also became forums of political conflict. In the latter years of Perestroika they were concerned with questions relating to the Party and its position on various political, social, economic and cultural issues. The resolutions were more concerned with these issues than with direct involvement in economic and agricultural sectors. The case was similar with conferences. In relation to the lower Party organisations, which had acquired autonomy, the Central Committee and the Party were no longer politically co-ordinated entities. Decisions might not even be brought to the notice of Party members and committees. The Central Committee no longer functioned as the centre for aggregation of interests and decision-making as in the past. It had lost its influence on the government.

Soviet society in the 1980s was qualitatively different from what it had been when the Soviet political system had emerged. The institutions of the State were under-developed and steeped in an quasi-authoritarian tradition. But the social structure of the contemporary Soviet Union was infinitely more complex than before. Soviet society was now an urbanised and highly educated one. The State system did adjust from time to time to the requirements of an ever more sophisticated society. Yet in the absence of an inbuilt mechanism of renewal due to its unrepresentative character these institutions lagged behind the times. This inbuilt mechanism would have been competitive elections. The absence of antagonistic classes did not warrant these, according to the Soviet explanation. It would have, however, allowed the expression and interplay of newly emerging social, political, cultural and economic interests, thus adjusting political institutions to the realities of a changing society. Soviet society was not a static one. Competitive elections could have updated and adapted the governing institutions to the social environment. But this would have undermined the politically privileged position of the Party and the State organisations. They had been inculcated with a political and organisational culture which was paternalistic and authoritarian. Such a culture bred inertia; hence the underdevelopment of both the representative and the executive wings of the State. The existing organisations and working of the Party proved inadequate to deliver the reforms. However, in the earlier years of Perestroika the Party's organisational mechanism was meant to play a more dominant role than the State and the government in the implementation of reforms. Economic questions required the involvement of the Central Committee. One of the consequences was that the Party and the Central Committee were held responsible for failure. The hierarchically organised system had curtailed the initiative of even the leading cadres. They ultimately paid a political price for that.

The representative wing, the Soviets, were generally dominated by their executive committees at the expense of the mandated deputies. This was not least because of the part-time nature of their work. However, the deputies contributed towards the working of the State system via the commissions. The executive side of the State, the ministries and the State committees, had burgeoned and had been particularly strong during most periods of Soviet rule. This was because of the imperatives set by industrialisation, central planning, external factors and the conscious project of building socialism. It was here that the Party became deeply involved in State matters. An underdeveloped State (here underdevelopment refers to the lack of capacity of the State to respond to the growing complexities of a society) led to the increased involvement of the Party in its affairs.

Although the Party remained a channel for the expression of various interests, its political and social role, a necessary feature of any political party and more so in a single-party system, was undermined. The proximity of the Party and the State resulted in a flawed recruitment process, which made career rather than political commitment the main reason for membership. Party admissions were artificially boosted. No adequate weighting was given to gender representation and ethnic composition. Target orientation was a key feature in this case as in all other aspects of Soviet life. This was also a logical consequence of a single-party system. However, a distinction has to be made here between the Party as a whole and the Party organisation. The committees of both the Party and the Soviets were effective executives. The flaw in this system was that however well intentioned they might be, the input in their decisions was limited. This was because of the restricted channels of articulation and general involvement of the Party members. This resulted in a disequilibrium in society and the political order. These committees quite often evaded responsibilities, thereby necessitating the intervention of the Central Committee.

The system of the Party organisation involved in matters of State had over a long period of time oriented the participation of its individual members. This in itself was restrictive and stifled initiative. The Party lacked a working mechanism of inner-party democracy. The centralist element of the principle of Democratic Centralism, the established interests of the Party organisation, a single-party system and most importantly the Party's involvement in the affairs of the State were factors contributing towards this lack of effective democracy inside the Party. Inner-party democracy would not only have given life to the sole political force but also provided a channel for open articulation of the entire diversity of an advanced society.

The reforms were designed to widen and consolidate the social base of Soviet democracy and ensure the replenishing of the Party's ranks. This inevitably resulted in increasing pressures for pluralism, for glasnost, thus undermining the monopoly of the Party and the State apparatuses over information and ideology. It should, however, be noted that several Party organisations positively opposed glasnost and pluralism, or did not allow them to become part of their functioning, especially in the first and second stages of Perestroika, i.e. up to the end of 1989. In any case the emerging economic pluralism was providing a basis for political pluralism. It would also give rise to social class differentiation, paving the way for a multi-party system. The Party as a political organism could have modified itself to represent the interests of the working class and other sections of society. Yet it could not have contained within its fold political forces representing nationalist aspirations or those of the newly emerging bourgeoisie. In that sense the multi-party system was inevitable, and the Party had the opportunity to become a broad-based mass party representing the interests of large sections of Soviet society, thus renewing its socialist character. Although it was already late and after the 19th Party Conference there was no turning back, yet it seems there existed a possibility of democracy within a one-party system based on a democratic consensus. The predominantly conservative Party and State organisations, however, sought to prevent this development. Instead of adjusting to the changes they attempted to reverse the process. The voice of civil society, which had acquired an autonomy of its own, was ignored. It was precisely because of this that the attempt at one-party democratisation failed.

Perhaps given a consensual approach allowing the emergence and settling down of responsive representative State institutions, i.e. the legislature, responsible and accountable executive institutions and a Party that could ensure at least the beginning of a working democracy within its ranks, one-party democratisation could have succeeded. Power could then have been transferred to the people and their plenipotentiary State organs away from the superimposed and authoritarian State machinery dominating the public life. Then it would have been the democracy of the majority defending the basic interests of the working people. This was the most important political dimension of Perestroika. In practice, however, no historical precedent of such a one-party democratisation had ever existed. In this sense the experiment of Perestroika and one-party democratisation was unique. With continuing economic reforms social-class differentiation would have ultimately emerged, and with it a multi-party system. Perhaps by then a renewed Party might have consolidated itself as a Party representing a coalition of interests of the major sections of the society and prepared to participate in a multi-party system.

However, the problem which the reformists faced at this stage was not one of the impending emergence of social-class differentiation, but that of opposition from within the Party. It seems it was possible for the Party to incorporate most if not all newly emerging interests at this stage precisely because of its unique position as the single dominant political force in a one-party system. Although a multi-party system was on the horizon it was still some way off. The Party could have represented the interests of the working class, the peasantry, the co-operators, the leaseholders, the professionals and various social and political groups with a communist and socialist perspective. It did attempt to do that as shown by the nature of the membership of the Central Committee elected in 1990. However, the Party programme of the 28th Party Congress, instead of clearly defining the new social base of the Party, gave the vague formulation of the Party defending the interests of the labourers. The absence of a clear-cut definition of interests further added to the prevailing confusion and conflicts in the Central Committee and the Party. Instead of harmonising the conflicting interests, this exacerbated the existing vertical and horizontal divisions.

Two more significant and interconnected political dimensions of the changing nature of the relationship of the Party and State emerged. One was that the revival of the Party as a political organism also meant the rehabilitation of the individual as a political being. This contrasted with the atomised and alienated individual who was the part of the leviathan called the Soviet State. Political individuals would have been restored to a political and social community being shaped and reshaped by them. This would also have restricted violations of social justice, a phenomenon all too frequent in Soviet society which had necessitated the intervention of the Central Committee. The latter would then have not only provided a forum articulating various social and economic interests, but also political leadership for such an endeavour. The other aspect would have been a State in which the principle of electivity operated, institutions were accountable, power was decentralised and a separation of powers existed. Such a State could also have helped the revival of the individual as a political person. A renewed complementarity of the Party and the State would thus have continued to exist in the reformist project. This, however, would have been a qualitatively different one from that which had existed over long periods of Soviet history. Such a transformation could only have been brought about by a consensual approach and a continuing coalition of moderate conservatives and moderate reformists.

The relationship between the individual and the State was a component feature of Party and State relations. Socialist democracy had been infringed, if it existed at all, thus the stipulation of individual liberty in statutes and in practice became an important issue. The question of the democratic rights of the people vis-à-vis their own State became crucial. Freedom of the individual within the collective, an inalienable component of socialism, was subordinated to freedom from exploitation. It was deemed that freedom from exploitation had automatically resulted in individual liberty. A mechanism to safeguard the individual from the malevolence, arbitrariness and administrative deficiencies of the State and its personnel was not guaranteed. Increasing bureaucratism made such a guarantee all the more crucial. The task of the State was to defend the interests of the people, not to act against them. It was here that the Soviet State was deficient. The political essence of the reforms was thus to restore its character as the State of the people. It could only be done by making the institutions of the State legally accountable. Such a State could have prioritised choices and endeavoured to fulfil them at various levels. The Party as the only political force and its Central Committee could have ensured this.

Thus the separation of the Party and the State constituted the central political reform and the reformist leadership seemed intent on implementing it. The areas of competence in both institutions had to be clearly defined and governed by regulatory norms at all levels. This central question was linked to the issue of political tendencies in the Central Committee and Party. If this separation was to be effective, then for the success of the reformist forces the conservative elements of the Party and the leadership, which favoured the integration of the Party and the State, had to be replaced, particularly in the leading bodies of the Party. Conservative elements, particularly moderate ones, would go some way with such a reform in the expectation that it would strengthen the position of the Party in which they were dominant. However once such a reform really started working, it would by its inherent logic lead to a disintegration of institutions and institutionalised practices. This would result in conservative opposition and the breakdown of any consensus between conservatives and reformists. A further polarisation and differentiation of political tendencies would take place, given the nature of the Soviet system. The further deepening of reforms in general, and the separation of the Party and the State in particular, would lead to a crisis situation because of the period of transition. This would result in the collapse of any consensus later on, spelling doom for official Perestroika or controlled reforms. The reforms had gone far enough for the conservatives to make the break up of this consensus inevitable. The emergence of an aggressively vocal civil society as a result of the attempts of the reformist section to draw sustenance and strength from protest movements probably showed the awareness of the reformists that beyond a certain stage in the reforms, the consensus would inevitably come under strain. The coalition would eventually snap and they would come into conflict with the conservatives. In addition, with the unprecedented involvement of civil society in the reforms, reformers became more and more radicalised and conservatives more and more revivalist resulting in the shrinking of the centrist coalition. This seems to explain the eventful rupturing of the Central Committee and the Party and its subsequent disintegration.

The Soviet leadership had two alternatives - one that the existing system was retained and perfected and the other that it was reorganised on more democratic lines as a responsive system. The former choice was not possible in an urban, highly educated, complex, sophisticated society with the multitude of interests that the USSR had become. Responding adequately to these complexities was the problem the Soviet leadership faced, hence the need for the reforms. The latter was the only feasible option. In this option the question of Party and State relations and their reorganisation had to be fundamentally addressed. What Gorbachev embarked upon was thus a process of simultaneous de-institutionalisation and re-institutionalisation. The system as it existed had to be de-institutionalised with all its ramifications, and a new one created, in which the nature of the different component institutions of the two would be modified, their relationship, organisation and working redefined and re-institutionalised. The Party had to be rescued from its existing organisational system and the State as an independent institution with relative autonomy rebuilt. Given the transitional nature of this period the two processes had to take place simultaneously.

The reforms in the Central Committee of the CPSU have to be viewed in this context. They were a concomitant and inherent part of the central reform of the separation of the Party and State. Changing the composition of the Central Committee was a necessary though not adequate measure to this end. It would not radically alter the character of the Central Committee though it would bring in members more amenable to the reforms. It was after all these new members who helped prepare the ground for further reform. The changes in personnel were thus an important part of the strategy of reform. Reform of the job-slot system of representation was a significant change of far-reaching consequences which was again consistent with the overall separation of Party and the State. The representation of the State and government institutions was no longer tenable if an effective separation was to be undertaken. Because the Soviet political system was in transition, some leading State and government institutions were still represented. Nevertheless power seemed to have effectively shifted away from the Central Committee and to State institutions, although the link was not completely severed.

The existing institutions of the Central Committee - the Central Secretariat and the Central Apparatus - also had to be reformed. They had to be re-adjusted to discharge the task of providing political leadership rather than share the job of administering the country with State institutions. Hence the necessity for the new organisation of Central Committee Commissions. Changing the composition of the Central Committee was necessary because individuals are carriers of values and ideas. However values and ideas do not exist in isolation of, and are conditioned by, existing institutions, making change in them imperative. But the primary force spurring on such transformations, be it the institutions or the individuals, was that of irrevocable social change. The working of the Central Committee had to change for the same reason. It had to function more as the leading organ of a political party.

At one level Gorbachev was undertaking the process of de-institutionalisation by reforming the existing institutions, including the Central Committee, that had taken root in the Stalin era. On the other he was attempting a process of re-institutionalisation by building new institutions both inside and outside the Party. This was done by attempting to democratise and build up new institutions which might provide scope for incorporating new interests in society in the mainstream political processes and bring institutions in tune with the realities of a society ever more complex and lagging behind economically. All this entailed a clear-cut demarcation of the Party and State. The reforms in the Central Committee were an intrinsic part of this process. However, it was precisely in this transformation that the reasons for its inexorable decline and disintegration lay. A vacuum of power and authority occurred. The question of to whom they would be devolved remained unresolved. New institutions and institutional practices did not have time to evolve and consolidate. The emerging cleavages in a transitional system undermined the reforms and the system itself. A democratic consensus within the coalition, incremental changes and malleability of the Party, its institutions and its leaders, might have saved the day for the Party and the Central Committee. Deprived of their traditional role of administration, however, they lost their *locus standi* in society and the political system, and collapsed.

Therefore the separation of the Party and the State resulted in the unravelling of and disintegration of the Soviet political system leading to the emergence of fifteen independent nation-states with distinctive political identities from within the political-geographical boundaries of the former Soviet Union. The CPSU and its institutions firstly surrendered their monopoly over political power and their control over the instrumentalities of the Soviet State which in any case was an incomplete state-formation because of the integration of the Party and the State and thereby systematically dismantling and deinstitutionalising the once formidable Soviet political system. The institutions of the Party and the State ultimately succumbed to the subalteran and subterranean forces hitherto lying dormant and their political manifestations such as the resurgent nationalisms and sub-nationalisms and a disintegrating economy coupled with a state of socio-cultural entropy.

The basis of these changes were laid down with the inception of the Soviet Union and its political-ideological roots preceded the birth of the Soviet State in historical terms. Most of the diverse ideologies that defined the open pluralism of Perestroika and subsequent post-Soviet era had recorded their existence in the early years of the Soviet regime and even before. A single -Party system precluded their interplay. However they existed broadly as conservatism and reformism during the entire Soviet era. Some of these were driven underground and led an illegitimate existence until the pluralism and glasnost of the Perestroika period allowed them to resurface and start influencing the Soviet political system. During Perestroika, particularly in its later years, the more liberal political dispensation under Gorbachev, who himself was undergoing major transformation in his political-ideological thinking and positions, as were most of those who constituted the political leadership of the Soviet Union, the political pluralism became manifest and several hitherto subterranean ideologies started reasserting themselves. Nationalist and sub-nationalist aspirations, which had been subdued for decades, reasserted and not only defined the political discourse but revealed the fault lines along which the Soviet Union disintegrated. The parameters of the economy and the economic system were laid down during this period and the successor states more or less adhered to them. Even the political leadership which came to rule these successor states was largely drawn from the erstwhile ruling sections of the former Soviet Union, many of whose political ideas and practices had mutated. However they still continued to be influenced by the practices, if not the ideas of the past and therefore there remained a noticeable continuity in the legacy of the past and the political institutions and the praxis of the present, in all spheres of the political and economic system as well as in the socio-cultural organisation, alongwith that of the individuals who constituted the political leadership.

Note

[1]T. Bottomore, 1987, pp. 482-3.

Bibliography

Ali R.(1990) 'CPSU In Search of Lost Identity, Review of Twenty-eighth Congress of Soviet Communists', *Mainstream*, vol xxvii, no. 46, 8 September 1990.

Armstrong J.A. (1973) *Ideology, Politics and Government in the Soviet Union-An Introduction*, Nelson, London, pp. 87-93.

Beissinger M.R. (1988) The Leadership and the Political Elite, in James Cracraft, ed. *The Soviet Union Today-An Interpretive Guide,* Chicago, pp. 37-52 and p.38.

Biriukova A. (1988)'Priority Direction of Social Policy', *Kommunist*, no. 5, March 1988.

Bogomolov O.(1989) 'The Changing Image of Socialism', *Kommunist*, no.11, 1989.

Bottomore T. (1987) *A Dictionary of Marxist Thought*, Oxford University Press, Delhi, pp. 360-61.

Brovkin V. (1990) 'Revolution From Below: Informal Political Associations in Russia 1988-1989', *Soviet Studies,* vol. 42, no. 2, April 1990.

Brown A. H. (1974) *Soviet Politics and Political Science,* Macmillan, London, p. 62.

Brown A. H. (1989) The Soviet Leadership and the Struggle for Political Reform in Paul Lerner (ed) *The Soviet Union- Essays From the Harriman Institute Forum 1988,* Crane Russak, New. York, pp. 54-56 and pp. 51-67.

Brown A., Kaser M. and Smith G. S. (eds), (1994) *The Cambridge Encyclopaedia of Russia and the Former Soviet Union*, Cambridge University Press, Cambridge.

Buzgalin A.V.(1993), *Belaia Vorona, Poslednii God Zhizhni TsK KPSS: Vzgliad I znutri*, Znanie, Moscow.

Centre for Applied Political Studies, *INDEM (INformation for DEMocracy) Data Base*, Moscow.

Chebrikov V.(1989) 'Legal Policy: An Active Part of Perestroika,' *Kommunist*, no. 8, May 1989.

Chiesa G. (1990) 'The 28th Congress of the CPSU', *Problems of Communism*, July-August 1990.

Churchward L.G. (1975)*Contemporary Soviet Government,* Routledge and Kegan Paul, London, pp. 206-237.

Cohen S. F. (1980) The Friends and Foes of Change: Reformism and Conservatism in the Soviet Union in S. F. Cohen, A. Rabinowitch and R. Sharlet (eds), *The Soviet Union Since Stalin,* Macmillan, London, pp. 11-31.

Daniels R.V. (1989) 'Political Processes and Generational Change' in Archie Brown (ed.) *Political Leadership in the Soviet Union*, Macmillan, p. 97 and pp. 96-126.

Devlin K. (1988) 'Soviet Journalist Describes El'Tsin's Struggle Against Party 'Mafia", *Radio Liberty (hereafter RL) 206/88*, 20 May 1988, p. 4.

Editorial : 'Revolution, Perestroika, Humanism', *Kommunist*, no. 15, October 1988.
Editorial: 'Ideology of Thought and Action', *Kommunist*, No. 5, March, 1988.
Editorial: 'Political Vanguard of Society', *Kommunist*, no. 1, January 1988.
Editorial: 'Towards New Image of Socialism', *Kommunist*, no. 13, 1989.
'End of the Beginning', The Second Russian Revolution, *BBC Television, Channel 2,* 5 July 1991.
'Enter Gorbachev', The Second Russian Revolution, *BBC Television, Channel 2*, 31 May 1991.
Fainsod M. (1963) *How Russia is Ruled*, Harvard University Press, Cambridge, Massachusets, pp. 179-99, pp. 201-204.
Farmer K.C. (1992) *The Soviet Administrative Elite*, Praeger, London, p. 109.
From "Culture" of Battle to Culture of Accord - Y. Prokofiev, Member Central Committee CPSU, First Secretary Moscow Party Committee', *Kommunist*, no. 13, September 1990.
Gehlen M.P. (1969) *The Communist Party of Soviet Union-A Functional Analysis,* Indiana University Press, London, pp. 40-70.
Gehlen M.P. and McBride M. 'The Soviet Central Committee: an Elite Analysis', *American Political Science Review*, vol. LXII, no. 4.
Gill G. (1987) Khrushchev and Systemic Development in Martin McCauley, ed. *Khrushchev and Khrushchevism,* Macmillan Press in association with the School of Slavonic and East European Studies, University of London, London, pp. 39-40.
Gill G. (1994)*The Collapse of a Single-Party System, The Disintegration of the Communist Party of the Soviet Union,* Cambridge University Press, Cambridge, p. 140.
Gorbachev M. 'Socialist Idea and Revolutionary Perestroika', *Kommunist*, no. 18, November 1989.
Gorbachev's Political Report', *Current Digest of Soviet Press*, vol. XXXVIII, no. 8, 1986.
Gorbachev's Report Sizes Up Restructuring', *Current Digest of Soviet Press*, vol. XL, no. 26, 1988.
Hahn J.W. (1990) The Soviet State System in Stephen White, Alex Pravda and Zvi Gitelman eds., *Developments in Soviet Politics,* Macmillan, London, pp. 87-103.
Hahn J.W.'Power to the Soviets?', *Problems of Communism,* January - February 1989.
Hahn W. (1982) *Post-war Soviet Politics* , Cornell University Press, London.
Hammer D.P. (1986) *The USSR: The Politics of Oligarchy*, Westview Press, pp. 85-119.
Harasymiw B. 'Changes in the Party's Composition: The 'Destroyka' of the CPSU', *The Journal of Communist Studies,* Vol. 7, June 1991, no. 2.
Harris J. 'The Public Politics of Aleksander Nikolaevich Yakovlev, 1983-1989', no. 901, *The Carl Beck Papers in Russian And East European Studies*, University of Pittsburgh Centre For Russian and East European Studies, December 1990.

Hill R. J. 'The CPSU: From Monolithic to Pluralist?', *Soviet Studies*, Vol. 43, no. 2, 1991.
Hill R.J (1990) The Party, in Stephen White, Alex Pravda and Zvi Gitelman (eds) *Developments in Soviet Politics*, Macmillan, London, pp. 67-86.
Hill R.J and Frank P. (1986)*The Soviet Communist Party*, Allen and Unwin, London, pp. 64-70 and pp. 107-124.
Hill R.J. and Rahr A. (1985)*Soviet Union-Politics, Economics and Society-From Lenin to Gorbachev*, Frances Pinter, London, p. 85.
Hill R.J. and Rahr A. (1988) The General Secretary, the Central Party Secrateriat and the Apparat, in Lane D. ed., *Elites and Political Power in the USSR*, Edward Elgar, (Hants) pp. 49-72
Hough J.F. (1971) The Party Apparatchiki in H.G. Skilling and F. Griffiths (eds), *Interests Groups in Soviet Politics,* Princeton University Press, New Jersey, pp. 47-92.
Hough J.F. (1982) Changes in Soviet Elite Composition, in S. Bialer and T. Gustafson ed., *Russia at Crossroads: The 26th Congress of the CPSU,* George Allen and Unwin, pp. 39-64.
Hough J.F. and Fainsod M. (1979) *How Soviet Union is Governed*, Harvard University Press, pp. 409-466.
Koptyug V. 'Democratisation of the Party - Democratisation of Society', *Kommunist*, no. 7, 1988.
Kramer M. 'The Role of the CPSU International Department in Soviet Foreign Relations and National Security Policy', *Soviet Studies*, Vol. 42, July 1990.
Lane D. (1978) *Politics and Society in the USSR,* Martin Robertson, London, pp. 272-73.
Lane D. (1985) *State and Politics in the USSR*, Basil Blackwell, pp. 162-163.
Lane D. (1992) Soviet Elites, Monolithic or Polyarchic? in D. Lane ed., *Russia in Flux, The Political and Social Consequences of Reform,* Edward Elgar, Hants, pp. 3-23.
Lane D. (1992) *Soviet Society Under Perestroika,* Routledge, London, 1992 pp. 80-83.
Lane D. and Ross C. 'The Composition of the Politburo of the CPSU: 1966 to 1991'(unpublished paper).
Lane D. and Ross C. 'The CPSU Ruling Elite 1981-1991: Commonalities and Divisions'. (unpublished paper).
Lane D. and Ross C. (1994) 'The Social Background and Political Allegiance of the Political Elite of the Supreme Soviet of the USSR: The Terminal Stage, 1984 to 1991', *Europe-Asia Studies (Formerly Soviet Studies),* Vol. 46, no. 3, 1994.
Lenin V.I. Better Fewer, But Better, *iSelected Works-111*, pp. 836-37.
Lenin V.I. How We Should Reorganise the Worker's and Peasants Inspection, *Selected Works-111*, Foreign Languages Publishing House, (Moscow), pp. 824-25.
Lentini P. (1993) 'A Note on Women in the CPSU Central Committee, 1990', *Europe-Asia Studies* , vol. 45, no. 4, 1993.
Lewin M. (1988) *The Gorbachev Phenomenon - A Historical Interpretation,* University of California Press, Berkeley.

Ligachev E.K.(1991), 'Iz Vospominanii', *Argumenti i fakti*, no. 3.
Ligachev E.K.(1992), *Zagadka Gorbacheva*, Sibirskii Centre, "Inter Book", Novosibirsk.
Mann D. (1988) 'Party Report and Election Campaign Winds Down', *RL 59/88*, 27 January 1988.
Materials of the 19th All-Union Conference of the Central Committee of the CPSU', *Kommunist*, no. 10, June 1988.
Materiali delegatu XIX Vsesoiuznoi Konferentsii KPSS, (1988) Moskva.
Mawdsley E. (1991) 'The 1990 Central Committee of the CPSU in Perspective', *Soviet Studies*, vol. 43, no. 5, 1991.
Mawdsley E. (1992) Portrait of a changing elite: CPSU Central Committee full members, 1939-1990, in S. White, ed. *New Directions in Soviet History,* Cambridge University Press, Cambridge, pp. 193-96.
McCauley A. (1992) Poverty and Underprivileged Groups, in D. Lane (ed) *Russia in Flux*, Edward Elgar, Hants, pp. 204-5.
McCauley M, (1987) Khrushchev as Leader in McCauley M., (ed), *Khrushchev and Khrushchevism,* Macmillan Press in association with the School of Slavonic and East European Studies, University of London, London, p. 27.
McCauley M. (1987) Gorbachev as Leader, in McCauley M. (ed), *The Soviet Union Under Gorbachev,* Macmillan, pp. 20-27.
McNeill T. (1985) 'Gorbachev Strengthens His Hold', *RL 134/85*, 26 April 1985.
McNeill T. (1985) 'Nikolai Ryzhkov-- Gorbachev's New Economic Overlord', *RL 146/85,* 8 May, 1985.
McNeill T. (1985)'Grigorii Vasil'evich Romanov - The Other Heir Presumptive?', *RL 24/85,* 25 January, 1985.
Medvedev V. (1988) 'Towards Cognition of Socialism', *Kommunist*, no. 17, 1988.
Medvedev V. (1990) 'A Test by History', *Kommunist*, no. 17, November 1990.
Medvedev, R. (1980) The Stalin Question in S.F. Cohen, A. Rabinowitch and R. Sharlet (eds) *The Soviet Union Since Stalin,* Macmillan, London, p. 33.
Meyer A.G. (1965) *The Soviet Political System-An Interpretation*, Random House Inc., New York, pp. 152-178.
Miller J.H. (1987) How Much of a New Elite?, in R.F. Miller, J.H. Miller and T.H. Rigby (eds), *Gorbachev at the Helm-A New Era in Soviet Politics,* Croom Helm, London, pp. 61-89.
Moore Barrington, Jr. (1961) Development and Functioning of the Party (1944) in A. Inkeles and K. Geiger, (eds) *Soviet Society, A Book of Readings,* Constable and Co. Ltd., London, p. 135.
Nenashev M (1993), *Posledenoe Pravitelstvo SSSR, Lichnosti Sviditelstva Diialogi,* Moskva, AO, <KROM>.
Panov V. G. (1987) (ed), *Ezhegodnik Bolshoi Sovetskoi Entsiklopedii*, 1987, Sovetskaia Entsiklopedia, Moscow.
Perestroika, Chapter 4, in J. L. Black, (1989) (ed), *USSR Documents Annual, 1988, Perestroika-The Second Stage*, Academic International Press, Gulf Breeze, FL, 1989, pp. 183-208.
Plenary Conference of the CPSU Central Committee, 27-28 January 1987', *Kommunist*, no. 3, 1987.

Plenary Conference of the CPSU Central Committee, February 17-18, 1988', *Kommunist*, March 1988.
Plenary Meeting of the CPSU Central Committee, January 27-28, 1987', *Kommunist*, no. 3, 1987.
Plenary Session of the CPSU Central Committee, 23 May 1988', *Kommunist* , no. 9, June 1988.
Rahr A. (1985) 'Changes at the Top in Moscow', *RL 218/85*, 3 July, 1985.
Rahr A. (1985) 'More Personnel Changes in the Offing', *RL 341/85*, 10 October 1985.
Rahr A. (1985) 'The Party's Darling', *RL 102/85*, 29 March 1985.
Rahr A. (1986) 'Boris El'tsin: Moscow's Champion of Glasnost', *RL 2/87*, 19 December 1986.
Rahr A. (1987) 'Gorbachev's Champion of Glasnost' Threatens to Resign', *RL 443/87*,
Rahr A. (1987) 'Ligachev Versus Gorbachev?', *RL 325/87*, 12 August 1987.
Rahr A. (1987) 'The Ouster of Boris El'tsin -- The Kremlin's 'Avant gardist'', *RL 506/87*, 18 December 1987.
Rahr A. (1987) 'Turnover in the Central Party Apparatus', *RL 256/87*, 9 July 1987.
Rahr A. (1988) 'Gorbachev Changes Party Structure', *RL 519/88*, 30 November 1988.
Rahr A. (1988) 'Turnover in the Soviet Nomenklatura?', *RL 238/88*, 5 June 1988.
Rahr A. (1989) 'Who Is in Charge of the Party Apparatus?', *Report on the USSR*, 14 April 1989.
Rahr A. (1990), *A Biographical Directory of 100 Leading Soviet Officials*, Westview Press, RFE/RL.
Rahr A. (1991) 'The CPSU in the 1980s: Changes in the Party Apparatus', *The Journal of Communist Studies,* Vol. 7, June 1991.
Rahr A. (1991) 'The Soviet Leadership on the Eve of the Coup', *Report on the USSR,* 23 August, 1991.
Razumovski G. (1987) 'To Improve the Training and Retraining of Leading Party Cadres', *Kommunist*, no. 9, 1987.
Razumovski G. (1989) 'To Lead the Perestroika Effort, To Generate the Energy of Renewal', *Kommunist*, no. 4, March 1989.
Revolution from Below', The Second Russian Revolution, *BBC Television, Channel 2,* 21 June 1991.
Rigby T.H.(1980) A Conceptual Approach to Authority, Power and Policy in the Soviet Union in T.H. Rigby, Archie Brown and Peter Reddaway (eds), *Authority, Power and Policy in the USSR-Essays Dedicated to Leonard Schapiro,* Macmillan, London, pp. 9-31.
Rigby T.H.(1990) *Political Elites in the USSR*, Edward Elgar, Hants, p. 52 and p. 56.
Robinson N. (1992) 'Gorbachev and the Place of the Party in Soviet Reform, 1985-91', *Soviet Studies,* Vol. 44, no. 3, 1992.
Ross C. (1990) Party-State Relations, in Eugene Huskey (ed), *Executive Power and Soviet Politics-The Rise and Decline of the Soviet State,* M.E. Sharpe Inc.,

London, pp. 49-82.
Rutland P. (1990) Economic Management and Reform, in S. White, A. Pravda, Z. Gitelman (eds), *Developments in Soviet Politics,* Macmillan, London, pp. 161-62.
Sakwa R. (1989) *Soviet Politics, An Introduction,* Routledge, London, pp. 133-36.
Schapiro L. (1960) *The Communist Party of the Soviet Union*, Eyre & Spotiswoode, London, pp. 241-45.
Schapiro L. (1963) The New Rules of the CPSU in L. Schapiro (ed), *The USSR and the Future-An Analysis of the New Program Of the CPSU,* Frederick A. Praeger, London pp. 179-194.
Schapiro L. (1973) *The Government and Politics of the Soviet Union*, Hutchinson, London.
Scott D.J.R. (1969) *Russian Political Institutions*, George Allen and Unwin, London pp. 141-153.
Shakhnazarov G. (1990) 'Renewal of Ideology and Ideology of Renewal', *Kommunist,* no. 4, March 1990.
Shevardnadze E. (1991), *The Future Belongs to Freedom*, Translated by C. A. Fitzpatrick, Sinclair-Stevenson Ltd., London.
Shlapentokh V. (1988) 'The XXVII Congress- A Case Study Of the Shaping of a New Party Ideology', *Soviet Studies*, vol. Xl, no. 1, January 1988.
Sliunkov N. (1988) 'Restructuring and Party Guidance on Economy', *Kommunist*, no. 1, January 1988, no. 1.
Smith G.B. (1992),*Soviet Politics- Struggling with Change,* Macmillan, pp. 111-114.
Speech of Gorbachev to 18 February 1988 Central Committee Plenum - Towards Revolutionary Perestroika - The Ideology of Renewal', *Kommunist*, , no. 4, March 1988.
Surovell J. (1994) 'Gorbachev's Last Year: Leftist or Rightist?', *Europe-Asia Studies*, vol. 46, no. 3, 1994.
Teague E. (1985) 'Gorbachev Consolidating His Position', *RL 201/85*, 20 June 1985.
Teague E. (1985) 'Gorbachev Picks Up Where Andropov Left', *RL 78/85,* 14 March, 1985.
Teague E. (1985) 'The Process of 'De-Brezhnevisation' Gets Under Way', *RL 386/85*, 18 November 1985.
Teague E. (1986) 'Gorbachev Attacks Opponents of Reform', *RL 232/86,* 18 June 1986.
Teague E. (1986) 'Gorbachev's First Year: Domestic Policy', *RL82/86,* 19 February 1986.
Teague E. (1986) 'Gorbachev's Speech to the Twenty-Seventh Party Congress: More Carrot and More Stick', *RL 96/86*, 25 February 1986.
Teague E. (1986) 'Moscow Party Organisation Under Grishin Set Itself 'Above Criticism'', *RL 54/86*, 31 January 1986.
Teague E. (1986) 'Pockets of Opposition to Kremlin Policies?', *RL 39/86*, 22 January 1986.
Teague E. (1987) 'Central Committee Resolution Fudges Issue of Party Elections',

RL 42/87, 29 January, 1987.
Teague E. (1987) 'El'tsin Sacked as Moscow Party Boss', *RL 453/87*, 11 November 1987.
Teague E. (1987) 'Gorbachev Answers His Critics', *RL 280/87*, 15 July 1987.
Teague E. (1987) 'Gorbachev Discusses Personnel Policy', *RL 38/87*, 28 January 1987.
Teague E. (1987) 'Personnel Changes in the Politburo', *RL 233/87*, 26 June 1987.
Teague E. (1987) 'Signs of a Conservative Backlash', *RL 474/87*, 18 November 1987.
Teague E. (1988) 'Gorbachev Counter Attacks in Tashkent', *RL161/88*, 13 April 1988.
Teague E. (1988) 'Gorbachev Says Ligachev's Position is Secure', *RL 233/88*, 1 June 1988.
Teague E. (1988) 'Ligachev's Position in Doubt', *RL 178/88*, 22 April 1988.
Teague E. and Mann D. (1990) 'Gorbachev's Dual Role', *Problems of Communism*, January -February 1990.
The Battle for Glasnost', The Second Russian Revolution, *BBC Television, Channel 2*, 7 June 1991.
The Yeltsin File', The Second Russian Revolution, *BBC Television, Channel 2*, 14 June 1991.
Ulrich-Joachim Schulz-Torge(1992) (ed), *Who was Who in the Soviet Union,* K. G. Saur, London.
Voslensky M. (1984) *Nomenklatura-Anatomy of the Soviet Ruling Class,* The Bodley Head, London.
White S. (1989), The Soviet Political Leadership and Soviet Power, in Menon R. and Nelson D. N. (eds), *Limits to Soviet Power*, Lexington Books, Toronto, pp. 49-68.
White S. (1990),*Gorbachev in Power,* Cambridge University Press, Cambridge,
White S. (1991) 'Reformulating the Programme and Rules' in Profile, The Twenty-Eighth CPSU Congress, *The Journal of Communist Studies,* Vol. 7, March 1991.
White S. (1994), Pluralism, Civil Society, and Post Soviet Politics in C. R. Saivetz and A. Jones ed., *In Search of Pluralism, Soviet and Post Soviet,* Westview Press, Oxford, pp. 5-26.
White S. G. Gill and D. Slider (1993) (eds)*The Politics of Transition, Shaping a Post-Soviet Future*, Cambridge University Press, Cambridge, p. 127, Chapters Three and Eight.
White S., Gill G., Slider D.(1993) (eds),*The Politics of Transition-Shaping A Post-Soviet Future,* Cambridge University Press, Cambridge, pp. 212-229 and Chapter Nine.
Willerton, Jr. J.P. (1990) The Political Leadership, White S., Pravda A. and Gitelman Z. (eds) *Developments in Soviet Politics,* Macmillan, p. 57-65.
XXVI Syezd Kommunisticheskoi Partii Sovetskovo Souiza otchet, no. 2.

XXVIIth CPSU Congress, Report by M. Gorbachev', (1990) Soviet Land Booklets, Moscow, pp. 9-10.

Yakovlev A.N. (1988) The Philosphy of Perestroika, in Aganbegyan A. (ed), *Perestroika Annual,* Futura Publications, London, p. 38

Yakovlev A.N.(1992), *Predislovie Obval Posleslovie,* Novosti, Moscow.

Yasmann V. (1987) 'Yakovlev Sets Out Gorbachev's Ideological Platform', *RL 322/87,* 18 August 1987.

Zaslavskaia T. (1988) Friends or Foes? Social Forces Working For and Against Perestroika, in Aganbegian A. (ed), *Perestroika Annual*, Futura Publications, London, pp. 255-78.

Index